The Promise of Human Rights

PENNSYLVANIA STUDIES IN HUMAN RIGHTS

Bert B. Lockwood, Jr., Series Editor

A complete list of books in the series is available from the publisher.

The Promise of Human Rights

Constitutional Government,
Democratic Legitimacy, and International Law

Jamie Mayerfeld

PENN

UNIVERSITY OF PENNSYLVANIA PRESS

PHILADELPHIA

Copyright © 2016 University of Pennsylvania Press

All rights reserved. Except for brief quotations used for purposes of review or scholarly
citation, none of this book may be reproduced in any form by any means without
written permission from the publisher.

Published by
University of Pennsylvania Press
Philadelphia, Pennsylvania 19104-4112
www.upenn.edu/pennpress

Printed in the United States of America on acid-free paper
10 9 8 7 6 5 4 3 2 1

Library of Congress Cataloging-in-Publication Data
ISBN 978-0-8122-4816-6

for Peter Mack

C o n t e n t s

"Men can never be secure from Tyranny, if there be no means to escape it, till they are perfectly under it: And therefore it is, that they have not only a Right to get out of it but to prevent it."
—John Locke, *Second Treatise of Government*, 1689

"No man is allowed to be a judge in his own cause."
—James Madison, *The Federalist*, 1787

The Promise of Human Rights

Introduction

I argue in this book that human rights require not only domestic but also international protections. The reasons why a country should adopt constitutional democracy as a form of government are also reasons why it should become integrated into an international human rights regime. It should incorporate international human rights law into its domestic legal system and accept international oversight of its human rights commitments. Contrary to the view that international human rights law undermines constitutional government by undermining state sovereignty, I argue that international human rights law is a necessary extension of domestic checks and balances, and therefore necessary for constitutional government itself. To put it another way, constitutional democracy is incomplete unless domestic human rights institutions are bolted into a system of international guarantees.

The justification for international human rights institutions typically offered to Western audiences is "outward looking"—that such institutions can improve the human rights practices of other countries. I instead present the "inward looking" argument that international human rights institutions can improve the human rights practices of one's own country. International human rights institutions are an element of domestic governance: they allow democratic and democratizing states, through mutual criticism and oversight, to strengthen the domestic constitutional order. I do not minimize the importance of outward-looking motives. Indeed, the inward-looking rationale presupposes their existence: countries must take an interest in improving one another's human rights practices in order for participating countries to reap the benefits of the system. But the inward-looking justification merits more attention than it has received.

Faith in the sufficiency of domestic human rights institutions is one mistake; belief that international human rights institutions can function unaided is another. The role of international human rights institutions is not to replace but rather to strengthen their domestic counterparts. When they ensure that domestic rights institutions honor their mandate, they not only provide individuals an additional layer of protection from abuse, but also make the domestic institutions more secure. By the same token, democratic states are needed to safeguard the integrity of international human rights institutions. In this way, the mutual oversight mechanisms of domestic checks and balances are reproduced (though not in identical form) at the transnational level. The fundamental point is that human rights require the protection of multiple guardians, exercising concurrent responsibility and holding one another to account.

The United States as a Case Study

Although the argument of this book is general in application, the United States figures prominently in the discussion. Recall that the United States came into being with a declaration of universal human rights, a claim that all human beings[1] are endowed "with certain unalienable rights" and that governments exist "to secure these rights." The Founders reaffirmed their commitment to human rights in language contained in the original Constitution and Bill of Rights, a commitment strengthened in subsequent amendments abolishing slavery, obligating states to respect due process and uphold the equal protection of the laws, and extending suffrage to racial minorities and women. The Constitution that frames the U.S. system of government was famously defended in *The Federalist Papers* as one best suited to the protection of human rights.

Given the historical association of the United States with the idea of human rights, one might have expected it to seek integration into the international human rights institutions that developed after World War II. Those institutions, largely derived from the 1948 Universal Declaration of Human Rights, include a growing number of UN-based and regional treaties, together with their respective courts, commissions, and monitoring committees. Contemporary international human rights law has sources in custom as well as treaty, and is enriched by international humanitarian law, whose sources include the Nuremberg and Tokyo trials following World War II, the 1949 Geneva Conventions and their Protocols (1977), the war crimes tribunals for the former Yugoslavia and Rwanda, and the Rome Statute of the International Criminal Court (1998).

Yet the relationship of the United States to international human rights law is ambivalent. While often eager to apply international human rights law to other countries, it has consistently sought to minimize the impact of such law on its own laws and policies.[2] It has refused to ratify several major human rights treaties, and ratified others only after a long delay. Even when ratifying human rights treaties, it uses "reservations, understandings, and declarations" to cancel any obligations requiring a change in its own laws and policies and to block American judges from enforcing treaty provisions in their judgments. It has declined to accept the jurisdiction of the International Criminal Court and the Inter-American Court of Human Rights. It has questioned the binding force of customary international law, including that pertaining to human rights and armed conflict, on the president and Congress.

Resistance to U.S. adoption of international human rights law began very early.[3] In the late 1940s, as the United Nations proclaimed the Genocide Convention and began work drafting a human rights covenant, Frank Holman, president of the American Bar Association, led a campaign to block U.S. ratification of any human rights treaties. He found a tireless champion in Senator John Bricker, Republican of Ohio, who introduced a constitutional amendment that would bar U.S. treaties from becoming domestic law in the absence of congressional legislation. The amendment failed to win the necessary two-thirds vote in the Senate, but the campaign elicited a promise from President Dwight Eisenhower not to submit any human rights treaties for Senate approval. The United States waited forty years (until 1988) to ratify the Genocide Convention and twenty-six years (until 1992) to ratify the International Covenant on Civil and Political Rights; ratification of both treaties was heavily qualified with reservations, understandings, and declarations.

Arguments by Holman and Bricker have been restated ever since: that the adoption of international human rights law is unnecessary in view of the deep U.S. commitment to rights and that it would undermine the Constitution, subvert democracy, and violate U.S. sovereignty. The arguments gained fresh impetus in the 1990s with the rise of the New Sovereigntists,[4] a group of prominent legal scholars and Republican administration officials who recommended sharply limiting the impact of international law on U.S. law and policy. The New Sovereigntists have expressed particular concern about international human rights law, warning that its domestic incorporation not only would be imprudent and antidemocratic, but may violate the Constitution.[5] Their arguments have influenced judicial opinions.[6] Most New Sovereigntists belong to the right, but some of their arguments are echoed by scholars on the left.[7] Parallel critiques are raised in other countries[8]—the issues are general in scope.

I argue that the critiques are misplaced. Because domestic human rights protections in the United States are both fragile and incomplete and because international human rights law offers much-needed reinforcement, it does not undermine but rather shores up the Constitution. It supports democracy, because respect for human rights is a core purpose of democracy. Democracy does not mean unfettered choice, and the Founders wisely rejected such an understanding of popular government. Learning from James Madison, we should envisage democracy as a joint commitment to uphold justice, including human rights, where popular participation in government is the primary but not exclusive device used to block unjust policies. Nor must we rely on Madison: other arguments show that the best understanding of democracy is one that incorporates effective rights protections, and this view now informs standard uses of the term "democracy." Because human rights require international as well as domestic protections, international human rights institutions complete the democratic project. They place limits on state sovereignty, but such limits are no cause for regret. The limits do not contravene democratic or other moral values.

A leading criticism of international human rights law is that it is antidemocratic because it limits the policies that citizens of a nation-state might otherwise choose to adopt. To rebut this criticism, I develop two arguments. The gentler argument (made in Chapter 6) is that international human rights law prohibits policies countries should not consider anyway, so these prohibitions constitute no loss for democracy. This argument is compatible with diverse theories about the meaning of democracy, and is not overturned by the fact that people may disagree about the content of human rights. The bolder argument (made in Chapter 2) advances a particular theory about the meaning of democracy. As an institutional matter, democracy requires popular government, but that leaves open the question what the purpose of democracy is. It is often assumed that its purpose is to realize the people's will. I argue instead that its purpose is to secure justice. I defend what I call a "Madisonian" conception of democracy, understood as a promise among citizens and officials to hold one another accountable in a shared project of crafting and enacting policies that promote justice, where justice necessarily includes a commitment to human rights. The fundamental institutional logic of democracy is checks and balances, where citizens and officials monitor each other to prevent the misuse and abuse of political power. Popular government is the most important of these checks, but not the only one; it is a necessary but insufficient element of democracy. On this account, democracy requires, and is not in tension with, international human rights law. I hope readers may be persuaded by the Madisonian conception of democracy, but if not, the gentler argument mentioned above is still sufficient to establish the democratic legitimacy of international human rights law.

I make no claims for international law as a whole. Let me state what should be obvious: international law can reinforce human rights and democracy but can also undermine them.[9] This book addresses the international law of human rights, not international law in general. Nor is international *human rights* law infallible. Sometimes it may harbor a false conception of human rights or adopt flawed means of implementation. The politicized resolutions process of the UN Human Rights Council (and its predecessor, the Human Rights Commission), in which some notorious human rights abusers have been shielded from criticism, reminds us that human rights institutions sometimes fall short of their mandate.[10] We should also be vigilant against attempts to corrupt international human rights institutions from within, attempts that sometimes use the language of human rights to subvert human rights.[11] In the worst case, if corruption becomes too pervasive, withdrawal may be necessary. But we may succeed in defeating (or at least limiting) attempts at sabotage, and we may be able to improve flawed human rights institutions or replace them with better ones. A theme of this book is that democratic states have a responsibility to enhance and maintain the integrity of international human rights institutions. Moreover, it is important to point out that some international human rights laws and institutions have made great contributions, and that constitutional democracies, including the United States, can harness those contributions for their own good.

When I claim that constitutional democracies should become integrated into an international human rights regime, therefore, I do not mean any international regime bearing that label. There can be false international human rights institutions no less than false constitutional democracies. The main danger is the influence of abusive governments wishing to subvert rather than support human rights and their ability to commandeer international human rights institutions to their purposes. One example is the Independent Permanent Human Rights Commission of the Organization of Islamic Cooperation, which some observers fear is little more than an exercise in window dressing for an anti-human rights agenda by the organization's most powerful member states.[12] What complicates the picture is that repressive governments may sometimes become trapped in their own human rights pledges, however insincere. A well-known case is the Helsinki Final Act of 1975, briefly discussed in Chapter 3: the Soviet Union and its allies agreed to what they thought were *pro forma* human rights commitments, not anticipating that the declaration would boost the human rights movement throughout the Eastern Bloc, eventually contributing to the fall of the Berlin Wall. But entrapment is not inevitable; forewarned states may prevent it. Among the factors that contribute to the effectiveness of international human rights institutions are the inclusion of democratic states, a platform for human rights nongovernmental organizations, and an independent staff that cares about human rights and can resist member-state pressure.[13] International human rights institutions are not a *deus ex machina*; their success depends on the supportive action of dedicated participants.

The United States should not incorporate international human rights law in a blind or mechanical way. On the contrary, it should reject treaty obligations and institutional arrangements if it has good reason to believe that they would undermine human rights. Such critical engagement can promote an international dialogue from which all parties can learn. Instead of taking this path, however, the United States has rejected the incorporation of international human rights norms whenever it perceives that such norms would require a change in its national law or policy. The message conveyed by the self-exemption policy is that the United States has nothing to learn from others, and that others may learn from it through imitation but not dialogue.[14]

Learning from Europe

Europe demonstrates what international human rights institutions can achieve. Since the end of World War II, it has built an international regime under which participating states hold one another accountable to respect human rights. In effect, European countries have become co-guardians of human rights within each national jurisdiction. The dramatic advancement of human rights throughout the region would have been impossible if Europe had rejected the multilateral approach and left each country to be final judge of its human rights policies. The European human rights system adopts central principles of Madisonian constitutionalism and proves their power to promote justice.

The success of the European regime should not be exaggerated. Grave human rights problems persist. Progress has been slow in some areas, nonexistent in others. I do not attempt a global comparison of respect for human rights in the United States and Europe. Instead, my claim is that respect for human rights in Europe is significantly stronger than it would have been in the absence of a strong transnational human rights regime. Even after 9/11, when officials in some European countries colluded in the U.S. torture program, there can be little doubt that regional human rights institutions prevented what would otherwise have been a worse unraveling of human rights. They exerted a significant, albeit inadequate, restraint on government conduct.

Serious problems cloud the future of human rights in Europe. These include the Eurozone crisis and its political fallout, the rise of extreme right-wing parties, the persistence of anti-immigrant and anti-Roma sentiment, authoritarian entrenchment in Russia and Azerbaijan, Russia's aggression against Ukraine, the authoritarian turn in Hungary and Turkey, the refugee crisis, and terrorism. One threat is recurrent opposition to the regional human rights regime itself. Echoing American critics of international human rights law, some European citizens, politicians, and media accuse the regime, especially the European Court of Human Rights, of being antidemocratic and infringing state sovereignty. I seek to rebut this line of criticism by establishing the democratic legitimacy of international human rights institutions and by reminding readers of the invaluable contributions made by Europe's regional institutions to the protection of human rights.[15]

Lessons from the "War on Terror"

The "War on Terror" reveals the dangers of the U.S. self-exemption policy. When tested by the shock of 9/11, U.S. human rights institutions failed dramatically. Practices that should have been unthinkable, "enhanced interrogation techniques" constituting torture in all but name, were authorized by the president and members of his cabinet. The government's senior lawyers vowed that the practices broke no laws, a finding that gave officials the assurance they needed to continue using torture and that hindered the ability of future administrations to put those officials on trial. Government lawyers similarly enabled the policy of using "extraordinary rendition" to have individuals tortured by foreign officials.[16]

U.S. officials designed and implemented interrogation methods calculated to cause pain, terror, humiliation, and despair.[17] The avowed goal was "learned helplessness," to be achieved by patient and methodical destruction of the victim's sense of agency and self-worth. Victims sometimes thought they would die under torture, and several did.[18] Their harrowing testimonies have been confirmed by the internal government communications of those who tortured them.[19]

Some of the victims had no connection to terrorist activity. False statements elicited by torture were used to justify the 2003 Iraq War, a moral and strategic catastrophe that has set off a careening escalation of violence with no end in sight.[20] As symbols of U.S. torture, Abu Ghraib and Guantanamo became a rallying cry for terrorists worldwide.[21]

Back in the United States, the architects of the torture policy found themselves with a personal stake in defending its legitimacy. They have mounted a vigorous campaign aimed at weakening the torture taboo and propagating the false belief that torture benefited U.S. efforts to combat terrorism.[22] The CIA destroyed video recordings of its interrogation sessions, then fiercely resisted the Senate Intelligence Committee's investigation into its treatment of detainees, to the point that it spied on Committee staffers and sought to have them prosecuted (but publicly denied these actions).[23] U.S. law was rewritten to immunize several acts constituting torture from criminal prosecution.[24] At the urging of both the George W. Bush and Barack Obama administrations, courts have blocked lawsuits by victims of U.S. torture, and the reasoning on which judges have based their findings of official immunity suggests that there are weak institutional restraints against the future resumption of systematic torture in the name of national security.

I consider the U.S. torture policy in depth in Chapters 4 and 5, but take this opportunity to recall a few of its many victims. In the fall of 2002, Maher Arar of Canada was seized by U.S. agents at JFK Airport in New York, then delivered to Syria, where he was tortured and kept in a grave-like cell for ten months.[25] After his release, a Canadian commission of inquiry produced a three-volume report clearing him of all ties to terrorism. The Canadian government formally apologized for providing U.S. officials misleading information about Arar and awarded him $9 million in compensation, but when he attempted to sue U.S. officials responsible for his rendition to torture in Syria, U.S. judges blocked his case from going to trial.[26] He remains on a terrorist watch list that bars his entry into the United States.

In December 2001, Murat Kurnaz of Germany was seized by Pakistani police and sold for a $3,000 bounty to the United States. At Kandahar Airbase in Afghanistan, U.S. interrogators beat him, suffocated him by forcing his head under water, administered electric shocks, and suspended him by his hands for days. He was sent to Guantanamo, where a tribunal justified his detention on the grounds that his friend had carried out a suicide bombing in Istanbul. In fact, his friend never took part in the bombing, but was alive and well in Germany. Although internal Pentagon documents dating from 2002 stated there was no evidence linking Kurnaz to Al Qaeda or terrorist activity, he was kept in detention and tortured over the next four years.[27]

Lakhdar Boumediene, an Algerian resident of Bosnia, was arrested by Bosnian police at the request of U.S. authorities claiming that he was part of a plot to blow up the U.S. and British embassies. Bosnia's highest courts ordered his release when they could find no evidence to support the allegations, but U.S. authorities spirited him to Guantanamo, where he endured harsh interrogation including torture for over seven years, and was force-fed during a two-year hunger strike. After the Supreme Court ruled in 2008 that Boumediene had a constitutional right to habeas corpus, the government was obliged to justify his designation as an "enemy combatant" in court. No longer alleging a plot to attack the embassies in Bosnia, the government submitted as its sole evidence a document reporting a statement by an unnamed informant that Boumediene planned to travel to Afghanistan to fight the United States. A U.S. judge, finding that the reliability of the informant could not be established, ordered Boumediene's release.[28]

In June 2002, U.S. citizen Jose Padilla was placed in indefinite detention in a South Carolina military prison without charge or trial. Federal authorities claimed he was part of an Al Qaeda plot to explode a radioactive "dirty bomb" inside the United States. Kept in extreme solitary confinement for over three years, Padilla reports that he was subjected to stress positions, sleep deprivation, temperature extremes, and noxious fumes, as well as hooded, denied urgent medical care, given mind-altering drugs, and threatened with torture, mutilation, and execution.[29] For over two years he was denied access to a lawyer. As the Supreme Court was considering whether to review the legality of his indefinite detention, the government transferred him to the criminal justice system. No longer charged with the dirty bomb plot, he was instead accused and convicted of conspiring to murder, kidnap, and maim people outside the United States.[30] His repeated attempts to sue those responsible for his torture have been thrown out of court.[31]

In March 2002 Abu Zubaydah, a Saudi Arabian citizen who helped administer a jihadist military training camp in Afghanistan, was captured by U.S. agents in Pakistan. Described by President Bush as "al Qaeda's chief of operations" and "one of the top three leaders in al Qaeda,"[32] Abu Zubaydah became a test subject for the CIA enhanced interrogation program. He was kept naked, subjected to extreme cold, deprived of solid food, denied pain medicine for wounds received in his capture, kicked and beaten, shackled in uncomfortable positions, slammed into walls, blasted with loud music, confined in a small box (causing his wounds to reopen), prevented from sleeping (once for over two weeks), and waterboarded eighty-three times in one month.[33] In September 2006, he was transferred to Guantanamo. In habeas corpus proceedings in 2009, the government dropped its earlier claims that he was a member of Al Qaeda and that he had helped plan the attacks of September 11.[34] His lawyer has reported that Abu Zubaydah's "mental grasp is slipping away," partly because of a head injury suffered in the 1990s and partly because of his treatment by the CIA.[35] Abu Zubaydah remains in Guantanamo, having never been charged with a crime by the U.S. government.

How could the United States, following 9/11, institute a policy of torture, and even maintain it after the secret was revealed? This question will require years of empirical and intellectual detective work. We need to understand not only the individual decisions and bureaucratic and legal maneuvers that constructed the policy but also the background conditions that made it possible. Though several outstanding journalistic, scholarly, and investigative works have been written,[36] the question needs vastly more attention. One obstacle to full engagement is the still widespread assumption, even among those who acknowledge the fact of officially sponsored torture, that the United States is a rights-respecting polity. "This is not who we are" is a common response to revelations of U.S. torture. (In President Bush's words: "The values of this country are such that torture is not a part of our soul and our being.")[37] Because the self-image of the United States as a non-torturing nation is preserved, Americans seem to feel less need to understand the program's underlying causes.[38]

As I show in Chapters 4 and 5, one of the major contributing factors— though of course not the only one—was the U.S. marginalization of international human rights law. As it turns out, legal choices previously made by executive, legislative, and judicial officials in furtherance of the self-exemption policy made a direct and decisive contribution to the U.S. authorization of torture; they facilitated the task of Bush administration officials charged with authorizing "enhanced interrogation techniques." The pre-9/11 legal choices that smoothed the subsequent path to torture included the substantive exceptions attached to U.S. ratification of the Torture Convention and International Covenant on Civil and Political Rights; the decision to block U.S. judges from enforcing U.S. treaty obligations; the general unwillingness to implement human rights treaty obligations through congressional legislation; the position taken by the executive branch and federal appeals courts that a policy decision by the president or a cabinet-level official overrides customary international law; and the refusal to ratify or domestically incorporate the Rome Statute of the International Criminal Court.

U.S. marginalization of international human rights law must therefore figure into an explanation of the U.S. torture policy, a policy that in the words of the U.S. Senate Armed Services Committee "damaged our ability to collect accurate intelligence that could save lives, strengthened the hand of our enemies, and compromised our moral authority."[39] Because the self-exemption policy remains in effect, the return of "enhanced interrogation techniques" cannot be excluded.[40] The price for American exceptionalism is paid in terms of other human rights violations, not just torture. (I shall give some attention to rights violations committed in the U.S. criminal justice system.) Yet the torture program reveals the cost of American exceptionalism with special clarity.

The Effectiveness of International Human Rights Law

The embrace of international human rights law has inhibited human rights violations in Europe, while its marginalization has facilitated human rights violations in the United States. These findings, elaborated in Chapters 3 through 5, are powerful evidence for the practical value of international human rights law. Obviously, international human rights law does not stop all abuses (and some governments seem quite indifferent to their own international human rights promises), but when used well it can exert a significant restraint. Constitutional democracies should employ it as one device among others to prevent the abuse of power.

In recent years, studies have appeared claiming that ratification of international human rights treaties is not correlated with improved respect for human rights.[41] On the basis of these studies, it is sometimes asserted that international human rights law is ineffective—that it makes little or no meaningful contribution to the protection of human rights.[42] However, this inference is unwarranted for several reasons.

First, several studies report a statistical correlation between human rights treaty ratification and improved respect for human rights under certain conditions. For example, Beth Simmons reports such a correlation among the large group of countries that are neither stable democracies nor stable autocracies.[43] Other studies report such a correlation for democratic states,[44] a result consistent with my argument that international human rights law strengthens respect for human rights in constitutional democracies.

Second, it now appears likely that the negative statistical findings are the result of misleading social science datasets. Because the principal datasets report an overall stationary or slightly declining respect for human rights, and because of the large increase in human rights treaty ratifications, it is fairly easy to demonstrate a noncorrelation between treaty ratification and respect for human rights. But the datasets are derived from yearly reports by human rights monitors (primarily Amnesty International and the U.S. State Department) that over time have been able to obtain more information about human rights violations and have defined such violations more broadly. This results in a stricter standard of accountability, such that actual improvements are underreported in the datasets.[45] The pattern is accentuated in states genuinely committed to the respect of human rights, since such commitment entails openness to human rights scrutiny.[46] The existence of a "changing standard of accountability" is confirmed by the political science methodologist Christopher Fariss, who shows statistically that it offers the best way to make sense of a wide array of human rights information sources.[47] He goes on to show that once the social science datasets are corrected for the changing standard of accountability, they reveal a *positive* correlation between ratification of major human rights treaties and respect for physical integrity rights.[48]

Third, the skeptical statistical studies use an overly simple test to measure the adoption of international human rights law. They check whether a country has ratified one or another human rights treaty, but as I emphasize in the following chapters, adoption of international human rights law involves much more than treaty ratification. [49] A country like the United States may ratify human rights treaties and then undercut ratification through reservations, understandings, declarations, and other actions. Beyond ratification, the adoption of international human rights law includes measures such as legislative implementation of human rights treaty provisions, authorization for the enforcement of human rights treaty provisions by domestic courts, screening of proposed legislation for compliance with international human rights commitments, the establishment of national human rights institutions,[50] and respect for customary international human rights law. Such measures have the potential to strengthen respect for human rights, and in many cases they plainly do.

Fourth, those who deny the effectiveness of international human rights law typically overlook its potential to influence domestic law.[51] Since the adoption of international human rights law is partly a matter of its incorporation into domestic law, it largely misses the point to claim that international human rights law is ineffective per se. If that claim is true, we have all the more reason to incorporate international human rights law into domestic law. In any event, the influence of international human rights law on domestic law is extensive. The rights provisions of the 1948 Universal Declaration of Human Rights and 1966 International Covenant on Civil and Political Rights (ICCPR) have been widely reproduced in national constitutions.[52] A recent study shows that countries that ratify the ICCPR are likelier to incorporate its provisions into their constitutions and that their decision to do so is associated with improved respect for physical integrity rights.[53] Human rights treaty provisions are often written into domestic legislation.[54] As discussed in Chapter 3, the European Convention on Human Rights is domestic law in all forty-seven member states. The growing influence of international human rights law on domestic law, a much-studied phenomenon,[55] shows that ratifying international human rights treaties can have significant consequences for domestic practice.

Finally, international human rights law provides human rights advocates an important resource to advance their cause.[56] The availability of the resource is important in itself, notwithstanding the frequent difficulty of knowing if or when or how its use will bear fruit in the form of legislative, judicial, and bureaucratic change. As an analogy, we may think of the role of the Equal Protection Clause (ratified as part of the Fourteenth Amendment to the U.S. Constitution in 1868) in mobilizing legal advocacy against racial discrimination, even though it took many decades to translate those efforts into lasting legislative and judicial victories. As Geoff Dancy and Christopher Fariss observe, we need to attend to the "slow-burning and hard-to-observe improvements in state behaviors" associated with "sustained human rights legal activism over time."[57] In this and other ways, large-N cross-national studies, if used in isolation, may miss important developments in the struggle for human rights.

Brief Summary of the Book

My discussion is roughly divided between empirical and theoretical chapters (though there is some mixture of empirical and theoretical material throughout). Chapters 3 through 5 contrast Europe and the United States to demonstrate the benefits of international human rights law and the costs of its marginalization. The remaining chapters build the case for the moral necessity and political legitimacy of international human rights law. I argue that we should affirm universal human rights (Chapter 1); that adoption of international human rights law is a corollary of the human rights idea (Chapter 1); that participation in an international human rights regime is required by sound principles of constitutional design such as those that guided the founders of the United States (Chapter 2); that international human rights law does not subvert but, on the contrary, bolsters democracy (Chapters 2 and 6); and that international human rights law can be criticized as an infringement of sovereignty only on an implausibly strong conception of sovereignty that we should reject anyway (Conclusion).

Parts of the empirical discussion in Chapters 3–5 are highly detailed. Readers wishing to focus on the theoretical storyline might want to limit their reading of those chapters to pages 73–78, 89–93, 105–10 (chap. 3), 111–17, 120–24, 142–46 (chap. 4), and 147–51, 155–59, 164–70, 180–85 (chap. 5), while skimming or skipping the rest.

More Detailed Summary

Chapter 1 addresses the meaning and justification of human rights. I propose that rights are grounded in a set of principles that can be held by people holding diverse philosophical and religious doctrines. The principles recognize our shared interest in security and freedom and shared status as equal and inviolable persons. Human rights have an institutional dimension, because they embrace not only primary entitlements but also social arrangements that protect those entitlements. Because of the many ways national rights protections may fail, international protections are a necessary supplement; they are the logical completion of the human rights idea. In this chapter, I also consider controversies relating to cultural relativism, socioeconomic rights, and the proper addressee of human rights claims.

Chapter 2 develops a justification of international human rights

institutions based on James Madison's constitutional philosophy. A democratic constitution as envisaged by Madison is a promise to hold one another
accountable in a shared project to promote justice, above all the protection of
human rights. Madison's consistent strategy against tyranny was to break up
concentrated power and replace it with a system of divided powers and mutual oversight. As Madison was aware, however, checks and balances can be
undermined by faction—that is, by groups of people organized to pursue a
collective interest or passion at the expense of justice. His famous solution to
this problem involved the skillful geographic redistribution of decision-making authority. During the debates over the ratification of the U.S. Constitution, he argued that a federal union would limit the harm caused by faction in
the separate American states. In our own time, when nation-states (especially
the United States) wield a degree of power unlike anything Madison ever
knew, and when profound social transformations have made national factions a formidable threat to individual liberty, Madisonian constitutionalism
calls for international oversight of national policy.

Chapter 3 shows what a Madisonian system of transnational human
rights protections might look like in practice. Over the last seventy years,
Europe has built a powerful human rights regime that adheres to Madisonian
principles of constitutional design. The fundamental idea is that the protection of human rights is a collective task—that all European states and all European citizens are simultaneously responsible for the protection of human
rights in each national jurisdiction. The significant achievements of this regime show why a multilateral approach is necessary for the effective protection of human rights.

Chapters 4 and 5 examine the U.S. refusal to integrate itself into international human rights institutions. Since World War II, the United States has
kept itself practically exempt from international human rights law, in the belief that its domestic institutions give rights sufficient protection. But this policy of "American exceptionalism" has created loopholes, blind spots, and a
lack of accountability resulting in grave abuses of human rights. Chapter 4
begins by reviewing the emergence of American exceptionalism, the U.S. involvement with torture before 9/11, and the prohibition of torture under U.S.
constitutional and international law. It then examines the United States' authorization of torture in the "War on Terror," with special attention to the
so-called torture memos written by senior lawyers in the Bush administration. In Chapter 5, I show how specific features of American exceptionalism
(treaty loopholes, nonincorporation and nonjusticiability of treaties,

demotion of customary international law, and nonratification of the International Criminal Court treaty) created a legal environment more conducive to the authorization of torture.

Chapter 6 responds to complaints that international human rights law, by limiting policies that states might otherwise adopt, is antidemocratic. I add new arguments to those made in Chapter 2 for the democratic legitimacy of international human rights law. Because democracy is not group license, because it can never include permission to violate human rights, international human rights law bars only those policies that governments should not consider anyway. Some will object that this reasoning overlooks cross-national disagreement about the meaning of human rights. I do not deny such disagreement, but argue that international human rights law offers a constructive response to disagreement about human rights.

In the conclusion I consider how international human rights law stands in relation to the norm of national sovereignty. I show that international human rights law is compatible with a moderate conception of sovereignty. Only an expansive conception of sovereignty is rejected by international human rights law, but since such a conception represents a false political ideal, this is no cause for regret.

Human Rights and Shared Governance

I argue not only for a strong international human rights regime but also for the need to give it a decentralized character. States must preserve enough authority and independence to monitor each other's human rights policies and to safeguard the integrity of the system overall.[58] What is needed is a model of shared governance built on the cooperation of international institutions, democratic states, and civil society.

If we look beyond human rights (or civil and political rights, which are the primary focus of my book), there are urgent reasons to strengthen global (not just transnational) governance. Climate change, nuclear proliferation, and world poverty are global crises requiring global solutions.[59] (Other global crises could be added to this list.) The world cannot afford to let individual states block just and necessary solutions to these crises, and these solutions may require a greater degree of centralization than is necessary and appropriate for international monitoring of human rights. (That is to say, the proper degree of centralization may vary according to policy issue.) These matters, however, lie outside the scope of my book.

By means of international human rights institutions, states can remind one another of their domestic and international human rights pledges, and correct one another's errors, blind spots, and biases. The "War on Terror" has reminded us of the fragility of human rights, even in constitutional democracies. Human rights are too important to be left to the sole care of one's government. If all human beings are "endowed with certain unalienable rights" and governments exist "to secure these rights," then it is incumbent on governments to provide both internal and external safeguards. Transnational institutions form part of the necessary architecture of human rights.

Chapter 1

Human Rights

Human rights are enshrined in international law and the domestic law of most countries. A vast network of local and transnational organizations is dedicated to their defense. All over the world, people believe in and struggle for human rights.

Many scholars have written about the meaning and justification of human rights. Heated debate on particular controversies masks broad areas of agreement. Appropriating the wisdom of past and present thinkers, I offer a brief account that is neither new nor distinctive but that I hope is persuasive. Toward the end of this chapter and in the rest of the book, it will help us draw out the institutional implications of human rights.

I claim that human rights are based on a set of principles that can be shared by people holding diverse philosophical and religious views. Highlighting this widely sharable conception of human rights is the main purpose of the chapter. In addition, I argue, albeit briefly, that human rights can withstand the cultural relativist critique, that they do not conflict with one another, that they include certain socioeconomic rights, that they entail both institutional and interpersonal duties, that they are mutually supportive, and (anticipating the larger argument of the book) that they require international protections. Though some of these claims may court controversy, they lead us, I believe, to a sounder understanding of human rights.

As the term implies, human rights are rights that we have because we are human. They are not conditional on nationality, race, religion, sex, or other group memberships. The guiding thought is that each person is a moral center whose perspective matters and whose interests must be accorded significant weight and respect. Think of the child who (as you are reading this sentence) was most recently born into the world. What kind of life may this child expect? What opportunities will he or she enjoy, and what harms and dangers will he or she endure? Will he or she have enough to eat, enjoy adequate health care, receive an education, be protected from violence and persecution, and be permitted to chart the direction of his or her life? Such questions remind us of the person's vulnerability to the individual and collective choices of other people. They focus our attention on the minimal entitlements to which we give the name human rights.

Human rights are distinct from legal rights.[1] In the American South before the Civil War, the law gave whites the right to own slaves and denied slaves the right to be free. The first was a legal right that was not a human right; the second was a human right that was not a legal right. At most, the law recognizes human rights; it does not create them.[2] The law is nonetheless important to human rights for the following reasons: (1) many human rights require legal backing; (2) some of those legal protections are themselves human rights; (3) the law can transmit the values of human rights; (4) the law provides a forum where we can negotiate provisional (though fallible) agreement about human rights; (5) a well-designed legal system, by structuring thoughtful deliberation, can improve our understanding of human rights.[3]

Which rights are human rights? I make the working assumption that the 1948 Universal Declaration of Human Rights moves us toward the right answer. The Declaration remains the primary inspiration and reference for the contemporary human rights movement. If the Declaration is far off base, then the contemporary human rights movement is far off base. However, I do not believe the Declaration is far off base. Its values and commitments are those we should look for in a conception of human rights.

The Declaration earns much of its prestige from the circumstances of its creation. It was drafted with the tragedies of the 1930s and 1940s fresh in people's minds, and emerged from a painstaking and protracted deliberation that drew on the participation of individuals and organizations from around the world. When put to a vote, it was approved without dissent by the General Assembly of the United Nations. Its content has been admired ever since, and its provisions incorporated into numerous national constitutions and international treaties.

It is a human creation, and therefore unlikely to be perfect. There are few (if any) who on reflection would agree with all its provisions. The real issue is its overall adequacy as a conception of human rights. You may think that it approximates the best overall conception. But even if you prefer a different conception, you may still think that it captures an important part of the truth.

Those, for example, who question the six articles (of a total of thirty) that assert the existence of social and economic rights may still find inspiration and enlightenment in the remaining twenty-four, which deal with rights to physical integrity, legal due process, personal liberty, and political participation.[4] (Below I defend the inclusion of social and economic rights, but most of my book is concerned with the protection of civil and political rights.)

Of course, the Declaration does not stand alone. It draws on earlier rights charters and philosophical explorations of rights. Subsequent legal instruments appropriate but also supplement and adjust the Declaration, and it has generated extensive critical commentary. One may regard it as an important moment in a continuing deliberation on human rights.

Content and Justification

Human rights are concerned with the interests of individual persons; they adopt the perspective of the individual. This does not imply atomistic individualism, since human rights also protect a wide range of social activity. But human rights value social groups because of their benefits to people, not the other way round. The starting point is the vulnerability of the individual; the main object, to protect individuals from various kinds of harm. These harms are often inflicted by groups, although one of the principal harms inflicted is to deprive individuals of the benefits and rewards of social life.

Belief in human rights does not imply a rejection of animal rights. Indeed, animals may have rights for some of the same reasons that humans have rights. Though I do not pursue the point here, a belief in human rights may lead to a deeper appreciation of animal rights, and even to the recognition of values beyond human and animal values.[5] In any event, it is worth emphasizing that human rights claims do not exhaust the domain of morality, or even justice. A society that fully respects human rights could still be unjust in a number of ways.

Human rights, despite their superficial variety, possess an underlying rationale. There is a point to human rights. If we look, for example, at the Universal Declaration and the entitlements asserted over the course of its thirty articles, we can perceive some unifying themes and persistent concerns. The following is an attempt to render the basic values that underlie human rights. The precise wording is unimportant: other people may prefer different formulations that convey the same general idea.

On the account I present, human rights may be tied to the following four principles:

1. *Persons have a fundamental interest in security.* There are some fates that everyone has a reason to avoid. They include untimely death, severe injury, physical confinement, torture, terror, disease, chronic or severe pain, hunger, starvation, abandonment, forced isolation or separation, social humiliation, and lack of basic education and socialization. Everyone should be protected from these fates. Of the main principles that support the human rights idea, this is the least contested. Stuart Hampshire writes, "There is nothing mysterious or 'subjective' or culture-bound in the great evils of human experience, re-affirmed in every age and in every written history and in every tragedy and fiction: murder and the destruction of life, imprisonment, enslavement, starvation, poverty, physical pain and torture, homelessness, friendlessness. That these great evils are to be averted is the constant presupposition of moral arguments at all times and in all places."[6]

2. *Persons have a fundamental interest in autonomy.* Everyone should be allowed to lead a life of one's own choosing. Persons should be allowed to think their own thoughts, make their own plans, and choose their own company.[7] The principle of autonomy recognizes that, once our most basic needs are guaranteed, individuals should be given considerable scope to define what is, for each, the most desirable life.[8] In the world as a whole, belief in individual autonomy is somewhat less robust than belief in individual security. It encounters resistance from traditional societies (which believe individuals should adhere to prescribed roles), conservative religious groups (which seek the enforcement of scriptural rules limiting religious freedom, sexual freedom, and women's freedom), and autocratic governments (which limit freedom of expression and association). When critics complain about the "Western" bias of human rights, they generally have in mind the importance attached to personal autonomy.

3. *Persons are inviolable.* Persons may not be treated as means only. They may not be used as a mere instrument for the pursuit of other goals, however worthy. That includes the goals of furthering other people's security or autonomy. In an example well known to moral philosophers, a surgeon may not kill a healthy man to save the lives of five other people in need of the man's transplanted organs. For the same reason, the police may not suspend due process and thereby condemn a certain number of

innocent people to punishment, even if doing so will save a larger number of citizens from violent crime. Inviolability affirms our status as creatures *whom it is morally forbidden* to injure in certain egregious ways. Although philosophers debate how best to explain the principle of inviolability, it is politically indispensable for blocking the consequentialist rationales used by governments to justify all manner of cruelties.[9]

4. *Persons deserve to be recognized and treated as equals.* This principle goes beyond noting our equal inviolability and equal interest in security and autonomy. It upholds a claim to be accorded equal standing in the communities, especially the political communities, to which we belong. The principle excludes arbitrary or invidious discrimination, social caste systems, and stigmatization of entire groups. It bars the political subordination of one group of people to another. Equality is a recurrent principle of human rights charters and national constitutions. It is emphasized by the Universal Declaration and the International Covenant on Civil and Political Rights, as well as the Fourteenth Amendment to the U.S. Constitution. It is trumpeted in the classic human rights texts of John Lilburne, John Locke, and Thomas Jefferson. Practically speaking, it is a crucial condition for the respect of one's other rights (though that may not be the only reason to uphold it).[10]

Security, autonomy, inviolability, and equality are the point of human rights. If we are asked, why human rights? these are the principles we can invoke. Their powerful appeal explains why the idea of human rights is so difficult to resist.

This may not be the most philosophically rigorous explanation of human rights. Yet it has important virtues. For want of a better term, I shall call it a "public conception" of human rights.[11] That is, it is an argument for human rights with which a great many people can agree, although their reasons for supporting it may vary.[12] Do we want a deeper, philosophically more rigorous justification? There are a great many to choose from: Kantianism, consequentialism, contractualism, intuitionism, sentimentalism, conventionalism, constructivism, discourse ethics, Aristotelian perfectionism, natural law, and various religious traditions. Each has been identified as providing the strongest basis for human rights. All have inspired discussions that enrich our understanding and appreciation of the values underlying what I call the "public conception." All the same, they tend to place heavy demands on our intellects—that is, they can be difficult to understand, and each is premised on the denial of at least some of the others. So focusing on these deeper justifications can bring uncertainty and dissension. It is worth recalling the existence of an "overlapping consensus"[13] on a set of core principles that make sense of, help explain, and render coherent the human rights idea, even if the search for reasons behind the principles leaves us perplexed and divided.

Some people, struck by the clash of different people's philosophical and religious worldviews, may say that collective human rights discourse should avoid talk of justification altogether. This goes too far in the opposite direction, and threatens to make belief in human rights seem accidental, arbitrary, contingent, and optional. Without a public justification, we cannot explain to one another the point of human rights, or have a shared basis for determining which items do and do not belong in a list of human rights, and our confidence that people really have human rights may begin to fade.

The fact is that we do care about people's vulnerability to calamity, and people's ability to make their own choices in life (not have others decide for them). We care that people be spared the most severe griefs, terrors, and humiliations. We care that their capacity to think, decide, and act not be forced down by the overriding preferences of others. For some of us, this is a moral starting point; for others, an inference from prior moral, religious, or philosophical premises. In either case, these are robust convictions, difficult to shake, which we have little reason to doubt, and which supply their own motivating power.

As befits a public conception of human rights, nothing about this story is original. The idea that security and autonomy are the two fundamental interests underpinning human rights has been invoked by many thinkers, though in different ways. Ronald Dworkin writes, "Government must treat those whom it governs with concern, that is, as human beings, who are capable of suffering and frustration, and with respect, that is, as human beings who are capable of forming and acting on intelligent conceptions of how their lives should be lived."[14] George Kateb echoes this idea, though he notes as a third feature of the human condition our capacity to treat others as equals: "Public and formal respect for rights registers and strengthens awareness of three constitutive facts of being human: every person is a creature capable of feeling pain, and is a free agent capable of having a free being, of living a life that is one's own and not somebody else's idea of how a life should be lived, and is a moral agent capable of acknowledging that what one claims for oneself as a right one can claim only as an equal to everyone else."[15] The idea makes clear and immediate sense. Major human rights declarations and manifestos acquire a new coherence when they are understood in terms of security, autonomy, inviolability, and equality.

In distinguishing between public and philosophical conceptions of human rights, I do not mean to disparage the latter. To review: a public conception justifies human rights by reference to a widely (not universally) shared set of principles but suspends inquiry into the justification of those principles themselves. A philosophical conception seeks to supply human rights with a deeper and more rigorous justification. (Both approaches may be contrasted with a "superficial" approach that forswears justification altogether.) The disadvantage of each approach corresponds to the strength of the other. The benefit of a public conception is that it commands wider (though of course not universal) agreement. This benefit is enormously significant, because human rights become more secure as more people believe in them. Widespread principled agreement allows us to get on with the task of teaching, promoting, defending, implementing, and enforcing human rights. The cost is that deeper inquiry into the meaning of human rights is suspended. While the cost of a philosophical conception is the narrowing of consensus, the potential gain is enhanced understanding, which may improve and bolster the public conception over the long term (but which is valuable even if it does not). Moreover, we face difficult questions when it comes to the full specification of human rights, and philosophical conceptions may help us arrive at the best answers. Though I rely on a public conception of human rights in this discussion, philosophical conceptions are also needed in public deliberation.[16] Both approaches are needed; both influence and inform each other; and it would be impossible to draw a sharp line between them.[17]

The Relativist Challenge

Is the idea of universal human rights undermined by appeal to cultural relativism? The claim would be that it shows insufficient respect for cultural diversity. Packed into that claim are several premises: (1) that the world contains distinct cultures; (2) that some cultures reject the idea of human rights, at least in part; and (3) that it is wrong or unreasonable to assert the universality of human rights over the dissent of particular cultures.

I believe each of these premises is mistaken. The third premise presupposes that cultures should have the final say on questions of morality. But every culture is a mixture of good and bad. The aspects of a culture that permit or require human rights violations are among the aspects that ought to be reformed. Awareness that cultures are flawed is one reason why cultures can change from within—why, for example, feminists have made progress in challenging patriarchal norms embedded in their own cultures. If one denies that cultures contain anything bad, one must say that internal criticism of a culture is always mistaken and that no reform achieved through internal criticism, for example, the promotion of sex equality, represents progress. These claims are implausible.

The problem with the second premise (that some cultures reject human rights) is that it presupposes the first (that the world contains distinct cultures). Reference to "cultures" in the plural[18] conveys a picture of a world in which social groups (typically defined by nation, region, tribe, ethnicity, or religion) are the bearers of stable, coherent, and distinctive systems of belief. Implied is an essentialist understanding of culture—culture as a belief system that one inherits along with one's group membership. (Individuals may switch cultures, along with group membership, but this is the exception, and requires special effort.) Individuals receive their beliefs from the groups to which they belong.[19]

This is a misleading picture. It denies or discounts the ability of individuals to learn from, influence, and be influenced by members of other groups. Worse, it denies the ability of individuals to think for themselves, to question and sometimes reject the views of local authorities. Yet these things happen, and they make a cumulative impact. The observable result is heterogeneity of belief within groups and overlap of belief across groups.[20] The longer the process unfolds, the less meaningful it becomes to speak of "cultures" as corresponding to social groups defined by nation, region, tribe, ethnicity, and religion. (Moreover, some people prefer not to be identified with ascriptive groups at all.)

Cultural essentialism is least persuasive when it claims that the idea of human rights is culturally bounded. Belief in human rights travels with particular ease: wherever human rights can be discussed without threat of violence or sanction (and sometimes even in the face of these threats), there will be people who believe in human rights. If some of us believe in freedom of religion or the wrongness of the death penalty while local religious or political authorities believe the opposite, what is the position of "our" culture? So long as "culture" refers to our nation, region, tribe, ethnicity, or religion, there is no coherent answer to the question. To avoid such indeterminacy, cultural essentialism tends to associate culture with authority and tradition. It carries a conservative bias, and does not seem bothered that the traditional views are often shored up by coercion.

Why are people still drawn to cultural relativism? One reason is the grip of cultural essentialism. Once the picture takes hold of the world as a mosaic of different cultures, it appears difficult to shake. I would mention two other factors: (1) group identity, and (2) a generalized reluctance to pass moral judgment.

First, group identity. The thought is that if human rights are a "Western concept," non-Westerners cannot embrace the idea as their own. To this we should reply that human rights are *not* a Western concept: they are an idea understood and embraced by people all over the world. Yet someone might answer back that, if fully worked-out theories of human rights first *emerged* in the West, that is enough to mark the idea as Western: a non-Westerner strongly identifying with his or her non-Western group therefore has reason to regard the idea as alien.[21] Such a preoccupation with the historical pedigree of ideas, though unnecessary and unfortunate, exerts surprising influence (and is a major source of cultural essentialism).

Second, some people are shy about making moral assertions in the face of potential disagreement. They fear that there is something arrogant about passing judgment on the behavior of others. Yet urgent matters are at stake. Should prisoners be spared cruel and humiliating treatment? Do the accused have the right to a fair trial? Should girls be educated? To withhold judgment is to act from a misplaced sense of decorum. When those otherwise withholding judgment have their attention drawn to actual people whose lives are affected by these questions, their principled detachment tends to fade (as it should).

Behind the reluctance to condemn or dismiss views contrary to human rights may lie a worthy impulse, namely, an openness to dissent and disagreement. Trouble emerges when, striving to be humble, we allow dialogue to become deference, and when, in deference to "what other people think," we no longer challenge each other to think harder, or no longer encourage thinking at all. An "emperor's new clothes" aspect can creep into these discussions. The worst is to subsume people under their "cultures," and to defer to cultures rather than people. The practice becomes internalized when people refuse to think for themselves, and leave all thinking to be done by their "culture."

Cultural relativism about human rights is sometimes related to guilt over the history of Western crimes against non-Western peoples. Guilt is appropriate, but rejecting universal human rights is not, since the crimes were themselves massive violations of human rights, and need to be condemned as such. It is of course true that efforts to promote human rights transnationally can become self-defeating or destructive when the local context is poorly understood or when talk of human rights masks a hidden agenda (and not only then). There is a potential for human rights discourse to abet overbearing, even imperialist, policies, and indeed policies that entail serious violations of human rights. I do not think this problem is a reason to reject human rights per se, but it obliges us to think more carefully about the responsible promotion of human rights.[22] My book is intended as one contribution to this effort. I argue that one check on the danger of overbearing policies is the construction of reciprocal human rights regimes in which participating countries understand that standards applied to others can also be applied to themselves.

The human rights idea, as has often been pointed out, is not a totalizing doctrine. It is not a comprehensive blueprint for what to think or how to live. It deliberately leaves many areas open for individual and collective judgment, valuing people's ability to decide important matters on their own. It is therefore compatible with a wide range of ethical, political, and religious viewpoints. All it does is erect certain limits: not to impose great suffering, not to stifle individual autonomy, not to treat persons as mere means, and not to deny equality of moral status.

Of course not everyone believes in human rights. Personal freedom is the value most frequently contested—whether in the name of tradition, community, or religion. Some of the fiercest and most determined opposition comes from religious fundamentalists who believe themselves authorized to coerce others into scripturally required forms of belief and behavior. This is a tyrannical attitude, rightly resisted, because it forces other people to conform their own lives to religious views they do not share. On the other hand, the conflict between autonomy and tradition is sometimes exaggerated. The right to autonomy does not prohibit individuals from adopting traditional lifestyles; it prohibits their being *forced* to do so. To those readers who might question a universal human right to autonomy, I would ask: Would you be willing to give up the right to autonomy, to let someone else dictate how you should live your life? If not, why would you be willing to deny that right to others?

It is a curious fact that arguments against universal human rights often draw inspiration from a principle central to the human rights idea. The principle is autonomy: living according to one's own values. The idea of universal human rights is accused of being coercive, by imposing some people's values on others. This gets things backwards. The human rights idea claims that individuals should be allowed to pursue their own vision of a good life.[23] Insisting on universal human rights is not about imposing some people's values on others. It is about *preventing* the imposition of some people's values on others.[24]

The Force of a Human Rights Claim

Some people claim that human rights routinely or frequently conflict.[25] For example, it is claimed that the right to privacy conflicts with the right to freedom of expression, or that the right to economic subsistence conflicts with the right to private property, or that the right to be presumed innocent conflicts with the right to protection from violent assault. However, I do not think this is the best way to understand human rights.

We name human rights by the interests they protect, but the content of a human right is defined by (1) the moral permissions granted to the rights bearer ("correlative permissions") and (2) the duties assigned to other people ("correlative duties"). Neither correlative permissions nor correlative duties are unlimited. My right to life implies that I may defend myself from a violent attacker, that you have a duty not to kill me, and that a nearby police officer has a duty to protect me from being killed. But it does not permit me to raid other people's bodies for their organs. Nor does it give you a duty to donate your liver or to block the assassin's bullet with your body. Your reasonable interest in staying alive and remaining healthy limits the risk and sacrifice you must bear for the sake of my life. Diverse moral considerations extending beyond the interests of the rights bearer determine the content of the correlative permissions and duties.

When we say that someone's human rights have been violated, our exact meaning is not that the rights bearer is unable to enjoy the substance of his or her right but rather that someone else has violated a correlative duty owed to the rights bearer. (Correlative duties tend to be more salient than correlative permissions in human rights discourse, because we usually have our attention drawn to human rights by the fear that they will be violated.) The concept of human rights violations refers not to *prima facie rights* (defined by the interest of the rights bearer) but to *all-things-considered rights* (defined by the boundaries of the right, that is, the reach of the correlative permissions and duties).[26] The key point is that the characterization of an all-things-considered right, and therefore the definition of a human rights violation, is *preceded* by a consideration of all relevant moral factors. This is why human rights claims have a morally conclusive character. To cite a human rights violation is to classify the behavior and policy in question as morally unacceptable. Defenses are not allowed, because all defenses were considered prior to our classification of the behavior as a violation of human rights.

The articles of famous human rights charters sometimes limit themselves to the statement of a prima facie right. An example is the right to life in the Universal Declaration. Article 3 states: "Everyone has the right to life, liberty and security of person." While the correlative duties are not spelled out, there is a tacit understanding that we know and agree what some of them are and could uncontroversially state them if asked. We find a more complete (though not fully complete) description of correlative duties in human rights treaties, constitutional bills of rights, legislative statutes, and judicial rulings. Even in the major charters, however, some correlative duties are spelled out. For example, Article 4 of the Universal Declaration states, "No one shall be held in slavery or servitude," while Article 5 states, "No one shall be subjected to torture or to cruel, inhuman or degrading treatment or punishment." This means that it is always wrong to practice slavery or inflict torture or ill-treatment. Note, however, that this is not all that the articles convey, because state officials have additional positive duties to protect persons from being enslaved and subjected to torture or ill-treatment. Several of these duties are spelled out in the 1926 Slavery Convention and the 1984 Convention Against Torture and Other Cruel, Inhuman or Degrading Treatment or Punishment.

In ordinary discourse, if it is accepted that a policy violates human rights, this means that the matter is settled, morally speaking: the policy is wrong and must be ended. One implication of this is that human rights cannot (except very rarely) conflict with one another. Since violating human rights is morally unacceptable, it must be possible to live our individual and collective lives in ways that do not (except very rarely) violate human rights. If human rights routinely conflicted, violating human rights would become unavoidable, and we would lose the sense that doing so is morally unacceptable. So we must work out a conception of human rights in which the enumerated rights are mutually compatible. If we discover routine conflicts between human rights as we have conceived them, our conception needs to be revised, perhaps by pruning the correlative duties attached to certain rights, or by removing some rights from the catalog altogether.

It is sometimes said that courts are asked to resolve conflicts between human rights. I think it is more helpful to say that courts are called on to determine the contours of rights, where this sometimes entails tracing the boundary between rights. Suppose that a court denies a request from parents on religious grounds to deny a life-saving blood transfusion to their young child. Assuming that we agree with the ruling, how should we characterize it? Some might say that in this case the child's right to life overrides the parents' right to freedom of religion, but I think it is clearer to say that the parents' right to freedom of religion *does not include* the right to deny a life-saving blood transfusion to their young child. I suggest that other apparent "conflicting rights" cases should be redescribed in this way.

The only occasion that could justify talk of conflicting human rights is a tragic conflict between two immovable moral considerations. The clearest case would be a conflict, in extreme cases, between two duties such that any action you choose would be morally wrong. In such a case, it is not just that each of the available actions has bad consequences, but that each act *itself* deserves moral condemnation: you cannot emerge from the situation morally unscathed. Perhaps there also exist, in extreme cases, conflicts between an undefeated obligation (e.g., not to harm another) and an undefeated moral permission (e.g., not to sacrifice a core interest). Some people deny, while others accept, that morality admits irresolvable conflicts of these kinds. If there are ever conflicts between human rights, they would manifest themselves in such situations.[27]

Tragic conflicts aside, human rights do not conflict. The more general point is that human rights should be asserted only with caution. Something's being morally desirable does not make it a human right. Something can be a human right only if its violation is morally wrong (and of course not every wrong act is correlated to a human right).

Some writers have disputed this picture.[28] They say we should become used to the idea of human rights being in conflict, that the identification of a human right marks the beginning, not the end, of a moral discussion. We should (in this view) recognize the existence of plural and competing values and the moral quandaries in which they land us; human rights discourse should incorporate the truth of moral pluralism into its own terms. But this proposal represents too abrupt a departure from ordinary usage. It drains the concept of human rights of its moral force. Sooner or later we would have to coin a new term to do the work now done by "human rights," and such linguistic reshuffling would be an unnecessary invitation to confusion and misunderstanding. The concept of human rights does not deny (or affirm) that values conflict. It merely says that some ways of treating human beings are morally unacceptable. Since that happens to be true, the existing usage is worth preserving.

Socioeconomic Rights

The Universal Declaration of Human Rights asserts several social and economic rights. They include economic subsistence (adequate provision of food, clothing, housing, and health care); security against destitution from old age, disease, disability, and unemployment; safe and dignified conditions of work (with the right to form trade unions as a necessary protection of this right); opportunities for rest and leisure; and education.

The existence of socioeconomic rights has been denied. The only true human rights, some claim, are civil and political. The skeptical position has been strongly rebutted in philosophical arguments made over the past forty years.[29] Here I confine myself to some cursory remarks. Note that I am not interested in challenging economic libertarianism in general, but only the strong version of it that denies that there are any socioeconomic rights.

We should first notice the extreme nature of the skeptical position. It implies that no one's human rights are violated if children are deprived of an education, or workers are subjected to unsafe working conditions, or trauma victims are denied emergency medical services, or orphans, the severely disabled, the unemployed, or the unemployable are left to starve.

Socioeconomic rights are grounded in the same values as civil-political rights. They are necessary to a minimally decent existence; some of them (such as food and basic health services) are necessary to any existence at all. Like protection from violent assault, they honor our fundamental interest in security. They are also necessary for autonomy: their deprivation confines one to a set of severely reduced, often grim opportunities, or no opportunities at all. To deny people these goods—to let them go hungry, or permit their deterioration from easily cured disease, or leave them unattended when no cure is available, or refuse them shelter, or subject them to slave-like work, or keep them illiterate—is to deny their basic dignity.

Skeptics posit fundamental differences between civil-political and socioeconomic rights. It is claimed, for example, that civil-political rights imply negative duties (duties not to inflict harm) whereas socioeconomic rights imply positive duties (duties to provide help); or that civil-political rights are less demanding than socioeconomic rights; or that unlike socioeconomic rights they can be universally fulfilled; or that they lend themselves more easily to legal enforcement; or that civil-political rights imply individual duties whereas socioeconomic rights imply collective ones; or that the duties implied by civil-political rights are clear and determinate while those implied by socioeconomic rights are vague and indeterminate. These differences, it is claimed, constitute the line between genuine and spurious human rights.

If the differences seem real at first glance, they fade on closer inspection. Begin with the alleged distinction between negative and positive rights. As several scholars have shown, all human rights imply a package of both negative and positive duties. The right not to be violently assaulted entails more than a moral obligation of fellow citizens and government agents not to commit assault. It requires positive measures by government to protect citizens from assault. When governments leave certain private groups free to terrorize a particular segment of the population, those governments are properly accused of violating human rights.[30] An effective police force, functioning system of criminal and civil justice, and competent regulatory regime are measures necessitated by our rights to physical safety and security of property. And while the negative duty of governments not to harm the innocent and not to inflict excessive harm on the guilty is central to any human rights conception, this obligation is reinforced by an elaborate system of positive duties, including habeas corpus and the numerous undertakings that constitute the guarantee to a fair trial. Moreover, rights imply remedies. If there are no rights without a remedy, then civil-political rights no less than socioeconomic ones entail positive duties.[31]

Just as civil-political rights imply positive duties, so socioeconomic rights imply negative duties. One reason for emphasizing socioeconomic rights is precisely that they prohibit grievous inflictions of harm. Humans have long inflicted starvation through blockade, siege, and seizure. During the 1932–33 terror-famine that killed millions of Ukrainians, Soviet officials seized food from the homes of starving peasants. Three-quarters of a million people or more died in the Nazi siege of Leningrad. Nor should we forget that land seizures by white settlers caused vast numbers of American Indians to die from hunger; that Mao Zedong's grain requisitions in the Great Leap Forward killed millions of Chinese; that crushing taxes and shredding of local safety nets by agents of the British Empire caused severe famines in colonial India; or that food blockages to starving civilians are still used as a method of war in Africa.[32] Evictions and housing demolitions cause widespread homelessness,

often depriving those affected of access to employment and basic social services.[33] Large numbers of people lose access to safe drinking water through
government or private company diversion of traditional water sources or
through the industrial pollution of the water supply.[34]

The deprivation of socioeconomic goods, in other words, often takes an
active rather than a passive form. But, in addition, the very distinction between active and passive deprivation is systematically misperceived. In all
societies, property, whether private or communal, is constituted by norms
that are coercively enforced.[35] The authorities in Stalin's Soviet Union did
not permit agricultural workers to dissolve collective farms into private
plots, just as U.S. authorities today do not permit landless farmhands to
establish their own plots on large commercial estates. What looks superfi-
cially like passive deprivation—people not owning or not being able to purchase or not being given particular resources—is in fact a case of active
deprivation whereby human agents use force or the threat of force to enforce institutionalized rules determining who owns what. The wealthy land-
owner who evicts the starving poacher from his orchard, or the baker who
hauls Jean Valjean to the police for stealing a loaf of bread to feed his sister's
starving children, may not be perceived as engaging in an act of positive
deprivation, but that is exactly what they do. Similarly for all those who
assisted the export of grain from famine-stricken Ireland, India, Ukraine,
and rural China while local people died from hunger. Institutions are
human arrangements and therefore involve human agency and choice,
however much we take them for granted. To prevent someone from taking
something (or to force him to return what he has taken) is a form of action.
If we think that individuals who lack some good *should* be prevented from
taking it, we must make our case on grounds other than the distinction
between active and passive behavior. (For example, we might argue on
other grounds that the good is the rightful property of the current posses-
sor. The appeal to private property as a reason for rejecting socioeconomic
rights is discussed below.)

Other alleged differences between civil-political and socioeconomic
rights fare no better. Consider the socioeconomic right to safe working conditions. This right is legally enforceable. It creates obligations for individual
employers and managers (obligations that are often negative in character, for
example, not to expose workers to dangerous chemicals or block safety exits).
It is less costly to guarantee than several civil-political rights, such as the right
to a fair trial. And it can be specified with some precision.

It has been claimed that physical scarcity makes it impossible for certain socioeconomic rights such as the right to food to be universally fulfilled. If such rights cannot be universally fulfilled, some argue, then calling them universal human rights cheapens the meaning of the term. This argument may be criticized on both empirical and conceptual grounds. The view that the world cannot produce enough food for its inhabitants finds little acceptance among contemporary experts. Nobel Prize economist Amartya Sen has convincingly argued that world hunger does not result from a global shortfall in food production but rather from the inability of vulnerable populations, under existing institutions, to command access to sufficient food.[36] How to distribute the blame between domestic and global institutions is a matter of continuing dispute; plausibly, both levels of institutional failure are intertwined.[37]

But let us accept that, for whatever combination of institutional and natural causes, it would be *difficult* to quickly supply all the world's inhabitants with sufficient food. To say that this disproves a universal human right to food rests on a conceptual confusion. The need for food makes access to food a morally urgent matter and establishes it as a universal human right. That right generates various duties on the part of individuals and institutions to help ensure that everyone has enough food. The human right to food is cashed out in terms of those duties. That does not mean, however, that if someone lacks sufficient food you and I are necessarily guilty of having violated that person's right to food, for you and I may have done everything that could reasonably be expected of us to guarantee that person sufficient food. As Henry Shue writes, human rights call for "some reasonable level of guarantee."[38] We recognize this well enough in the case of civil-political rights. The right not to be enslaved is enshrined in international law and in the Thirteenth Amendment to the U.S. Constitution. Even so, there are several million slaves in the world, and several thousand in the United States. Even if every government did all that could be reasonably expected of it to end slavery, its complete elimination would be unlikely. These facts do not negate the right not to be enslaved. The right not to be enslaved gives institutions and individuals a package of negative and positive duties whose underlying rationale is the prevention of slavery. The equivalent is true of the right to food. Some of these duties are more absolute than others: the duty not to practice slavery or deprive someone of food is more absolute than the duty to prevent slavery or prevent hunger (though, as explained above, we tend to draw the line between inflicting and not preventing hunger in a confused manner). The crucial point is that an individual or institution may fully respect the human right not to be enslaved and the human right to food even if slavery and hunger are not fully eliminated.

It may be objected at this point that socioeconomic rights are excessively vague. We may have a clearer image of what is meant by the duty to prevent slavery, say, than the duty to prevent hunger. There is some merit to this challenge, because the duties implied by many welfare rights are still being worked out: the jurisprudence on socioeconomic rights is younger than that on, say, the right to a fair trial. We should not exaggerate the contrast, however. No human rights are perfectly transparent, which is why their meaning is continually reexamined in court decisions and why those decisions are themselves subjected to critical scrutiny. Some civil-political rights are famously vague: for example, the right to liberty, to equal protection of the laws, to the presumption of innocence, and to be spared cruel and unusual punishment. The task of specifying these rights—that is, clarifying the content of their correlative duties—is an immense labor both intellectual and political, and one that is never at an end. Considerable progress has been made in specifying the duties implied by socioeconomic rights, thanks to the rulings of national courts; treaties such as the International Covenant on Economic, Social and Cultural Rights and the European Social Charter; the general comments and concluding observations of the International Committee on Economic, Social and Cultural Rights; nongovernmental organizations such as Oxfam and Amnesty International; and international law commissions and conferences.[39] But there is no doubt that far more progress is needed, especially in clarifying those correlative duties that are transnational in scope.[40]

Socioeconomic rights place restrictions on the right to private property. They authorize taxes for education and basic welfare, and limit the conditions employers may impose on workers. Opposition to socioeconomic rights has therefore come from those who believe in what I shall call a maximal right to private property—one that excludes taxation for most (or all) functions other than the military, courts, and police and forbids most forms of regulation. Some even claim this as a human right.

As a general proposition, the claim that we have a maximal right to private property is not credible. It implies that Jean Valjean should let his sister's children starve rather than steal a loaf of bread. With regard to the present discussion, it implies that the tax policies of almost all existing governments—certainly those of all economically advanced countries—are violations of human rights. But the idea that taxes levied for education or food stamps or Medicare (or, for that matter, roads or medical research or the arts) constitute human rights violations is difficult to take seriously. Democratically authorized, nonarbitrary taxes do not jeopardize people's safety or deny them the chance to live autonomously. Deprivation of food, shelter, education, and basic health care, on the other hand, does have these effects. To deny the latter rights in the name of a maximal right to private property is a grotesque disordering of priorities.

For these reasons, the claim that our human rights include a maximal right to private property is difficult to maintain. The following difficulties may also be noted.

1. The claim of a maximal right to private property is not self-evident, but must be plausibly derived from human values and interests. Recall that the historically most influential defense of private property emphasized the universal benefits it provides. According to John Locke, private appropriation is permitted only if "enough and as good" is left for others, a condition satisfied in commercial society, Locke thought, because the resulting gains in productivity operate to the benefit of everyone, particularly the worst-off. Thus Locke claimed that the rural poor derive more benefit from ten fertile acres in commercial England than one hundred fertile acres in precommercial America. Even then, the property owner must acknowledge the right of the starving man to the "surplusage of his goods, so that it cannot justly be denied him, when his pressing wants call for it," for "charity gives every man a title to so much out of another's plenty, as will keep him from extreme want, where he has no means to subsist otherwise."[41] Locke makes the legitimacy of private property depend on its ability to guarantee universal subsistence; if modifications of that right are necessary to better guarantee universal subsistence, those modifications are morally required.

2. It is not plausible to defend a maximal right to private property in the name of self-ownership, because moderate taxation is compatible with autonomy and because our pre-tax holdings do not flow from our choices alone. As Kateb writes, it seems "impossible to conceive of us as having nerve endings in every dollar of our estate. A person's holdings and level of income are so bound up with the changeable and culturally contingent rules and arrangements of the system of property, with the channels and opportunities for activity *created* by state action or permission, that it should be strange to look on all one's dollars as exactly and entirely one's own."[42]

3. No one came by his or her present possessions through a pure sequence of free market transactions. Preceding centuries of conquest, plunder, slavery, and government intervention shape current holdings. Until we enact a massive redistribution of goods to rectify past involuntary transfers, it is doubtful to suppose on libertarian grounds that your pre-tax holdings are more genuinely yours than your post-tax holdings.

4. Wealth creation is a social process. I did not create my own clothes, food, shelter, office space, computer, Internet service, car, train service, or medical care. My money has value only because of the labor of vast numbers of people, past and present (much of that labor performed under exploitive conditions). This undermines the claim that I am entitled to maximum control of my current holdings.[43]

It may be claimed that recognition of socioeconomic rights undermines individual self-reliance. It transfers the responsibility of guaranteeing subsistence from the individual to society, thereby weakening the sources of personal effort and initiative. This argument moves too swiftly. To assert a right to subsistence is not to exempt the ablebodied from the necessity of working for such subsistence. As Stuart White notes, the right to subsistence must be understood as a right to "reasonable access" to subsistence.[44] Moreover, since most people are not satisfied with subsistence alone, they will have ample incentive to struggle for higher levels of economic well-being not guaranteed to them as a human right. It is only an extreme view which holds that individuals benefit from the self-reliance learned by struggling to subsist when there is not enough work for everyone or some of the available jobs provide too little to live on. The notion that malnourished children and adults are better treated for having no one come to their assistance is a reductio ad absurdum. And if self-reliance is this important, there is no reason to stop here. Why not let people fight for physical safety as well as economic subsistence? No doubt the necessity of single-handedly fending off attackers may sharpen one's wits and build up one's courage, but that is no reason to reinstate the law of the jungle. We lose sight of human rights when self-reliance becomes our ruling ideal.

Why do some Americans resist the idea of socioeconomic rights? One reason is that their education often leads them to think about rights in terms of the U.S. Bill of Rights, the first ten amendments to the Constitution. The Bill of Rights emphasizes civil-political rights to the neglect of socioeconomic rights. Americans often forget that the constitutions of all fifty states establish a right to education. They overlook the fact, too, that socioeconomic rights are enshrined in the Universal Declaration of Human Rights, several international treaties, and an increasing number of national constitutions. Countries whose bills of rights enshrine socioeconomic rights have developed a growing jurisprudence on the legal implications of such rights. Though some theorists deny the practicality of constitutionalized socioeconomic rights, experience is proving them wrong. Courts have articulated interpretive guidelines and principles, and governments have adjusted their policies in response. In Kim Scheppele's words, "what isn't supposed to work in theory actually does seem to work in practice."[45]

It would be foolish to claim that civil-political and socioeconomic rights are indistinguishable. They are different in several ways. What they have in common is that their acknowledgement is a necessary component of treating one another with respect. If there are any human rights, they include socioeconomic as well as civil-political rights.

Who Is Responsible?

For a harm or deprivation to count as a human rights violation, does it matter who the agent is? If a police officer beats a prisoner in his custody, we would all agree that a human rights violation has occurred. What if a husband beats his wife? What if a private citizen beats a stranger on the street? Are these human rights violations, too?

There are, broadly speaking, three views. On one view, human rights are claims against governments and their agents only, so that only governments and their agents can violate human rights. On a second view, human rights are claims against institutions more broadly defined, including not only governments but also (for example) insurgencies, criminal organizations, businesses, families, intergovernmental organizations, religious institutions, voluntary associations, and cultural practices, so that all individuals acting as part of an institution can violate human rights. On a third view, human rights are claims not only against governments and other institutions but against individuals in general, so that all persons whether or not they act as part of an institution can violate human rights. We may call these the state-centric,[46] the broad institutional,[47] and the institutional-and-interpersonal[48] conceptions respectively. I shall sometimes refer to "institutional" versus "inclusive" conceptions to contrast the first and second with the third.

I believe that the simplest and most inclusive view is the best one. If we are interested in human rights because we want to protect human beings from grave injuries and indignities, we should recognize that the relevant injuries and indignities may count as human rights violations whether caused by governments, institutions, or individuals. A celebrated quote by Eleanor Roosevelt captures the heart of the matter:

> Where, after all, do universal human rights begin? In small places, close to home—so close and so small that they cannot be seen on any maps of the world. Yet they are the world of the individual person; the neighborhood he lives in; the school or college he attends; the factory, farm, or office where he works. Such are the places where every man, woman, and child seeks equal justice, equal opportunity, equal dignity without discrimination. Unless these rights have meaning there, they have little meaning anywhere. Without concerted citizen action to uphold them close to home, we shall look in vain for progress in the larger world.[49]

In John Tasioulas's apt words, "what is in question is not merely a legal-institutional structure, but a human rights *ethos* that pervades our lives, cutting across boundaries between public and private, society and state."[50]

Though institutional conceptions do not (I claim) represent the best understanding of human rights, one can understand their persistent influence in human rights discourse. When international human rights organizations like Amnesty International and Human Rights Watch emerged in the 1960s and 1970s, they limited their efforts according to a rough division-of-labor logic. They would monitor government abuses on the assumption that governments would remain vigilant against ordinary crimes. Only later did human rights organizations recognize the need for a wider focus, given that insurgencies commit human rights atrocities of their own, that women suffer pervasively from violence in their homes and communities, and that national and multinational corporations subject workers to inhuman and degrading conditions. Though it is not plausible to view governments as the sole violators of human rights, we remain partly under the spell of the classic model of human rights activism, understandably so in view of the massive violence and terror that governments continue to unleash.

Another factor is the influence of legal discourse, specifically, our tendency to associate human rights with international human rights treaties and the judicial enforcement of constitutional bills of rights, both of which place primary responsibility on governments. Traditionally, international treaties are addressed to states and assign obligations only to states. Most human rights treaties follow this tradition. A telling example is the Convention on the Elimination of All Forms of Discrimination Against Women. While recognizing that sex discrimination is rooted in cultural prejudices and stereotypes, the treaty assigns the obligation of eliminating harmful prejudices and stereotypes only to states (art. 5). At the same time, when domestic courts enforce constitutional rights provisions, they almost always address their rulings to legislative and executive officials. They do so not only when the immediate agents of the harm are identified as government officials but also when they are identified as nonstate actors. In the latter, so-called horizontal rights cases, it is government officials who are given responsibility for ensuring that the nonstate actors desist from the harm.

Another factor (one that encourages institutional conceptions in general) is that institutions are undeniably important and require our sustained attention. Many scholars properly devote their careers to understanding the ways in which institutions cause or prevent personal harms. Because of the huge importance of institutions, we may feel that we can exert greater leverage—that is, achieve broader and more lasting results—by seeking to improve institutions than by seeking to improve the behavior of individuals as individuals. It is easy to slide from the thought that "institutions are important" to the thought that "institutions alone are important." But to think that institutions alone are important is to obscure the large role that individual agency plays in our lives.

Why prefer the inclusive conception of human rights? Notice, in the first place, that the state-centric conception produces odd distortions and displacements when nonstate actors are the primary agents of harm. Consider domestic violence against women. On the state-centric conception, we must adopt one of two implausible views—either that no human rights are violated, or that they are violated not by the aggressors but by the government agents who fail to take appropriate preventive action. The sad fact is that the state-centric conception of human rights has contributed to the invisibility of violence against women. Note, too, that the state-centric conception encourages the view that government is the solution to our problems. To be sure, sometimes government is the solution, but sometimes it forms only part of the solution or no part of the solution at all; we should not prejudge the question. African NGOs such as Tostan have discovered that female genital cutting (FGC) is more successfully combated through education and consciousness-raising than through legal sanctions.[51] Imagine someone who combats FGC or domestic violence through education and who decides that, given the circumstances, her efforts will be most successful if undertaken without government participation or support. Surely she does not cease, by virtue of her preferred strategy, to be a human rights activist. We can emphasize the responsibility of governments to respect, protect, and promote human rights without claiming that this responsibility belongs to government alone. To reserve the term "human rights" for government's responsibilities while using other language to designate the responsibilities of nonstate actors produces an unnecessary linguistic complication, one with the potential to sow moral misunderstanding.

I believe confusion also arises under the broader institutional conception of human rights. One danger of viewing human rights as claims against institutions but not individuals is that individual responsibility may be effaced. While the man who beats his wife may be an agent of patriarchy, he is also an individual who fails to respect the dignity of his victim. And certain harms are plausibly viewed as human rights violations even in the absence of institutional complicity. A beating is a beating whether delivered by a random stranger or a police officer: the wrongness of either act is ultimately based on the same set of reasons, an impermissible disregard for the status and interests of the victim.[52] Thus classic rights thinkers like John Locke and Thomas Jefferson plausibly assumed that unaffiliated individuals can violate one another's human rights outside an institutional setting (in a "state of nature").

I suggest that the proper perspective for thinking about human rights is as individuals with responsibilities toward one another, on the assumption that institutions are an important but not the only means by which those responsibilities are honored or betrayed. (Of course, many interpersonal responsibilities, like many institutional responsibilities, do not involve human rights.) Institutions are human creations, dependent on human choices, whether acknowledged or not. The values that should govern institutions cannot be divorced from those that properly govern individuals in their relations to one another, and we ought to preserve a flexible attitude regarding which mix of institutional and noninstitutional approaches is best suited to protecting individuals from grave injuries and indignities. The risk of an institutional conception of human rights is a form of alienation, in which institutions are seen as leading an existence separate from that of individuals and are invested with a kind of moral responsibility from which individuals feel personally exempt. A wiser approach is one in which individuals feel simultaneously responsible for their institutional and personal choices. An inclusive conception that broadens responsibility for human rights directs our attention to more diverse sources of harm; it helps avoid the backlash that can arise when individuals harmed by entities that are not institutions feel that their experience is left out of the language of human rights; and it gives us a richer understanding of the contributions that civil society can make to the protection of human rights, as a watchdog of government and potential replacement for some of its functions as well as an agent of social change outside government and the institutional sphere more broadly conceived. The inclusive conception I have defended here bears affinities to the theory of "concurrent responsibility" for human rights to be explored later in this book.

The Right to Have Rights

Human rights form an organized whole. They are related to each other in a particular way, and their mutual relations form a particular structure, or architecture, of internal support. Some rights take the form of primary entitlements. They include, among others, life, freedom from torture, freedom from assault, adequate nutrition and health care, education, and freedom of religion. A second category of rights exists to *protect* primary entitlements. Consider the right to a fair trial. The primary entitlement at stake is the presumption of innocence: the right of innocent individuals not to be imprisoned, fined, or otherwise punished. The elements of the fair trial—publicity, the right to counsel, the right to summon witnesses, cross-examination of witnesses, no coerced confessions, possibility of appeal, the reasonable doubt rule—are all designed to save innocent individuals from erroneous convictions, even at the price of letting some guilty people go free.[53]

The redundant character of these protections may try the patience of some citizens, but their very redundancy is integral to the idea of due process. A large package of overlapping protections is needed because any smaller package could fail. It is a crucial feature of this arrangement that higher-level protections improve the effectiveness of lower-level protections. Police may be trained to respect the due process rights of criminal suspects, but even so they are less likely to infringe these rights when they know that suspects have competent counsel, enjoy a right to habeas corpus, and can appeal convictions.

Similarly, public officials are less likely to abuse their power when they must anticipate the judgment of a free press and an independent legislature.

Some rights function as primary entitlements and instrumental protections simultaneously. Liberty is one such right, as Locke emphasized in the *Second Treatise of Government*. It is both valuable in itself and indispensable to other goods; nothing valuable is secure, not even our lives, when freedom is withheld.[54] Examples can be multiplied. Education, among its many benefits, teaches us awareness of our rights, and gives us resources to defend them. A right to economic subsistence, valuable in itself, arms individuals against blackmail used to perpetuate abuse (such as domestic violence against women and servants). Freedom of speech is both a primary entitlement and a means of protesting the denial of other rights.

If human rights include both primary entitlements and their protections, they also include protections of those protections, and protections of human rights generally. A series of outer walls is erected to minimize the danger of erosion or attack. The logic of mutually reinforcing supports is well displayed in the Universal Declaration of Human Rights. "Everyone has the right to recognition everywhere as a person before the law" (art. 6) and to the "equal protection of the law" (art. 7), "to equal protection against any discrimination in violation of this Declaration" (art. 7), "to an effective remedy by the competent national tribunals for acts violating the fundamental rights granted him by the constitution or by law" (art. 8), and "to a fair and public hearing by an independent and impartial tribunal, in the determination of his rights and obligations" (art. 10). These protections, though they may sound arid and legalistic, prove indispensable when fundamental entitlements are threatened.

It is significant that many protections of rights are themselves counted as human rights, not just as means to the fulfillment of human rights. To leave fundamental entitlements without protection is to leave persons exposed and thus to harm their dignity. A falsely accused person who is denied a fair trial but is still acquitted—say, because of luck, or a sympathetic judge, or friends helping behind the scenes—is not treated with the dignity she deserves, because she is denied the fully panoply of protections that is her due; her safety, preserved for now, remains contingent. We are entitled not only to the enjoyment of our rights, but to their *secure* enjoyment. We have a right to take our rights for granted.

The ideal posited here is independence, where independence means not having to fight, scheme, barter, or plead for one's rights. Rejected, obviously, is a vision of extreme self-reliance, in which rights themselves must be achieved through struggle. Struggle, of course, is built into any society that honors human rights, since people face the stress of making their own choices in life, and must inevitably compete for scarce prizes and positions. But human rights are not something to be earned; they are not a reward for superior virtue, fortitude, and pluck. The "survival of the fittest" is foreign to the idea of human rights, its entry into rights discourse a sure sign that the discourse has been corrupted. Human rights are anchored by "the right to have rights," as Hannah Arendt correctly insisted, not the right to *seek* rights.[55] That is why rights include the protections of our rights.

Why Human Rights Require International Protections

Human rights are both a moral and a political concept. As a moral concept, they imply a set of moral permissions for oneself and duties for others. But among the duties owed one by others is the duty to organize or coordinate their behavior in suitably helpful ways. Human rights imply the need for certain kinds of social institutions, and that is why they are a political, not just a moral, concept. This point has been well understood at least since the seventeenth century, when the classic social contract theorists argued that human rights entitle their bearers to institutional protections. Social contract theorists envisaged such institutions within the frame of the nation-state, which could protect individuals from each other, but could also, of course, violate human rights on a much larger scale. To guard against this danger, Locke advocated the creation of representative democracy, in which the enforcement of human rights was entrusted to "collective bodies of men," chosen by the people, who would dedicate themselves to upholding the law of nature.

But human rights are not adequately fulfilled if we entrust their protection to the nation-state alone. The state has too many opportunities to betray human rights. Or it may lack the resources to fulfill important human rights even if it wanted to. International rights institutions are needed to correct the failures of nation-states—for example, to compensate for the resource deficiencies of poor states, or to oppose national policies that violate or threaten human rights. The moral principle is well captured in the Universal Declaration of Human Rights, whose Article 28 proclaims, "Everyone is entitled to a social and international order in which the rights and freedoms set forth in this Declaration can be fully realized."

Hence the effort since World War II to create an effective international human rights regime. Despite formidable obstacles and demoralizing delays, the human rights movement has succeeded in establishing a system of inter-locking protections in the form of multilateral declarations, treaty commit-ments, monitoring committees, investigative bodies, reporting procedures, fact-finding missions, regional human rights courts, and international crimi-nal courts. It goes without saying that human rights continue to be violated on a massive scale, and that some states still demonstrate an astonishing ca-pacity for cruelty. But international human rights institutions have had some impact on the calculations and self-understandings of states and public offi-cials. While the maleficent potential of the state has not been removed, it has often been inhibited, and in some parts of the world significantly reduced.[56] I examine some contributions of international human rights institutions in the chapters to follow.

When international institutions reinforce national protections of human rights, they recapitulate the domestic process of institutional reinforcement whose necessity has long been understood. The secure enjoyment of human rights within any society depends on the presence of multiple overlapping protections. A democratic state mindful of its constitutional mission should therefore welcome the oversight and assistance that international human rights institutions provide. When a state refuses international checks on its human rights practices, it negates our right to the reliable protection of our rights. The international protection of human rights is the logical completion of the human rights idea.

Chapter 2

Madison's Compound Republic and the Logic of Checks and Balances

Learned men pledged to the defense of individual rights forged political institutions for the new United States. They constructed forms of government not seen before, thus transforming our understanding of politics itself. The U.S. Constitution was the culmination of their efforts, and James Madison the principal genius behind its creation. Alexander Hamilton boasted that the original constitution was itself a bill of rights (*Fed.* 84, p. 477),[1] even before the first ten amendments. Although the original constitution contained grave flaws, above all the accommodation of slavery, its underlying principles inspired many to seek improvements, efforts that bore fruit in subsequent amendments abolishing slavery and requiring equal protection of the laws. Our current understanding of human rights owes an immense debt to American innovations in the art of government.[2]

Gratitude for the theoretical contributions of the Founders, and Madison in particular, has nourished the view that U.S. institutions do not stand in need of international human rights law. There is a sense that Madison and his colleagues solved the main difficulties, that to institutionalize external supervision of U.S. human rights practices or incorporate international human rights law into America's domestic legal system would be to tinker with the Founders' wise design, a move both ungrateful and imprudent. Mixed with these feelings is the pride of vicarious authorship (the thought that the Founders' achievement is ours, too) and an attachment to strong national sovereignty as a matter of principle. Belief in the sovereign right of Americans to govern their affairs without external supervision and belief that the Founders made the *correct* institutional choices are mutually reinforcing.

I propose that such thinking leads us astray, and that Madison shows us why. The political theory presented in his *Federalist* essays furnishes an argument for the integration of constitutional democracies, not least the United States, into a transnational human rights regime. He leads us toward the theory of cosmopolitan republicanism, by which I mean the view that individual freedom depends on a particular configuration of domestic and international institutions working in tandem.[3] Aside from passing suggestions, Madison does not make this view explicit, understandably so, given that neither international institutions nor other large-scale republics existed in his time. But his writings lend theoretical support to the view.

I develop this argument in the course of an examination of Madison's constitutional philosophy. Along the way, I hope to correct what I regard as certain common misconceptions about Madison's own political thought and, with Madison's help, to challenge widespread, but I think mistaken, ways of understanding democracy. Specifically, I shall argue that Madison is a democratic thinker; that he wisely provides democracy with a nonvoluntarist justification, valuing popular government not as an end in itself but as an indispensable means to the end of justice; that he properly warns us against an adversarialist, self-interest-based model of political action; and that he sensibly grounds checks and balances on a logic of concurrent responsibility, in which different institutional actors ensure one another's compliance with the dictates of justice.

I argue that Madison leads us toward a worthier conception of democracy, thus placing its legitimacy on firmer ground.[4] One of my purposes is to show that there is no conflict between democracy on the one hand and constitutional bills of rights or international human rights law on the other. Madison's nonvoluntarist conception of democracy helps us make this argument. However, not everyone may be persuaded to adopt a nonvoluntarist conception of democracy. In Chapter 6 I shall argue for the democratic legitimacy of international human rights law (and of constitutionally entrenched rights) without assuming a nonvoluntarist conception of democracy.

Madison as a Democrat

Madison is remembered as a theorist of checks and balances, divided powers, federalism, and representative government. He is less often remembered as a friend of democracy. Bernard Manin writes that "for Madison, representative government was not one kind of democracy; it was an essentially different and furthermore preferable form of government."[5] With notable exceptions,[6] this is the prevailing view.

I want to consider a different possibility—that Madison, instead of rejecting democracy, invites us to redefine it. Perhaps we are mistaken about democracy and Madison can set us straight. Madison is committed to popular government, but not on the voluntarist grounds that have come to dominate democratic theory. Preventing the misuse and abuse of power is his aim. "Checks and balances" are the central device—understood not as an "invisible hand" mechanism that renders personal virtue unnecessary to the common good, but as a means of harnessing moral impulses that are distributed among the citizenry at large. They are the core of a civic ethic that extends beyond interbranch relations and federalist arrangements to the construction of civil society, popular political participation and debate, and the act of voting.

Inspired by Madison, we can think of democracy as a system designed to ensure the responsible exercise of power by means of checks and balances, in which popular participation through voting is the most important but not the sole check. In democracy rightly understood, citizens reinforce and enhance one another's efforts to comply with justice and seek the common good. Realization of the people's will is not the purpose of democracy. (By the common good, I have in mind outcomes that are beneficial and morally desirable, though not required by justice—for example, a policy that takes a good educational system and makes it even better. Justice takes precedence over but does not exhaust the common good. Both are proper ends of democracy. I shall sometimes use the term "justice" as shorthand for both.)

Like Locke and Rousseau, Madison does not call himself a democrat.[7] But he earns the title of democrat as that term is now ordinarily used, because he declares himself a friend of popular government and takes it for granted that "the people are the only legitimate fountain of power" (*Fed.* 49, p. 313). Though he favors republics over democracies (the latter being impossible in any territory larger than a city-state), he defines both as a species of popular government: "in a democracy the people meet and exercise the government in person; in a republic they assemble and administer it by their representatives and agents" (*Fed.* 14, p. 141). America's glorious gift to posterity and the world (p. 144) was the discovery that by means of representation, governments of large territories (for example, both the individual American states and the contemplated union) could remain "wholly popular" in character (p. 141).

Europe originated the principle of representation, but "America can claim the merit of making [it] the basis of unmixed and extensive republics" (p. 141).

Of course, Madison does not idealize the people. He worries about the propensity of popular government to mobilize faction, and he seeks institutional arrangements that will allow a virtuous few, chosen by the people, to carry out the main tasks of government. Yet to call him an elitist is misleading. Though he believes that some people possess more virtue than others, he does not regard virtue as the exclusive property of any class (*Fed.* 57, pp. 343–44). Public officials should be chosen by the people or their elected representatives, not assigned by heredity. He follows the republican tradition of placing all social classes under suspicion: the rich have their vices no less than the poor.[8] If the emboldened state legislatures of the 1780s heightened his distrust of the people, his subsequent break with the Federalists and horror at the Alien and Sedition Acts reawakened his fear of arrogant elites. Even in *The Federalist* (written when the recent excesses of empowered majorities were freshest in his mind), there is a straightforward reason for his preoccupation with majority tyranny that has nothing to do with aristocratic leanings.[9] The reason is that there is an obvious solution to minority tyranny, namely popular government and majority rule, whereas the solution to majority tyranny is harder to figure out (*Fed.* 10, p. 125).

Madison illuminates the value and purpose of popular government. Contemporary readers are sometimes bothered by the rude things he says about the people. How can someone with such a dim view of the people believe in their right to govern? But that is precisely the point. Madison does not trust the people, because he does not trust anyone. Or more precisely, he does not trust any collectivity defined by a shared interest or identity. His constant fear is that power will be misused or abused. Participation in government is not a prize to be distributed for our enjoyment, but a responsibility whose burden should be keenly felt. If widespread character flaws threaten the proper exercise of power, those flaws should be constantly kept in mind so that we can more adequately correct and counteract them. Self-distrust, like mutual distrust, is a necessary precondition of good government.

To ensure the responsible exercise of power, we must enlist one another's help in exposing and correcting our errors. Since partiality hinders perception of our own faults, we need others to help point them out. Mutual criticism protects society, not only by exposing error to public view, but also by encouraging virtue, since to avoid the shame of external criticism and correction, we become more self-critical. Madison embraces what I call the principle of concurrent responsibility, according to which each actor must ensure that all actors (oneself and the rest) exercise their power responsibly. Concurrent responsibility is another name for checks and balances and forms the heart of "Madisonian democracy," by which I mean the engagement to hold one another accountable in a shared project of crafting and enacting policies that promote justice and the common good.

The reason why concurrent responsibility, or checks and balances, implies democracy is that popular control is the most important of all checks. "A dependence on the people is, no doubt, the primary control on the government" (*Fed.* 51, p. 320). Madison does not pause to defend the claim—perhaps it struck him as obvious.[10] Let us say the following. Because respect for individual rights is the chief element of justice, all individuals must be given a voice. Self-interest makes us vigilant custodians of our own rights. Empathy and a sense of justice as well as self-interest (violations visited on others may be visited on us next) motivate us to protect the rights of others.[11] The virtues of empathy and justice receive encouragement when the people can express their views not only through voting but also through voluntary associations and the press.[12] In a thriving and inclusive civil society, new perspectives demand attention; errors are challenged; and those who want to view themselves and be viewed by others as good, fair, and decent must work harder to prove the case. Not least, popular government models the equality and universal respect that are inseparable from the idea of individual rights.

Madisonian Checks and Balances

Though dependence on the people is the primary control on government, "experience has taught mankind the necessity of auxiliary precautions" (*Fed.* 51, p. 320). Most obviously, a majority may perceive a shared interest in oppressing a minority. In *Federalist* 10, Madison devises a sociological remedy and in *Federalist* 51 an institutional one. First, construct a polity in which no faction is likely to embrace a majority of the people. Second, divide and disperse power so that public officials can monitor and check each other's behavior. The latter solution (on which I shall focus for the time being) is the principle of checks and balances. As I stated above, checks and balances should be understood as the "concurrent responsibility" of each actor to ensure that all actors exercise their power responsibly.

Concurrent responsibility is woven into the design of the U.S. Constitution. Members of Congress "and all executive and judicial Officers" take an oath to support the Constitution (U.S. Const., art. VI). If an unconstitutional bill is introduced in the Congress, legislators have a duty to reject it. If passed in one house, legislators in the other must block it. If they do not, the president has a duty to veto it, and if he or she fails to do so, or Congress overrides his or her veto, the federal courts have a duty to declare it unconstitutional.[13] We can tell similar stories about the concurrent responsibility of the three branches to block unconstitutional acts by the executive and judiciary.

If Congress does its duty, the matter will not come before the president or the courts, but their independent power to block unconstitutional laws in case of congressional malfeasance reminds Congress of its constitutional obligations. Checks and balances thus perform an educative and reforming function. They serve not merely as an insurance mechanism, but as a means of habituating actors into virtuous behavior and thus (in good Aristotelian fashion) making them virtuous. They foster dialogue, thus creating possibilities for mutual learning and assistance as well as mutual supervision. In a constitution of divided powers and mutual checks, John Adams wrote, "a general emulation takes place."[14]

We must stay clear of two persistent confusions, one regarding institutional design and the other regarding the motivation of the parties. The first is an identification of checks and balances with a strict separation of powers scheme in which functionally defined branches enjoy undisturbed authority within their respective spheres. An example of this view is the theory of the unitary executive, supported by a selective (and mistaken) reading of Alexander Hamilton's *Federalist* essays, which in its most extreme version holds that the president has sole decision-making power on executive matters.[15]

The question is how we should understand the concepts of separation of powers and checks and balances. I do not intend to pit these two concepts against each other, since the meaning of both is what needs to be determined. Theorists often define one in terms of the other, and this is to be expected, because on the most plausible accounts they are functionally related. The question is which model ought to underlie both concepts. For our purposes, I shall distinguish between a "strict separation model"[16] and a "mutual interference model," and argue for the latter over the former.

Not only is the strict separation model contradicted by numerous provisions in the U.S. Constitution that institutionalize interbranch monitoring and control, but Madison clearly rejects it in his theoretical writings, and for sound reasons. He ties his view to that of Montesquieu, who (Madison tells us) understood the separation of powers as prohibiting only those arrangements in which "the *whole* power of one department is exercised by the same hands which possess the *whole* power of another department." Montesquieu "did not mean that these departments ought to have no *partial agency* in, or no *control* over, the acts of each other" (*Fed.* 47, p. 304, emphasis in original). What is required is a modified rather than strict separation of powers.

Strict separation is impossible in practice: "unless these departments be so far connected and blended as to give to each a constitutional control over the others, the degree of separation which the maxim requires, as essential to a free government, can never in practice be duly maintained" (*Fed.* 48, p. 308). An unmodified separation of powers leads to its own collapse. But the purpose of mutual controls is not merely to preserve a partial separation between the branches. As the discussion in *Federalist* 48 of Pennsylvania's recent troubles makes clear, their purpose is to prevent constitutional violations in general, including violations of individual rights.

More worrying to Madison than the blurring of functional boundaries is the concentration of power itself. The "encroaching nature" of power (*Fed.* 48, p. 309) means that no department should acquire disproportionate strength. The early history of the American states had convinced Madison that, in republics, "the legislative authority necessarily predominates" and should therefore be divided in two (*Fed.* 51, p. 320). Soon after the federal union was created, he learned to fear the power of the executive branch, and adjusted his constitutional strategy accordingly.[17] His interest in devising cross-departmental checks, evident at the Philadelphia Convention, persisted after the national constitution was drafted. In 1788 he recommended that Virginia adopt a "Council of Revision" drawn from members of the executive and judiciary branches with the power to veto "precipitate," "unjust," or "unconstitutional" laws passed by the state legislature.[18]

Separation of powers is not an end in itself. The reason not to combine legislative and executive power, Locke and Montesquieu argued, is that officials could otherwise enact oppressive legislation, serene in the knowledge that it would not be applied to themselves.[19] Virtuous government involves distinct tasks: enactment of good laws and faithful interpretation and enforcement of the law. While some division of labor is necessary, so that each task is carefully distinguished and thus conscientiously carried out, the overall enterprise is cooperative in nature, and the separate branches can help each other fulfill their duty. An outsider's perspective may more easily identify errors and abuses, while the consciousness of external monitoring encourages scrupulous performance of each task. Note that some interbranch independence is necessary for these checks to remain in place. Madisonian checks and balances entail mutual interference between the branches as a necessary precondition for virtuous government.

The second confusion to be avoided is an overly "adversarialist" reading of Madison's theory of checks and balances. I have in mind the attribution to Madison of the view that, given the right institutional setting, virtuous motivation is not needed to steer political actors to just and wise policies. In the following paragraphs, I first comment on adversarialism and remind readers that it is not Madison's view, and then argue that implicit in his actual view is a call on citizens and officials to intensify rather than relax their sense of individual moral responsibility.

Adversarialism is the belief that, in certain contexts, the vigorous pursuit of one's self-interest leads by an "invisible hand" to the common good. While some applications of the theory are true, many are not. Too often, it becomes a license to engage in predatory and exploitive behavior with a clear conscience. Thus encouraged, corporate lobbyists deceive public opinion and obtain legislative favors, politicians mislead voters and rouse or pander to unreasonable passions, citizens demand pork barrel appropriations and low taxes, advertisers manipulate consumers, cartels block competition, businesses resist health and environmental regulations, corporations use scorched-earth legal tactics to protect or increase profits, employers exploit workers, powerful countries bully weak ones, and prosecutors use extortion and deceit to maximize convictions. The adversarialist theory is not the only source of these practices, but it lends them powerful support, loosening the restraints of conscience and distorting our moral compass. Harmful practices are conducted openly, without embarrassment—sometimes indeed with righteous satisfaction, as vice assumes the mantle of virtue.

Invisible hand arguments that convert self-interest or adversarial contest into public good earn our trust when their causal mechanisms are clearly explained, their enabling conditions fully recalled, their claims carefully tested, and their limits duly noted. These requirements are often evaded, however, as we succumb to the counterintuitive charm and flattering convenience of the central idea. A theory that yields important insights when properly circumscribed propagates harmful myths when reduced to a simple form. Background conditions on which the logic depends (for example, free entry and full information in the market context, equality of arms in the legal context, a shared recognition that certain strategies are off-limits) are forgotten, or it is forgotten that their preservation requires other than self-interested motives. When the theory becomes ideology—when it is imposed on rather than tested by experience—pathologies appear. The costs of generalized self-interest go unseen (because they do not fit the theory) or even cease to be regarded as costs. (Social Darwinism is the extreme example of this tendency.) A Panglossian circularity enters our reasoning. The result is that our characters are warped—our ends altered, and habits of self-restraint (on which most valid forms of the theory depend) eroded. Vice parades as virtue, while true virtue is mocked as self-indulgent preening. Responsibility is dissipated, because the "system makes everything turn out all right."

The adversarialist reading of Madison draws on the famous passage in *Federalist* 51 arguing that, since men are not angels, a well-designed constitution uses "opposite and rival interests" to supply "the defect of better motives." "Ambition must be made to counteract ambition," Madison writes. "The interest of the man must be connected with the constitutional rights of the place." Offices should be arranged in such a manner that "the private interest of every individual may be a sentinel over the public rights" (*Fed.* 51, pp. 319–20). We should not misconstrue these remarks, however.

Hume held it "a just political maxim that every man must be supposed a knave."[20] Montesquieu argued that no republic could survive without virtue.[21] On this question, Madison sides with Montesquieu. His *Federalist* essays are saturated with references to virtue. His constant fear is that men of deficient virtue will be chosen for positions of political authority, and this in fact becomes one of his main arguments for an extended republic in *Federalist* 10. His adherence to Montesquieu is made plain in the conclusion to *Federalist* 55:

As there is a degree of depravity in mankind which requires a certain degree of circumspection and distrust, so there are other qualities in human nature which justify a certain portion of esteem and confidence. Republican government presupposes the existence of these qualities in a higher degree than any other form. Were the pictures which have been drawn by the political jealousy of some among us faithful likenesses of the human character, the inference would be that there is not sufficient virtue among men for self-government; and that nothing less than the chains of despotism can restrain them from destroying and devouring one another. (p. 339)

In the Virginia ratifying convention, he rebuked the adversarialist conceit in the clearest terms:

> I go on this great republican principle, that the people will have virtue and intelligence to select men of virtue and wisdom. Is there no virtue among us? If there be not, we are in a wretched situation. No theoretical checks—no form of government can render us secure. To suppose that any form of government will secure liberty or happiness without any virtue in the people, is a chimerical idea.[22]

These words echo the assertion in the 1776 Virginia Declaration of Rights that "no free government, or the blessings of liberty, can be preserved to any people but by a firm adherence to justice, moderation, temperance, frugality, and virtue and by frequent recurrence to fundamental principles." I find no hint in Madison's writings that the effort to be virtuous may ever be relaxed. Deviations from angelic motivation and understanding are to be expected and planned for, not celebrated or encouraged. The view, widespread in contemporary American political culture, that self-interest legitimately determines the political choices of citizens, candidates, and elected officials is wholly opposed by his theory.

Madison writes in the peroration of *Federalist* 51: "Justice is the end of government. It is the end of civil society" (p. 322). I take it that this is the attitude proper to citizens and officials, not just those watching from the outside. We should elect representatives "whose enlightened views and virtuous sentiments render them superior to local prejudices and to schemes of injustice" (*Fed.* 10, p. 128) and "whose patriotism and love of justice will be least likely to sacrifice [the interest of their country] to temporary or partial considerations" (p. 126). We should reject "Men of factious tempers, of local prejudices, or of sinister designs" who "may by intrigue, by corruption, or by other means first obtain the suffrages and then betray the interests of the people" (p. 126). In *Federalist* 57: "The aim of every political constitution is, or ought to be, first to obtain for rulers men who possess most wisdom to discern, and most virtue to pursue, the common good of the society; and in the next place, to take the most effectual precautions for keeping them virtuous whilst they continue to hold their public trust" (p. 343).

When Madison writes, "No man is allowed to be a judge in his own cause, because his interest would certainly bias his judgment, and, not improbably, corrupt his integrity" (*Fed.* 10, p. 124), he implies that the attitude appropriate to elected officials and the citizens who choose them is that of an impartial judge, seeking only to attain a just outcome as determined by the rights of all parties: "what are many of the most important acts of legislation but so many judicial determinations, not indeed concerning the rights of single persons, but concerning the rights of large bodies of citizens?" The task of *Federalist* 10 is to devise a system that selects political officials genuinely motivated by justice and that minimizes their temptations to deviate from justice.

Let us note that Madison's preoccupation with justice is by no means limited to the rights of property. The man who wrote the "Memorial and Remonstrance Against Religious Assessments," drafted the Bill of Rights, and sought to mobilize state resistance against the Alien and Sedition Acts is animated by a far broader conception of human dignity. In the ringing defense of unalienable rights that concludes the 1785 Memorial (a passage Lance Banning calls the most explicit statement of "the consistent core of fundamental principle that guided him through all the turns of his career"),[23] Madison invokes freedom of the press and trial by jury but not property. Property may receive the emphasis Madison gives it in *Federalist* 10 because recent economic conflicts raised its salience in readers' minds. Even in the warning against majority tyranny that concludes *Federalist* 10, however, fear of religious persecution is mentioned before fear of paper money (p. 128). Madison does not favor unlimited accumulation of wealth, and he retains the traditional republican fear of sharp economic divisions. In 1792 he argued that the spirit of party faction should be combated by (among other means) opposition to "an immoderate, and especially an unmerited, accumulation of riches" and "by the silent operation of laws, which, without violating the rights of property, reduce extreme wealth towards a state of mediocrity, and raise extreme indigence towards a state of comfort."[24] We should take Madison at his word when he claims his primary allegiance is to justice.

If his conception of justice is in some respect mistaken, we should correct it, as he himself would desire. He would hardly claim immunity from the forces that distort opinions about justice. (Madison's compromises with slavery—he did not free his own slaves, sold some of them to another master, and although professing opposition to slavery argued that the solution lay in the removal of freed blacks to Africa—are a reminder that he was all too fallible.)[25] In his preoccupation with human fallibility and his belief that a well-designed political system rescues collective deliberation from the worst effects of interest and passion, we see a hint that our understanding of justice can improve over time. Madison suggests that constitutional democracy is conducive to moral progress. I find his political philosophy hard to reconcile with theories of constitutional interpretation that wed us to understandings of moral and political concepts prevalent at the time of ratification.[26] As Justice Kennedy writes of those who drafted the Due Process Clause in the Fifth and Fourteenth Amendments, they did not presume to know "the components of liberty in its manifold possibilities," for "They knew times can blind us to certain truths and later generations can see that laws once thought necessary and proper in fact serve only to oppress."[27]

The sources of human fallibility are complex. Our political judgment is warped by self-interest, ambition, pride, opinion, religious zeal, and personal loyalties.[28] These give rise to factional allegiances so intense that we often prefer to harm our adversaries rather than seek mutual advantage (*Fed.* 10, p. 124). It is not enough to be motivated by justice. We may be taken in by the noble rhetoric of cynical leaders.[29] More important, our opinions about justice are distorted by self-interest and pride: "As long as the connection subsists between [man's] reason and his self-love, his opinions and his passions will have a reciprocal influence on each other; and the former will be objects to which the latter will attach themselves" (pp. 123–24). In addition, the intrinsic difficulty of political questions (emphasized in *Fed.* 37) renders inevitable the emergence of deep-seated disagreement, which self-interest and pride easily fan into mutual animosity and distrust.[30]

Avowed self-interest is not the main issue. Rather, self-interest is one of several motives that distort our judgment. The antisocial motives are often disguised as demands for justice. This is a problem—the antisocial motives are harder to unmask—but also an opportunity—we find ourselves arguing about justice, and thus potentially in a position to be influenced by reason.

We should strive ever harder to comply with justice. We are not angels, however, and humility requires acknowledgment of our imperfection. Virtue is proven by our acceptance of checks that raise the standard of our deliberations.

Why does Madison say that "ambition must be made to counteract ambition" and that "the private interest of every individual may be a sentinel over the public rights"? (*Fed.* 51, pp. 319, 320). I propose the following account. Under a well-designed constitution, officials chosen for their virtue and wisdom are pledged to uphold the constitution, defend justice, and seek the common good. Seeking a reputation for public probity and effectiveness, they have reasons of pride and political ambition as well as duty to honor their commitment. Scrutiny by an informed electorate and by the independent branches raises the level of performance needed to maintain a favorable reputation. It is to be expected, moreover, that officials will form some identification with their own department. Conscious of its contributions to the public order, and eager to demonstrate their personal abilities, they will have self-interested as well as principled reasons to resist improper encroachment on their constitutional responsibilities. Ambition thus sharpens their perception of their rivals' misdeeds. But any claims made against the other branches must be presented on impersonal legal and moral grounds. Conscientious officials will internalize this requirement, impartially evaluating the counterclaims of the rival branches, and asking themselves whether their own arguments are truly sound. Ambition and interest contain a moral element: we can take pride in satisfying high moral standards, while interest makes us sensitive to injustices that others inflict on us. Madisonian checks and balances harness the moral side of interest and ambition as one strategy among others to heighten our sense of moral responsibility. Madison's view is the opposite of the adversarialist position with which it is often confused.

Constitutional theory has become a haven for two fallacies—the adversarialist conceit that a well-designed system reliably directs self-interest to the public good, and the related institutionalist conceit that a well-designed system will yield good results without the determined efforts of the parties. Madison emphatically rejects both: "To suppose that any form of government will secure liberty or happiness without any virtue in the people, is a chimerical idea." If the people be not virtuous, "No theoretical checks—no form of government can render us secure."[31] The Constitution is not a "machine that would go of itself."[32] It is not a machine at all. It is a mutual commitment to seek justice and the common good, in which we not only pledge our own efforts to that end but hold one another accountable for doing the same. Recognizing our imperfection, we employ one another to correct our errors, but external oversight does not relieve us of the burden of striving to act and judge as justice requires. When Senator Arlen Specter voted for the 2006 Military Commissions Act despite his belief that its denial of habeas corpus to military detainees "was patently unconstitutional on its face," stating as his excuse that the Supreme Court "will clean it up," he was led by a false constitutional morality to violate his constitutional oath of office.[33] Waiting for the Supreme Court to clean up our mess was never Madison's idea of checks and balances.

Madisonian Democracy

Democratic theorists often locate the value of popular government in the empowerment of the people's will. To let the people decide public policy is to realize the good of self-government or public autonomy. Madison takes a different approach. On his view, popular government is an indispensable means to justice. Because it is not sufficient, however, "auxiliary precautions" are needed. He supports a combination of popular government and other institutions that are collectively needed to secure justice. Constitutional democracy is the term we now use for this arrangement. (Of course, there are also non-Madisonian arguments for constitutional democracy.)

We can agree with Madison that the purpose of popular government is to secure justice without binding ourselves to his own conception of justice. For example, we can insist more clearly than Madison that justice requires equal universal adult suffrage. (The mature Madison moved toward endorsement of universal adult (white) male suffrage, but continued to show some sympathy for the argument that only property holders should be allowed to vote for the upper house.)[34] To deny some adults an equal vote is an affront to justice, because it denies their status as equal members of the community, entitled to an equal voice. Principled support for equal universal suffrage can be fitted into a "Madisonian" conception of democracy. It is different from saying that the purpose of popular government is the realization of the people's will, because (1) equal universal suffrage forms only one element of the larger end of justice, and (2) the purpose of political power, in whosoever hands it is placed, is to secure justice.

Why not say that the purpose of popular government is public autonomy or the realization of the people's will, regarded as an end in itself? I believe that references to public autonomy or the people's will obscure the central fact that popular government, like all forms of government, is a system of rule. Popular government is not continuous with individual autonomy, because some people are obligated to obey rules they do not in fact agree with. The stakes are high, every decision produces winners and losers, and the potential to harm others unjustly is always present. It is hard to believe that *choice* is a value when the choice being exercised affects the vital interests or decides the fate of other people. What is valuable is the avoidance, by means of the *correct* choice, of injustice or misfortune.

If we are honest, popular government always entails rule over others.[35] The use of the term "self-government" as a synonym for popular government is enormously misleading.[36] Because decisions must be made, minorities must defer to majorities. There is not enough role-switching to lend this practice the semblance of self-government even over the long term. Decisions are continually made regarding specific groups of people—farmers, factory workers, teachers, welfare recipients, homeless people, drug addicts, and so on—by people who do not belong and do not expect to belong to the affected categories. Even if we grant the fiction of a collective "self," there is a vast range of policy making that still cannot fall under the description of self-government. It is not *self*-government when countries undertake foreign policy, or adopt policies affecting children, or future generations, or animals, or the rest of nature. In an interdependent world, moreover, externalities loom large: our decisions affect outsiders even when the outsiders do not enter our thinking. A domestic energy or industrial policy, or lack of such a policy, may exacerbate global climate change, causing catastrophic floods and droughts elsewhere in the world, or the loss of agricultural lands and densely populated areas, even entire countries, to rising seawaters. Domestic deliberations on such matters cannot be termed an exercise in self-government. And this is not even to mention the effects on children, future generations, animals, and the rest of nature.

When we realize that popular government is not self-government, we ought to be nervous about its legitimacy. What gives the people the right to govern if their decisions reach far beyond themselves? The answer is that popular government offers necessary protection against the unjust and unwise use of power. Once we have enunciated this thought, however, we are reminded that the people can abuse power, too: a majority can mistreat a minority, and a community can mistreat outsiders. Additional protections are needed to forestall these dangers. We might say that the "auxiliary precautions" are the security the people must offer in exchange for their necessary but also dangerous exercise of political power.

This is a nonvoluntarist conception of democracy. The point of popular government is not to realize the people's will (whether taken as given or refined through deliberation) but instead to foster just and wise policy. Democracy is a system designed to ensure the responsible exercise of power by means of checks and balances, with popular participation through majority voting serving as the most important check, but not the only one. Justice and the common good, not self-interest or group interest, should determine the political choices of citizens and officials alike. Of course, citizens should be on guard against policies that would cost them unjustly; our talent for

identifying such policies is one of the principal reasons for democracy. However, we should always strive to distinguish between those personal costs that
justice forbids and those that it permits or even requires. We may advocate
our interests as far as justice and the common good permit, but no farther.
Virtuous citizens in a democracy strive to honor the distinction and help one
another do the same.

A venerable tradition in democratic theory has sought to reconcile the
concepts of popular government and justice. The true will of the people (on
this view) is that which can receive everyone's reasonable consent, and to pass
such a test is to comply with the demands of justice. Rousseau's *Social Contract* is a classic statement of this argument, but it echoes among many heirs
to the social contract tradition. The emphasis that democratic theorists often
place on reciprocity as a norm of collective decision making—rotation of office, a general will that abstracts from the particular will, public reason, orientation toward consensus, inclusive deliberation—may be seen as an attempt
to yoke collective will formation to the demands of justice. I agree that we
should support institutional devices that steer public deliberation toward justice (indeed, that is what I am arguing). I think it is wisest, however, to keep
justice analytically distinct from the popular will. We otherwise run the danger of misrepresenting the people's will to make it conform to justice, or rede-
fining justice to fit the people's will. The strain is evident in Rousseau's
argument. We all know that the *actual* will of the people easily diverges from
justice. If we turn from actual to hypothetical consent—that is, what it would
be reasonable for the people to consent to—it is difficult to define "reasonable" without importing norms of justice (reached independently of the people's will). When we recall that justice also governs our treatment of those not
included in the deliberative process—foreigners, children, future generations,
animals, and the rest of nature—it becomes still harder to posit a conceptual
identification of justice with the popular will.

One possible response to this line of argument is that since justice is a
contested concept, we must refer the question of its meaning and application
and weight relative to other values to a process of political deliberation. Such
a view (though widespread in contemporary political theory) carries epistemic modesty too far. It does little good to pretend that we (you and I) know
nothing about justice. Even though our understanding can be improved—
and public debate is necessary for its improvement—we already know a great
deal. We know that justice requires respect for human rights (under a conception not too distant from that of the Universal Declaration of Human

Rights), respect for the rights of animals (implying, at a minimum, the prohibition of systematic cruelty to animals undertaken to maximize economic profits), and abstaining from policies that consign future generations to conditions of life significantly worse than our own. (Of course, we know much more about justice than these minimal propositions.)[37]

The question that should guide the citizen's political choices is not, what do I want?, or what do we want?, but instead, what does justice require? (And to the extent that justice is not at stake, what does the common good, broadly understood, require?) Of course, you may be mistaken about what justice requires. Because your opinion is fallible, you should reexamine it and expose it to the force of other people's criticisms. A well-designed political system encourages critical reflection on our views regarding justice. It also strives to ensure that the policies actually adopted will be just. Madison's constitutional theory is a major contribution to the science of designing such institutions. It would be a mistake, however, to say that the outcome of any constitutional process is just by definition. True regard for justice forbids any such complacency. In a proper checks-and-balances system, justice remains an independent standard for evaluating any policies proposed or adopted.

Some people may deny that Madison really articulates a theory of democracy. But why not? It is true that he defends popular government mostly as a means rather than an end, yet he regards it as an indispensable means. His commitment to popular government is firm.

Some may argue that Madison is less than democratic because he believes that laws should be made by the people's chosen representatives rather than the people themselves; because he expects that (at least in the federal union) elected representatives on average will be superior in virtue and wisdom to the people at large; and because he wants representatives to develop a perspective partly independent from that of their constituents, even though the latter, at periodic intervals, can remove them from office.

Are such views undemocratic? Not according to contemporary usage, for we now take it for granted that in "democracies" laws are made by the people's representatives, and the idea that the people should choose representatives of better than average character and judgment is viewed as common sense rather than as a rejection of democracy. Yet some argue that contemporary usage has gone astray, that if we recall the original meaning of the word, we should at least acknowledge that the move from direct to representative democracy is a move toward less democracy. My goal has been to show that this view is not obligatory—that, with help from Madison, we can think about democracy in a different way. The inclination to view representative democracy as less democratic is part of a general inclination to view any impediment to the people's will as a diminution or limitation of democracy. We can shed this assumption if we think that the purpose of popular government is to secure justice. Popular government is necessary, but the reason why it is necessary is the reason why a robust system of checks and balances is also necessary. If our goal as a people is justice, we will insist on holding power and also insist on a system of limits, restraints, separations, divisions, checks, revisions, and vetoes to block unjust policies. We do so because we appreciate both our capacities and our limitations, and recognition of our limitations is one of our capacities. Because this theory firmly commits us to popular government, because it articulates a rationale for constitutional systems that contemporary ordinary (that is, nonacademic) usage considers "democratic," and because it provides a superior account of political legitimacy, we are permitted to say that it gives us the true meaning of democracy. (I know that some readers will persist in saying that I am making an argument to reject rather than redefine democracy.)

This conception of democracy (inspired by Madison) does not envisage a passive or docile citizenry. The quest for justice is no less demanding or inclusive than the articulation of the people's will. There is a need for communication, information, criticism, debate, airing of multiple perspectives, reflection, and revision. Difference becomes a resource rather than a complication. A free media and vigorous civil society, supported by a strong educational system, help complete the constitutional order. They train their gaze not only on the political sphere but also on areas of social life where political institutions do not and sometimes should not intrude. What is needed above all is a critical posture toward oneself and others, a moral alertness. Hence the need to institutionalize challenges from those who are differently situated, including minorities, and to stand ready to offer an account of oneself. Madison writes, "Had every Athenian citizen been a Socrates, every Athenian assembly would still have been a mob" (Fed. 55, p. 336). Socrates says the same in Plato's Apology, when explaining why he could not continue to participate in politics without sacrificing his integrity. Like Socrates, Madison fears that in large assemblies group sentiment will replace individual judgment and conscience will fall asleep.[38] Responsibility is dissipated in crowds. Though respect for character may be a strong motive in individuals, "In a multitude its efficacy is diminished in proportion to the number which is to share the praise or the blame."[39]

Madison rejects direct democracy because he views it as impractical on anything other than a local scale, where parochialism and group think pose grave dangers to justice, and because he cannot imagine how to supply the necessary checks against majority tyranny. He also thinks that many adults lack qualifications to decide complex policy questions; they are better able to choose suitable lawmakers than to make laws themselves. Though he recognizes the problems of direct democracy, he appears less alert to those of representative democracy. He should have known better than to assume that in a system based on geographic representation, voters would choose lawmakers "whose wisdom may best discern the true interest of their country and whose patriotism and love of justice will be least likely to sacrifice it to temporary or partial considerations" (*Fed.* 10, p. 126). Experience has proven what common sense would predict. When representatives are beholden to geographic constituents, who are not institutionally constrained to justify their preferences to other citizens, parochialism asserts itself with a vengeance and lawmakers are under pressure to flout justice. Direct democracy at least has the advantage that all citizens are present to challenge one another's demands. One attempt to address this dilemma is the consensus model of democracy, which by stipulating that government policy should secure the widest possible agreement seeks to raise the standard of public justification.[40] Some of the devices characteristic of this model (bicameralism, judicial review) are familiar to American citizens, others less so (proportional representation, multiparty systems, coalition cabinets, multiparty appointment of judges). Political scientists debate the merits of the consensus model of democracy, but it deserves our attention as one attempt to remedy the deliberative defects of geographic representation.

Madison's Cosmopolitan Republicanism

Other commentators have noted the cosmopolitan logic implicit in Madison's thought.[41] By "cosmopolitanism," I mean support for international institutions that constrain national policy in the interest of justice and the common good. Of course, Madison does not expound the idea; he does not follow his thought to its logical conclusion. This is unsurprising, for international institutions did not exist at the time, and it took the genius of Kant to theorize their possibility.[42] (Kant's "Perpetual Peace" appeared seven years after *The Federalist*.) Yet Madison's thought points unmistakably in a cosmopolitan direction.

Madison's cosmopolitanism springs from three sources: his support for cooperative solutions to otherwise insoluble problems, his commitment to avoiding injustice toward minorities (tyranny of the majority), and his commitment to avoiding injustice toward outsiders.

Madison (writing in 1788) believes that closer political integration of the American states is necessary, because it offers security against foreign danger and against "contentions and wars" among the states, and because it guards states against "violent and oppressive" internal factions and against military establishments poisonous to the foundation of liberty (*Fed.* 45, pp. 292–93). To object in the name of the sovereignty of the individual states is to make a fetish of particular institutions, no wiser than the old attitude that "the people were made for kings, not kings for the people" (p. 293). "Peace, liberty, and safety" should not be sacrificed so that the governments of the individual states "might enjoy a certain extent of power and be arrayed with certain dignities and attributes of sovereignty." Instead, "the public good, the real welfare of the great body of the people, is the supreme object to be pursued," and "no form of government whatever has any other value than as it may be fitted for the attainment of this object" (p. 293).

Madison's views are worth keeping in mind today when the world's safety, freedom, and welfare are imperiled by global climate change, weapons of mass destruction, and financial interdependence. Our response must take the form of close international cooperation, with institutional mechanisms to ensure that countries honor their commitments. We now have many generations' worth of experience with international institutions and understand that their benefits could not have been secured by other means. If thicker international institutions are the rational solution to looming disaster, emotional attachment to strong state sovereignty must not bar the way.

Madison has no patience for institutional inertia. The spirit of innovation, informed by reason and experience, is famously celebrated in *Federalist* 14. "Hearken not to the voice which petulantly tells you that the form of government recommended for your adoption is a novelty in the political world; that it has never yet had a place in the theories of the wildest projectors; that it rashly attempts what it is impossible to accomplish." The glory of the people of America is "that, whilst they have paid a decent regard to the opinions of former times and other nations, they have not suffered a blind veneration for antiquity, for custom, or for names, to overrule the suggestions of their own good sense, the knowledge of their own situation, and the lessons of their own experience" (*Fed.* 14, p. 144). In *Federalist* 49 Madison warns against *frequent* invitations to constitutional transformation, as destabilizing, dangerous, and unnecessary. This does not contradict the clear implication of *Federalist* 14 that revisions should be undertaken when circumstances require.

It may be objected that Madison's argument depends on a sense of national belonging, which gives us reason to support national integration but to *resist* the cosmopolitan project. It is true that in *Federalist* 14 (from which I have just quoted) and *Federalist* 45 appeals are made to a shared American identity. Madison writes that "the kindred blood which flows in the veins of American citizens, the mingled blood which they have shed in defense of their sacred rights, consecrate their Union and excite horror at the idea of their becoming aliens, rivals, enemies" (*Fed.* 14, p. 144; see also *Fed.* 45, p. 293). But we do not have to choose: cosmopolitanism, as I use the term, does not imply the disappearance of the nation-state. It envisages international institutions that constrain national policy for the sake of justice and the common good. In fact, as I argue in my next chapter, some cosmopolitan goals may prove unattainable without the preservation of the nation-state.

We should also recall the purpose of Madison's remarks. Responding to those who think a federal union is impractical, he argues that a sense of national identity (recently reinforced by the shared sacrifice of the War of Independence) is sufficient to guarantee the enterprise. He does not claim it is necessary. It is worth noting that appeals to national belonging take up very little space in his *Federalist* essays. His case for the federal union rests on justice and the need to solve shared problems. Nowhere does he say these reasons are insufficient to motivate action, and the view should not be imputed to him. Unlike Hamilton, moreover, he is not guided by a desire for national self-assertion.

The second source of Madison's cosmopolitanism is his fear of majority tyranny. The perennial threat to justice is faction, defined as any majority or minority group "united and actuated by some common impulse of passion, or of interest, adverse to the rights of other citizens or to the permanent and aggregate interests of the community" (*Fed.* 10, p. 123). Republican government solves the problem of minority faction but not that of majority faction. Madison's famous solution to the latter involves the geographic redistribution of decision-making authority. His epiphany is that majority faction is disarmed in large republics, because factional interests and passions are less likely to command a majority, and, if they do, coordinated action is more difficult (p. 127). Where force of numbers no longer avails, rational persuasion must be tried instead. "In the extended republic of the United States, and among the great variety of interests, parties, and sects which it embraces, a coalition of a majority of the whole society could seldom take place on any other principles than those of justice and the general good" (*Fed.* 51, p. 322). In a large and heterogeneous republic, there are enough parties with critical distance from sectional disputes to constitute an impartial judge. Let us call this the sociological argument.

Madison's pessimism about small republics can be severe. Rhode Island is doomed to majority tyranny or dictatorial usurpation unless it joins a federation (*Fed.* 51, p. 322). It must choose between complete independence (strong sovereignty) and republican government; it cannot have both. Without the federal union, we lack a "disinterested and dispassionate umpire in disputes between different passions and interests in the state."[43] Not only does the extended republic create the possibility of an impartial judge, but the Constitution, recognizing the fragility of republican institutions at the state level, provides formal guarantees. Under Article IV, "the United States shall guarantee to every State in this Union a Republican form of Government," while under Article I, Section 10, no state shall "pass any Bill of Attainder, ex post facto Law, or Law impairing the Obligation of Contracts, or grant any Title of Nobility." Although these rights are promised in most state constitutions, "Our own experience has taught us, nevertheless, that additional fences against these dangers ought not to be omitted" (*Fed.* 44, pp. 287–88). Chief Justice John Marshall called Article I, Section 10 "a bill of rights for the people of each state."[44] The Constitution is, among other things, an early human rights treaty.

The importance of the sociological argument cannot be overstated. Critics of Madison's checks and balances model have faulted him for not anticipating the rapid emergence of party politics—which, ironically, he took a lead in creating not long after *The Federalist* appeared. But I think Madison in *The Federalist* is aware of the danger. His very awareness that no system of checks and balances is foolproof causes him to make his last stand with the sociological argument. On it depends the success of his project. Hence his fear that constitutional checks and balances are insufficient to prevent majority tyranny in the unfederated states; his belief that territorial enlargement is the main reason why faction becomes less dangerous in republican than in democratic government;[45] and his decision to conclude *Federalist* 51, the locus classicus of his institutional checks and balances argument, with a recapitulation of *Federalist* 10.

The sociology of *Federalist* 10 must be updated, however. Let us admire *The Federalist* without pretending that time stopped in 1788. Madison himself predicts the growing homogenization of the United States: "increased intercourse among [citizens] of different States . . . will contribute to a general assimilation of their manners and laws" (*Fed.* 53, p. 329). This admission, damaging to the argument that the diversity of an enlarged republic will allow rational discourse to replace factional dominance, should have set alarm bells ringing in his head. Of course, the succeeding centuries have effected deeper transformations than he could ever imagine. Today, mass parties, instant communications, modern broadcast technology, and the concentration of enormous economic and media power in a few hands allow political mobilization to quickly outrun rational discourse, and they make it all too easy for majority and minority factions to seize control of the policy process. In addition, the national security state has concentrated vast unchecked powers in the executive branch. In such an environment, individual rights, justice, and the common good are easily overwhelmed.

The conditions that in Madison's time threatened justice in direct democracies and small republics are today reproduced and exacerbated at the national level. To ignore this problem is to risk the fate of Rhode Island. *Federalist* 10 teaches us to seek help from the outside. In our own time, Madisonian constitutionalism calls for international oversight of national policy—in other words, the creation of a strong international human rights regime. Under such a regime, national policy is monitored by those with both the institutional and psychological independence, the means and the motive, to act as an impartial judge. International monitoring not only offers an additional check against injustice, but provides needed reinforcement for domestic checks and balances.[46] Of course, the monitors must be guided by a genuine commitment to human rights, and the regime must incorporate mechanisms of mutual accountability to prevent corruption and political manipulation.

I argue in the next chapter that the transnational human rights regime developed in Europe over the last seventy years offers a model of how such a regime might be constructed. The United States can learn from Europe's example. I do not wish to be misunderstood: there are obvious differences between an international human rights regime and the kind of compound republic that Madison aimed to achieve by means of a closer union of the original American states. An international human rights regime (of the kind found in Europe) is unlike a national government, because it lacks its own legislature and military or police apparatus, and because its mandate extends only to human rights rather than the much wider set of purposes entrusted to national governments (though as in Europe it may be enmeshed in regional organizations exercising broader governance responsibilities). However, it provides the advisory, admonitory, deliberative, and adjudicative functions that Madison argued in *Federalist* 10 and 51 were necessary for the promotion of justice. It rests on Madisonian principles of wise constitutional design.

Because of his commitment to justice, Madison is pledged to the rights of outsiders. This is the third source of his cosmopolitanism. The third, fourth, and eleventh *Vices of the Political System of the United States* are, respectively, "Violations of the law of nations and of treaties," "Trespasses of the States on the rights of each other," and "Injustice of the laws of States."[47] The rights of minorities and outsiders are closely connected; both groups stand as outsiders to legislative majorities with the power to dispose of their fates. In discussing the "Injustice of the laws of States," Madison comments: "Is it to be imagined that an ordinary citizen or even an assembly-man of R. Island in estimating the policy of paper money, ever considered or cared in what light the measure would be viewed in France or Holland; or even in Massts or Connect.?"[48] Madison wrote to George Washington on April 16, 1787, that in the absence of institutional reform "the States will continue to invade the national jurisdiction, to violate treaties and the law of nations & to harass each other with rival and spiteful measures dictated by mistaken views of interest."[49]

The legal education of the time was steeped in the law of nations, and Federalists held it in highest regard. They were alarmed to see widespread violations of the law of nations by individual states under the Articles of Confederation, and viewed the prevention of such violations as one of the chief purposes of the Constitution.[50] When presenting the Virginia Plan to the Constitutional Convention, Edmund Randolph listed among the defects of the Articles "that they could not cause infractions of treaties or of the law of nations, to be punished."[51] Madison's first question in response to the New Jersey Plan was:

> Will it prevent those violations of the law of nations & of Treaties which if not prevented must involve us in the calamities of foreign wars? The tendency of the States to these violations has been manifested in sundry instances. The files of Congs. contain complaints already, from almost every nation with which treaties have been formed.

Hitherto indulgence has been shewn to us. This cannot be the permanent disposition of foreign nations. A rupture with other powers is
among the greatest of national calamities. It ought therefore to be ef-
fectually provided that no part of a nation shall have it in its power to
bring them on the whole.[52]

John Jay asserted in *Federalist* 3 that "it is of high importance to the peace of
America that she observe the law of nations towards [foreign] powers" (p. 95).

Madison glimpsed the need for transnational oversight to restrain transnational injustice. He wrote in *Federalist* 63 (p. 369): "What has not America
lost by her want of character with foreign nations; and how many errors and
follies would she not have avoided, if the justice and propriety of her measures had, in every instance, been previously tried by the light in which they
would probably appear to the unbiased part of mankind?" In describing the
problem, Madison reveals the solution: the relevant policies should be evaluated "by the unbiased part of mankind." He writes in the same passage that
"in doubtful cases, particularly where the national councils may be warped by
some strong passion or momentary interest, the presumed or known opinion
of the impartial world may be the best guide that can be followed."[53] And in
Federalist 43, he allows himself to hope that the federalist solution to inter-
state conflict might find an international analogue:

In cases where it may be doubtful on which side justice lies, what better umpires could be desired by two violent factions, flying to arms,
and tearing a State to pieces, than the representatives of confederate
States, not heated by the local flame? To the impartiality of judges,
they would unite the affection of friends. *Happy would it be if such a
remedy for its infirmities could be enjoyed by all free governments; if a
project equally effectual could be established for the universal peace of
mankind!* (p. 283, emphasis added)

Madison's cosmopolitan intimations are remarkable because they predate the
creation of international institutions that could serve as a model, and because
his fear of the injustices America may inflict on outsiders long precedes its
rise to global hegemony. In our own time, when the problem is incomparably
more grave and the path to a remedy easier to discern, Madison's cosmopolitan reasoning should be carefully heeded.

Do international institutions suffer from a democratic deficit? (For if so, the cosmopolitan and democratic readings of Madison may be in tension with each other.) I argue in Chapter 6 that international *human rights* institutions, like constitutional bills of rights, do not subvert democracy because they bar policies that governments should not consider anyway. What about international institutions that address issues of justice and the common good beyond human rights? The question may be too complex to admit a straightforward answer. On the one hand lie fears that decision-making power is delegated to supranational bodies too little dependent on the popular will, and that participation may be extended to nondemocratic governments that do not allow popular input at all. On the other hand lie arguments that in democratic states the people in fact exercise some control over international institutions, and that international institutions *remedy* a democratic deficit inherent in a Westphalian system, namely, the ability of states to affect the lives of outsiders without the latter's consent. Exploration of this important controversy, however, lies beyond the scope of this book.

It is customary to cite Kant as a source of cosmopolitan thought. I close with the suggestion that Kant's essay on "Perpetual Peace" and Madison's *Federalist* essays provide a necessary complement to each other. Madison theorizes a compound republic in which the union can harness the critical energies of its component parts to check injustice. But the main part of his theory is constructed within a national frame. He intimates but does not render explicit the cosmopolitan tendency of his thought. Kant theorizes the possibility of international institutions, yet his understanding of such institutions is circumscribed. For example, he grasps that lasting peace depends on the emergence of republican constitutions, but does not call on international institutions to encourage the emergence or guarantee the preservation of such constitutions. The closest he gets to the topic is to state his categorical opposition to the forcible interference by one nation with the constitution and government of another.[54] Kant and Madison supply the missing elements of each other's vision. Kant shows that countries can form not only treaties but also international institutions to promote peace and justice. Madison shows that separate polities can create an overarching structure that consolidates and promotes republican institutions at the unit level.[55]

The lesson to be drawn from a careful reading of Madison's political theory is that democratic states should help one another live up to their constitutional commitments. How this idea might be implemented in practice is the subject of my next chapter.

Chapter 3

Europe and the Virtues of International Constitutionalism

Constitutional democracy, when confined to the national level, is a fragile arrangement. If a leader or party targets constitutional restraints that stand in its way, domestic opponents may lack the power to stop it. Even when constitutional processes are formally left in place, human rights may be violated if the responsible guardians do not rise to their defense. Fear, xenophobia, sectarianism, prejudice, indifference, and political intrigue are powerful solvents of constitutional commitments. History offers many examples of formal democracies that have allowed systematic human rights violations or even slid into dictatorship.

It stands to reason that if internal safeguards are vulnerable, help should be sought from the outside. External monitoring and constraint provide domestic checks and balances with the backing needed to operate most effectively. This is an argument for the internationalization of constitutional democracy. The claim I am making is not that transnational problems require democratic decision making at the transnational level (though that also is true), but rather that a commitment to preventing human rights violations by *one's own* government makes the involvement of international institutions necessary. We often think of international human rights institutions as a means for certain countries to improve the human rights records of other countries. But international human rights institutions also help democracies fulfill their own constitutional commitments. They complete the domestic constitutional order.

I develop the argument in this chapter through an examination of the regional system of human rights protection in Europe.[1] There can be no doubt that this system has contributed dramatically to the protection of human rights. I do not offer a simple celebration. There have been major shortcomings and outright failures. But honesty requires recognition of the regime's achievements as well as its shortfalls. The plain fact is that it has altered the political course of many countries for the better and ensured the safety and well-being of large numbers of people.

The regime's success has depended on a partnership connecting international institutions, states, and civil society. The regional bodies give nongovernmental actors new means to demand human rights improvements from states; committed states strengthen the powers and raise the standards of the regional bodies, and these in turn oblige states to honor their commitments. The regime has accomplished what few if any European states could have done on their own, even within the domestic sphere. It mirrors, reproduces, reinforces, and is in turn reinforced by the human rights commitments of the more democratically advanced states. It showcases the power and promise of cooperative constitutionalism.

Several lessons from the European experience are anticipated in the constitutional philosophy of James Madison. What I have in mind are the following broad themes: a belief that good constitutional design brings out the best while suppressing the worst in human nature; a simultaneous commitment to popular government and the protection of individual rights; an insistence on dividing power and duplicating responsibility so as to encourage deliberation and deter abuse; an appreciation for both the institutional and pedagogical value of bills of rights;[2] an awareness that human rights face dangers from emboldened majorities on the one hand and privileged minorities on the other; an understanding that a plurality of interests and identities is a resource rather than a problem, and is indeed necessary to avert injustice; a flexible and experimental attitude that welcomes improved means to secure one's constitutional objectives.

I presented the "Madisonian" case for strong international human rights institutions in the preceding chapter. Madison believed that checks and balances are necessary to prevent the abuse and misuse of political power. Yet checks and balances may be insufficient to withstand the pressure of faction, defined as a collective passion or interest unconstrained by justice. Madison famously argued that factions that might otherwise introduce injustice or tyranny in the individual states could be held in check by a compound republic. In the last few generations at least, history has offered some vindication of his theory. Federal institutions in the United States (federal courts, Congress, and the Department of Justice) have overruled or preempted state and local policy in order to uphold freedom of speech and religion, privacy rights, rights of the accused and prisoners' rights, freedom from police brutality, freedom from discrimination, and the right to vote and to equal representation. While federal checks on local abuses are seriously incomplete (and have often arrived tragically late), and while they do not cancel abuses perpetrated by the center itself, their importance cannot be ignored.

But how do we guard against faction at the national level? How do we prevent national factions from permitting grave abuses in the states and introducing abuses of their own? Madison argued on sociological grounds that the problem was already solved. In a large federation, the principle of popular government would prevent tyranny by minority faction, while the heterogeneity of interests and identities would prevent strong majority factions from forming. Unable to appeal to group interests or passions, officials would be obliged to follow reason and principle. "In the extended republic of the United States and among the great variety of interests, parties, and sects which it embraces, a coalition of a majority of the whole society could seldom take place on any other principles than those of justice and the general good."[3]

These words sound naïve today, when mass parties, mass media, and concentrated economic power make it all too easy for a majority or minority faction to take control of government. Moreover, contemporary countries are all vulnerable to nationalism, which may itself be considered a kind of faction, visibly so when it asserts itself against the just claims of foreigners and ostracized citizens. (One of Madison's main reasons for supporting the union was his belief that it would lead to fewer American violations of the law of nations.)[4] It is a notable advantage of international human rights institutions over domestic rights institutions that, due to the greater heterogeneity of their population base, they are less vulnerable to capture by faction. The fear of faction that led Madison to support a federal union over two hundred years ago becomes an argument, in today's altered circumstances, for the international supervision of national policy. When Madison asked, "how many errors and follies would [America] not have avoided, if the justice and propriety of her measures had, in every instance, been previously tried by the light in which they would probably appear to the unbiased part of mankind?" he reminded us that nations are not fit to be judge in their own cause. Participation in a strong international human rights regime helps guard us from moral error. Europe has taken this lesson to heart.

Concurrent Responsibility as a Principle of Democracy

Though I emphasize the contributions of international human rights institutions, I want strenuously to avoid the implication that they should function unaided. States (countries) remain responsible for the protection of human rights. When a state enlists the support of international institutions, the support should take the form of reinforcing and assisting commitments that the state has previously lifted onto its shoulders. The idea is not to displace responsibility upward, but rather to reaffirm one's responsibility (as a state) by increasing the number of *other* entities that are *simultaneously* responsible for fulfilling a shared commitment to human rights.

The key concept is "concurrent responsibility." I defined this in the last chapter as the responsibility of each member in a group to ensure that all exercise their power responsibly. More precisely, it refers to a situation in which several actors share an obligation, each is independently capable of fulfilling the obligation or ensuring that it is fulfilled, and each stands ready to do so if the others do not. An example discussed in the previous chapter is the concurrent responsibility of the U.S. president, Congress, and judiciary to block unconstitutional laws. Another example is the complementarity principle of the International Criminal Court (ICC). Under this principle, states are expected to prosecute genocide, war crimes, and crimes against humanity perpetrated by their citizens or occurring on their territory. (In truth they are expected to prevent such crimes from being committed in the first place.) However, if they fail to launch criminal proceedings, whether from a lack of will or capacity, the ICC is empowered to take action in their stead. One benefit of the ICC's complementary jurisdiction, it has been argued, is that it will encourage states to take their human rights responsibilities more seriously.[5]

We can see concurrent responsibility at work in a certain understanding of civil society. Alexis de Tocqueville and John Stuart Mill celebrated the civic initiative of American communities—their readiness when necessary to organize collective tasks normally entrusted to the state—because they believed it made citizens both less dependent on the state and better qualified to participate in government.[6] But concurrent responsibility is central to democratic citizenship at a still deeper level, for it is implicit in the very idea that political decisions should be made by the people. Every citizen casting a vote has the responsibility to support the best policy, defined not in terms of one's personal interests, but in terms of justice and the common good. Other citizens' participation serves as insurance against the possibility that I may fail my responsibility by voting incorrectly. Popular elections are the original checks and balances. When democracy succeeds in cultivating virtuous citizens, the correct policies will tend toward unanimous support.[7]

It might be objected that concurrent responsibility ignores the benefits that flow from task specialization. Theorists from Aristotle to Mancur Olson have warned that when everyone is responsible, no one is responsible.[8] Concurrent responsibility (it may be argued) raises the specter of shirking on the one hand and wasteful duplication of efforts on the other hand. But we know that when vital goods are at stake, multiple guardians are often necessary. In a well-designed system of checks and balances, the sharing of responsibility does not dissipate but instead reinforces the sense of individual responsibility. What is necessary is that each party knows what it is expected to do, knows that fulfilling its responsibility is morally required, and knows that other parties stand ready to help, by providing oversight and advice. Accountability mechanisms can shore up the incentives of the parties.[9] A working division of labor is compatible with mutual oversight and residual shared responsibility; parties may be instructed to withhold action unless other parties neglect or betray their assigned task. Decision procedures can encourage participation and deliberation, enabling diverse parties to screen out unjust policies, while still permitting a determinate result.

In Europe (as I intend to show) responsibility for protecting human rights is held concurrently by states and international institutions. Or to look at it another way: responsibility for protecting human rights within the jurisdiction of each state is held concurrently by that state and other European states. European states are co-guardians of human rights within each national jurisdiction. That at any rate is the principle on which the system is founded, a principle that to a considerable and increasing degree is reflected in practice.

The purpose of these remarks is to correct the common tendency of thinking that responsibility for protecting human rights rests either in one place (the state) or another (international institutions). There can be little doubt that Europe's regional institutions have enhanced respect for human rights. There can be equally little doubt that respect for human rights varies according to the commitment demonstrated by particular states.[10] The most committed states have maintained the best record at home, but have also worked to strengthen the human rights dimension of regional institutions. These in turn have led individual states to deepen their commitment to human rights. International institutions and rights-respecting states have endeavored to improve their own performance and that of each other, and in the process they have spread the culture of rights over a larger geographic area, increasing the number of rights-respecting states.

The European Human Rights Regime

The European human rights regime is a complex system that embraces different regional organizations and a multitude of overlapping initiatives. The guiding principle is that the protection of human rights is a collective task—that all European states and all European citizens are simultaneously responsible for the protection of human rights in each national jurisdiction. This principle has inspired unprecedented forms of transnational cooperation in the human rights field, including the establishment of supranational institutions that exert increasing influence over national policy. Since the character and extent of this cooperation are not universally known, I offer a bird's-eye view in the pages that follow.

In addressing this topic, I do not confine my attention to the European Convention on Human Rights (ECHR). Although the ECHR is rightly regarded as the linchpin of the system, it does not function alone. It is one of several human rights instruments of its parent body, the 47-member Council of Europe (COE), whose impact cannot be understood in isolation from the decisive contributions of the 28-member European Union (EU), the 28-member North Atlantic Treaty Organization (NATO), and the 57-member Organization for Security and Cooperation in Europe (OSCE). I examine these organizations in turn.

European Union

The purposes of today's EU extend well beyond the original goal of economic integration: the 1992 Treaty of Maastricht subsuming the old European Economic Community (EEC) under the broader mandate of a "European Union" is only one part of a long-term trend. The promotion of human rights is now a core mission of the EU. Since Maastricht, respect for human rights has been defined as a foundational principle of the Union and demanded of all member states.[11] Article 7 of the Treaty on European Union (EU Treaty) establishes procedures under which the Union may declare a member state to be in serious and persistent breach of human rights and, as a last resort, may suspend certain of the state's rights under the Treaty, including the right to vote in the Council of Ministers.

The powerful European Court of Justice (ECJ), responsible for interpreting EU law, has since 1969 recognized respect for fundamental rights as one of the general principles of law that guides its jurisprudence.[12] This commitment has been enshrined in the EU Treaty since Maastricht. (Specific articles in the founding Treaty of Rome had also empowered the ECJ to promote certain kinds of human rights, for example, the labor rights of women.)[13] A Charter of Fundamental Rights, adopted by the EU in 2000, became formally binding on EU institutions with the entry into force of the Lisbon Treaty in December 2009. The Lisbon Treaty also declares that the EU will itself become a party to the ECHR.

Within the EU, human rights conditions are monitored (though inadequately, some have argued)[14] in periodic reports by the European Parliament and the Council of Ministers. In 1997, a European Monitoring Center on Racism and Xenophobia was created to focus attention on one of the gravest sources of human rights violations in the region. It was succeeded in 2007 by the EU Agency for Fundamental Rights, authorized to provide "the relevant institutions and authorities of the Community and its Member States . . . with assistance and expertise relating to fundamental rights." In its foreign relations, the EU has made respect for human rights a criterion of development assistance and trade concessions, and has more than once sanctioned foreign countries for persistent violations.[15] The European Parliament has become an outspoken advocate for the promotion of human rights inside and outside the EU.[16]

Significantly, Article 49 of the EU Treaty, following the Copenhagen Criteria of 1993, makes respect for human rights a condition for the admission of new countries into the EU. A stream of EU guidelines and progress reports keeps candidate states aware of the requisite reforms.[17] Among scholars there is near-universal consensus that the "membership conditionality" practiced by the EU has played a decisive role in encouraging, reinforcing, and consolidating human rights reforms in several central and eastern European countries.[18] A kind of symbiosis has thus developed between the EU and the ECHR. The material rewards of EU membership lead states to take the ECHR more seriously, while the ECHR and its case law lend content and legitimacy to the human rights demands of the EU.

Some observers have been less than fully impressed by the EU human rights policy, arguing that it involves more show than substance.[19] A common criticism is that the Union seems to subject candidate states to greater human rights scrutiny than it does to its own members. The recent moves toward one-party dictatorship in Hungary lend force to this criticism. There are fears that EU counterterrorist measures adopted in the wake of 9/11 have encroached on individual liberties.[20] The EU, it should also be noted, took its time before officially embracing human rights. Only after a threatened rebellion by the German and Italian constitutional courts in the late 1960s did the ECJ promise it would make respect for human rights a guiding principle of its jurisprudence.[21] The episode serves as a reminder of the role that individual states can play in strengthening the multilateral protection of rights.

North Atlantic Treaty Organization

Because NATO makes democracy and respect for human rights a criterion of admission, it has played a role similar to the EU in central and eastern Europe.[22] The prospect of NATO membership has provided a significant incentive for democratic reforms, and scholars who study the relation between democratization and "membership conditionality" often study EU and NATO accession policies in tandem. Below I note an example of successful human rights diplomacy by NATO, specifically, the role of its secretary general in helping to repeal legal discrimination and defuse ethnic tensions in Latvia.

In its own conduct, on the other hand, NATO's impact on human rights is decidedly mixed. After 9/11, it provided a logistical framework that facilitated collusion by various European officials with the torture and extradition policies of the Bush administration.[23] NATO bombing raids have killed many civilians in Afghanistan. NATO's role in the Balkan wars of the 1990s is the subject of enduring controversy. NATO offensives halted genocide in Bosnia and ethnic cleansing in Kosovo. But the former action followed three years of half measures during which more than a hundred thousand people were killed, while the latter involved bombing tactics in apparent violation of international humanitarian law. In 2001 NATO sent troops to halt an incipient civil war in Macedonia. In both Bosnia and Kosovo large NATO deployments monitored the peace and assisted the process of reconstruction.

Organization for Security and Cooperation in Europe

The OSCE is constituted differently from both NATO and the EU. Because membership is extended to all European countries and former Soviet republics (alongside Canada and the United States), the OSCE includes several dictatorships and quasi dictatorships with severe human rights problems. Membership conditionality is thus not part of the OSCE repertoire. (Since the OSCE is not a treaty organization, not even formal ratification is required.) Nonetheless, the OSCE has made dramatic contributions to human rights.

When the OSCE, originally the Conference on Security and Cooperation in Europe (CSCE), was created to reduce tensions between the Soviet bloc and the West, its founding document, the Helsinki Final Act of 1975, included a generally worded commitment to human rights and fundamental freedoms. The results took everyone by surprise.[24] Dissidents in the East organized to monitor the human rights pledges made by their own governments. Sympathetic Westerners formed watchdog groups in support. One of these was a U.S. group calling itself Helsinki Watch. Thus was born the powerful NGO today known as Human Rights Watch—a salient reminder of the catalyzing potential of international human rights agreements. The Eastern dissidents and their international backers used subsequent meetings of the CSCE to train a spotlight on communist repression. The "Helsinki Process," as it has come to be known, contributed to the downfall of the communist system and strengthened the democratic orientation of the dissident movement, thus giving human rights a more prominent role in the political settlements that followed the fall of the Berlin Wall.

The CSCE acquired a permanent institutional structure in the early 1990s, with a new name (OSCE) to mark the change. Under the 1990 Charter of Paris for a New Europe, it solemnly committed itself to human rights, democracy, and the rule of law, spelling out the human rights obligations of member states with new precision. Today's OSCE is chiefly devoted to the connected tasks of conflict prevention, democratization, and human rights. It mediates disputes, organizes fact-finding missions, observes human rights conditions, advises governments how to run successful elections, monitors elections, teaches courses on democratization, and trains civil society organizations in international human rights law.[25]

Every year in Warsaw the OSCE convenes a two-week meeting to review the human rights performance of all member states. An innovative feature of the meeting is the equal participation of state delegations and human rights nongovernmental organizations (NGOs). For NGOs it is a rare opportunity to present criticisms directly to offending governments. According to a past participant, "the tone can often be very sharp between certain states not used to hearing democratic criticism, and NGOs like Human Rights Watch or the Helsinki Committee."[26]

In 1992 the OSCE established a High Commissioner on National Minorities (HCNM) with the task of defusing ethnic tensions before they erupt into violent conflict. The initiative reflected the lesson of the Yugoslav tragedy (and many past conflicts) that ethnic wars, "once started[,] are difficult to stop."[27] Its guiding norm is "integration," meant to avoid "the extremes of forced assimilation on the one hand and separatism on the other."[28] The legal authorities to which the HCNM appeals include the International Covenant on Civil and Political Rights and the Framework Convention on National Minorities of the Council of Europe.

Governments that resist the Commissioner's recommendations have been known to back down when NATO, the EU, and the COE have adopted the recommendations as conditions of accession. It is difficult to know how many wars have been prevented by the HCNM. However, knowledgeable observers believe that his efforts have been crucial.[29] Thus the first HCNM, Max van der Stoel, was widely credited with helping to defuse a dangerous standoff in the Baltic states in the 1990s between the dominant ethnic groups and the Russian minority that could have provoked military intervention by the Russian Federation.[30]

Council of Europe

The COE was an early attempt to promote the economic and political integration of Europe. The broad aims announced in the 1949 Statute—to achieve greater unity, facilitate economic and social progress, and promote human rights and fundamental freedoms—papered over tensions between those seeking a federated Europe and those (led by the UK) favoring a more limited form of integration.[31] As it turned out, economic integration and policy coordination would be entrusted to the European Coal and Steel Community, which evolved into today's EU. The greatest achievement of the COE remains the Convention for the Protection of Human Rights and Fundamental Freedoms adopted in 1950 and entering into force in 1953. Today the COE devotes itself almost exclusively to the promotion of human rights.

That mission has been sustained by painful memories and persistent fears. The motivation for founding the Council was both to prevent a revival of European fascism and to provide a bulwark against Soviet-inspired communism, which was then consolidating its grip on central and eastern Europe and posing a threat to countries further south and west. The 1970s brought the accession of Spain, Portugal, and Greece, for whom Council membership both symbolized and safeguarded their recent liberation from dictatorship. (Greece had been an early member of the Council but withdrew after the military coup of 1967.) The pattern was repeated after 1989 with the accession of formerly communist countries in central and eastern Europe. The Yugoslav tragedy soon put an end to complacent assumptions about the inevitability of peace and democracy following the end of the Cold War.

The principal statutory organizations of the COE are the Committee of Ministers and the Parliamentary Assembly,[32] which like the European Court of Human Rights (ECtHR) are based in Strasbourg, France. The Committee of Ministers, an intergovernmental body consisting of the member states' foreign ministers and their permanent representatives, has the power to admit and expel members, open treaties for signature, and issue recommendations to member states. Under the ECHR, it oversees compliance with judgments of the ECtHR. The Parliamentary Assembly is a deliberative and advisory body whose members are chosen by and drawn from national parliaments in proportion to national population. The Committee of Ministers and Parliamentary Assembly promote human rights by means of various public resolutions, reporting requirements, monitoring activities, and independent investigations. It was the Parliamentary Assembly that commissioned the major June 2007 report confirming the existence of torture centers run by the CIA in Poland and Romania.

Other COE institutions play an important role. A Commissioner for Human Rights, established in 1999, is given broad discretion to highlight serious patterns of human rights violations, promote human rights education, advise governments, and facilitate communications between member states and the Council. The so-called Venice Commission (officially the European Commission for Democracy through Law) develops expertise and offers advice on the adoption of democratic constitutions and legal practices. The COE secretary general, among his or her other roles, functions as a public advocate for human rights.

According to the COE's Statute, Council membership is limited to states that honor "the rule of law" and "human rights and fundamental freedoms" (art. 3), and member states that violate these principles can be expelled (art. 8). Admission of new states has often been delayed until basic human rights standards are fulfilled; the Council thus applies a form of membership conditionality reminiscent of but less stringent than that of the EU and NATO. Standards have varied, and some admissions have been controversial.[33] The Council has struggled over what to do with already admitted states that revert to authoritarianism. In 1969, two years after a military coup in Greece, the Committee of Ministers was considering a motion for suspension when Greece preemptively withdrew.[34] Motions to suspend the voting rights of Turkey and Russia on human rights grounds have at various times been introduced and even adopted (though rarely for an extended time).[35] Today, all countries in geographic Europe (including Turkey, Russia, and the Caucasus states) belong to the Council, with the exception of authoritarian Belarus.

Much Council activity deals with the adoption and implementation of treaties, now some two hundred in number.[36] The European Court of Human Rights, until 1998 assisted by the European Commission of Human Rights, rules on alleged violations of the ECHR and its protocols. Other COE human rights treaties do not involve the direct participation of the Court, however. These include the European Social Charter (encompassing social and economic rights), the Framework Convention on National Minorities, and the European Convention for the Prevention of Torture (discussed below).

Without doubt, the ECHR has had the most impact of any COE treaty.[37] It is the foremost symbol of the Council's commitment to human rights, and the primary point of reference for Council officials charged with defending human rights. The Convention recognizes the right to life, the right not to be subjected to torture or ill-treatment, the right not to be enslaved, the right not to be arbitrarily detained, the right to a fair trial, the right against retroactive punishment, the right to privacy, the right to freedom of religion, the right to freedom of expression, the right to freedom of assembly and association, the right to marry, the right to a remedy for the violation of one's rights, and the right not to suffer discrimination in the enjoyment of one's rights. Protocols adopted subsequent to the ECHR establish rights to private property, education, free elections, freedom of movement, equal treatment of spouses, the appeal of a criminal conviction, and compensation for wrongful conviction, as well as rights against capital punishment, double jeopardy, imprisonment for debt, expulsion of citizens, arbitrary expulsion of aliens, and legalized discrimination. Ratification of the ECHR and the procedural protocols adapting its machinery has become a condition of admission into the Council of Europe. Ratification of the substantive protocols is not universally mandated, though there has been heavy pressure to ratify some of them (such as the prohibition of the death penalty).

The prestige of the ECHR owes much to the vigor of its Court. Originally, all cases first went before the Commission of Human Rights, which issued nonbinding opinions. Some of these cases could then be referred to the

Court, which issued legally binding judgments. No member state could block another from lodging a complaint against it before the Commission, but the choice was left to each state whether individuals had a similar right to lodge complaints, and whether to recognize the jurisdiction of the Court. Protocol 11 to the Convention, which entered into force in 1998, streamlined the process by abolishing the Commission, and making the jurisdiction of the Court and the right of individuals to bring complaints before the Court compulsory for all member states. Protocol 11 reflected and reinforced the growing clout of the Court, which had resembled a "sleeping beauty"[38] during its early years, but delivered a series of bold decisions beginning in the late 1970s and saw a dramatic increase in its caseload in subsequent years. In 2014 the Court delivered nearly nine hundred judgments.

The Court may hear a case when domestic remedies have been exhausted (art. 35). If it finds that a member state has violated the Convention, it can order financial compensation to the injured party (art. 41). Judgments of the Court are final and legally binding (arts. 44 and 46). States almost always comply with all financial awards ordered by the Court, though sometimes after a considerable delay.[39] Many states routinely alter their policies in response to adverse rulings. The COE's Committee of Ministers monitors compliance with Court rulings, and brings pressure to bear on noncompliant states. Most national judiciaries routinely harmonize their domestic rulings to the Court's jurisprudence.[40] Several states endeavor to conform their policies to the overall jurisprudence of the Court, heeding decisions against other states, not only themselves.[41] Where some rights are concerned (though not the right against torture and ill-treatment), the Court grants the defendant state a "Margin of Appreciation," deferring to the state's interpretation of the rights provision within reasonable limits.

Compliance is by no means universal, as witnessed by the persistence (and sometimes increase) of serious and systematic violations in several states.[42] Russia is stubbornly resistant to reform. As the ECtHR continued to find extreme human rights violations in the North Caucasus, Russia paid the ordered compensation while refusing to take steps to end the violations,[43] and in its recent aggression against Ukraine, it has declared its open defiance of European institutions. Turkey, having made progress on torture and prisoners' rights, has lately veered toward repression,[44] while the formerly communist states of eastern and southeastern Europe present a mixed pattern. Among the more established democracies, Italy and France are known for their failure to correct abuses that have earned repeated rebuke in Strasbourg, although the situation appears to be changing in France.[45] Factors that contribute to noncompliance in these countries include the absence of a human rights ethic among political elites, the cultural reluctance or legal inability of national courts to apply ECHR law, the absence of an effective complaints mechanism under domestic law for individuals whose rights have been violated, and well-entrenched systems of criminal and civil justice that prove refractory to human rights reform.

These failures notwithstanding, observers agree in recognizing the far-reaching impact of the ECHR. Michael Goldhaber samples the reviews:

> Among the world's systems of human rights, it has been dubbed "the most advanced and effective"; "pre-eminent"; the "most successful"; certainly the most fully developed and the best-observed"; "no doubt the most developed and successful." The diplomat and scholar Antonio Cassese proclaims, "no other human rights treaty can claim the level of influence of the European Convention." Another professor calls the Strasbourg tribunal "a sort of world court of human rights."[46]

Laurence Helfer writes: "It is no exaggeration to state that the Convention and its growing and diverse body of case law have transformed Europe's legal and political landscape."[47]

The Court would never have acquired its current power without the vigorous participation of civil society. The overwhelming majority of cases are brought to the Court not by states but by nongovernmental actors. Human rights advocates exploit favorable decisions of the Court in legal, political, and educational venues, thereby magnifying its prestige.[48] In Europe, as in the rest of the world, they supply information, publicity, petitioners, and political pressure needed for the actual functioning of formal human rights institutions. They breathe life into a system that would otherwise remain largely inert.[49] Of course, human rights advocates derive much of their effectiveness and clout from favorable rulings of regional and national courts. Courts and civil society have formed a powerful partnership.[50] The judicial empowerment of civil society has led some scholars to speak of a new model of democracy, in which individuals enjoy more direct means of influencing public policy than that traditionally offered by parliaments and parties.[51]

It would be a mistake, however, to identify the Convention wholly with the Court. The heart of the Convention is the set of human rights obligations it contains. States promise, when ratifying the Convention, to honor these obligations. As the treaty's first article declares, "The High Contracting Parties shall secure to everyone within their jurisdiction the rights and freedoms defined in . . . this Convention." States need not and should not wait for an adverse Court ruling to strive for complete adherence to the Convention. All forty-seven members have acted appropriately, therefore, in incorporating the Convention into their domestic law. Ideally, the Court should have nothing to do, since states will have previously acted to correct and prevent possible violations of the Convention. As a tribunal of last resort, it serves to remind states of obligations they have previously assumed. Moreover, states can adopt institutional measures beyond treaty ratification and domestic incorporation to promote national compliance with the Convention. In several states, parliamentary committees, executive-branch legal advisors, courts, independent human rights committees, or national ombudsmen screen proposed legislation and monitor executive conduct for compliance with the Convention and Strasbourg case law.[52]

Because the ECHR is now incorporated into the domestic law of all member states, judicial oversight occurs at the national as well as transnational level. In some countries (such as Russia), domestic incorporation is more nominal than real.[53] But in others, the process is far advanced. Helen Keller and Alec Stone Sweet, leaders of a major collaborative study, report that as a result of ratification and incorporation, "national officials are being steadily socialized into a Europe whose Convention not only binds the State, as a matter of international law, but also binds domestic officials, as a matter of enforceable national law."[54] In several countries, the Convention has altered the domestic institutional landscape, enhancing the power of courts, encouraging the practice of judicial review, and promoting a domestic jurisprudence more favorable to human rights.[55] As compliance becomes more automatic, there arises what Fionnuala Ní Aoláin calls, with reference to prohibition of torture and ill-treatment, a "process of circular enforcement": "As European states have become accustomed to external legal scrutiny, and their legal systems have accordingly bent to preempt and/or accommodate such review, it has become much easier for the Court to extend both the depth and breadth of its jurisprudence in the context of article 3."[56]

The UK illustrates the value of placing international human rights commitments under the oversight of domestic judges. Though it was the first country to ratify the ECHR, the UK waited several decades before incorporating it into domestic law. In the meantime, individuals were obliged to seek relief in Strasbourg for British violations of the Convention. (The absence in the UK of a domestic constitution exacerbated the problem.) The Human Rights Act (HRA), which passed in 1998 and took effect in 2000, empowered British courts to enforce compliance with the ECHR by public officials, interpret ambiguous legislation in a manner consistent with the ECHR, and declare legislation to be incompatible with the ECHR. In principle, Parliament may ignore an incompatibility declaration, but with one exception it has always responded by passing corrective legislation.[57]

The significance of the HRA became manifest after 9/11, when British courts used the Act to exert a partial, albeit inadequate, check on the government's counterterrorism policies. Under the HRA, British courts ruled in the seminal *Belmarsh Prison* case against a law authorizing the indefinite detention without trial of foreigners suspected of involvement in terrorist activity,[58] a decision later backed by the European Court of Human Rights.[59] After *Belmarsh*, British courts used the HRA to subject the government's use of "control orders" (a range of restrictions up to a modified form of house arrest) to significant limitations.[60] Because of these limitations, Parliament replaced the control orders system with a milder system of Terrorism Prevention and Investigation Measures in January 2012.[61] British judges ruled that the ECHR extends to British treatment of detainees abroad, thus obligating the government to investigate reports of prisoner abuse in Iraq,[62] a decision upheld and expanded in subsequent rulings by the ECtHR.[63] Guided by past rulings of the Strasbourg Court, British courts have blocked some deportation orders against foreigners with alleged ties to terrorism, on the grounds that they face a risk of torture or persecution in the receiving countries.[64] In December 2005, UK judges banned the use of tortured confessions in legal proceedings, although this ruling rested primarily on common law rather than the Human Rights Act.[65]

UK courts may be criticized for not doing nearly enough to protect human rights against the government's counterterror initiatives.[66] Yet it seems clear that human rights would be less secure in the absence of the HRA. Stephen Gardbaum finds it "hard to deny that rights are better protected under the HRA" inasmuch as the Act has created greater rights-consciousness "among citizens, courts, public officials, Parliament and government," and has extended legal protection to a wider class of rights. He observes that "Pre-HRA, there would likely have been no plausible legal claim for the UK courts to consider in the *Belmarsh Prison* case."[67] A pattern has arisen in which UK courts and the ECtHR appeal to one another's rulings when invalidating counterterrorist initiatives—an example of the "circular reinforcement" described by Ní Aoláin—though in general the ECtHR has issued bolder rulings. As Fiona de Londras emphasizes in her indispensable study, it took the resistance of domestic and international courts acting together under authority of the ECHR to block a wide range of repressive counterterrorism policies promoted by the British government—a resistance all the more remarkable given the concerted opposition of the British government and heightened fears of terrorism in the public at large.[68] When it comes to the effectiveness of the HRA and ECHR in restraining counterterror policies, we may say that the glass is partly full, without thereby implying that it is nearly or completely full.

Upon winning a parliamentary majority in May 2015, the Conservative Party announced it would pursue its election promise to replace the Human Rights Act with an as yet undrafted British Bill of Rights and Responsibilities.[69] The Bill would free UK judges from an obligation to consider Strasbourg precedent in their decisions, and would establish that Strasbourg rulings do not require changes in UK law, a move that party leaders acknowledge might trigger the UK's withdrawal from the Convention.[70] Under the Bill, a real risk of torture or ill-treatment would no longer be a sufficient bar to deportation, and the judicial protection of human rights would no longer extend to UK military actions abroad.[71] A study by prominent legal scholars concluded that "a plausible effect of the Bill of Rights is a limitation of existing rights" and that withdrawal from the ECHR would cause "a substantial reduction of human rights protection, in particular for minority and vulnerable groups."[72] It remains to be seen if the government will carry out its plan.[73]

The European Human Rights Regime as a Whole

Together the EU, NATO, OSCE, and COE form a complex set of complementary and overlapping mechanisms for the promotion of human rights. The methods include standard-setting and codification, lawmaking and adjudication, exhortation and shaming, monitoring and reporting, investigation and inspection, training and education, capacity-building and advice-giving, dialogue and diplomacy, material rewards and membership incentives, conflict prevention and peacemaking. The key is not to confine oneself to one method, but to use several in combination.[74]

The potential of this strategy to effect fundamental change may be illustrated by the evolution of Latvia's citizenship and election laws during the

1990s.[75] At independence in 1991, the Latvian government limited citizenship to those who were Latvian citizens before 1940 and their descendants. The law excluded one-third of the population—most of them ethnic Russians—from citizenship. Max van der Stoel, the first OSCE High Commissioner on National Minorities, made it a priority to end this discriminatory arrangement. Over the next few years he made frequent visits to Latvia and drew up detailed proposals for reform. The Council of Europe made similar recommendations. In 1995 the Latvian government agreed to a partial liberalization of the law as the necessary price for admission into the COE. Further liberalization was enacted in 1998 as a condition of accession into the EU. The reforms provided citizenship to large numbers of people (most of them formerly stateless) and greatly speeded up the naturalization process.

Meanwhile, laws passed in 1994 and 1995 had decreed that only citizens demonstrating the highest level of proficiency in the Latvian language could run for local or national office. The laws were rescinded in 2002, however, after an adverse ruling from the European Court of Human Rights, and after the NATO secretary general warned during a visit to Latvia that they jeopardized Latvia's chance of admission into NATO. Both the citizenship and election reforms were achieved despite strong domestic opposition. Thus did European regional organizations defeat a policy of legalized discrimination and defuse a dangerous set of ethnic tensions at the domestic and international levels.

The European human rights regime is not confined to regional mechanisms. Most European states (especially in the EU) have ratified and given strong support to global treaties such as the International Covenant on Civil and Political Rights, the Torture Convention, and the Rome Statute of the International Criminal Court. (The European Parliament and the Parliamentary Assembly of the COE also encourage ratification of these treaties outside Europe.)

What is the state of human rights in Europe today? If we look at the forty-seven countries that have ratified the ECHR, we see continuing violations in all member states (as in all countries of the world), with the worst pattern of violations in certain southeastern European countries and former Soviet republics and dangerous moves toward one-party dictatorship in Hungary.[76] Russia has intensified government repression, continued harsh counterinsurgency tactics in the North Caucasus, and waged military aggression against Ukraine.[77] Turkey saw significant human rights reforms in the late 1990s and early 2000s, followed by a surge of repression in recent years (including harassment of journalists, politicized prosecutions, and police brutality).[78] Some countries permit the widespread torture and ill treatment of prisoners. Certain groups (immigrants, Muslims, and Roma) are at heightened risk of state abuse (ill-treatment, prolonged detention without trial, expulsion).[79] These are grave failures, but it remains the case that the great majority of member states offer a bright picture in comparison both to their own past and to the world as a whole. As of 2014, Freedom House gave its strongest "Civil Liberties" score (1 on a scale of 1 to 7) to twenty-nine of the forty-seven. Eight more received a score of 2, and only four scored below 3. (Azerbaijan came last with a score of 6, preceded by Russia with 5.)

Europe has come a long way since 1949, when dictators ruled eastern and central Europe and the Iberian Peninsula. Today, in most (sadly not all) European countries, a return to authoritarianism is unthinkable. The language of human rights is now deeply internalized in Europe's national and international institutions, and five decades of human rights judgments from Strasbourg have altered public perceptions of the boundaries between acceptable and unacceptable government behavior. The progress toward freedom in central, eastern, and southeastern Europe over the past two decades is particularly striking. There can be no doubt that Europe's supranational human rights institutions contributed significantly to this transformation. We can register our disappointment with the failures of the European human rights regime without losing sight of its real and remarkable achievements.

New challenges have arisen in recent years. The fear of international terrorism in the wake of 9/11 has tested the resilience of the system, contributing to persistent anti-immigrant and anti-Muslim sentiment, and prompting serious abuses associated with the detention, interrogation, deportation, and transfer of terrorist suspects. The refugee crisis poses a tremendous challenge, to which European states have responded in an uneven, inadequate, and often cruel manner. The prolonged Eurozone crisis has ravaged the safety net in indebted countries, triggered the rise of extreme right-wing parties, sown divisions between Eurozone states, and battered the prestige of the EU, damaging its ability to sustain democratic institutions inside and outside its borders. It remains to be seen whether a distracted EU can turn back the antidemocratic measures of the ruling Fidesz party in Hungary, an EU member state. Not the least reason to regret the gamble of the common currency (a gamble seemingly encouraged by a simplistic vision of regional integration) is the threat posed by the current crisis to the regional protection of human rights.

Under President Vladimir Putin, Russia has repressed dissent, shut down independent media, harassed civil society organizations, and legislated persecution of gays and lesbians. Tensions between Russia and Europe developed into open confrontation when Ukraine's president Victor Yanukovych acceded to Putin's request not to sign the EU Association Agreement, and Russia intervened in Ukraine following the Maidan Revolution that removed Yanukovych from power. Yanukovych had been a corrupt and increasingly autocratic ruler; his unexpected rejection of the EU agreement alarmed many Ukrainians who viewed the EU accession process as the last hope to save democracy in Ukraine. It would appear that Russia is using military means in an attempt to veto Europe's pro-democratization efforts in Ukraine.

The European Court of Human Rights has suffered strains as well. Because of a staggering caseload, judgments on the small minority of cases deemed admissible by the Court have been delivered an average of five years after initial filing.[80] Such delays undermine the Court's role as an agent of justice and guardian of rights.[81] The overload is due in part to the growing fame and influence of the Court, and in part to the problem of repetitive violations—countries failing to correct patterns of violation identified in previous Court rulings. As of July 2014, five countries—Ukraine, Italy, Russia, Turkey, and Romania—accounted for two-thirds of pending cases.[82] Protocol 14 introduced streamlined procedures in 2010, and the Court has devised its own strategies to improve efficiency. In a small but increasing number of cases, it not only directs the violating state to pay financial compensation to the victims but orders it to desist from the violation.[83] It has also begun using "pilot judgments" to address similar cases: under this procedure, the Court issues a ruling on a representative "pilot" case and directs national authorities to settle remaining cases in accordance with the pilot ruling.[84] Significant progress has been made—the number of pending cases has been reduced from a high of over 160,000 in September 2011 to 70,000 in December 2014[85]—but the problem is far from vanquished.

The Court has also faced open resistance. Relations with the United Kingdom, historically rocky, have worsened under Conservative prime minister David Cameron, in power since 2010. The Conservative Party, the UK Independence Party, and sectors of the media have subjected the Court to a barrage of criticism. In advance of the 2012 Brighton Conference on the future of the European Convention on Human Rights, a draft declaration leaked to the public revealed British government proposals that could have significantly narrowed the jurisdiction of the Court. The final declaration emerging from the Conference proved far milder, but the UK has prodded other member states to accept a proposed Protocol 15 adding language to the Convention

Preamble that could be interpreted as encouraging the Court to show greater deference to member states.[86] As noted above, the majority Conservative government elected in May 2015 has stated its intention to replace the Human Rights Act with a weaker Bill of Rights and Responsibilities and to reduce the legal authority of the European Court of Human Rights in the UK.

The European Anti-Torture Regime: Achievements, Failures, Challenges

In this section, I examine the successes and failures of the European human rights regime in preventing torture and ill-treatment. Overall, the regime has greatly limited the use of torture, though alongside progress there have been dramatic failures. (This is a long section, and may be skipped by those wishing to focus on the chapter's core argument.)

Although judicial torture was abolished throughout Europe by the end of the eighteenth century, ill-treatment often amounting to torture persisted in prisons, police stations, and military barracks. The imperial powers used severe forms of torture to maintain control of their overseas possessions.[87] The unrestrained cruelties of Hitler's Gestapo, Stalin's NKVD, and the Japanese Kempeitai caused general horror, and became a powerful spur to the human rights revolution following World War II.[88]

The unequivocal language of the European Convention (which closely follows that of the 1948 Universal Declaration of Human Rights) was intended to draw a sharp break with the past. Beginning in 1951, ratifying states have pledged in Article 3 that "no one shall be subjected to torture or to inhuman or degrading treatment or punishment." The prohibition is stated in absolute terms: unlike most other rights asserted in the Convention, it admits no exceptions. The prohibition may not be suspended even during an emergency "threatening the life of the nation" (art. 15[2]). It also extends beyond torture to include all inhuman or degrading treatment or punishment, thus forbidding brutality in all its forms and removing the temptation to fiddle with the meaning of the word "torture." Moreover, for the first time in human history the prohibition was to be enforced by a permanent international commission and court.

The UK, France, and Belgium kept their overseas empires until the early 1960s. France's systematic use of torture during the Algerian War of Independence predated its ratification of the Convention in 1974. Belgium ratified the

Convention in 1955, but chose to forego the option, available under Article 63 of the original treaty, of applying the Convention to its African colonies.[89] The UK, which in 1951 became the first country to ratify the Convention, applied the Convention to most of its imperial territories,[90] but did not recognize the right of individual petition or the jurisdiction of the Court until 1966, and then only for Britain and Northern Ireland.[91] UK officials made extensive use of torture against independence movements throughout the Empire.[92] It came as a shock to the British government when in 1956 and 1957 Greece accused it before the Commission of Human Rights of systematic torture among other human rights violations in Cyprus—then still a British colony. The Commission began proceedings, but these were dropped as part of negotiations leading to Cyprus's independence in 1960.[93]

Ten years after the Cyprus cases it was Greece's turn to be accused. Following the military coup of 1967 and the brutal repression that ensued, Greece was charged before the Commission with a long list of human rights violations in a joint complaint filed by Denmark, the Netherlands, Norway, and Sweden. In 1969 the Commission ruled that Greece had violated numerous Convention provisions, including Article 3. More than three hundred pages of its report were devoted to accounts of torture. As the Committee of Ministers was considering a motion to expel Greece from the Council of Europe, Greece announced its own decision to withdraw.[94]

The landmark case of *Ireland v. UK* addressed the "Five Techniques" the British government had authorized in 1971 during its antiterrorist campaign in Northern Ireland.[95] The techniques referred to wall-standing, hooding, loud noise, food deprivation, and sleep deprivation, although these descriptions understate the brutality of the treatment actually used. In 1976, the Commission unanimously held that the treatment constituted torture. The Court, delivering its judgment in 1978, determined that the treatment did not amount to torture, but that it did constitute inhuman and degrading treatment and was therefore still a violation of Article 3. Accounts by the victims make it clear that the Commission made the more accurate assessment.[96] The Court suggested as much in *Selmouni v. France* (1999), stating that "the Court considers that certain acts which were classified in the past as 'inhuman and degrading treatment' as opposed to 'torture' could be classified differently in future."[97] In December 2014, the Irish government asked the Court to reopen the *Ireland v. UK* case, based on newly revealed documents regarding the severity of the techniques. Legal scholars believe that the Court is likely to rehear the case and to rule that the techniques did, in fact, constitute torture.[98]

Torture has long been a problem in Turkey, the subject of concerted campaigns by international human rights NGOs. Though a member of the Council of Europe since 1949, Turkey was to some degree sheltered from intergovernmental human rights criticism by Cold War politics. In 1982, two years after a military coup that unleashed mass arrests and widespread torture, five states (Denmark, Norway, Sweden, the Netherlands, and France) accused Turkey of torture before the Commission, but the complaint was withdrawn in 1985, possibly under U.S. pressure.[99] Turkey did not permit individual petitions until 1987, nor did it recognize the jurisdiction of the Court until 1990. Thereafter, a large number of cases were filed in Strasbourg, especially from the Kurdish southeast. In the 1996 case of *Aksoy v. Turkey*, the Court issued its first finding of torture.[100] Between 1995 and 2004 the Court issued fifty-one rulings against Turkey for violations of Article 3.[101]

Turkey was slow to take action until its political landscape began to change at the turn of the century.[102] In 1999 the government captured Abdullah Öcalan, leader of the insurgent Kurdish organization PKK, who called on his followers to abandon the use of violence. The same year, the EU named Turkey an official candidate for membership in the Union, increasing the likelihood that eventual membership would be the reward of serious human rights reform. In the next few years, the government took steps to reduce the political power of the military and broaden rights for the Kurdish minority. Reforms accelerated after the Justice and Development Party won national elections in 2002. New laws further enhanced civilian control of the military, expanded human rights training for the police, decreased the period of incommunicado detention, banned blindfolding of prisoners, and beefed up prosecution of officials guilty of ill-treatment. Human rights organizations agree that torture has greatly decreased in Turkey, though it remains a serious problem.

Russia remains a problematic case. A new Criminal Procedure Code, enacted in 2001, established several safeguards intended to prevent torture. According to Amnesty International, the measures have caused some improvement, but police still regularly use torture to extract confessions from criminal suspects.[103] Lack of police training, pressure to produce convictions, and new ways of circumventing the anti-torture safeguards have lessened the impact of the 2001 reforms. In the meantime, torture long continued in Chechnya,[104] although the slowing pace of the conflict decreased the number of new victims. In March 2007 the European Committee for the Prevention of Torture (discussed below) took the rare step of issuing a public statement to condemn Russian authorities for allowing the continued use of torture in Chechnya.

The European Court of Human Rights has developed a rich jurisprudence on torture and ill-treatment. Among the practices held by the Court to violate Article 3 are disproportionate use of force during arrest, inadequate accommodations for detainees with physical or mental disabilities, inadequate medical care for detainees, housing of prisoners in overcrowded or unsanitary conditions, complete sensory deprivation, aggressive strip searching, expulsion or threatened expulsion to countries where a person faces a significant danger of ill-treatment, premeditated destruction of homes without warning and without respect for the feeling of the homeowners, capital punishment following an unfair trial, corporal punishment of children by judicial authorities, and inadequate measures to prevent the domestic abuse of children.[105] The Court has established that under Article 3 governments are obligated to investigate credible complaints of ill-treatment (including torture),[106] abstain from deporting individuals to countries where they face a real risk of ill-treatment,[107] and take reasonable measures to protect individuals from being subjected to ill-treatment by other private individuals.[108] While countries such as Turkey and Russia account for a disproportionate share of Article 3 violations, countries with better human rights reputations have not been spared; thirty-eight of the forty-seven member states have been held in violation of Article 3.[109]

For much of its history, the ECtHR did little to challenge prison conditions in the region.[110] However, in the past few decades, two major Council of Europe initiatives inspired by Article 3 of the ECHR have sought to improve prison conditions and in the process encouraged greater intervention from the Court.[111] In 1987 and again in 2006, the Committee of Ministers of the Council of Europe issued a set of detailed guidelines for the treatment of prisoners. The European Prison Rules are not legally binding, and conditions in several countries are far from anything approaching compliance. (They are often appalling, as European Court of Human Rights cases like *Kalashnikov v. Russia* [2002] and *Dougoz v. Greece* [2001] attest.)[112] The Rules nonetheless represent a collective effort to flesh out the meaning of Article 3, and provide a normative standard against which national policies can be assessed. The nine principles that introduce the 2006 Rules are worth quoting in full, because of their evident commitment to the dignity of prisoners:

  1. All persons deprived of their liberty shall be treated with respect for their human rights.

2. Persons deprived of their liberty retain all rights that are not lawfully taken away by the decision sentencing them or remanding them in custody.

3. Restrictions placed on persons deprived of their liberty shall be the minimum necessary and proportionate to the legitimate objective for which they are imposed.

4. Prison conditions that infringe prisoners' human rights are not justified by lack of resources.

5. Life in prison shall approximate as closely as possible the positive aspects of life in the community.

6. All detention shall be managed so as to facilitate the reintegration into free society of persons who have been deprived of their liberty.

7. Co-operation with outside social services and as far as possible the involvement of civil society in prison life shall be encouraged.

8. Prison staff carry out an important public service and their recruitment, training and conditions of work shall enable them to maintain high standards in their care of prisoners.

9. All prisons shall be subject to regular government inspection and independent monitoring.

Among the specific rules:

17.1. Prisoners shall be allocated, as far as possible, to prisons close to their homes or places of social rehabilitation. . . .

18.2. In all buildings where prisoners are required to live, work or congregate: *a.* the windows shall be large enough to enable the prisoners to read or work by natural light in normal conditions and shall allow the entrance of fresh air except where there is an adequate air conditioning system. . . .

18.7. As far as possible, prisoners shall be given a choice before being required to share sleeping accommodation. . . .

20.2. [Prison] clothing shall not be degrading or humiliating.

The document also states: "Solitary confinement shall be imposed as a punishment only in exceptional cases and for a specified period of time, which shall be as short as possible" (rule 60.5).

A second major initiative was the adoption in 1987 of the European Convention for the Prevention of Torture and Inhuman or Degrading Treatment or Punishment. Now binding on all forty-seven COE member states, the convention establishes an interdisciplinary committee (known for short as the Committee for the Prevention of Torture, CPT, or Anti-Torture Committee) with the power to inspect any detention center of its choosing.[113] Following country visits, the CPT communicates its recommendations to host governments in the form of confidential reports, which are now voluntarily published by all Council of Europe countries except Russia, and which thus become a resource for human rights advocates. On the rare occasions when the CPT determines that a government is withholding cooperation, either by interfering with visits or refusing to implement the committee's recommendations, it can issue a public statement describing its concerns. Both the CPT and the European Prison Rules have influenced the judgments of the European Court of Human Rights, which since 2001 has acted more assertively to correct abusive prison conditions.

The CPT has made hundreds of visits to the forty-seven member states. Local officials holding detainees in their custody know that they can receive a visit from the CPT at any time.[114] (Country visits are announced with a few weeks' notice, but committee members can visit detention sites of their choosing without warning.) Because of the CPT's recommendations, more countries grant detainees prompt access to legal counsel and medical attention, and improvements in the physical accommodation of detainees have been adopted.[115] The CPT helped spur major structural reforms in Turkey from the late 1990s onwards that led to a significant reduction, though far from an eradication, of torture. Less progress was achieved in Russia, however, and a trend in many countries toward higher incarceration rates, with consequent overcrowding, threatens several of the committee's achievements.[116]

Through general reports, in addition to communications with individual governments, the CPT has played a major role in setting regional standards for detainee treatment. It has popularized the formula that three basic rights—access to a lawyer, access to a doctor, and notification of one's detention to a third party of one's choosing—are vital to the prevention of ill-treatment in pretrial detention. To combat the problem of state denial, the committee has spelled out in detail the measures needed for ensuring that apparent cases of ill-treatment receive prompt and impartial investigation. The work of the CPT inspired much of the content of the 2006 European Prison Rules and has exerted a growing influence on the jurisprudence of the European Court of Human Rights.[117] Together, the Court, the CPT, and the Prison Rules have formed, in the words of Jim Murdoch, "a complex scheme of interwoven standard-setting and implementation machinery which draws upon international expectations and domestic practices and is given practical force through state goodwill and, when necessary, by the threat of judicial condemnation."[118] A major legacy of the European Convention for the Prevention of Torture is the establishment of a parallel global arrangement under the auspices of the 2002 Optional Protocol to the Torture Convention (discussed in Chapter 4).

After 9/11, European officials lent various forms of assistance to the U.S. torture program, leading Amnesty International to call Europe "the USA's partner in crime."[119] Several countries granted overflight and refueling privileges to the United States' extraordinary rendition flights. Other assistance has been more direct. Local authorities in Italy, Britain, Sweden, Macedonia, and Bosnia delivered or facilitated the transfer of citizens or temporary residents into the hands of U.S. officials, who sent them overseas for torture or severe ill-treatment. Intelligence officers from Britain, Germany, Turkey, and possibly France traveled to Guantanamo Bay to interrogate their countries' citizens and residents imprisoned there.[120]

It is a damning fact that the CIA located some of its primary "black sites" in Europe. From late 2002 to 2005, secret detention centers in Poland, Romania, and Lithuania were the setting for harrowing abuse such as waterboarding, longtime standing, hypothermia, extreme isolation, and a range of psychological methods intended to cause severe mental regression.[121] The interrogators were American CIA operatives, but the premises were supplied and secured by the host governments with the knowledge of high-ranking officials, whether or not they knew the details of the interrogation methods being used.

Where collusion occurred, it can be understood as the defeat of one kind of multilateralism by another, with European rights protections succumbing to the superior might of transatlantic security and intelligence networks.[122] A 2007 Council of Europe report on renditions and secret detentions in Europe analyzes in detail the role played by NATO agreements and procedures in facilitating the black sites and extraordinary renditions.[123] The showdown between the two multilateralisms appears starkly in Bosnia, where in October 2001 national police arrested six men at the request of the U.S. embassy. Months later, Bosnian courts ordered the men released (because the U.S. embassy refused to hand over evidence allegedly demonstrating a terrorist plot) and issued an order banning the deportation of four of the men. Nonetheless, on the day of their release, all six were promptly rearrested by Bosnian police and transferred to U.S. NATO troops for shipment to Guantanamo, where they were tortured.[124]

The UK government was deeply complicit in torture in the "War on Terror." Some of its conduct amounted to a policy of torture by proxy, because it cooperated with and sought to benefit from torture by other governments. Pakistan's notorious intelligence service seized and interrogated British citizens at the request of MI5 and MI6, which met and questioned the detainees but took no action in response to obvious signs that they were being tortured.[125] Despite knowledge of U.S. torture and ill-treatment, British authorities facilitated the rendition of British residents to Guantanamo Bay and Bagram prison in Afghanistan and conducted hundreds of detainee interviews in both locations.[126] British intelligence officials supplied Moroccan officials with questions for use in the torture of British resident Binyam Mohamed.[127] They similarly asked foreign intelligence organizations well known for using torture—including those of Pakistan, Algeria, Egypt, and Bangladesh—to share the results of detainee interrogations that actually involved torture.[128] The UK government arranged the involuntary return of two Libyan dissidents and their families to Libya, where the two men were severely tortured by Moammar Gaddafi's intelligence services. After Gaddafi's overthrow, human rights researchers in Tripoli discovered several pages of questions that MI5 and MI6 had supplied to the prisoners' Libyan interrogators.[129]

It has emerged that the "torture by proxy" policy was facilitated by secret MI5 and MI6 legal directives stating that under certain circumstances UK intelligence officials could request and receive information from foreign interrogators if they did not know but only foresaw a "real possibility" that the request would cause torture or mistreatment to be used. This was allowed if the foreign intelligence service furnished "credible assurances" that it would not engage in torture or mistreatment, or if (in the absence of trustworthy assurances) senior MI5 and MI6 management judged that the risk of mistreatment was outweighed by the value of the requested information.[130]

Victims have filed civil actions against UK officials, and in some cases won substantial settlements.[131] However, the government has often sought to impede investigation. In August 2011, ten leading human rights NGOs withdrew from the primary official inquiry, objecting that it was subject to excessive government control.[132] Amnesty International states, "There has been no genuinely independent, public inquiry into allegations of UK involvement in serious human rights violations of people detained overseas in the context of counter-terrorism operations."[133]

In Iraq, British soldiers applied torture themselves.[134] Between 2003 and 2008, they subjected hundreds of detainees to abuses that included hooding, sleep deprivation, deprivation of food and water, prolonged stress positions, forced exercises, beatings, mock executions, electric shock, and sexual humiliation. The "Five Techniques" of Northern Ireland fame figured prominently, notwithstanding their prohibition by the ECtHR in 1978 and the UK government's promise to discontinue them in the early 1970s. On September 14, 2003, Baha Mousa was one of ten men who were arrested in a hotel raid in Basra, then hooded, forcibly kept awake, placed in stress positions, and severely beaten. Thirty-six hours later Mousa was dead, having suffered at least ninety-three injuries. A public inquiry led to a 1,400-page report concluding that a "corporate" and "systemic failure" by the Ministry of Defense to establish proper guidelines for prisoner treatment was a contributing factor to Mousa's death.[135] In *Cruel Britannia*, Ian Cobain discusses four Iraqi detainees who died from torture in British custody. Lawyers representing victims' families claim that the real figure is much higher.[136] The UK government has paid several million pounds in restitution to Iraqi victims of UK torture.

In January 2014, two organizations, the European Center for Constitutional and Human Rights and Public Interest Lawyers, submitted a 250-page report to the International Criminal Court, formally requesting an investigation into the responsibility of high-ranking British officials—including a former secretary of defense and former armed forces minister—for widespread and systemic torture and inhuman treatment in Iraq.[137] The report stated that military commanders "knew or should have known" of abuses committed by their subordinates, while "civilian superiors knew or consciously disregarded information at their disposal, which clearly indicated that UK services personnel were committing war crimes." The report observed "clear patterns" of abuse "in a variety of different UK facilities . . . from 2003 to 2008," and offered evidence "that failures to follow-up on or ensure accountability for ending such practices became a cause of further abuse."

After 9/11, the European Court of Human Rights has generally reinforced the right against torture and ill-treatment, though sometimes moving in a backward direction. Crucially, it has taken several opportunities to reaffirm the absolute prohibition of torture and ill-treatment. In *Chahal v. UK* (1996), the Court had invoked Article 3 to uphold an absolute ban on the repatriation, or "*refoulement*," of any individuals, including suspected terrorists, to countries where they faced a serious threat of torture or ill-treatment.[138] In the 2008 case of *Saadi v. Italy*, Britain intervened as a third party to argue that the possibility of ill-treatment by a foreign state ought to be weighed against the danger of terrorist attack if deportation is blocked. In a unanimous opinion, the seventeen-judge Grand Chamber declared such balancing inadmissible.[139] The Court continues to block numerous deportations on Article 3 grounds.[140] In *Al-Skeini v. UK* and *Al-Jedda v. UK* (2011), it broadened the extraterritorial application of the Convention, ruling that the British detention without charge of an Iraqi civilian for over three years in Iraq violated the Convention, and that in Iraq the Convention covered not only detainees in UK custody but all individuals in territories where the UK had assumed authority and responsibility for the maintenance of security.[141]

In December 2012 the Strasbourg Court issued its much anticipated judgment in *El-Masri v. Macedonia*. Khaled El-Masri was a German citizen whom the U.S. government confused with a suspected Al Qaeda associate bearing a similar name.[142] He was secretly detained and abusively interrogated by Macedonian authorities for three weeks, then transferred to CIA officials, who brutalized him before flying him to a CIA black site in Afghanistan where he was subjected to four months of abuse. His family and friends were not told what had happened to him. When El-Masri later tried to sue CIA director George Tenet for kidnapping and torture, his case was thrown out by federal courts on grounds of the state secrets doctrine, and the U.S. Supreme Court refused to hear the case on appeal.[143]

When El-Masri brought a case against Macedonia before the European Court of Human Rights, a Grand Chamber of seventeen judges unanimously ordered Macedonia to pay restitution to El-Masri, ruling that Macedonia had violated El-Masri's rights to freedom from torture and inhuman or degrading treatment, freedom from unlawful detention, respect for his privacy and family life, and an effective remedy for the violation of his rights.[144] Among other findings, the Court ruled that U.S. officials tortured El-Masri at Macedonia's Skopje Airport, where he was severely beaten, stripped, sodomized with an object, placed in a diaper, shackled, hooded, subjected to total sensory deprivation, forced into a plane, thrown to the floor, chained, and forcibly tranquilized (§205).

The Court took the opportunity to reaffirm several principles established in its case law: that torture and inhuman or degrading treatment are absolutely forbidden, "even in the most difficult circumstances, such as the fight against terrorism" (§195); that governments are obligated to investigate serious claims of torture or inhuman or degrading treatment and to prosecute and punish those responsible (§182); that governments are obligated to take measures designed to protect individuals from torture or inhuman or degrading treatment by third parties (§198); that governments are forbidden to send individuals to countries where they face a serious risk of torture or inhuman or degrading treatment or flagrantly unlawful detention (§§212, 239); and that extraordinary rendition is forbidden as "anathema to the rule of law and the values protected by the Convention" (§239). It is striking that no U.S. court has enunciated these principles with respect to the U.S. government's conduct in the "War on Terror," or ruled that the U.S. government has violated the law by engaging in torture or extraordinary rendition.

In July 2014, the ECtHR handed down a pair of decisions on the clandestine imprisonment and interrogation of Al Nashiri and Abu Zubaydah at a CIA black site in Poland.[145] The Court ruled unanimously (7–0) that the enhanced interrogation techniques and unauthorized techniques used by the CIA constituted torture. It further ruled that Poland committed multiple violations of the Convention and its Protocols by enabling the CIA's use of torture, failing to conduct an effective investigation into the victims' allegations of torture, abetting clandestine and incommunicado imprisonment, and allowing the victims' transfer to possible prosecution before military commissions that would deprive them of the right to a fair trial and (in the case of Al Nashiri) pose a risk of capital punishment. Poland was ordered to pay restitution. As in the *Masri* case, the lack of any equivalent ruling in the United States, the country primarily responsible for these crimes, is striking.

Some judgments of the Strasbourg Court, however, have weakened the protective force of Article 3. In *Ahmad and Others v. UK* (2012), the Court took a major step backward when it granted Britain permission to extradite five individuals to stand trial on terrorism charges in the United States, despite concerns that they faced the prospect of Article 3 violations.[146] The unanimous (7–0) ruling held that prolonged solitary confinement in ADX Florence supermax prison did not constitute inhuman or degrading treatment or torture; that extradition to a possible U.S. sentence of life in prison without possibility of parole did not violate Article 3; and that a life sentence was not grossly disproportionate, even when, in the case of two plaintiffs, the principal charges involved the operation of a website that recruited Muslims to fight in Afghanistan and Chechnya and received classified information about U.S. naval activities in the Strait of Hormuz. Although the Court hinted that it would have applied stricter criteria to conduct by a state party, and the Grand Chamber subsequently ruled (*Vinter and Others v. UK*, 2013)[147] that a British sentence of life in prison without the possibility of parole violated

Article 3, the *Ahmad* judgment is correctly viewed as a major setback to prisoners' rights and the campaign against prolonged solitary confinement in particular. There is some evidence that the decision resulted from sustained pressure by the UK government on the Court to place fewer restrictions on British counterterrorist policy.[148] In another recent setback for human rights, the Court ruled in *Jones and Others v. UK* (2014) that Britain did not violate the Convention when it invoked the concept of sovereign immunity to block a lawsuit by four British citizens against Saudi state officials responsible for their torture in Saudi Arabia.[149]

The (mostly) courageous Article 3 judgments of the European Court of Human Rights pertaining to the "War on Terror" do not negate the extensive complicity of European officials in torture. This complicity, most pronounced on the part of the UK government, represents a disastrous failure of the European human rights regime. There needs to be, at both the national and regional level, a thorough examination of what went wrong, and robust reforms to address the problem. The malign influence exerted by U.S. officials committed to using torture is obviously central to the story, but it does not explain the full extent of European complicity, nor is it an excuse for the lack of more strenuous resistance.

Yet it would be obviously wrong to infer that the European human rights regime was devoid of value; there can be little doubt that the regime prevented what would otherwise have been an even worse deterioration of human rights after 9/11. *Ireland v. UK* established the bedrock principle that ill-treatment, let alone torture, may not be used for the purpose of combating terrorism. The principle, though skirted, is not publicly defied. To look no further than the UK, the ECHR brought an end to indefinite detention of terrorist suspects within Britain, whittled away use of control orders, mandated investigations into UK abuses in Iraq, and saved several individuals from deportation to countries where they faced a serious risk of torture or ill-treatment. Despite frequent resistance by the British government, there has been some accountability in the form of public inquiries, criminal investigations, civil lawsuits, and restitution to victims. The quest for justice has faced significant delays, obstructions, and limitations, but it has achieved real results, whereas in the United States far more flagrant crimes have escaped investigation, and all attempts by victims to sue government officials responsible for their torture have been thrown out of court. To repeat, none of this undoes the torture inflicted or abetted by British officials. We might say that although the European human rights system failed to prevent such torture, it moved the UK closer to a place where such torture *could* have been prevented. While this is no consolation to the victims, it is a reason to use the existing domestic and regional human rights regime as a base for building more effective protections against torture. The struggle continues.

The value of the Convention is proven by the resistance it has provoked in the UK. Government officials, echoed by some sectors of the media, have denounced a series of adverse Strasbourg rulings concerning prisoners' rights and counterterrorism policy, as well as British HRA-based rulings relating to the "War on Terror."[150] When in October 2014 the Conservative Party announced its intention to seek legislation repealing the Human Rights Act and weakening the legal authority of Strasbourg rulings in the UK, it made clear that one of its main purposes was to shrink existing protections of the right not to be subjected to torture or ill-treatment. The proposed "Bill of Rights and Responsibilities" would make it easier to deport individuals at risk of torture or ill-treatment, narrow the definition of "degrading treatment or punishment," and shield overseas UK armed forces from human rights lawsuits.[151]

The Virtues of Multilateralism

The system for the protection of human rights in Europe is a collective achievement, built over a long period of time. Successive protocols have strengthened the procedural mechanisms and expanded the substantive obligations of the European Convention of Human Rights, just as the Convention has widened its geographic reach from ten to forty-seven countries. The burgeoning jurisprudence of the Court has raised the minimum standard of acceptable state conduct, new human rights treaties have supplemented the ECHR and its protocols, and nonjudicial means of securing human rights have been developed. The COE and the OSCE have focused ever more exclusively on human rights, while the EU has made the protection of human rights one of its central goals, and all three organizations have become skilled at piggybacking on each other's accomplishments. NATO has participated in this process, too, although it has also taken actions destructive of human rights, especially after 9/11. In much of the continent, domestic courts have become more assertive defenders of human rights, while government officials (legislative, executive, and judicial) make increasing reference to the ECHR. The representative assemblies of the EU, COE, and OSCE denounce countries by name for their human rights failings. The fact that national leg-islators and cabinet officials help staff the governing organs of the regional organizations reinforces the feedback loop between international institutions and individual states.

We have here a story of continual experimentation, adaptation, and im-provement. Innovations have usually taken the form of strengthening, rather than weakening, the enforcement of human rights. Despite periodic setbacks and crises, the overall trajectory has been one of progress, and the cumulative contribution of the regime to the protection of human rights is, without ques-tion, enormous.[152]

What explains this success? A principal reason is the collective nature of the enterprise.[153] Europe demonstrates that states can do far more to strengthen domestic human rights by acting in concert than by acting apart. Certain vital protections of human rights are available only at the international level. That is why democratic states need international human rights institutions as much as international human rights institutions need democratic states. In the following paragraphs I identify some advantages of the multilateral approach.

A mutual pledge. When a country joins an international compact to pro-tect human rights (whether a formal treaty like the ECHR or a non-treaty agreement like the Helsinki Final Act), it creates a new class of promisees. The domestic contract is welded to an international contract; leaders must answer not only to citizens and citizens to each other, but leaders and citizens to leaders and citizens of other countries.[154] The international contract adds so-lemnity to domestically affirmed human rights. It reminds citizens that their rights are also universal human rights, which other countries properly care about and are pledged to protect. Citizens, knowing that their rights have an additional set of guardians, can assert their rights with greater confidence.[155]

An international pledge authorizes countries to hold each other to their human rights commitments. This involves more than reminding countries of the verbal formulas in the international agreements they have ratified. It means ensuring that countries follow through on these commitments, study-ing their implications, adhering to their full meaning, and applying them in all circumstances. The ECtHR is only the most visible of the many European institutions that carry out this task.

The speck in my neighbor's eye. If there is hope for humanity, it lies in our talent for perceiving the faults of others. A democracy should harness this talent by inviting other countries to identify its human rights failings. An international human rights regime institutionalizes this service and makes it reciprocal. We exercise our talent for criticizing others, on condition that they return the favor. This arrangement is on full display in the European system.

Leading by example. Just as parents must clean up their own act to encourage good behavior in their children, so countries must honor the human rights standards they expect others to follow. International institutions use the altruistic desire of certain countries to reform other countries as leverage for reforming the altruistic countries themselves. Several countries that ratified the ECHR did so in order to promote human rights abroad, not appreciating the domestic implications of their decision. In Britain, "The negotiation of the ECHR was conceived to be an aspect of foreign, not domestic, policy," while in Denmark human rights were regarded "as a good mainly suitable for export."[156] In the treaty's early years, "the leaders of most States assumed that ratifying the Convention would not require any meaningful adjustment on their part, in that they considered that the level of national rights protection was more than adequate."[157] When it turned out that domestic transformations would be required, the established democracies were not in a mood to pull the rug out from the collective enterprise. Self-improvement became the accepted price of improving others. A similar logic applies to the impact of the European Anti-Torture Committee.

Virtuous rivalry. Most states do not want to have a reputation as human rights violators. Close international monitoring and evaluation of a state's human rights policies increases pressure to enhance its reputation by actually having a good record. In the European system, reputations are also affected by a state's dedication to preserving the system itself, and by the importance it gives human rights in its foreign policy. Some states—especially Norway, Sweden, Denmark, and the Netherlands—have made it a matter of pride to promote human rights at the global and regional level, and therefore domestically as well.[158] International human rights institutions can exploit the rivalry between image-conscious states, none of which wants to be seen as less dedicated than the others.

Learning from others' mistakes. Judgments of supranational human rights institutions like the ECtHR and Anti-Torture Committee are increasingly treated as precedent by participating states. A ruling of the ECtHR against one state tends to be heeded by other member states as well. For example, the landmark case of *Ireland v. United Kingdom* established a region-wide precedent, no longer contested, that the prohibition of torture and other inhuman or degrading treatment may not be suspended even for purposes of combating terrorism. In this way, one country's mistake educates the rest, and removes the need for continual reinventing of the wheel.

Mutual education and assistance. International human rights institutions allow countries to share experience, expertise, and resources. We must remember that the international promotion of human rights is not always or even primarily an adversarial process. Many states genuinely want to improve their human rights records; but they need to learn how, and they need the resources that will enable them to do so. Capacity-building, education, and dialogue take up much of the actual work of the European human rights regime, and explain much of its success.

"They made me do it." When citizens or officials express opposition to human rights protections, the domestic guardians of human rights can reply that their hands are tied. International agreements become what game theorists call a "pre-commitment strategy." International institutions take on the role of a strict cop or stern parent whose purpose cannot be altered. This dynamic underscores the value of the Anti-Torture Committee. In many countries, Antonio Cassese observes, "there are bureaucratic barriers to inspection; the force of tradition is a hindrance, but so is public opinion—since there is a general clamour to ensure that 'criminals' receive the severest punishment, but little interest in possible abuse to which they can be subjected. This may be why these countries have eventually realized that it is easier to delegate the monitoring of places of detention to an international body."[159]

Showing up is nine-tenths of success. After decades of deepening institutionalization, the promotion of human rights occupies the attention and structures the daily work of large numbers of regional and national officials. These officials form a powerful and knowledgeable constituency, not easily circumvented, much less dislodged. They are committed for professional and often public-spirited reasons to doing their job and doing it well. A large human rights bureaucracy is another legacy of strong international human rights institutions. So is the emergence of a powerful civil society sector devoted to human rights.

Others to lift me when I fall. A country that has been committed to human rights in the past may one day elect a government indifferent or even hostile to human rights. The monitoring and enforcement mechanisms of the European human rights regime help prevent such a government from effecting a permanent or even temporary erosion of human rights. The fact of separate electoral systems in different countries means that a hostile government is unlikely to pull down the regime as a whole, whereas there is a much greater chance that the regime will stop such a government from fulfilling its anti-rights agenda. Other countries can band together to head off the threat, with the crucial help of the system's powerful supranational institutions. They can coax the errant state back onto the democratic path, knowing that one day they may need similar assistance themselves. As Montesquieu wrote of confederate republics, "Should abuses creep into one part, they are reformed by those that remain sound."[160] It is a crucial virtue of the system that, in proper Madisonian fashion, it separates decision-making power from partisan allegiances and strong group identities.

Why International Human Rights Institutions Must Remain Decentralized

The collective protection of human rights envisages strong international institutions, but ones that take a decentralized form.[161] States must retain independent agency for the system to work; the positive dynamics described above could not otherwise occur. In the European model, states take responsibility for the protection of human rights within their own and one another's jurisdictions. While human rights require the protection of strong international institutions, the power of those institutions needs to be balanced as well as buttressed by similarly powerful states. An effective system of checks and balances at the international level requires the preservation of independent states.

European states have not only created, supported, and staffed the regional human rights organizations, but they have also acted as leaders, innovators, and critics on behalf of human rights. They have monitored one another's human rights performance, as well as that of the regional organizations, which have monitored their performance in turn. At crucial moments, states have reoriented regional organizations toward human rights. A prominent example (mentioned earlier) is the rebellion in the late 1960s by the German and Italian constitutional courts, threatening invalidation of EEC legislation or withdrawal from the Community if EEC law was found to violate constitutionally protected rights. The warnings motivated the ECJ to begin applying human rights principles in its jurisprudence, and thus prepared the ground for the EU Treaty articles that since Maastricht have made respect for human rights a binding obligation for the EU, the ECJ, and EU member states.[162]

It also bears noting that the European human rights regime embraces not one but several regional organizations. Like the individual states, they, too, exercise concurrent responsibility for human rights. They have achieved far more as separate organizations, reinforcing each other's contributions, than if they had been consolidated into a single organization. Decentralization offers several advantages. The organizations perform different but complementary roles, provide a rich menu of resources for human rights advocates, and preserve flexibility in the system as a whole. Over the years, states and civil society actors have created new regional organizations and reformed old ones as the need has arisen. Such institutional innovations and improvements are made easier by the decentralized nature of the regime.

Conclusion

The European experiment—like the eighteenth-century American experiment that helped inspire it—applies the Madisonian insight that individual liberty depends on the dispersal of power and duplication of responsibility. Human rights are vulnerable if the sovereign nation-state is their exclusive guardian. They require the protection of multiple guardians. Indeed, as I have argued, shared guardianship of human rights is fundamental to democracy itself.

The European experience shows that if we are serious about democracy at the domestic level, we should cultivate strong international human rights institutions. Such institutions preserve the checks and balances on which democracy depends. They embody the principle that we all share responsibility for the protection of human rights. A successful human rights regime is one in which state responsibility for protecting human rights is assisted, encouraged, monitored, and enforced by international institutions operating with the watchful support of democratic states and civil society.

Chapter 4

American Exceptionalism and the Betrayal of Human Rights, Part I: The Torture Memos

On June 2, 2003, Senator Patrick Leahy wrote to National Security Advisor Condoleezza Rice about abusive interrogations in the war on terrorism.[1] The media were reporting suggestions by anonymous officials that detainees had been subjected to "stress and duress" techniques, including "beatings, lengthy sleep and food deprivation, and being shackled in painful positions for extended periods of time." Leahy, the ranking Democrat on the Senate Judiciary Committee, sought assurance that the United States was treating detainees in accordance with its obligations under international and domestic law.

Rice referred the matter to Jim Haynes, general counsel to the Department of Defense, who answered Leahy as follows:

> we can assure you that it is the policy of the United States to comply with all of its legal obligations in its treatment of detainees, and in particular with legal obligations prohibiting torture. Its obligations include conducting interrogations in a manner that is consistent with the Convention Against Torture and Other Cruel, Inhuman, or Degrading Treatment or Punishment ("CAT") as ratified by the United States in 1994. And it includes compliance with the Federal anti-torture statute, 18 U.S.C. §§ 2340–2340A, which Congress enacted to fulfill U.S. obligations under CAT. The United States does not permit, tolerate or condone any such torture by its employees under any circumstances.
>
> Under Article 16 of the CAT, the United States also has an obligation to "undertake . . . to prevent other acts of cruel, inhuman, or degrading

treatment or punishment which do not amount to torture." As you noted, because the terms in Article 16 are not defined, the United States ratified the CAT with a reservation to this provision. This reservation supplies an important definition for the term "cruel, inhuman, or degrading treatment or punishment." Specifically, this reservation provides that "the United States considers itself bound by the obligation under article 16 to prevent 'cruel, inhuman or degrading treatment or punishment,' only in so far as the term 'cruel, inhuman or degrading treatment or punishment' means the cruel, unusual and inhumane treatment or punishment prohibited by the Fifth, Eighth, and/or Fourteenth Amendments to the Constitution of the United States." United States policy is to treat all detainees and conduct all interrogations, wherever they may occur, in a manner consistent with this commitment.[2]

The reply might seem to allay the senator's concerns, for it stated that the United States was honoring its obligations under international treaty law not to engage in torture or cruel, inhuman, or degrading treatment. Yet Haynes belonged to the self-described "War Council," a group of five administration lawyers that approved the techniques Leahy mentioned and others even more harrowing.[3] His letter was both a public cover-up and an insider's guide to the legal rationalization of torture. That's because the War Council took the position that the Torture Convention "*as ratified by the United States*" (Haynes's words, my emphasis) permitted painful and terrifying methods of interrogation, and that such techniques were barred neither by Congress nor by the Constitution.

Haynes and his associates were wrong: the notorious "enhanced interrogation techniques" were a violation of both U.S. and international law. But as I shall argue, the peculiar relation of the United States to international human rights law made it *easier* for the Bush administration to develop and sustain a fake legal justification of practices constituting torture. The Bush administration torture program reveals the high cost of the U.S. marginalization of international human rights law.

In Chapter 2, I drew on the constitutional philosophy of James Madison to argue that the prevention of injustice requires checks and balances both domestic and international. In Chapter 3, I illustrated the benefits of transnational checks through a case study of the European human rights regime. In the next two chapters, I examine the post-9/11 U.S. torture policy to show the terrible costs that can arise from a country's refusal to accept meaningful international checks on its human rights policies. Shortly after the revelation of U.S. abuses at Abu Ghraib, Secretary of State Colin Powell said, "Watch America. Watch how we deal with this. Watch how America will do the right thing. Watch what a nation of values and character, a nation that believes in justice, does to right this kind of wrong. Watch how a nation such as ours will not tolerate such actions."[4] The American founders, and Madison in particular, did not believe that moral virtue was sufficient to guarantee that America would do the right thing. Or rather, they believed the proof of moral virtue was acknowledgment of one's moral limitations and therefore the adoption of robust checks and balances to prevent moral backsliding and to hold public officials to a higher standard of justice. The United States' systematic dismantling of international human rights constraints on its own laws and policies facilitated official criminality exactly as Madison's constitutional philosophy would lead us to predict.

The Wages of American Exceptionalism

The proximate cause of the U.S. torture policy was the Bush administration's decision to authorize coercive interrogation (torture in all but name), deploying ingenious legal arguments to circumvent the clear prohibition of torture under domestic and international law. As for the context of this decision, we should note that the terrorist threat after the September 11 attacks made coercive interrogation newly respectable in the eyes of some public officials, that a general climate of fear and anger weakened the force of public opposition to torture, and that the Republican majority that controlled Congress until January 2007 chose, for both partisan and ideological reasons, to keep loose reins on the executive branch. Yet we expect the law to protect fundamental human rights against bureaucratic zeal, partisan calculations, and shifts in public sentiment. The 9/11 attacks may have increased the temptation of public officials to authorize torture, but an effective legal regime is one that prevents torture precisely when its use becomes most tempting. Since we normally expect the law to erect impregnable barriers against the use of torture, we must ask why, in this case, the barriers gave way so easily.

I argue that a principal (though not sole) cause of this failure was a policy of "American exceptionalism," adopted well before the inauguration of George W. Bush, whereby the United States chose to loosen the constraints of international human rights law on its own laws and policies. Legal obstacles that otherwise would have confronted the Bush administration had been re-moved by previous congresses, administrations, and court rulings. I develop this argument over two chapters. In this chapter, after briefly discussing the emergence of American exceptionalism, the history of the U.S. involvement with torture, the pattern of post-9/11 abuses, and the prohibition of torture under U.S. constitutional and international law, I examine the evolution and legal authorization of torture under the Bush administration. In Chapter 5, I pinpoint the connections between American exceptionalism and the legal ra-tionalization of torture.

A chief means by which the United States evaded international human rights law was the attachment of significant reservations, understandings, and declarations (RUDs) to its ratification in the early 1990s of the International Covenant on Civil and Political Rights (ICCPR) and the Convention Against Torture and Other Cruel, Inhuman or Degrading Treatment or Punishment (Torture Convention). The RUDs had two main effects. First, they watered down several treaty obligations, including those regarding the prohibition, prevention, and punishment of torture and other forms of ill-treatment. Sec-ond, they limited the ability of U.S. courts to enforce the treaties' provisions. Human rights groups denounced the RUDs from the start; their danger should have been obvious to everyone. Torture has hardly been absent from U.S. his-tory. Both history and common sense indicate the folly of carving out loop-holes in the international prohibition against torture and ill-treatment. As we shall see, the RUDs became a main pillar of the Bush administration's torture policy.

But the RUDs are not the full story. Executive branch officials also deter-mined, years before the 9/11 attacks, that the president has domestic legal authority to violate customary international law, a view encouraged by the leading modern court case to examine the issue. Bush administration lawyers invoked this doctrine to brush away customary international law prohibi-tions on torture and ill-treatment. Recently, Congress and the courts have taken action to bar the judicial enforceability of human rights treaties other than the ICCPR and Torture Convention. In support of these various mea-sures, leading U.S. legal scholars have mounted arguments challenging the legitimacy of international law, and international human rights law in partic-ular. Finally, nonratification of the Rome Statute of the International Crimi-nal Court helped the United States evade prohibitions placed on torture and ill-treatment by international criminal law.

I preface my discussion with a few caveats. I do not claim that the domestic incorporation of international human rights law is sufficient to create an effective anti-torture regime. Other steps are needed, and the black-letter text of international human rights law leaves some of these steps underspecified. Nor do I claim that even a comprehensive program of legal reform, one that goes beyond the domestic incorporation of international human rights law, is foolproof. When a sufficient number of public officials are united in their determination to use torture, even the strongest legal protections may prove ineffective.[5]

U.S. marginalization of international human rights law is far from being the sole cause of the torture policy, but it is a significant contributing factor. At work are various cultural, ideological, and political factors, along with the historical accident that brought certain people to power at a certain moment in time, and the way in which America's great power status encourages permissive attitudes about the use of violence.[6] Torture is a frequent temptation in war, perhaps especially for a global state accustomed to waging far-flung conflicts and achieving certain of its objectives by overwhelming force. The personalities of the Bush administration and the ethos of the national security apparatus must figure prominently in any causal account. Marginalization of international human rights law accompanies, reflects, and is nourished by other causes at the same time that it magnifies their impact.

American Exceptionalism Concerning Human Rights

In the years immediately following World War II, the general policy of the United States was to support the creation of new global human rights institutions while preventing them from acquiring too much power.[7] The ambivalence of the late 1940s gave way to steady resistance in the 1950s, as Southern segregationists, nativist Republicans, and militant anticommunists joined forces against a common perceived threat. Fear of international human rights law led Senator John Bricker of Ohio, with the encouragement of the American Bar Association's president, Frank Holman, to propose a constitutional amendment that would bar international treaties from having domestic legal effect unless implementing legislation was enacted. The amendment narrowly failed in the Senate, but only after President Dwight D. Eisenhower promised not to ratify any human rights treaties.[8]

The "ghost of Senator Bricker" still haunts U.S. policy.[9] The Genocide Convention, opened for signature in 1948, was not ratified by the United

States until 1988. The United States waited twenty-six years before ratifying the ICCPR, twenty-five years before ratifying the Convention on the Elimination of All Forms of Racial Discrimination (Race Convention), and ten years before ratifying the Torture Convention. It still has not ratified the Inter-American Convention on Human Rights, the Rome Statute of the International Criminal Court, or major treaties on socioeconomic rights, children's rights, landmines, forced disappearances, and discrimination against women. Even when it ratifies human rights treaties, the United States attaches reservations, understandings, and declarations (RUDs) that sharply reduce the impact of the treaties on U.S. policy and practice.

In recent years, an influential group of legal scholars and Republican appointees has challenged the legitimacy of international law and sought to limit its effect on U.S. policy. Peter Spiro called them the "New Sovereigntists" in a *Foreign Affairs* article published a few weeks before the inauguration of George W. Bush.[10] Among the figures he profiled were Berkeley law professor John Yoo and University of Chicago law professor Jack Goldsmith, both of whom would shape U.S. interrogation policy in the Justice Department's Office of Legal Counsel (OLC) under President Bush. After leaving the OLC, Yoo returned to Berkeley and Goldsmith went on to Harvard; they continue to press sovereigntist arguments in numerous writings.

New Sovereigntists express grave reservations about international human rights law. Goldsmith writes that human rights treaties "strike at the heart of domestic self-governance"[11] and may violate the Constitution.[12] Jeremy Rabkin of Cornell Law School writes that human rights treaties "cannot be constitutional if they are understood as establishing an authority above that of American government institutions, empowered to direct the American government in its treatment of American citizens." They are constitutional only "as registers of common opinion, having no effect on actual American practices."[13] David Rivkin and Lee Casey, senior legal officials to successive Republican administrations, decry a "'new' international law" that "purports to govern the relationship of citizens to their governments" and consequently "is profoundly undemocratic at its core." "Any limitation on sovereignty as an organizing principle," they write, "is an abdication of the right of the citizens of the United States to be governed solely in accordance with their Constitution."[14]

These views are sometimes connected to deep skepticism about international law in general. John Bolton, later appointed by President Bush as U.S. ambassador to the United Nations, stated: "It is a big mistake for us to grant any validity to international law even when it may seem in our short-term interest to do so, because over the long term, the goal of those who think that international law really means anything are those who want to constrict the U.S."[15] In their 2005 book *The Limits of International Law*, Jack Goldsmith and University of Chicago law professor Eric Posner argue that international law lacks both motivating power and moral authority.[16] That is to say, it neither constrains nor *should* constrain the behavior of states. When states comply with international law, on this view, they do so only from a calculation that the legally compliant acts serve the national interest.[17] The authors apply these claims to both customary international law and ratified treaties. Notice the implication that, for example, the United States may violate the Geneva Conventions whenever it perceives that doing so would serve the national interest.

Accompanying the U.S. self-exemption policy is a widespread belief that the United States has no need of international human rights law because its own rights protections are sufficient. According to this belief, the purpose of U.S. ratification of human rights treaties (assuming their legitimacy in the first place) is to encourage human rights improvements in *other* countries. Among Americans, belief in the sufficiency of U.S. rights law is largely unquestioned. The view permeates not only popular culture and political rhetoric but also scholarly and legal analyses of the relation of the United States to international human rights.[18] The United States assured the Human Rights Committee, the international body charged with monitoring state compliance with the ICCPR, that "fundamental rights and freedoms protected by the [ICCPR] are already guaranteed as a matter of U.S. law . . . and can be effectively asserted and enforced by individuals in the judicial system on those bases."[19] New Sovereigntists echo the view. Goldsmith writes: "the United States remains one of the greatest protectors of individual rights in the world by virtue of its domestic constitutional and democratic processes. . . . [It] does not need external legal processes or the threat of external sanctions in order to provide its citizens and residents with prodigious human rights protections."[20]

The Bush administration's embrace of torture should cast doubt on this view. That the United States' legal institutions permitted this most paradigmatic of human rights violations, coordinated from the highest centers of power and continued long after public exposure, suggests that American rights protections are not all they are cracked up to be. Whether the myth of America as a beacon of rights is dislodged by notorious facts to the contrary or proves impervious to them (as myths sometimes do) remains to be seen.

United States Involvement in Torture Before 9/11

There is an understandable impulse to say that the United States' recent use of torture is something entirely new. Unfortunately, the truth is otherwise. At various times in its history, the United States has allowed, encouraged, and even participated in torture.[21] As this history reveals, the U.S. legal system was broken even before 9/11.

Torture is part of America's domestic past. It was integral to the institution of slavery and the practice of lynching. Local police forces used torture to elicit confessions through the first third of the twentieth century, and fifty years ago wardens in southern prisons still tortured inmates.[22] Although there have been significant improvements, the mistreatment of prisoners remains a grave problem, an issue to which I return in Chapter 5.

At various times the United States has used torture as a counterinsurgency tactic abroad. U.S. troops tortured Philippine insurgents during the rebellion of 1899–1902.[23] In Vietnam, South Vietnamese troops tortured many suspected Viet Cong members, sometimes with the assistance and direct participation of U.S. personnel.[24] During the Cold War, the United States adopted a policy of "torture by proxy," supporting military regimes in Asia and Latin America that it knew practiced torture. The CIA kept on its payroll some officials from these regimes who it knew practiced or ordered torture, in effect paying them for information extracted by torture. We now know that the CIA instructed Latin American security officials in the use of certain torture methods, and even sent its U.S. employees to supervise torture.[25]

Early in the Cold War, the CIA launched a vast secret research project, codenamed MKUltra, into the possibilities of "mind control." Experiments to observe the effects of sensory deprivation, many of them conducted on mental patients without their consent, demonstrated the considerable power of such techniques to disturb the human psyche, while LSD was given to unsuspecting mental patients, prostitutes' clients, and even government scientists, with disastrous effects.[26] The results of these studies made their way into the 1963 *Kubark Counterintelligence Interrogation* handbook,[27] containing 128 pages of detailed instructions for the interrogation of individuals detained against their will. The purpose of coercive interrogation, the manual explained, is to produce mental regression "to whatever earlier and weaker level is required for the dissolution of resistance and the inculcation of dependence,"[28] and the possible techniques include "arrest, detention, the deprivation of sensory stimuli, threats and fear, debility, pain, heightened suggestibility and hypnosis, and drugs."[29]

Themes of the Kubark manual resurfaced in a CIA manual used for training Honduran officers, titled *Human Resource Exploitation Training Manual— 1983*, which stated that the interrogator should be in a position to "manipulate the subject's environment, to create unpleasant or intolerable situations, to disrupt patterns of time, space, and sensory perception."[30] In 1988, a member of the Honduran intelligence unit known as Battalion 316 reported what he and his colleagues learned from U.S. Army and CIA instructors at a training camp in Texas: "They taught us psychological methods—to study the fears and weaknesses of a prisoner. Make him stand up, don't let him sleep, keep him naked and isolated, put rats and cockroaches in his cell, give him bad food, serve him dead animals, throw cold water on him, change the temperature."[31] As cruel as these tactics were, members of Battalion 316 went on to commit far more extreme methods of torture, with the knowledge of the U.S. Embassy and close involvement of the CIA.[32]

The CIA appears to have lost interest in the Kubark methods after the late 1980s, so that "by the time of the 9/11 attacks, the CIA's capabilities in this realm were a thing of the past."[33] But the CIA's earlier experiments were an indirect source of the post-9/11 torture program, because they informed the development of the military training program known as Survival, Evasion, Resistance and Escape (SERE), which the Bush administration used to design and justify "enhanced interrogation techniques" in the "War on Terror."[34]

Despite historical antecedents, the post-9/11 period marked a new phase in the United States' relation to torture. Under President Bush, torture became centralized, systematized, and rationalized as never before. What distinguished Bush administration policy from the Cold War era was the direct authorization and close monitoring of torture by the highest officials of government; the creation of an international network of U.S. interrogation centers where detainees were brought to be tortured and often held for long periods of time; the large-scale enlistment of U.S. military and CIA personnel, not just foreign intermediaries, to carry out torture; the frequent transshipment of prisoners across international borders to be tortured; the greater frankness about torture on the part of public officials (using transparent euphemisms such as "questioning" and "alternative procedures"); the elaborate new legal rationalizations of torture; and the insistence on using torture in defiance of what had become over the preceding decades a much stronger international legal prohibition against torture and other forms of ill-treatment.

Torture in the "War on Terror"

After 9/11, U.S. military and intelligence officials abused prisoners in Afghanistan, Guantanamo Bay, Iraq, and CIA secret prisons or "black sites" operated in various countries.[35] As the American Civil Liberties Union reported, detainees were "beaten; forced into painful stress positions; threatened with death; sexually humiliated; subjected to racial and religious insults; stripped naked; hooded and blindfolded; exposed to extreme heat and cold; denied food and water; deprived of sleep; isolated for prolonged periods; subjected to mock drownings; and intimidated by dogs."[36] The United States also sent individuals to be tortured by foreign security forces under the so-called extraordinary rendition program.[37] Through extraordinary renditions, "black sites," and cooperation from foreign security services, the CIA created an unknown number of "disappeared" persons who were shuttled from one clandestine torture center to another and who were cut off from any protection of the law.[38] Some detainees were tortured for weeks, months, or even years.

In Camp Nama in Iraq, a U.S. sergeant reports that one prisoner

> was stripped naked, put in the mud and sprayed with the hose, with very cold hoses, in February. At night it was very cold. They sprayed the cold hose and he was completely naked in the mud, you know, and everything. [Then] he was taken out of the mud and put next to an air conditioner. It was extremely cold, freezing, and he was put back in the mud and sprayed. This happened all night. Everybody knew about it. People walked in, the sergeant major and so forth, everybody knew what was going on, and I was just one of them, kind of walking back and forth seeing [that] this is how they do things.[39]

Ameen Sa'eed Al-Sheikh, a former prisoner at Abu Ghraib, recounts:

> The guards started to hit me on my broken leg several times with a solid plastic stick. He told me he got shot in his leg and he showed me the scare and he would retaliate from me for this. They stripped me naked. One of them told me he would rape me. He drew a picture of a woman to my back and makes me stand in shameful position holding my buttocks. Someone else asked me, "Do you believe in anything?" I said to him, "I believe in Allah." So he said, "But I believe in torture and I will torture you. When I go home to my country, I will ask who-

ever comes after me to torture you." Then they handcuffed me and hung me to the bed. They ordered me to curse Islam and because they started to hit my broken leg, I cursed my religion. They ordered me to thank Jesus that I'm alive. And I did what they ordered me. This is against my belief. They left me hang from the bed and after a little while I lost consciousness.[40]

Binyam Mohamed describes what happened when three masked men came to his Moroccan prison cell, where he had been sent by the CIA: "One stood on each of my shoulders and a third punched me in the stomach. It seemed to go on for hours. I was meant to stand, but I was in so much pain I'd fall to my knees." On subsequent occasions guards made cuts in his penis, drawing copious blood.[41] At Guantanamo, Mohammedou Ould Slahi was blindfolded, forced to drink salt water, beaten until he bled from his mouth and nose and could not speak, bound so tightly around his chest he could barely breathe, and covered with ice.

> They stuffed the air between my clothes and me with ice cubes from my neck to my ankles, and whenever the ice melted they put in new hard ice cubes. Moreover, every once in a while, one of the guards smashed me, most of the time in the face. The ice served both for pain and for wiping out the bruises I had from that afternoon. Everything seemed to be perfectly prepared. . . . There is nothing more terrorizing than making somebody expect a smash every single heartbeat.[42]

Several detainees died in U.S. custody as a result of torture or ill-treatment.[43] At a CIA prison in Afghanistan, Gul Rahman was placed in a near-freezing room, where he was stripped from the waist down, shackled with his hands over his head, and soaked with water. He froze to death.[44] In Abu Ghraib Prison in Iraq, Manadel al-Jamadi was shackled in a stress position after beatings that accompanied his arrest. Within hours he had died from asphyxiation.[45] At Forward Operating Base Tiger in Iraq, Abed Hamed Mowhoush died from asphyxiation after he was beaten, then wrapped in a sleeping bag while his interrogator sat on his chest and intermittently covered his mouth or nose.[46] At Bagram Prison in Afghanistan, Habibullah and Dilawar were shackled and beaten until they died.[47]

There were different pathways to abuse. Some service members acted on their own initiative, though often with tacit encouragement from their superiors, who did little to rein in abuse, pressured service members to gain intelligence by aggressive means if necessary ("the gloves are coming off" was a widely circulated directive), and announced that terrorist suspects and insurgents were not entitled to the protections of the Geneva Conventions.[48] In other cases, CIA and military personnel received direct orders to abuse prisoners. The common enabling factor was a set of legal findings that asserted in contrast to long-standing official U.S. policy that abusive forms of detention and interrogation, variously referred to as "coercive interrogation," "enhanced interrogation techniques," or an "alternative set of procedures," were now legally permitted. For hierarchical organizations like the U.S. military and the CIA, the switch to a new legal framework had a profound impact.

Much of the abuse is rightly called torture. By torture, I mean the intentional infliction of severe physical or mental pain or suffering. This language comes from the canonical first article of the Torture Convention. That the techniques were intended to cause severe pain or suffering is underscored by the Bush administration's own insistence that tough measures were needed to obtain information from detainees, especially those purportedly trained to resist interrogation.[49] Several of the authorized techniques—including sleep deprivation, forced standing, and waterboarding—are infamously associated with the Gestapo, Stalin's secret police, and the Inquisition.[50] The Bush administration, though insisting that it did not torture, used methods that the United States has called torture when practiced by other governments.[51] In 2013, a bipartisan task force commissioned by the Constitution Project to study detainee treatment concluded that "it is indisputable that the United States engaged in the practice of torture."[52]

The anomaly of U.S. policy was cast into relief by a June 10, 2004, exchange between a reporter and President Bush, a few days after the first of the notorious "torture memos" was leaked to the press.

> James Harding of the *Financial Times*: "Mr. President, I want to return to the question of torture. What we've learned from these memos this week is that the Department of Justice lawyers and the Pentagon lawyers have essentially worked out a way that United States officials can torture detainees without running afoul of the law. So when you say you want the United States to adhere to international and United States laws, that's not very comforting. This is a moral question: Is torture ever justified?"
>
> President Bush: "Look, I'm going to say it one more time. . . . Maybe

I can be more clear. The instructions went out to our people to adhere to law. That ought to comfort you. We're a nation of law. We adhere to laws. We have laws on the books. You might look at these laws, and that might provide comfort for you. And those were the instructions . . . from me to the government."[53]

President Bush waited twelve days before clarifying that he did not condone torture,[54] but he never disavowed the claim, implicit in the June 10 exchange and defended in his administration's earlier memos, that he was legally permitted to order its use. (After the memos were leaked, Bush administration lawyers withdrew that claim but, like the president, were careful never to disavow it.) And Bush's June 22 claim that he "never ordered torture"[55] was rendered hollow by his administration's vanishingly narrow definition of the word "torture." (This wordplay, discussed below, is most infamously exemplified in the August 1, 2002, Department of Justice memo stipulating that interrogation techniques do not constitute torture unless they inflict pain as severe as that which accompanies crippling injury, organ failure, or death.)

The torture program cast a broad net. In the accurate summation of Larry Siems, who has written one of the most comprehensive studies of the program,

> [U.S. officials] tortured innocent people. They tortured people very likely guilty of terrorism-related crimes, but ruined all chance of prosecuting these people thanks to the torture. They tortured the innocent and the likely-guilty alike when the torture had nothing to do with imminent threats: they tortured people based on bad information extracted from people they had tortured . . . they tortured to get specific information they wanted, as when detainees were pressed about links between Saddam Hussein and Al Qaeda; they tortured to hide their mistakes, as when they used coerced statements by Guantanamo detainees to build cases against fellow detainees they had no business holding in the first place. They tortured people to break them, pure and simple.[56]

In Iraq and Afghanistan, U.S. torturers made little effort to distinguish "terrorists" from those fighting U.S. troops, and many victims were not militants at all.

Two days after taking office, President Obama publicly broke with the interrogation policies of his predecessor. In a series of executive orders, he prohibited the use of "enhanced interrogation techniques," rescinded the Bush administration interrogation memos, mandated the closure of CIA prisons, and required access by the International Committee of the Red Cross to individuals detained in armed conflict. In the judgment of the Constitution Project Task Force on Detainee Judgment, "the Obama administration has ended the most inhumane treatment of detainees, though some troubling questions about current policies remain unanswered."[57] Over a hundred detainees remain in Guantanamo, only a handful of whom have been charged with a crime—an outcome of both administration policy and restrictive congressional legislation. In Afghanistan, several detainees were tortured after they were transferred by U.S. authorities to the Afghan National Directorate of Security, even though U.S. officials knew or should have known of the danger. There have been several reports of abusive U.S. interrogations of individuals temporarily detained at the "Black Jail" in Bagram Air Base in Afghanistan. At Guantanamo, U.S. authorities continue to subject hunger-striking prisoners to an aggressive and painful regimen of force-feeding that the Constitution Project Task Force has deemed "a form of abuse" that "must end."[58]

I take it for granted that torture is wrong: no one should be subjected to the pain and terror that torture entails. Questions of "effectiveness" are beside the point, because torture is wrong even when it "works."[59] In any case, its effects in the "War on Terror" were the opposite of those imputed by its apologists. By inflaming the enemy, deterring voluntary cooperation, generating false information, and fabricating a pretext for the catastrophic Iraq War—statements extracted by torture were the main basis for a claimed link between Saddam Hussein and Al Qaeda—it made the United States and the world more vulnerable to terrorist attack.[60] It inflicted horrendous suffering, shattered lives, and loosened the international taboo against torture. In the words of the U.S. Senate Armed Services Committee, "the abuse of detainees in U.S. custody . . . damaged our ability to collect accurate intelligence that could save lives, strengthened the hand of our enemies, and compromised our moral authority."[61]

The Prohibition of Torture Under the U.S. Constitution and International Law

The world "torture" does not appear in the U.S. Constitution, presumably because the Founders thought it both unnecessary and shameful to name something so far outside the bounds of legality. Torture is foreign to the English common law. Its use by the early Stuart monarchs increased their infamy in the eyes of those who fought repeated revolutions to establish parliamentary rule. "Cruel and unusual punishments" were banned in the English Bill of Rights of 1689.

The Constitution contains several provisions intended to eliminate any thought of torture.[62] These include the protection of habeas corpus in the original articles, the Fourth Amendment prohibition of unreasonable searches and seizures, the Fifth Amendment prohibition of compulsory self-incrimination, the Sixth Amendment right to a fair trial, and the Thirteenth Amendment prohibition of slavery. Together, the Fifth and Eighth Amendments constitute a blanket prohibition of torture: the Eighth Amendment prohibits cruel and unusual punishments, while the Fifth Amendment forbids the government to deprive anyone of liberty without due process of law, and torture constitutes an obvious deprivation of liberty.[63] As Justice Kennedy wrote in *Chavez v. Martinez*, "[use] of torture or its equivalent in an attempt to induce a statement violates an individual's fundamental right to liberty of the person."[64] The abovementioned obligations also apply to the individual states, by virtue of their own constitutions and the Due Process Clause of the Fourteenth Amendment. Other constitutionally guaranteed civil and political rights, together with the checks and balances architecture of the political system, help prevent torture by arming the individual against state abuse.

International law places an absolute legal prohibition on torture. The charters of the Nuremberg (1945) and Tokyo (1946) Tribunals, along with the four Geneva Conventions of 1949, reaffirmed that torture is an international crime, for which individuals can be punished.[65] The Universal Declaration of Human Rights of 1948 announces simply, "No one shall be subjected to torture or to cruel, inhuman, or degrading treatment or punishment." This language was deliberately crafted to block any resort to a narrow definition of torture as a means of justifying inhumane treatment.[66] It reappears verbatim in Article 7 of the International Covenant on Civil and Political Rights (ICCPR), and forms the complete title of the Convention Against Torture and Other Cruel, Inhuman or Degrading Treatment or Punishment. Torture is prohibited in the European, African, and Inter-American human rights conventions.[67] The ICCPR, Torture Convention, and European and Inter-American Conventions declare that the prohibition of torture may never be suspended, even in an emergency that threatens the life of the nation.[68] In

1975 the UN General Assembly unanimously adopted a resolution condemn-ing torture under all circumstances.[69] In the *Pinochet* decision of 1999, the British House of Lords held torture to be an inherently criminal act incapable of official legitimation.[70] Torture continues to be prosecuted as a war crime and crime against humanity in the International Criminal Tribunals for Rwanda (ICTR) and the Former Yugoslavia (ICTY), and is punishable under the Rome Statute of the International Criminal Court (ICC).[71] Today the pro-hibition against torture is widely recognized as a *jus cogens* norm that cannot be overridden even by treaty or international custom.[72] The prohibition against torture is one of the clearest and strongest obligations to be found in all of international law.

Moreover, international law unequivocally prohibits *all* forms of cruel, inhuman, or degrading treatment or punishment, even those that might be alleged not to rise to the level of torture. The ban on ill-treatment[73] is also a requirement of customary international law.[74] Like the prohibition against torture, it may not be suspended even during the direst emergencies. This non-derogability requirement, as it is known, appears in the ICCPR, the Inter-American and European Conventions, and the 1975 UN General As-sembly Resolution.[75] It is not made explicit in the Torture Convention, where the paragraph that bans emergency exceptions (art. 2(2)) refers only to "tor-ture." However, since the Torture Convention makes a point of stating that nothing in its text may be construed to weaken or narrow preexisting prohi-bitions of ill-treatment ("The provisions of this Convention are without prej-udice to the provisions of any other international instrument or national law which prohibit cruel, inhuman or degrading treatment or punishment," art. 16(2)), it may not be invoked to override the non-derogable prohibition of ill-treatment as established in other treaties or in domestic law. Thus, at a minimum, the 168 countries including the United States that have ratified the ICCPR are still barred from suspending the prohibition of ill-treatment under any circumstances. Moreover, the Committee Against Torture, estab-lished by the Torture Convention to monitor member-state compliance with the treaty, has determined that the treaty's non-derogability requirement should be read to cover all forms of ill-treatment:

The obligations to prevent torture and other cruel, inhuman or degrad-ing treatment or punishment (hereinafter "ill-treatment") under article 16, paragraph 1, are indivisible, interdependent and interrelated.... Experience demonstrates that the conditions that give rise to ill-treatment frequently facilitate torture and therefore the measures required to prevent torture must be applied to prevent ill-treatment. Accordingly, the Committee has considered the prohibition of ill-treatment to be likewise non-derogable under the Convention and its prevention to be an effective and non-derogable measure.[76]

Inhuman treatment is utterly forbidden in the law of armed conflict. The charters of the Nuremberg and Tokyo Tribunals classify inhuman treatment as a crime against humanity, with the Nuremberg Tribunal Charter further labeling such treatment a war crime.[77] The prohibition of inhuman treatment permeates the Geneva Conventions, and reappears in the 1977 Protocols to the Geneva Conventions, the statutes for the ICTY and ICTR, and the Rome Statute of the ICC.[78] Conservative international law experts concur. A 2004 amicus brief submitted by leading conservative law scholars *in support* of the Bush administration position in the Guantanamo case of *Rasul v. Bush* cited the Martens Clause, customary international law, and the Geneva Conventions, to note: "Without dispute, all detainees are entitled to humane treatment."[79]

The prohibition of all forms of ill-treatment in the law of armed conflict is significant. War allows forms of violence permitted nowhere else. Nations fight wars only when they perceive vital interests to be at stake; indeed, today's wars are almost always fought in the name of national security. If international law forbids ill-treatment in the context of armed conflict, we can infer that it is forbidden in all circumstances.

Beyond placing a prohibition on torture and ill-treatment, international law requires effective measures of prevention. Civil and political rights as a whole (rights to physical integrity, legal due process, personal freedom, participation in the social and political life of the community, and effective remedies for the violation of one's rights) are essential protections against torture. (The same may be argued with respect to socioeconomic rights.) Enshrined in most democratic constitutions, they are reaffirmed in the Universal Declaration of Human Rights, the ICCPR, the Forced Disappearance Convention, and the European, American, and African human rights conventions, among other rights charters. The drafters of these documents understood how important these protections were in shielding individuals from state brutality.

The 1984 Torture Convention stipulates further measures. States are obligated to make torture a criminal offense (art. 4), and are forbidden to send individuals to other countries "where there are substantial grounds for believing that [they] would be in danger of being subjected to torture" (art. 3). The Convention establishes universal jurisdiction over the crime of torture (arts. 5–9), meaning that if a state finds a torturer on its territory, then regardless of where the torture was committed and regardless of the nationality of the perpetrator and victim, the state must either prosecute the torturer itself or extradite him or her to prosecution in another country.[80] In addition, states must educate public officials regarding the prohibition of torture and ill-treatment (art. 10), regularly review detention and interrogation practices with a view to preventing torture and ill-treatment (art. 11), guarantee victims of torture and ill-treatment the right to make a complaint and have their case promptly examined by the authorities (art. 12), compensate victims of torture and ill-treatment (art. 13), and abstain from introducing into criminal proceedings any statement elicited by torture or ill-treatment (art. 14).[81] A total of 158 countries, including the United States, have ratified the Convention.

The Third and Fourth Geneva Conventions contain several provisions designed to prevent inhuman treatment, including the right of detainees to elect representatives (GC III, art. 79, GC IV, art. 102) and make complaints (GC III, art. 78, GC IV, art. 101) and a requirement that the International Committee of the Red Cross be granted full access to all facilities where war captives are kept (GC III, art. 126, GC IV, art. 143). Under the Conventions' "grave breaches" provisions, member states (now literally every country in the world) are obligated to prosecute acts of torture or inhuman treatment. Two international treaties are dedicated exclusively to the prevention of torture and ill-treatment. As discussed in Chapter 3, the 1987 European Convention for the Prevention of Torture and Inhuman or Degrading Treatment or Punishment establishes a regional committee of independent monitors with the power to visit detention centers and interview inmates, communicate recommendations to governments for the elimination and prevention of torture and ill-treatment, and issue critical public statements if governments fail to cooperate. The 2002 Optional Protocol to the Torture Convention establishes a similar committee at the global level, and further obligates member states to establish domestic monitoring committees ("national preventive mechanisms") also charged with visiting detention centers and issuing recommendations to their respective governments. Eighty countries have ratified the Optional Protocol (not including the United States).

The goal of these treaties is to ensure that every person in the world is safe from torture and ill-treatment. Police, military, and other public officials who exercise authority over confined individuals should be made "torture proof."

They should be taught that torture and ill-treatment are against the law, and trained in methods of interrogation and confinement that preclude the use of such treatment. Superiors should regularly monitor and enforce compliance with the required procedures, and any individuals who allege they have been subjected to torture or ill-treatment should be granted the right to prompt investigation of their complaints by impartial officials. Independent monitors, both domestic and international, should be authorized to visit detention centers, interview detainees, and communicate their findings to government officials and the public.

Effective criminalization is the indispensable backbone of the anti-torture regime. (For this reason, it forms the centerpiece of the Torture Convention.) States should enact, publicize, and apply criminal penalties for all individuals who inflict, order, aid, abet, or knowingly contribute to torture or ill-treatment. Such penalties concentrate the minds of officials who might otherwise flirt with permitting abuse, and they remind officials of the need to vigorously maintain preventive measures. Further, criminalization prevents the guilty from ducking responsibility: under principles of individual responsibility made famous at Nuremberg, perpetrators can no longer shift blame to the "state," superior orders, or unruly subordinates.[82]

Effective civil remedies are also vital. Victims of torture and ill-treatment must be able to sue not only immediate perpetrators but also public officials who fail to implement or to abide by laws designed to prevent torture. The great value of civil actions is that they can be initiated by ordinary individuals, whereas in many countries such as the United States criminal prosecutions can be initiated only by governments. Governments should not be allowed to block anti-torture lawsuits merely by invoking national security or sovereign immunity. Thus the ICCPR (art. 2(3)) obligates governments to ensure that victims of human rights violations, including torture and ill-treatment, "shall have an effective remedy, notwithstanding that the violation has been committed by persons acting in an official capacity."

The "Legalization" of Torture Under President Bush

The Bush administration went to great lengths to insist that its interrogation methods were legal. (Recall Bush's incantation: "The instructions went out to our people to adhere to law. . . . We're a nation of law. We adhere to laws. We have laws on the books.") Because the authorized methods *seemed* patently illegal, administration lawyers set to work arguing the contrary. This task put them in control of important decisions, to such an extent that in the words of the Constitution Project's Bipartisan Task Force on Detainee Treatment, the post-9/11 conflicts

> could be thought of as "The Lawyers' War." From the beginning, the detention and interrogation of prisoners was less dependent on the decisions of generals, and more influenced by government attorneys. Both those in uniform and those in the CIA looked to government lawyers to guide them and set limits. Never before in the history of the nation had attorneys, and the advice they provided, played such a significant role in determining the treatment of detainees.[83]

Speaking of two powerful administration lawyers, an anonymous colleague said, "It's incredible, but John Yoo and David Addington were running the war on terror almost on their own."[84]

Controversial topics pitted legal moderates against legal hardliners. The hardliners generally prevailed, because they had the support of President Bush and Vice President Dick Cheney; because under the guidance of Cheney's counsel, David Addington, they outmaneuvered the opposition, sometimes locking them out of the discussion; and because they were well represented in the Justice Department's Office of Legal Counsel (OLC), which issues legal opinions binding on the executive branch. Dissenters included the Navy's general counsel, Alberto Mora, several senior members of the Judge Advocate General Corps, and the legal advisor to the State Department, William H. Taft IV. At the cabinet level, there was no consistent opponent of ill-treatment. Secretary of State Colin Powell opposed the legal finding that the Geneva Conventions did not apply to the conflict in Afghanistan, but he did not protest the use of "enhanced interrogation techniques" by the CIA.

A stream of voluminous secret memos from the OLC cleared the path for extreme tactics. In the formative period between 9/11 and the spring of 2003, the memos were almost all written or coauthored by Deputy Assistant Attorney General John Yoo, the OLC's expert on foreign policy and national security matters, though some of Yoo's most important memos bore the signature of the OLC director, Assistant Attorney General Jay Bybee. Before joining the OLC in summer 2001, Yoo was known for publications that defended sweeping presidential war powers and challenged the international law commitments of the United States. His scholarship is marked by egregious distortions of the historical record, most notoriously his claim that in spite of the "Declare War" Clause, the Constitution entrusts to the president rather than Congress the decision whether to go to war.[85] Yoo did not act alone in preparing the interrogation memos. He enjoyed the support of the "War Council" (the five-member legal team that planned the hardliners' bureaucratic strategy) and the drafting assistance of other OLC staff members, not to mention the approval of his boss, Jay Bybee. After Yoo and Bybee left the OLC in 2003, some of their memos were withdrawn, but memos by subsequent OLC directors continued to justify the use of extreme interrogation tactics.

The timing of the memos' release has clouded understanding of their impact. In June 2004, the *Washington Post* published a secret fifty-page memo from August 1, 2002, signed by Bybee and written by Yoo, that gave the president broad authority to order interrogation methods constituting torture (though not acknowledged as such). This memo seized the attention of a public still reeling from the late April 2004 revelation of photographed U.S. abuses in Abu Ghraib. When the media reported in late June that the administration would withdraw the memo, it was natural to infer a shift in government policy, an impression reinforced by the government's public adoption in December 2004 of a replacement memo criticizing several of the arguments made in the Bybee-Yoo memo. It was not until the Obama administration released several additional Bush era memos in 2009 that the full story was made plain (though the existence of some of the memos had been reported earlier).[86] Bybee had signed a second memo (written by Yoo) on August 1, 2002, that spelled out the authorized techniques in horrifying detail. *This* memo was never rescinded by the Bush administration, and between 2005 and 2007 acting OLC director Steven Bradbury wrote several secret memos once more describing the techniques and upholding their legality. Thus, notwithstanding the public withdrawal of the leaked Bybee-Yoo memo in 2004, the administration continued to insist, with the backing of other secret memos, that the originally authorized techniques were legal. But because the public's attention had largely moved on by 2009, the earlier impression was not fully corrected.

How the coercive interrogation policy took shape may be briefly summarized as follows. (What we know is still limited by government withholding of key information, including several OLC memos.)

On September 17, 2001, shortly after the terrorist attacks, President Bush issued an order, still classified, authorizing the CIA to capture and detain terrorist suspects in secret prisons outside the United States.[87] Beginning in

December 2001, the CIA and Defense Department requested advice on interrogation strategy from current and former officials linked to the Survival,
Evasion, Resistance, and Escape (SERE) program, a training regime which
exposes selected military personnel to harsh treatment as preparation for
possible abuse by the enemy.[88] These consultations led to the development of
the so-called "enhanced interrogation techniques," which over time included
slapping, sleep deprivation, stress positions, forced standing, wall-slamming,
blaring music, confinement in coffin-sized boxes, food deprivation, hosing
with cold water, leaving shackled prisoners to urinate and defecate themselves in diapers, and waterboarding.[89] James Mitchell and Bruce Jessen, former SERE psychologists contracted by the CIA, took a leading role in the
development of the new techniques.

Between September and November 2001, the OLC produced a series of
memos, written or coauthored by Yoo, that granted the president sweeping
powers in the "War on Terror."[90] Among other findings, the memos held that
Congress could not "place any limits on the President's determinations as to
any terrorist threat, the amount of military force to be used in response, or
the method, timing, and nature of the response."[91] Not all these memos have
been released: it is thought that a still-classified memo from November 21,
2001, was the first to address detainee treatment.[92]

In January 2002 the OLC waged a fierce debate with the State Department
over whether the Geneva Conventions applied to the conflict in Afghanistan.
On January 9, Yoo and OLC lawyer Robert Delahunty produced a forty-two-
page memo arguing that Al Qaeda and Taliban detainees held no rights under
the Geneva Conventions.[93] (The memo also asserted that the president was
not bound by customary international law, and that he had the constitutional
power to unilaterally suspend, contravene, or terminate treaties.)[94] If the Geneva Conventions did not apply, as White House Counsel Alberto Gonzales
explained to the president, then U.S. officials could not be prosecuted under
the War Crimes Act for subjecting Al Qaeda and Taliban members to inhuman treatment. The memo's novel and far-fetched arguments were forcefully
rebutted in a January 11 memo from State Department legal advisor William
H. Taft IV.[95] But Yoo had the support of Bybee, Gonzales, and Attorney General John Ashcroft. On January 18, President Bush agreed with Gonzales's recommendation that Al Qaeda and Taliban detainees were not covered by the
Geneva Conventions, and the next day Secretary of Defense Donald Rumsfeld instructed the Joint Chiefs of Staff that the Geneva Conventions did not
apply to the war in Afghanistan.[96]

The debate culminated in President Bush's secret policy-setting memo of February 7, 2002,[97] which determined that Al Qaeda and Taliban prisoners were entitled neither to prisoner-of-war status under the Third Geneva Convention nor to the minimum standards of humane treatment required by Common Article 3 of the Geneva Conventions. To make these harsh findings seem less ominous, Bush added the following paragraph (emphasis added):

> Of course, our values as a Nation, values that we share with many nations in the world, call for us to treat detainees humanely, *including those who are not legally entitled to such treatment.* Our Nation has been and will continue to be a strong supporter of Geneva and its principles. As a matter of policy, the *United States Armed Forces* shall continue to treat detainees humanely and, *to the extent appropriate and consistent with military necessity,* in a manner consistent with the *principles* of Geneva.

As the emphasized words show, the commitment to providing humane treatment was less than might initially appear. The paragraph left understood that Al Qaeda and Taliban prisoners "are not legally entitled" to humane treatment. It addressed the humane treatment directive only to the armed forces; CIA officials were repeatedly told that the directive did not apply to them.[98] The memo's promise to honor the "principles of Geneva" (an undefined term with no currency in international law) freed the United States from compliance with the actual requirements of the Geneva Conventions. And even this promise would be waived when reasons of "military necessity" so dictated.

Because the humane treatment of prisoners was regarded as a *policy choice* rather than a *legal requirement*, the president could change his mind any day. And the statement's sincerity is called into question by frequent assertions that the administration would do anything permitted by law.[99] In any event, the Bush administration adopted a relaxed understanding of the word "humane." A Defense Department investigation into alleged abuses at Guantanamo Bay cleared the Pentagon of the charge of subjecting detainees to inhumane treatment. Addressing the case of the detainee Mohamed al-Qahtani, who had been stripped naked, forced to wear women's underwear, sexually accosted by female guards, led around the room by a leash, forced to perform dog tricks, and hosed with water while being interrogated twenty hours a day for over two months, the report concluded that while Qahtani's treatment might be considered abusive or degrading it was not "inhumane."[100]

The government's policy of extraordinary rendition to torture received a legal green light in a secret thirty-four-page OLC memo signed by Bybee on March 13, 2002, claiming that there were no legal limits on the president's transfer of detainees across international borders.[101] The memo set aside the Geneva Conventions' restrictions on detainee transfers, by arguing that the Conventions did not apply to members of Al Qaeda or the Taliban. It set aside the Torture Convention prohibition on sending individuals to countries where they faced a serious danger of torture, by arguing that this prohibition did not extend to individuals seized outside U.S. territory.[102] The memo further claimed that Congress is constitutionally forbidden to restrict the president's power to dispose of war captives as he sees fit, citing as an authority for this proposition Henry V's order in 1415 for the mass execution of French prisoners of war.[103]

Abu Zubaydah, then alleged to be a high-ranking member of Al Qaeda involved in planning 9/11, was captured by U.S. forces in Pakistan on March 28, 2002, and flown to a secret prison in Thailand a few days later. Within days, while still suffering from severe injuries, he became an experimental subject in the CIA's new interrogation program:

> I was transferred to a chair where I was kept, shackled by hands and feet for what I think was the next 2 to 3 weeks. During this time I developed blisters on the underside of my legs due to the constant sitting. . . .
>
> I was given no solid food during the first two or three weeks, while sitting on the chair. I was only given Ensure and water to drink. At first the Ensure made me vomit, but this became less with time.
>
> The cell and room were air-conditioned and were very cold. Very loud, shouting type music was constantly playing. It kept repeating about every fifteen minutes twenty-four hours a day. Sometimes the music stopped and was replaced by a loud hissing or crackling noise. . . .
>
> I could not sleep at all for the first two to three weeks. If I started to fall asleep one of the guards would come and spray water in my face.

The mistreatment continued with variations, before the CIA subjected him to a twenty-day stretch of newly approved "enhanced interrogation techniques" in August 2002:

> About two and a half or three months after I arrived in this place, the

interrogation began again, but with more intensity than before. Then the real torturing started. Two black wooden boxes were brought into the room outside my cell. One was tall, slightly higher than me and narrow. Measuring perhaps in area 1m x 0.75m and 2m in height. The other was shorter, perhaps only 1m in height. I was taken out of my cell and one of the interrogators wrapped a towel around my neck, they then used it to swing me around and smash me repeatedly against the hard walls of the room. I was also repeatedly slapped in the face. As I was still shackled, the pushing and pulling around meant that the shackles pulled painfully on my ankles.

I was then put into the tall back box for what I think was about one and a half to two hours. . . . They put a cloth or cover over the outside of the box to cut out the light and restrict my air supply. It was difficult to breathe. . . .

After the beating I was then placed in the small box. They placed a cloth or cover over the box to cut out all light and restrict my air supply. As it was not high enough even to sit upright, I had to crouch down. It was very difficult because of my wounds. The stress on my legs held in this position meant my wounds both in the leg and stomach became very painful. . . . It was always cold in the room, but when the cover was placed over the box it made it hot and sweaty inside. The wound on my leg began to open and started to bleed. I don't know how long I remained in the small box, I think I may have slept or maybe fainted.

I was then dragged from the small box, unable to walk properly and put on what looked like a hospital bed, and strapped down very tightly with belts. A black cloth was then placed over my face and the interrogators used a mineral water bottle to pour water on the cloth so that I could not breathe. After a few minutes the cloth was removed and the bed was rotated into an upright position. The pressure of the straps on my wounds was very painful. I vomited. The bed was then again lowered to a horizontal position and the same torture carried out again with the black cloth over my face and water poured on from a bottle. On this occasion my head was in a more backward, downwards position and the water was poured on for a longer time. I struggled against the straps, trying to breathe, but it was hopeless. I thought I was going to die. I lost control of my urine. Since then I still lose control of my urine when under stress.[104]

CIA cables confirm the details of Abu Zubaydah's account.[105] His interrogation sessions were recorded on ninety-two videotapes, which reportedly showed him "vomiting and screaming," and which the CIA later destroyed, despite judicial inquiries into their existence.[106]

Prior to initiation of the August 2002 interrogation session, CIA officials insisted to other executive branch officials that the new techniques were necessary to elicit life-saving information from Abu Zubaydah, yet they admitted among themselves that he might already have divulged everything he knew: "Our assumption is the objective of this operation is to achieve a high degree of confidence that [Abu Zubaydah] is not holding back actionable information concerning threats to the United States beyond that which [Abu Zubaydah] has already provided."[107]

Nor did the CIA possess evidence in support of its claims to other executive branch officials that Abu Zubaydah was a top figure in Al Qaeda, participated in every major Al Qaeda terrorist operation, and helped plan the 9/11 attacks.[108] Today, Abu Zubaydah is a U.S. prisoner in Guantanamo, having never been charged with a crime. FBI interrogator Ali Soufan considers him a "major terrorist facilitator,"[109] but the U.S. government no longer claims that he belonged to Al Qaeda, had "any direct role in or advance knowledge of the terrorist attacks of September 11, 2001," or indeed "had knowledge of any specific terrorist operations" against the United States.[110]

In July 2002, National Security Advisor Condoleezza Rice approved use of "enhanced interrogation techniques" against Abu Zubaydah, contingent on a Department of Justice finding that they were lawful.[111] President Bush claims he provided similar approval.[112] (By September 2003, Vice President Cheney, Secretary of Defense Donald Rumsfeld, and Secretary of State Colin Powell were also briefed on the program.)[113] Legal authorization of the techniques came in the form of two lengthy OLC memos dated August 1, 2002. The first of these (the Bybee-Yoo Torture Memo)[114] stated that interrogation methods constituted torture only if the pain they inflicted was equivalent to that accompanying crippling injury, organ failure, or death; that torturers might seek acquittal by arguing they inflicted torture in defense of the nation; and that anyway neither congressional statutes (the Torture Statute) nor international treaties (the Torture Convention) could deprive the president of his constitutional authority, as commander in chief, to order torture in the interests of national security. The second (the Bybee-Yoo Techniques Memo)[115] used the reasoning of the first memo to approve ten techniques for use by the CIA, including facial slaps, slamming the prisoner against a wall, confinement in small boxes, forced standing, stress positions, continuous sleep deprivation up to eleven days, and waterboarding. It provided clinical descriptions of the techniques, while bizarrely downplaying their cruelty:

> The waterboard, which inflicts no pain or actual harm whatsoever, does not, in our view, inflict "severe pain or suffering." Even if one were to parse the statute more finely to attempt to treat "suffering" as a distinct concept, the waterboard could not be said to inflict severe suffering. The waterboard is simply a controlled acute episode, lacking the connotation of a protracted period of time generally given to suffering.

Waterboarding has become a symbol of how broadly the Bush administration viewed its legal prerogative. The technique may be thought of as "accelerated drowning," because water is forced into the air passages.[116] (When conservative radio host Erich "Mancow" Muller subjected himself to waterboarding in order to show it wasn't torture, he stopped the procedure after six or seven seconds, saying, "It was instantaneous . . . and I don't want to say this: absolutely torture.")[117] As described by M. Gregg Bloche:

> Water is poured over a cloth that covers the trainee's nose and mouth. This creates an airtight seal, making it impossible to inhale. This sensation triggers reflexive terror. Subjects gasp and flail about. The mind is useless as a defense. Trainees know that it's just an exercise and that their "interrogators" will remove the soaked cloth in seconds. Yet they experience drowning and think they will die. The craving for air overpowers all.[118]

Bloche's description refers to the practice used in U.S. military SERE training. Unlike U.S. military service members, of course, the CIA detainees were not voluntary participants, were not prepared by sympathetic trainers, and could not know that their captors did not intend to kill them.[119] Moreover, they were subjected to a far more aggressive version of the technique, leading CIA officials to acknowledge that "the SERE waterboard experience is so different from the subsequent Agency usage as to make it almost irrelevant."[120] (The Bybee-Yoo Techniques Memo assumed there was no difference between the SERE and CIA waterboarding. It is worth noting that the military stopped waterboarding its own personnel after 2007.) CIA officials reported that the waterboarding of Abu Zubaydah "resulted in immediate fluid intake and involuntary leg, chest and arm spasms" and "hysterical pleas." One session caused him to lose consciousness: he "became completely unresponsive, with bubbles rising through his open, full mouth."[121] The key point is that while SERE techniques are used to strengthen prisoners' resistance, CIA techniques were used to break prisoners' resistance, to induce "learned helplessness" as the interrogation program's architects boasted.[122] And used, it seems safe to say, to exact revenge. Abu Zubaydah was waterboarded eighty-three times in one month, Khalid Sheikh Muhamed 183 times.[123]

The Bybee-Yoo Torture Memo also influenced the armed forces. In late September 2002, military intelligence officers flew from Guantanamo to Fort Bragg, North Carolina, to receive instruction in the enhanced interrogation techniques. After returning to Guantanamo, they met on October 2, 2002, with Jonathan Fredman, chief counsel to the CIA Counterterrorism Center, who conveyed the outlines of the OLC position. These were incorporated in an October 11 memo by Staff Judge Advocate Diane Beaver that gave legal endorsement to all methods requested by military interrogators, including stress positions, isolation up to thirty days, hooding, twenty-hour interrogations, nakedness, manipulation of phobias, death threats against detainees and their family members, cold temperatures, cold water, and waterboarding.[124] Rumsfeld approved most of the techniques in writing on December 2.[125] Senior uniformed military lawyers resisted the policy with little success, although Navy general counsel Alberto Mora's opposition led Rumsfeld to rescind his December 2 order and seems to have brought to an end the months-long torture of Mohamed al-Qahtani (discussed above).[126] But the approved techniques had already been communicated to military units in Afghanistan and continued to influence intelligence operations there and later in Iraq.[127] Rumsfeld then appointed an Interrogation Working Group, which on March 14 received advice from Yoo in the form of a secret eighty-one-page memo reproducing and expanding arguments from the Bybee-Yoo Torture Memo.[128] Based on the April 4 Working Group report,[129] which incorporated large portions of Yoo's legal analysis, Rumsfeld issued an April 16 order approving twenty-four interrogation techniques, including "environmental manipulation," "sleep adjustment," and isolation. When these techniques were put into practice, detainees found themselves subjected to prolonged sleep deprivation, blaring music, and shackling in extreme heat and cold, while being forced to urinate and defecate on themselves.[130] Rumsfeld also left the door open to additional unspecified techniques, stating in his April 16 order that "If, in your view, you require additional interrogation techniques for a particular detainee, you should provide me, via the Chairman of the Joint Chiefs of Staff, a written request describing the proposed technique, recommended safeguards, and the rationale for applying it with an identified detainee." One such plan was adopted for Mohamedou Ould Slahi, whose testimony is quoted above. General Geoffrey Miller implemented the plan a month before he received approval from his superiors, who seem not to have minded his rush to action.[131] A few weeks later, he led a Guantanamo assessment team to Iraq to toughen U.S. treatment and interrogation of detainees.[132] As exhaustively documented by the Senate Armed Services Committee, the OLC opinions led directly and indirectly to widespread military abuses in Afghanistan, Guantanamo, and Iraq.[133]

In the spring of 2003, Bybee left the OLC to become a federal judge on the Ninth Circuit Court of Appeals, and Yoo to resume his faculty position at the UC Berkeley School of Law. In December 2003 Jack Goldsmith, Bybee's replacement as OLC director, withdrew the Yoo Military Interrogation Memo, while affirming the legality of the twenty-four techniques approved in Rumsfeld's April 16 order.[134] He left the Bybee-Yoo Torture Memo in place, not withdrawing it until a few days after it had been leaked to the press in June 2004. (His decision to withdraw the memo displeased key administration officials and helped precipitate his resignation a month later.)[135] Goldsmith never withdrew the Bybee-Yoo Techniques Memo, subsequently explaining, "I wasn't . . . confident that the CIA techniques could be approved under a proper legal analysis. I didn't affirmatively believe they were illegal either, or else I would have stopped them. I just didn't yet know."[136]

In December 2004, the OLC's next director, Daniel Levin, publicly issued a new memo to replace the discredited Bybee-Yoo Torture Memo.[137] Levin repudiated some, though not all, of the reasoning in the earlier memo, but in a footnote whose meaning was obscure to those not acquainted with the Bybee-Yoo Techniques Memo, he quietly upheld the legality of the CIA techniques. The following May, the OLC's next director, Steven Bradbury, produced three secret memos affirming that the techniques broke no laws. They did not violate the Torture Statute when used either singly[138] or in combination.[139] Nor did they violate the United States' obligation under the Torture Convention to abstain from cruel, inhuman, or degrading treatment.[140] The memos are ferociously detailed.[141] The Bradbury Techniques Memo of May 10, 2005, devotes eight single-spaced pages to a description of the techniques—for instance,

In no event is the detainee allowed to receive less than 1000 kcal/day. Calories are provided using commercial liquid diets (such as Ensure Plus).... [Nudity] is used to cause psychological discomfort.... Depending on the detainee's lack of cooperation, he may be walled one time during an interrogation session (one impact with the wall) or many times (perhaps 20 or 30 times) consecutively.... Wall standing ... is used only to induce temporary muscle fatigue.... The primary method of sleep deprivation involves the use of shackling to keep the detainee awake.... If the detainee is wearing a diaper, it is checked regularly and changed as necessary.... A cloth is placed over the detainee's face and cold water is poured on the cloth from a height of approximately 6 to 18 inches. The wet cloth creates a barrier through which it is difficult—or in some cases not possible—to breathe. A single "application" of water may not last for more than 40 seconds.

This is followed by sixteen single-spaced pages explaining why each technique does not constitute torture—for instance, "the physical distress caused by the waterboard would not be expected to have the duration required to amount to severe physical suffering."

In December 2005, after a long struggle with the administration, Senator John McCain won congressional passage with veto-proof majorities of an amendment prohibiting the "cruel, inhuman, or degrading treatment" of any person in the custody of the U.S. government.[142] However, at the administration's insistence, the legislation narrowed the legal remedies available to victims of torture, thereby undercutting the amendment's practical effect. One provision stated that a U.S. government agent is protected from criminal and civil liability for mistreating terrorist suspects if the agent "did not know that the practices were unlawful and a person of ordinary sense and understanding would not know the practices were unlawful"; the provision added that "good faith reliance on advice of counsel [a reference to the interrogation memos] should be an important factor, among others, to consider in assessing whether a person of ordinary sense and understanding would have known the practices to be unlawful."[143] The McCain Amendment was accompanied by another provision, known as the Graham-Levin Amendment, that limited the right of Guantanamo Bay inmates to challenge conditions of their detention.[144] The Bush administration soon invoked the Graham-Levin Amendment to block complaints of torture from being heard in U.S. courts.[145]

President Bush, unhappy over the ill-treatment ban, appended a signing statement implying that he did not consider it binding on his actions. He would construe the provision

> in a manner consistent with the constitutional authority of the Presi-
> dent to supervise the unitary executive branch and as Commander in
> Chief and consistent with the constitutional limitations on the judicial
> power, which will assist in achieving the shared objective of the Con-
> gress and the President . . . of protecting the American people from
> further terrorist attacks.[146]

The statement echoed the claim made in several OLC memos (and carefully bracketed in the Levin Memo) that Congress is constitutionally barred from restricting the president's conduct in matters relating to war and national se-curity. The signing statement sparked public outrage, but was something of a decoy, since the Bush administration was now quietly relying on Bradbury's May 2005 memo, which had affirmed that the CIA techniques were neither cruel, inhuman, nor degrading.

In June 2006, the Supreme Court delivered a major challenge to the ad-ministration's coercive interrogation policy when it ruled in *Hamdan v. Rumsfeld* that Common Article 3 of the Geneva Conventions protects mem-bers of Al Qaeda and other terrorist organizations.[147] Common Article 3 not only requires the basic elements of a fair trial (the immediate issue facing the Court); it also prohibits "cruel treatment and torture" and "outrages upon personal dignity, in particular, humiliating and degrading treatment." As the administration well knew, violations of Common Article 3 not only contra-vened international law, but constituted domestic crimes under the U.S. War Crimes Act.

The administration responded by (1) getting Congress to rewrite the War Crimes Act, and (2) obtaining a new memo from the OLC. The Military Commissions Act (MCA) of 2006 rewrote the War Crimes Act so that it no longer covers all violations, but only what it called "grave breaches," of Com-mon Article 3.[148] "Grave breaches" still include "cruel or inhuman treatment," but the definition of "cruel or inhuman treatment" is given such a narrow (and convoluted) definition[149] that it is no longer clear whether waterboard-ing, stress positions, hypothermia, sleep deprivation, and beating are punish-able under the War Crimes Act.[150] The 2006 MCA makes the change retroactive to 1997, thus providing immunity for post-9/11 interrogation practices (1997 was the year the War Crimes Act was expanded to cover violations of Common Article 3). To an alarming degree, the MCA inscribed the Bush OLC memos into the U.S. federal code.

The Act furthermore used various devices to deny judicial remedies to detainees at risk of ill-treatment or torture. The Geneva Conventions may not be invoked "as a source of rights in any court of the United States or its States or territories."[151] Habeas corpus rights were eliminated for foreign detainees who are either determined to be or *suspected* of being enemy combatants.[152] Moreover, "no court, justice, or judge shall have jurisdiction to hear or consider any other action against the United States or its agents relating to any aspect of the detention, transfer, *treatment*, trial or *conditions of confinement* of an alien"[153] detained as a possible enemy combatant (emphasis added). In June 2008 the Supreme Court overturned one piece of the 2006 MCA when it ruled that Guantanamo detainees have a constitutional right to habeas corpus.[154] But the amendments to the War Crimes Act and the provisions that bar judges from applying the Geneva Conventions or reviewing the treatment of suspected enemy combatants remain in place.[155]

In case there was any doubt, OLC director Steven Bradbury wrote a secret seventy-nine-page memo in July 2007 affirming that the CIA techniques were in compliance with the McCain Amendment and the amended War Crimes Act.[156] Bradbury still had to confront the *Hamdan* ruling that "War on Terror" detainees were protected by Common Article 3. Although the 2006 MCA withdrew federal criminal penalties from many acts constituting violations of Common Article 3, the United States is bound as a party to the Geneva Conventions to honor the article in its entirety. Accordingly, Bradbury devoted many paragraphs in the July 2007 memo to showing that practices such as slapping, 1,000-calorie-a-day diets, prolonged sleep deprivation, and leaving shackled, diapered prisoners to defecate and urinate on themselves did not violate the Common Article 3 prohibition on "humiliating and degrading treatment."[157] Thus stood the legal position of the U.S. executive branch until January 22, 2009, when a newly inaugurated President Obama revoked all Bush administration OLC memos relating to detention and interrogation in the "War on Terror."[158]

The Interrogation Memos and Their Impact

The Bush OLC interrogation memos are genuinely shocking. They sweep aside legal prohibitions against inhuman treatment, create permissive readings of the Torture Statute, and fill page after page with graphic descriptions of officially sanctioned torture. Several of them—the Bybee-Yoo Techniques Memo of August 2002 and the four Bradbury memos of May 2005 and July 2007—read like the smoking gun in a criminal trial, the "I can't believe what I'm seeing" proof of a deliberate plan to carry out torture.[159] They name their victims, state a motive for action, and spell out the crimes in morbid detail. All that stops these documents from sending their authors to prison is the authors' own assertion, as officers charged with interpreting the law for the executive branch, that the actions do not violate applicable international and domestic law. The conspirators built immunity into the crime. Theirs was "the perfect crime."[160]

The memos are not legally defensible.[161] They contain novel legal assertions disguised as settled law, misrepresentation of case law and legislative history, contrived readings of legal texts, glaring omissions of contrary evidence, phony footnotes, and flights of absurd reasoning—all to serve a predetermined agenda, that of justifying coercive interrogation. In a comprehensive report on the interrogation memos, the Justice Department's Office of Professional Responsibility concluded that both Bybee and Yoo had committed professional misconduct and that Yoo's misconduct was intentional.[162] The *OPR Report* did not conclude that Bradbury had committed misconduct, but it subjected his memos to sharp criticisms, one being that Bradbury relied on CIA factual assertions about its interrogation program despite knowing that the CIA had a history of misrepresenting the program.[163] The *OPR Report* was followed by a memo from senior Justice Department official David Margolis clearing Bybee and Yoo of misconduct.[164] Margolis's reasons for removing the misconduct charge are unpersuasive,[165] but he joined the Report in strongly criticizing the content of the memos, stating that they "contained significant flaws" and that Yoo and Bybee "exercised poor judgment" in composing them.

One of the more nonsensical arguments was that used in the Bybee-Yoo Torture Memo and Yoo Military Interrogation Memo to claim that interrogation methods would constitute torture only if they inflicted pain equivalent to that accompanying organ failure, crippling injury, or death. The purported evidence for this claim was a medical benefits statute that listed "severe pain" as a possible symptom of serious injury requiring emergency care. The argument is both illogical and meaningless—illogical because "X is a possible sign of Y" does not mean "X is defined by Y," meaningless because there is no determinate level of pain associated with serious injury. Everybody knows that excruciating pain sometimes occurs without major physical injury (a dentist's drill, passing a kidney stone) and that serious injury sometimes occurs without pain (a silent tumor, certain kinds of trauma). What the memo therefore insinuated was that interrogators *need not worry about pain at all* and could proceed so long as they did not (intentionally) inflict major injury—a point captured in the statement by CIA lawyer Jonathan Fredman to Guantanamo interrogators that physical torture is "anything causing permanent damage to major organs or body parts. . . . If the detainee dies you're doing it wrong."[166]

The interrogation memos are so brazen—the reasoning so contrived and in some cases nonsensical, the legal scholarship so distorted, and the conclusions so outrageous—that one cannot regard them as having been written in good faith. The OLC was under sustained pressure from White House officials to produce the desired conclusions.[167] Surviving email correspondence discussed in the *OPR Report* shows Yoo engaging in conscious deception.[168] The memos are best seen as forming part of a criminal conspiracy to commit torture.[169]

We know from the Senate Intelligence Committee report and other sources that techniques actually used by the CIA were often harsher than those described in the OLC memos.[170] But the practices authorized by the memos were horrific in their own right, and clearly constitute torture. Journalists Mark Mazzetti and Matt Appuzzo correctly observe that "some of the most shocking examples contained in the Senate Intelligence Committee report involved C.I.A. interrogations that were within the wide boundaries established by the Justice Department."[171] After the OLC crossed the threshold into licensing brutal treatment, a further descent into savagery is not surprising. The OLC's sweeping justifications, and its habit of retrospectively endorsing techniques introduced without prior authorization,[172] sent a message that the CIA enjoyed broad latitude and might venture beyond explicitly authorized techniques.[173]

It would be difficult to overstate the memos' impact. The torture program they enabled and sustained left a wake of human suffering, retaliatory violence, surging terrorism, and compromised intelligence; helped the Bush administration fabricate a leading pretext for the Iraq War; and gave other governments a precedent to justify their own torture. In the United States, the memos gave torture a veneer of legitimacy. For years, they enabled the U.S. president to say that techniques constituting torture (though not called "torture") were legal, a view that has now been internalized by a large portion of the American public and adopted by most of the Republican Party. They

caused the media to avoid saying "torture" when discussing systematic practices of torture, and even to detach the word from such iconic torture methods as waterboarding, sleep deprivation, and stress positions. In the
upside-down world created by the memos, one is suspected of trying to score
partisan points when calling torture by its real name.

The memos altered the U.S. Code by leading to provisions in the 2006
Military Commissions Act that shielded practices of torture from criminal
prosecution and that redefined "cruel and inhuman treatment" to the point of
incoherence in a newly weakened War Crimes Act. They created a culture of
torture in the CIA, which now fiercely resists efforts to establish accountability or clarify the historical record.[174] They immunized most participants in the
Bush administration torture program by making it harder to prosecute the
authorized practices. Having ushered in a policy of torture, they gave the implicated actors—the Bush administration, the CIA, and leading Republican
Party officials—powerful incentives of pride and individual and collective
self-interest to defend the legitimacy of torture. These actors have now dedicated themselves to making torture respectable, attempting nothing less than
a transformation of American culture; and with the help of conservative
media such as Fox News, they have disseminated false information to cultivate a widespread misperception that torture yielded valuable intelligence in
the "War on Terror."[175] The OLC memos have left a lasting mark on U.S. law,
institutions, and culture.

Having insisted that the memos are legally indefensible, I will argue in the
next chapter that they were facilitated by certain features of U.S. law. This
might seem to be a case of "having my cake and eating it, too." But although
the two claims are in some tension with each other, they are both in fact true,
and acknowledging them together is essential to understanding the whole
debacle. Though the U.S. marginalization of international human rights law
did not make the torture program legal, it assisted it in the following ways. (1)
It removed some of the several overlapping legal prohibitions of torture.
Other prohibitions remained in place, so that the proposition "torture and
ill-treatment are prohibited" remained the correct legal answer, but the upshot was that the memos acquired more plausibility than they should have
possessed, and their critics had to work harder than should have been necessary to reject them. (2) The symbolically most important prohibition, the U.S.
Torture Statute, contained significant loopholes derived from conditions attached to U.S. ratification of the Torture Convention, and these loopholes
handed the memos' authors a rhetorical advantage. It turns out that, because

of these loopholes, *some* of the outrageous arguments in the memos are not outrageous *as a statement of U.S. law*. (3) The U.S. practice of making international human rights commitments nonjusticiable (unenforceable in court) created a space in which the memos could operate, because it left interpretation of the U.S. international human rights commitments to the executive branch alone. The effect of this was to weaken certain laws by placing them outside the checks-and-balances system. We can say that the consequence of U.S. legal practice was not the legal authorization but the practical enablement of torture. Or in other words, U.S. law facilitated U.S. lawbreaking. (4) The aforementioned factors had deep institutional effects. Lawyers forgot or ignored whole branches of law, pernicious doctrines gained a foothold, and the criminal prosecution of those responsible for torture became harder to imagine.

The torture memos found a way to circumvent the international and domestic legal prohibition of torture, thus revealing the inadequacy of U.S. checks and balances. How the U.S. marginalization of international human rights law contributed to this constitutional failure is the subject of my next chapter.

Chapter 5

American Exceptionalism and the Betrayal of Human Rights, Part II: Enabling Torture

In the last chapter, we examined the legal maneuvers that enabled Bush administration officials to claim that interrogation methods constituting torture (though not acknowledged as such) were legally permitted. The heart of the story lies in the interrogation memos that managed the seemingly impossible feat of dismantling the absolute prohibition placed by international law on torture and cruel, inhuman, or degrading treatment. Beyond the human suffering and strategic calamity they produced, the memos inflicted lasting damage on U.S. law, institutions, and culture. They brought discredit to the legal system and the legal profession, by suggesting that lawyers, including those elevated to the highest rank in their field, are capable of deriving any legal finding, however outrageous. Their moral and legal wreckage will be with us a long time.

Blame for the torture policy does not rest entirely on the bad moral and intellectual judgment of the memos' authors and the policy makers who egged them on. This chapter will show how the torture policy (alongside certain other patterns of human rights violations) was facilitated by the U.S. marginalization of international human rights law. I focus on four areas: (1) the "reservations, understandings, and declarations" that qualify U.S. ratification of human rights treaties; (2) additional steps by Congress and the courts to marginalize international human rights law; (3) judicial and executive determinations that limit the binding force of customary international law; and (4) the U.S. failure to ratify the Rome Statute of the International Criminal Court. (Note to readers: discussion of the first topic will be quite lengthy, but I will move more quickly through the remaining three.) I end by juxtaposing the divergent approaches to international human rights law taken by Europe and the United States, particularly as regards the prohibition of torture and ill-treatment. The story of the Bush administration torture policy is a powerful refutation of the view that the United States does not stand in need of international human rights law.

It is also important to see the consequences of the U.S. marginalization of international human rights law beyond the Bush administration torture program. I shall mention some of these effects (where torture and ill-treatment are concerned) on U.S. immigration policy and the U.S. criminal justice system. In addition, the U.S. marginalization of international human rights law has made it easier for the U.S. government to resume torture in the future.[1]

The U.S. Self-Exemption Policy and Its Consequences: Treaty Law

After years of delay, the United States moved to ratify the Torture Convention and the ICCPR during the administration of the first President Bush. The Senate Foreign Relations Committee convened a hearing on the Torture Convention on January 30, 1990, and the full Senate voted to approve ratification on October 27, 1990. At President Bush's direction, formal ratification was postponed until Congress enacted legislation implementing Article 5 of the Convention. After Congress did so by passing the Torture Statute on April 30, 1994, ratification was formalized on October 21, 1994 (by which point Bill Clinton had become president). The ICCPR was taken up later but ratified earlier: the Senate Foreign Relations Committee conducted a hearing on November 21, 1991, the full Senate voted to approve ratification on April 2, 1992, and ratification was formalized on June 8, 1992.[2]

When ratifying the ICCPR and Torture Convention, the United States attached a set of "reservations, understandings, and declarations," or RUDs, whose acknowledged purpose was to ensure that the treaties, by themselves, would not require any changes to U.S. law and practice.[3] For decades, this has been standard practice for all human rights treaties submitted by the president for Senate approval.[4] The RUDs achieve their objective by two means. The first means is to attach self-exempting reservations or understandings to every substantive obligation in the treaty that potentially exceeds human rights protections already provided under U.S. constitutional or statutory law. As Richard Schifter, assistant secretary of state for human rights and humanitarian affairs, explained during the ICCPR hearing, "If the

Congress desires to change existing domestic laws, it will undoubtedly want to do so by statute, in the customary legislative process. Accordingly we should reserve on those few provisions of the covenant which are not in accord with existing law."[5]

A few of the reservations are intended to uphold constitutional rights. This includes a reservation stating that the mandated prohibition of war propaganda and group-targeting hate speech under Article 20 of the ICCPR must not infringe constitutionally protected rights to freedom of speech and association. At the ICCPR hearing, human rights organizations expressed support for this reservation. However, most of the reservations are intended not to uphold constitutional rights, but simply to cancel treaty-mandated rights for which no counterpart is found in U.S. law. Human rights organizations opposed such rights-weakening reservations, which include an exemption from the ICCPR prohibition of the juvenile death penalty (the execution of persons for crimes committed as children), because at the time of ratification the Supreme Court still allowed it.[6] The reservation proclaims that "the United States reserves the right, subject to its Constitutional constraints, to impose capital punishment on any person (other than a pregnant woman)."

The second means to avoid making changes to U.S. law is to accompany ratification of human rights treaties with a declaration announcing that the treaties' substantive provisions "are not self-executing," so that, in the words of a 2004 Supreme Court opinion, the treaties do not by themselves "create obligations enforceable in the federal courts."[7] Non-self-executing declarations accompanied ratification of the ICCPR, Torture Convention, and Race Convention (the three most significant human rights treaties ratified by the United States since 1990) and are now routinely recommended by the president in human rights treaties submitted to the Senate. The precise meaning of the phrase "not self-executing" is a matter of dispute,[8] but the bottom line is that judges virtually never apply provisions of the ICCPR, Torture Convention, or Race Convention in their rulings (except insofar as selected provisions of the Torture Convention have been incorporated in congressional legislation).[9]

Under international law, treaties are automatically binding between states.[10] Whether they may be enforced by domestic courts varies from country to country. In some countries, treaties automatically form part of the domestic law that courts may (in theory) enforce. In other countries, courts may not enforce treaties until the legislature has passed implementing legislation.[11] The United States is an intermediate case. Even though Article VI of the

Constitution states that all U.S. treaties form part of the "supreme Law of the Land" and Article III, Section 2, states that "the judicial Power [of the United States] shall extend to . . . Treaties made, or which shall be made, under [the United States'] Authority," the Supreme Court has ruled that some treaties are self-executing (judicially enforceable) while others are not.[12] The executive took this as a cue, starting in the late 1970s, to attach explicit "non-self-executing" declarations to human rights treaties submitted for Senate approval. Courts have consistently honored such declarations.

This practice is troubling, and can make ratification seem an exercise in bad faith. One can defend the idea of making treaties non-self-executing when they take the form of peace agreements, military alliances, and trade pacts; since treaties of this type have as their purpose the creation of interstate obligations, the judicial enforcement of domestic obligations carries secondary importance. But the primary purpose of human rights treaties is to assume domestic obligations, to restrict the ways in which governments may treat individuals under their power. When the United States declares human rights treaties non-self-executing, it therefore defeats the purpose of ratification. The practice would be less objectionable if Congress moved punctually to pass implementing legislation, but Congress has not passed any implementing legislation for the ICCPR or Race Convention, and as we shall see it has incorporated the Torture Convention only to a limited extent.

The legal upshot of the RUDs is that U.S. international human rights obligations are reduced in scope and are not, by themselves, judicially enforceable. This has the effect that executive and legislative officials (1) generally do not see themselves bound by treaty obligations that exceed the requirements of U.S. constitutional and statutory law, and (2) generally understand that their interpretations of human rights treaty obligations will not be subjected to judicial challenge. Further, because judges rarely consult the treaties, lawyers rarely invoke them and citizens have little incentive to study them. Their provisions are not well known. The RUDs have placed human rights treaties outside the U.S. legal system and legal culture.

The United States' expansive RUDs are not necessary to protect rights recognized in U.S. law. First, the United States can adopt narrowly tailored reservations withholding consent to treaty provisions that contradict or threaten human rights protected by its own laws, as it arguably did with regard to ICCPR Article 20. Second, it is a well-established principle of U.S. law that the Constitution prevails over a conflicting treaty provision.[13] (But in such cases the United States should still adopt a reservation to avoid assuming international obligations that it must then violate.) Third, the human rights treaties explicitly provide that their omissions may not be invoked to weaken rights recognized in domestic law. The ICCPR states in Article 5(2): "There shall be no restriction upon or derogation from any of the fundamental human rights recognized or existing in any State Party to the present Covenant pursuant to law, conventions, regulations or custom on the pretext that the present Covenant does not recognize such rights or that it recognizes them to a lesser extent."[14] In other words, the human rights treaties set a minimum floor, but states parties are free to establish higher standards in domestic law and in other treaties.[15]

At the Torture Convention and ICCPR hearings, senators and administration officials repeatedly affirmed that the United States did not allow torture and was already in compliance with the treaties' substantive obligations. Typical was the statement by Abraham Sofaer, State Department legal advisor, that "there is no need for the legal protections of the convention against torture in the United States" and that "we do not have a torture problem in the United States."[16] Little attention was paid to the warning from Human Rights Watch that "current conditions can change overnight. We leave our children vulnerable to abuses by future governments when we deny to them the full range of protections envisioned by the treaty."[17] Just as Human Rights Watch feared, the RUDs would prove harmful to human rights.

Reservations and Understandings

As I will show, U.S. treaty reservations and understandings (1) tightened the intent requirement for torture, (2) gutted the concept of mental torture, and (3) reduced the prohibition of ill-treatment to preexisting Supreme Court Fifth, Eighth, and Fourteenth Amendment jurisprudence. The resulting loopholes gave a big lift to the Bush administration's legal defense of enhanced interrogation techniques. And they have weakened human rights, including refugee rights and prisoners' rights, beyond the "War on Terror" context.

U.S. ratification of the Torture Convention was accompanied by several reservations and understandings limiting its application. One understanding stipulates that the Convention may not restrict or prohibit the United States' use of the death penalty or the period of confinement preceding its application.[18] Another makes it easier to deport individuals to countries where they face the danger of torture, stating that deportation is barred only if the resulting probability of torture is greater than 50 percent.[19] Other understandings narrow the meaning of official "acquiescence" to torture, limit civil liability to acts of torture "committed in territory under the jurisdiction" of a state party, and stipulate that torture refers only to actions taken against individuals in the offender's custody or physical control.[20]

The United States also narrowed the Convention's definition of torture. Article 1 of the Convention defines torture as the intentional infliction "of severe pain or suffering, whether physical or mental." Initially the Reagan administration had proposed attaching an understanding "that in order to constitute torture, an act must be a deliberate and calculated act of an extremely cruel and inhuman nature, specifically intended to inflict excruciating and agonizing physical or mental pain or suffering." When the first President Bush resubmitted the treaty for ratification, he discarded this redefinition in favor of another, which the Senate approved:

> the United States understands that, in order to constitute torture, an act must be specifically intended to inflict severe physical or mental pain or suffering and that mental pain or suffering refers to prolonged mental harm caused by or resulting from: (1) the intentional infliction or threatened infliction of severe physical pain or suffering; (2) the administration or application, or threatened administration or application, of mind altering substances or other procedures calculated to disrupt profoundly the senses or the personality; (3) the threat of imminent death; or (4) the threat that another person will imminently be subjected to death, severe physical pain or suffering, or the administration or application of mind altering substances or other procedures calculated to disrupt profoundly the senses or personality.[21]

The revised definition found its way into several U.S. statutes, including the Torture Statute of 1994 (making torture committed outside the United States a federal crime); the Torture Victim Protection Act of 1991 (allowing victims to sue foreign government agents responsible for torture or extrajudicial execution); Section 1242 of the Foreign Affairs Reform and Restructuring Act of 1998 (prohibiting the deportation of individuals to countries where they face a serious danger of torture); the War Crimes Act as amended by the Military Commissions Act (MCA) of 2006; and the 2006 MCA provision defining torture as a war crime punishable by military commission.[22] As Steven Bradbury correctly observed, the definitional requirements of the Torture Statute "closely track the understandings and reservations required by the Senate when it gave its advice and consent to ratification of the Convention Against Torture. They reflect a clear intent by Congress to limit the scope of the prohibition on torture under U.S. law."[23]

The U.S. understanding changes the Convention definition of torture in two ways: it tightens the intent requirement, and it significantly narrows the definition of mental torture.

The United States changed the mental state necessary for an act to qualify as torture from *intent* to *specific intent*.[24] Although the change was deliberate,[25] its implications are unclear, because the U.S. case law on the meaning of "specific intent" is muddled[26] and has never addressed the infliction of pain. Some judicial rulings have held that a person who causes a particular result acts with specific intent only if he or she consciously desires that result, seeking it as an end or a means to an end;[27] others have held that a person can act with specific intent simply by knowing that his or her action is likely to cause the result.[28] To distinguish different mental states, let us say that an action is *purposeful* when its likely effect is sought as an end or a means to an end, and otherwise *nonpurposeful*. In the torture context, we can say that the infliction of severe pain or suffering may be either:

- *sadistic*, meaning that the victim's suffering is the end of one's action;
- *instrumental*, meaning that the victim's suffering is sought as a means to one's end, say, collecting intelligence;
- *callous*, meaning that the infliction of severe pain or suffering is done knowingly, but not as an end or means to an end; or
- *reckless*, meaning that one acts with the awareness of exposing the victim to a significant risk of severe pain or suffering.[29]

Applying the previous distinction, we can say that the infliction of severe pain or suffering is *purposeful* when it is either sadistic or instrumental, and otherwise *nonpurposeful*.

The various interrogation memos charged with interpreting and applying the Torture Statute all draw attention to the "specific intent" requirement. That it represented a deliberate departure from the Convention text seemed to lend it added significance.[30] Although the memos are not fully clear or consistent about the term's meaning, it shapes their tone and conclusions. The Bybee-Yoo Torture Memo provided a detailed analysis—reproduced verbatim in the Yoo Military Interrogation Memo of March 14, 2003, and the Pentagon's Interrogation Working Group report of April 4, 2003—which begins by stating that specific intent is present only if the victim's severe pain or suffering is the agent's "precise objective" or "express purpose."[31] Whether this means that the infliction of pain must be sadistic or only purposeful is ambiguous, though several members of the administration took it to mean the former.[32] The "sadism" requirement is a clear misreading of U.S. case law, but the "purposefulness" requirement may not be. A few paragraphs later, the memo retreats to the view that specific intent may also be present in the nonpurposeful infliction of severe pain or suffering, but not if the interrogator acts in the good-faith (albeit mistaken) belief that his methods will not inflict severe pain or suffering.

The Levin Memo of December 2004 withdrew the "precise objective/express purpose" standard, but preserved the "good faith" standard.[33] The OLC had previously explained that the requisite good faith belief "may be established by, among other things, the reliance on the advice of experts."[34] It seems clear that the Bybee-Yoo and Bradbury techniques memos were regarded as providing the necessary expert confirmation that the enhanced interrogation techniques would not be expected to inflict severe pain or suffering, thus absolving U.S. officials of "specific intent" in case severe pain or suffering nonetheless resulted.[35] As a further guarantee of good faith, the memos stated that medical personnel would be present at interrogation sites, ready to intervene if the techniques proved more harmful than anticipated.[36] In this way, the "specific intent" requirement was used to help fashion the OLC "golden shield" protecting CIA and military officials from criminal liability.[37]

One receives the impression that the "specific intent" requirement, so insistently repeated in the interrogation memos, encouraged cavalier attitudes. There is an echo of the OLC's analysis in CIA lawyer Jonathan Fredman's notorious statement that "if the prisoner dies you're doing it wrong"[38] (suggesting you aren't liable for consequences you didn't deliberately seek). Years later, Jay Bybee, after he had become a federal appeals court judge, explained why the CIA official who caused Gul Rahman's death by ordering him to be soaked with water and left overnight semi-naked in a near-freezing cell might not be guilty of torture: "If Zirbel, as manager of the Saltpit site, did not intend for Rahman to suffer severe pain from low temperatures in his cell, he would lack specific intent under the anti-torture statute."[39] The senators and executive branch officials who had inserted the "specific intent" requirement as a condition of U.S. ratification of the Torture Convention may not have intended it to be used in this way, but they opened the door to creative interpretations through their ambiguous and unnecessary revision of the original treaty definition.

The consequences of the "specific intent" requirement extend farther than the Bush administration torture program. In 2008, Paul Pierre argued to a U.S. appeals court that his deportation to Haiti would violate the provision of the Foreign Affairs Reform and Restructuring Act that forbids the involuntary transfer of individuals to countries where they would be more likely than not to be tortured. As an ex-convict with a grave health problem, Pierre stated that he would be detained under conditions which would likely kill him and which prison officials knew were practically certain to cause him severe pain. In *Pierre v. Attorney General*, the Third Circuit Court meeting en banc relied on the concept of specific intent to argue that the brutal prison conditions feared by Pierre would not constitute torture:

> the specific intent requirement, included in the ratification history of the CAT [Convention Against Torture], requires a petitioner to show that his prospective torturer will have the motive or purpose to cause him pain or suffering. . . . Knowledge that pain and suffering will be the certain outcome of conduct may be sufficient for a finding of general intent but it is not enough for a finding of specific intent. . . . Under this standard, Pierre has failed to qualify for relief under the CAT because he has failed to show that Haitian officials will have the purpose of inflicting severe pain or suffering by placing him in detention upon his removal from the United States.[40]

Under the court's reasoning, even the most callous infliction of severe pain or suffering, provided it was not purposeful, would not qualify as torture. This holding has broad implications for what we consider torture in prison and other detention settings. After the decision appeared, Yoo claimed it vindicated his assertion in the Bybee-Yoo Torture Memo that the infliction of severe pain or suffering, in order to constitute torture, must be the interrogator's precise objective or express purpose.[41]

Such has been the impact of the U.S. stipulation that severe pain must be *specifically* intended in order to constitute torture. Even more damaging was language that gutted the concept of mental or psychological torture. The Torture Convention leaves the concept of "severe pain or suffering, whether physical or mental" undefined. The U.S. understanding similarly leaves *physical* pain or suffering undefined, but stipulates that *mental* pain or suffering refers to *the prolonged mental harm* that is *caused by* one of four practices: (1) the threatened or actual use of physical torture, (2) the threatened or actual use of mind-altering drugs "or other procedures calculated to disrupt profoundly the senses or the personality," (3) the threat of imminent death, or (4) the threat that another person will be imminently subjected to one of the aforementioned harms. What this means is that an agent who intentionally inflicts severe mental pain or suffering is not guilty of torture unless he applies one of the four specified practices, and then only if he specifically intends to produce prolonged mental harm by means of those practices. This revised definition was duly incorporated into the Torture Statute and other U.S. legislation pertaining to torture.

With this definition, it became remarkably easy for the OLC lawyers to argue that all manner of psychological torment did not constitute torture as defined by the Torture Statute, because it was not inflicted with the specific intention of causing prolonged mental harm. Whereas the interrogation memos must use brazen distortions to deny that the techniques cause severe *physical* pain or suffering, no equivalent distortions, thanks to the Torture Statute, are needed to deny that the techniques cause severe *mental* pain or suffering. The dirty secret about the memos is that some of their shocking conclusions, especially where psychological torment is concerned, emerge from a straightforward application of the Torture Statute.[42]

At the Torture Convention hearing in 1990, U.S. officials discussed the reasoning behind the inserted definition of mental pain or suffering. Deputy assistant attorney general Mark Richard explained that "Mental pain is by its nature subjective. Action that causes one person severe mental suffering may seem inconsequential to another person. Moreover, mental suffering is often transitory, causing no lasting harm."[43] This, Richard argued, rendered the Convention's definition of mental torture too vague, and since the Convention criminalizes torture, the United States would need to provide a more precise definition in order to safeguard the rights of the accused.[44] Richard never explained why the same concerns do not apply to physical pain, which also is subjective, variable from person to person, and often temporary in its effects.

The folly of the U.S. revision is well exposed by David Luban and Henry Shue.[45] It reveals a skeptical attitude toward mental pain, what Luban and Shue call a "materialist bias" that regards mental pain as somehow less real than physical pain. It performs a "substitution trick," such that mental pain and suffering "get defined through their causes and aftermath and not the experience itself." It is shaped by a "forensic fallacy," which allows the specter of unfair prosecution to block acknowledgment of a genuine crime, even though, as Luban and Shue remind us, the criminal law already contains vague or general concepts, such as the reasonable person standard, whose application requires our responsible judgment. [46] And the revision has the absurd consequence that psychological torture is limited to sadists, because it implies that "interrogators engaged in psychological abuse have not committed torture unless they specifically intend to prolong the severe pain or suffering beyond the interrogation."[47]

Torture means the intentional infliction of severe pain or suffering. The Convention gets it right: "whether physical or mental" is a way of saying that the characterization of pain or suffering as mental or physical does not matter for purposes of defining torture. That the perpetrator deliberately imposes severe pain or suffering is sufficient. Needless to say, much "physical torture" contains a strong psychological element. The victim may experience a combination of pain, terror, humiliation, dehumanization, hopelessness, helplessness, and self-loathing; torturers are aware of this and tailor their approach to increase the victims' suffering. To pry apart mental and physical distress is a largely artificial exercise, one that is carried to a ridiculous extreme in the interrogation memos, though they take their cue from the Torture Statute itself. To distinguish between different kinds of torment, and to specify that for certain kinds of torment one must intentionally produce certain aftereffects by means of certain techniques, is to leave the meaning of torture behind, replaced by a cloud of legal obfuscation.

The U.S. definition opens the door to every form of psychological torture, including mock execution; mock burial; entombment; immobilization by shackling or other means; forcing victims to defecate and urinate on themselves; psychotropic drugs; use of insects, dogs, or other animals to create fear; threats to loved ones; threats of torture; threats of disappearance; letting victims see or hear other people being tortured; all manner of humiliation, sexual and otherwise; sensory deprivation, such as hooding; sensory overstimulation; perpetual dark; isolation; manipulation of phobias; dehumanization; desecration of religion; and various techniques intended to create fear, guilt, or despair.[48] Although the U.S. definition appears to exclude some of these methods (such as mock execution), it readmits them if the interrogator does not use them with the specific intention of causing prolonged mental harm. A great many techniques, such as sleep deprivation and waterboarding, are simultaneously physical and psychological. And so the interrogation memos (to take one example) denied that waterboarding was torture, by arguing absurdly that it did not create severe physical pain or suffering, and then arguing, not so absurdly given the language of the Torture Statute, that it did not create severe mental pain or suffering (because interrogators did not practice it with the specific intention of creating prolonged mental harm).

At the Torture Convention hearing, Human Rights Watch gave a prophetic warning:

> The range of acts that constitute torture is limited only by the imaginations of those who seek to perpetrate them. In recent years governments that practice torture increasingly have sought to devise methods that cause intense pain but leave no marks. The era of psychological torture appears to be ahead of us. It would be a mistake for the U.S. to interfere with the Committee Against Torture's ability to respond effectively to these new and ever more cruel torture techniques.[49]

One of the terrible features of the Bush administration torture program was its psychological focus: its calculated use of insult, humiliation, despair, and terror to break prisoners, and its avowed intention, by means of mental and physical methods, to induce "learned helplessness" among detainees.[50] Professional psychologists played a leading role in the design and implementation of the program, their participation approved by senior officials of the American Psychological Association.[51] This approach recalls the CIA's Kubark-era fascination with mind control and psychological regression. Regrettably, the influence of the U.S. treaty understanding, via the interrogation memos, persists among those who have defended enhanced interrogation techniques on the grounds that they are "merely psychological." The editorial page of the Wall Street Journal declared in 2005:

> No one has yet come up with any evidence that anyone in the U.S. military or government has officially sanctioned anything close to "torture." The "stress positions" that have been allowed (such as wearing a hood, exposure to heat and cold, and the rarely authorized "waterboarding," which induces a feeling of suffocation) are all psychological techniques designed to break a detainee.[52]

But psychological torture is real and it is distinctly horrible, for reasons well captured by Luban and Shue. It threatens "the underlying psychological integrity necessary for having desires and beliefs that are one's own," not to mention "the psychological capacity (the agency) to act effectively on them."

Its evil resides in "its mercilessness—the limitlessness of the invasion of one person by others. Psychological torture is not finished until a person is broken. . . . It is government occupation of the human soul," and therefore "the ultimate assertion of arbitrary state power."[53]

The U.S. redefinition of torture is disturbing on several levels. It perpetrates an Orwellian distortion of language, allowing purveyors of carefully chosen methods of torture to claim that they do not torture, and causing the meaning of torture to become lost in a web of irrelevant distinctions. What is thrown out in the elaborately self-protective U.S. language is any sense that torture *as such* is morally unacceptable. The new definition not only wreaks havoc on the English language; it is also legally suspect. Since long before the United States ratified the Convention, torture has been recognized as a violation of customary international law. The Nuremberg and Tokyo Tribunals and the 1949 Geneva Conventions proclaimed it an international crime.[54] Its status as a violation of customary international law was reaffirmed by the 1980 U.S. case of *Filártiga v. Peña-Irala*[55] and many subsequent rulings. The *Filártiga* court applied the definition used by the UN General Assembly when it unanimously adopted the 1975 Declaration on Torture: "any act by which severe pain or suffering, whether physical or mental, is intentionally inflicted by or at the instigation of a public official." The United States cannot retroactively adjust a customary international law prohibition, much less *jus cogens*,[56] by substituting a new definition for the prohibited activity. One cannot redefine one's way out of a legal prohibition.

So much for the U.S. redefinition of torture. But international law forbids all cruel, inhuman, or degrading treatment, not just torture. Why didn't the broader prohibition restrain the Bush administration? Part of the answer is that, during the treaty ratification process, the United States tinkered with the broader prohibition as well.

U.S. reservations attached to both the Torture Convention and the ICCPR narrowed the prohibition of "cruel, inhuman or degrading treatment or punishment" to conduct prohibited by the Fifth, Eighth, and Fourteenth Amendments to the U.S. Constitution—meaning, in practice, the interpretation of these amendments by U.S. courts. The most relevant constitutional provisions are the Eighth Amendment prohibition of "cruel and unusual punishments," the Fifth Amendment prohibition of compulsory self-incrimination, and the Fifth and Fourteenth Amendment prohibition of the deprivation of liberty without due process of law. It can be argued that "cruel and unusual" punishment, rightly understood, is coextensive with "cruel, inhuman or degrading treatment or punishment." However, the Supreme Court has not interpreted the Eighth Amendment phrase this broadly.[57]

At the ratification hearings, U.S. officials claimed that the reservation was necessary to avoid ambiguity. Senator Larry Pressler stated, "I do not know what the terms 'cruel, inhuman and degrading' mean outside the U.S. Constitution."[58] State Department Legal Advisor Abraham Sofaer complained about the ambiguity of the term "degrading treatment."[59] He added that because the Constitution prohibits cruel and unusual punishment, interpreted by the courts as "the unnecessary and wanton infliction of pain,"[60] it "would prohibit *most (if not all)* of the practices covered in Article 16's reference to cruel, inhuman and degrading treatment or punishment" (emphasis added).[61] As a warning that Article 16 had too broad a sweep, Sofaer cited a recent ruling of the European Court of Human Rights that condemned the "death row phenomenon" as a form of inhuman or degrading treatment (even though a separate U.S. understanding exempted the death row phenomenon from the Convention's prohibitions).[62]

It is clear that the United States' objection to the ill-treatment prohibition was not its ambiguity but rather its breadth. The prohibition of "cruel, inhuman or degrading treatment or punishment" is no more ambiguous than U.S. constitutional provisions regarding liberty, due process, equal protection of the laws, and "cruel and unusual" punishment. Sofaer's objection to the term "degrading" (no more ambiguous than "cruel" or "inhuman") suggests a belief that degrading treatment should not always be off-limits. The dismissive response to the treaty text was regrettable. A dozen years after the United States refused to place an explicit prohibition on degrading treatment, U.S. officials in the "War on Terror" raised degrading treatment to an art form, humiliating prisoners by means such as forced nudity, sexual degradation, desecration of the Qur'an, leashing detainees, forcing them to defecate and urinate on themselves, dressing them in women's underwear, wrapping them in Israeli flags, and forcing them to perform dog tricks.

The accommodation of degrading treatment has deep roots in America's legal culture. In his magisterial comparison of American, French, and German criminal justice practices, James Whitman has argued that the stark transatlantic differences derive from an American conviction that punishment *should* be degrading and the equally strong European (or at least French and German) conviction that it must not be.[63] Even if (as Whitman himself argues) this difference has cultural sources deeper than any legal text, it nonetheless makes a big difference that the European commitment to dignified punishment is solemnized in a legal prohibition of "inhuman or degrading treatment or punishment" (art. 3 of the European Convention on Human Rights) that is now binding on 47 countries.

In the United States, there persists a widespread attitude that conditions of confinement not only may but should be degrading. Some prison officials boast openly of employing degrading measures. Inmates have been placed in tents in 110 degree heat, set in chain gangs, shackled, put in fetal restraints, housed naked in outdoor cages, forced to dance naked, and subjected to unnecessary body cavity searches.[64] Many prisoners endure overcrowding, filthy and unsanitary quarters, severely inadequate health care, continual threat of violence, and enforced inactivity.[65] Sexual violence by staff and other inmates is rampant.[66] Although U.S. case law makes clear that many of these abuses violate the Eighth Amendment, their persistence reveals the limits of the Amendment's protection in practice. Recurrent revelations of severe prison mistreatment arouse little protest. In James Forman's words, "We have allowed this sort of degradation and humiliation to become normal, acceptable, even inevitable. It has become the cost of doing business, a necessary incident to running such a large prison system full of incorrigibles."[67] This is in a country that, almost alone among Western democracies, preserves the death penalty, and that maintains the highest incarceration rate in the world.

Among the most merciless practices is the common use of solitary confinement, imposed on tens of thousands of American prisoners.[68] The suffering caused is so intense that some have called it torture.[69] Many of the most disturbing practices that have been used in Guantanamo Bay—confinement of inmates to their cells for twenty-three hours a day, deprivation of personal items, physically violent "extraction" of prisoners from their cells, indifference to mental illness caused or aggravated by such conditions—are in fact standard procedure at "supermax" facilities throughout the United States. Some American prisoners have been subjected to solitary confinement for over thirty years. We cannot understand the abuses of the "War on Terror" without grasping their connection to the pervasive cruelties of America's criminal justice system.[70] Courts have declined to rule that prolonged solitary confinement violates the Constitution.

The Eighth Amendment offers real protection. Some egregious abuses are investigated by the authorities and checked by the courts. In the 1960s and 1970s, state and federal courts ordered the comprehensive reform of a number of prison systems (mostly but not exclusively in the South) that had practiced torture, forced labor, and brutal overcrowding.[71] The Supreme Court recently ordered California to reduce overcrowding in its prison system from roughly 200 percent capacity to 137.5 percent capacity.[72] Yet the Supreme Court has set a high bar for prisoners claiming Eighth Amendment violations. Under current jurisprudence, prisoners claiming that they have been subjected to "cruel and unusual" punishment must demonstrate that responsible officials exhibit a "culpable state of mind."[73] Adverse treatment attributable to the "mere negligence" or "error in good faith" of prison officials does not qualify;[74] it must instead result from "deliberate indifference" (where prison conditions are concerned)[75] or "maliciously and sadistically" motivated conduct (where excessive force is concerned).[76] Human Rights Watch and the American Civil Liberties Union note that "this line of Eighth Amendment jurisprudence puts serious legal obstacles in the path of U.S. prisoners seeking to present claims under U.S. law," and that the international law prohibition of "cruel, inhuman or degrading treatment or punishment," canceled by the U.S. RUDs, offers "clearly stronger" protection.[77] Prisoners are also disadvantaged because the non-self-executing declaration attached to U.S. ratification of the ICCPR blocks judicial invocations of Article 10, which states that "all persons deprived of their liberty shall be treated with humanity and with respect for the inherent dignity of the human person." Since 1996, moreover, the Prison Litigation Reform Act has hindered the ability of prisoners to seek relief in federal courts.[78] One provision of the law bars prisoners from filing claim for "mental or emotional" injury unless a link to "physical injury" can be demonstrated (echoing the disparagement of mental suffering in the U.S. "understanding" altering the Torture Convention's definition of torture).

For the George W. Bush administration, the treaty reservation on ill-treatment was the gift that kept on giving. The government's attitude was captured in the candid summary of CIA lawyer Jonathan Fredman to Guantanamo interrogators: "The Torture Convention prohibits torture and cruel, inhumane and degrading treatment. The U.S. did not sign up to the second part, because of the 8th amendment (cruel and unusual punishment), but we did sign the part about torture. This gives us more license to use more controversial techniques."[79]

Administration lawyers derived various permissive arguments from Fifth and Eighth Amendment case law (setting aside the Fourteenth Amendment because it is directed to the states). One may criticize their reasoning on various grounds, but the crucial point is that because federal courts had never ruled (and still have not ruled) on the use of coercive interrogation methods to combat terrorism, administration lawyers had more room to maneuver. In Guantanamo, staff judge advocate Diane Beaver invoked several Supreme Court opinions to claim that techniques such as stress positions, death threats, and waterboarding did not violate the Eighth Amendment because they were used for a legitimate government objective and "not maliciously or sadistically for the very purpose of causing harm."[80] The government later deployed the simpler argument that the Eighth Amendment applies only to criminal punishment and that the Fifth Amendment does not extend to overseas aliens.[81] As a further argument that the Torture Convention's prohibition of ill-treatment does not restrict U.S. conduct overseas, the government read the Article 16 phrase "in any territory under its jurisdiction" as confining U.S. obligations to its own geographic territory.[82] (But note that this argument is not based on the treaty reservation.)

After a lengthy struggle, Congress in December 2005 overcame the concerted resistance of the Bush administration to pass the McCain Amendment, which prohibits the government from applying "cruel, inhuman, or degrading treatment or punishment" on any person in its custody, anywhere in the world. But legislators snatched defeat from the jaws of victory by adding (in the manner of the treaty reservation) that "the term 'cruel, inhuman, or degrading treatment or punishment' means the cruel, unusual, and inhumane treatment or punishment prohibited by the Fifth, Eighth, and Fourteenth Amendments to the Constitution of the United States." What is so reckless about this stipulation is that the Supreme Court *has never ruled* whether cruel, inhuman or degrading treatment (including torture) when used to gather intelligence in the name of national security is a violation of the Fifth, Eighth, and Fourteenth Amendments. One has to ask: If Congress wanted to ban cruel, inhuman, and degrading treatment, why didn't it ban cruel, inhuman, and degrading treatment? Why did it muddy the waters by applying a body of indirectly relevant Supreme Court jurisprudence?

The Bush administration was prepared for the McCain Amendment, because in a secret memo produced seven months earlier, OLC director Steven Bradbury had taken the precaution of arguing (in fifteen of the memo's forty single-spaced pages) that even if Fifth and Eighth Amendment standards were applied to U.S. conduct throughout the world, none of the enhanced interrogation techniques violated those standards.[83] As Bradbury noted, the Fifth Amendment right against self-incrimination only applies to the criminal justice context,[84] and the Supreme Court has ruled that the Eighth Amendment prohibition of "cruel and unusual" punishment refers only to *criminal* punishment.[85] More dubiously, he claimed that the enhanced inter-rogation techniques do not violate the Due Process Clause because, when used against a terrorist suspect in order to combat international terrorism, they do not "shock the conscience."[86] His reasoning contains grave distortions and omissions,[87] but could never have been launched in the first place if Congress had not hitched the ill-treatment ban to the Due Process Clause of the U.S. Constitution. Amnesty International captured the sinister logic of the administration's "shocks the conscience" argument:

> in contrast to the unequivocal and absolute international prohibition on torture or other ill-treatment, the door is opened to a sliding scale of legality in relation to acts that amount to such treatment against detainees viewed by their U.S. captors first and foremost as potential sources of intelligence. Under this paradigm, the higher the value that is placed on the information a detainee is claimed to possess, the more "enhanced" can be the interrogation techniques used against that in-dividual, and the less "conscience-shocking" the treatment will be held to be.[88]

By a weird alchemy, the ban on cruel, inhuman, and degrading treatment had been transformed, via Congress's insistence on filtering the ban through se-lected constitutional amendments, and the administration's creative applica-tion of the Fifth Amendment jurisprudence, into a "sliding scale" justification of torture.

To sum up, U.S. treaty reservations and understandings narrowing the definition of torture and ill-treatment helped Bush administration lawyers craft arguments that authorized the use of "enhanced interrogation tech-niques" constituting torture in all but name. Some of the arguments applying the treaty loopholes were contrived, though others were not. The loopholes lightened the justificatory burden and inspired new rationalizations for the torture memos' authors. And outside the "War on Terror," the loopholes have left prisoners and refugees more vulnerable to abuse.

Non-Self-Executing Declarations

Besides attaching reservations and understandings to its ratification of the ICCPR and Torture Convention, the United States declared that the sub-stantive articles of both treaties were not self-executing. This move was part of a larger policy to bar domestic judges from enforcing the ICCPR and to bar judges from enforcing the Torture Convention except at the margins. This policy of nonincorporation, as I shall call it, has weakened human rights in general, and is one of the factors that facilitated the U.S. adoption of torture after 9/11.

As the United States explained in its initial report to the Human Rights Committee, the international body that monitors state party compliance with the ICCPR, the non-self-executing declaration "did not limit the international obligations of the United States under the Covenant. Rather, it means that, as a matter of domestic law, the Covenant does not, by itself, create private rights directly enforceable in U.S. courts."[89] The United States explained its non-self-executing declaration regarding the Torture Convention in similar fashion.[90]

The United States also chose not to implement the substantive provisions of the ICCPR through Congressional legislation. As it explained to the Human Rights Committee,

> the fundamental rights and freedoms protected by the Covenant are already guaranteed as a matter of U.S. law, either by virtue of constitutional protections or enacted statutes, and can be effectively asserted and enforced by individuals in the judicial system on those bases. For this reason it was not considered necessary to adopt special implementing legislation to give effect to the Covenant's provisions in domestic law.[91]

In fact, some Covenant rights were *not* guaranteed by U.S. law. Wherever such gaps were to be found, the United States did not enact implementing legislation, as the above statement might lead one to expect, but instead adopted treaty reservations to withhold consent to the ICCPR's more generous provisions. The "logic" of the United States' position would appear to be: "We are already in compliance with the treaty, and therefore we do not need to bring our policies into compliance with the treaty."[92]

The United States also took the position that the ICCPR governs the conduct of states parties only within their respective territories.[93] It based this view on its reading of the Article 2 provision that "Each State Party to the present Covenant undertakes to respect and to ensure to all individuals within its territory and subject to its jurisdiction the rights recognized in the present Covenant." The Human Rights Committee and International Court of Justice (ICJ) have taken the contrary position that states parties are bound by the treaty also in relation to individuals under their power or jurisdiction outside national territory.[94] Scholars continue to debate the proper reading of Article 2.[95] Given the ambiguity of the Article 2 wording, the United States could have attached an understanding stating that the ICCPR governs the conduct of the United States outside its borders, or it could have adopted implementing legislation to that effect. It did neither. For a global power like the United States, the refusal to recognize the extraterritorial application of the ICCPR (under international no less than domestic law) has profound implications. The Bush administration would later invoke the customary U.S. interpretation to claim that the ICCPR gave the United States no obligation to constrain its behavior outside U.S. territory, including in Guantanamo.[96]

Congress has passed legislation implementing selected aspects of the Torture Convention. A 1998 law protects individuals from deportation to countries where they face a greater than 50 percent likelihood of being tortured. The 1991 Torture Victim Protection Act empowers victims of torture to bring civil actions in U.S. court, but only if the perpetrators are agents of foreign governments. The Torture Statute criminalizes torture outside but not inside the United States. Between October 2001 and October 2004, the Statute did not even criminalize torture by U.S. nationals in overseas U.S. military facilities, such as Guantanamo.[97] Explaining why it limited the Torture Statute to overseas acts, the United States stated that torture was already a criminal offense throughout U.S. territory.[98] Congress did not implement most of the treaty provisions relating to the prevention of torture (arts. 10–13 and 15), and its implementation of other provisions only addressed torture committed outside the United States or by agents of foreign governments. Notably, Congress did not pass implementing legislation that would allow individuals to sue U.S. officials responsible for torture, and the Torture Statute includes language stating that it cannot be used as the basis of civil proceedings.

For many years, Congress did not pass legislation implementing the Article 16 prohibition of ill-treatment, an omission that facilitated the administration's legal defense of enhanced interrogation techniques for use against terrorist suspects. Revelations of U.S. torture eventually led Congress to enact the December 2005 McCain Amendment prohibiting the infliction of cruel, inhuman, or degrading treatment or punishment on any person in U.S. custody.[99] The impact of this provision was limited, however, by simultaneous and subsequent legislation restricting the civil and criminal remedies available to foreign victims of U.S. ill-treatment, and (as we have seen) by the stipulation that "cruel, inhuman and degrading treatment or punishment" meant "the cruel, unusual, and inhumane treatment or punishment prohibited by the Fifth, Eighth, and Fourteenth Amendments."

The nonincorporation of the ICCPR and Torture Convention—the result of the non-self-executing declarations combined with little or no implementing legislation—has had profound consequences. First, lack of judicial enforceability gives the treaty obligations something of an ethereal existence, leaving many Americans uncertain whether international human rights law really is law. When not prevented from doing so, courts can play an important role in transmitting, teaching, and applying the law. U.S. human rights treaty obligations are largely excluded from the process of legal entrenchment that occurs by means of judicial litigation and enforcement. Consequently, they have not become part of our legal culture; neither legal, political and media elites nor ordinary citizens have internalized them.

Second, the nonincorporation policy removes an inducement to appropriately generous interpretations of our *constitutional* rights. While the Constitution forbids government brutality, the language of the relevant clauses is spare, and we depend on responsible constructions by humane judges to uphold their full meaning. That meaning is elaborated in the formulas of contemporary international human rights law that "no one shall be subjected to torture or to cruel, inhuman or degrading treatment or punishment," and that "all persons deprived of their liberty shall be treated with humanity and with respect for the inherent dignity of the human person." Judges used to applying these formulas would be steered toward the full meaning of the Constitution.[100] Because the framers were animated by a vision of natural or human rights, we should keep faith with their vision by reading the Constitution in the light of international human rights law.[101]

Third, the nonincorporation policy excludes from the body of judicially enforceable U.S. law the various procedural obligations under the Torture Convention (arts. 10–15)[102] designed to prevent the infliction of torture and ill-treatment at home and abroad. These include obligations to teach government and military personnel that torture and ill-treatment are illegal; to review interrogation, detention, and arrest practices with a view to preventing torture and ill-treatment; to ensure prompt and impartial investigation of credible reports of torture and ill-treatment; to guarantee that complaints of torture and ill-treatment are promptly and impartially investigated by competent authorities; to award fair and adequate compensation to victims of torture and ill-treatment; and to ensure that statements elicited by torture or ill-treatment will not be used in civil or criminal proceedings.

Fourth, the nonincorporation policy undermines the ability of torture and abuse victims to seek civil remedies in U.S. courts. Legislation implementing the Torture Convention carefully shielded U.S. officials from civil liability. While the Torture Statute creates criminal liability for torture committed outside U.S. territory, one great advantage of civil over criminal remedies in the U.S. legal system is that victims can initiate proceedings themselves, without waiting for the government to act. Obviously, President Bush's Department of Justice had no intention of prosecuting officials responsible for torture or abuse in the "War on Terror." By means of the interrogation memos, moreover, it constructed a "golden shield" to protect perpetrators from criminal proceedings under subsequent presidents. The effort has thus far succeeded: the Obama administration decided not to bring charges for abuses committed in the CIA interrogation program.[103] It is worth noting that only one person has ever been prosecuted under the Torture Statute: Charles "Chuckie" Taylor, convicted in 2008 of presiding over and participating in brutal torture in Liberia under the regime of his father, former president Charles Taylor.[104]

Torture victims in the "War on Terror" have been almost completely shut out of the U.S. legal system. At the urging of both the Bush and Obama administrations, courts have blocked every torture lawsuit against U.S. officials from going to trial. Victims denied justice include Maher Arar (extradited to torture in Syria), Jose Padilla (tortured in a South Carolina military prison), Khaled El-Masri (the German citizen sent to a CIA black site in Afghanistan in a case of mistaken identity), the family of Yaser Al-Zahrani (who claim their son died under torture in Guantanamo), and numerous other Guantanamo detainees.[105] Courts have ruled that the victims are not entitled to sue even if the allegations of torture (or homicide) are true, variously arguing that judges lack authority to review interrogation and rendition policies, that litigation would jeopardize state secrets, that the illegality of the alleged acts was not established at the time, that alleged enemy combatants are barred from filing torture lawsuits under the 2006 Military Commissions Act, or that the defendants acted "within the scope of their employment." An effort to sue private contractors for torture in Abu Ghraib and other U.S. prisons in Iraq was recently allowed to proceed after many years of judicial delay.[106] But when Binyam Mohamed and four other victims tried to sue a Boeing subsidiary for facilitating CIA extraordinary rendition flights sending them to torture, the suit was dismissed on state secrets grounds.[107]

The nonincorporation policy reflects and reinforces a general U.S. trend toward the expansion of presidential power and erosion of judicial oversight.[108] In matters deemed to affect national security, courts have invoked various doctrines (including sovereign immunity, state secrets, and the political question doctrine) to dismiss a large number of suits brought by victims of government abuse.[109] Presidents fighting judicial oversight are assisted by the nonjusticiability of human rights treaties. Victims cannot invoke the United States' obligation under the Torture Convention (art. 14) to ensure that victims have "an enforceable right to fair and adequate compensation, including the means for as full rehabilitation as possible" or the United States' obligation under the ICCPR (art. 2(3)) "to ensure that any person whose rights or freedoms as herein recognized are violated shall have an effective remedy, notwithstanding that the violation has been committed by persons acting in an official capacity." Although the United States is bound by these obligations, judges cannot enforce them. Thus are domestic checks and balances undermined by the circumvention of international human rights law.[110]

The absence of domestic case law on U.S. international human rights obligations is one factor among others that explains the OLC's free rein in the "War on Terror." Goldsmith notes that "most legal issues of executive branch conduct related to war and intelligence never reach a court, or do so only years after the executive has acted"; as a result, he claims, the OLC "is subject to few real rules to guide its actions."[111] In the national security realm, the OLC "has little or no oversight or public accountability."[112] The Justice Department Office of Professional Responsibility notes of the OLC that "many of its opinions will never be reviewed by a court or disclosed publicly and are made outside of an adversarial system where competing claims can be raised."[113] It is generally agreed that OLC opinions demonstrate proexecutive bias. Some defend this state of affairs by arguing that in a checks and balances system each branch's biased interpretation of its legal prerogatives leads via the adversarial process to a legally correct outcome.[114] The obvious problem with this argument is that owing to the sparseness of judicial oversight on matters of national security, the OLC largely operates outside the checks and balances system.

Unencumbered by judicial precedent addressing the international human rights obligations of the United States, the Bush administration made what looks like a decision to ignore its treaty obligations, though it never admitted doing so, and though it took the precaution of producing secret memos that argued that actions apparently in violation of those obligations were not what they seemed. If we ask why Bush administration lawyers advanced such implausible arguments, part of the answer is that they faced little constraint from past U.S. case law and little danger of judicial challenge in the future. The lawyers were well aware of this. In his May 30, 2005, memo arguing that waterboarding and other enhanced interrogation techniques did not violate the U.S. obligation under the Torture Convention to abstain from cruel, inhuman, or degrading treatment, OLC director Steven Bradbury noted that "we cannot predict with confidence that a court would agree with our conclusion," but added reassuringly that, because of the U.S. non-self-executing declaration, "the question whether the CIA's enhanced interrogation techniques violate the substantive standard of United States obligations under Article 16 is unlikely to be subject to judicial inquiry."[115]

The nonincorporation policy has produced some startling results. At Guantanamo, detainees facing military commission trials for terrorist acts were for some time prohibited from publicly discussing the torture they suffered at CIA black sites. When they objected that the gag order violated their rights under Articles 12 through 14 of the Torture Convention to submit complaints of torture, obtain prompt investigation of their complaints, and seek adequate compensation for their torture, Colonel James Pohl, the chief presiding officer for the military commissions, dismissed their plea on the grounds that the Senate had declared Articles 1–16 of the Convention not self-executing and that none of the relevant provisions had been legislatively implemented.[116] Recently, the gag has been largely lifted, though this was done at the prosecution's request.[117]

Congressional and Judicial Marginalization of International Human Rights Treaty Law

Congress and the courts have taken actions beyond the RUDs to marginalize international human rights treaty law. In the 2006 Military Commissions Act (MCA), Congress barred courts from enforcing rights provisions of the Geneva Conventions, and in the 2008 case of *Medellín v. Texas*, the Supreme Court raised potential new barriers to the judicial enforcement of human rights treaties. I now look at these developments.

The United States ratified the Geneva Conventions in 1955, decades before it came up with the idea of non-self-executing declarations. One question hovering over the post-9/11 torture litigation was the status of the Conventions in U.S. domestic law. If the Conventions were judicially enforceable, courts would be able to rule on the administration's claim that Taliban and Al Qaeda members possessed no rights under the Conventions to humane treatment.

When Salim Hamdan challenged the legality of his military commission trial in Guantanamo, courts divided over the justiciability of the Conventions. The district court ruled that they were justiciable,[118] while the D.C. Court of Appeals ruled that they were not (in a ruling joined by John Roberts shortly before President Bush nominated him to the Supreme Court).[119] The Supreme Court took no position on this question, reasoning that such a determination was unnecessary because the Conventions are incorporated in the Uniform Code of Military Justice (UCMJ).[120]

Article 21 of the UCMJ grants permission for military commissions that are authorized by statute or "by the law of war." These five magic words gave the Court the opening it needed to consult the Geneva Conventions, and thereby to overrule the administration's claim that Common Article 3 of the Convention (requiring humane treatment as well as fair trials) did not apply to members of Al Qaeda or the Taliban.[121] If Congress had not invoked the law of war in Article 21 of the UCMJ, and if Hamdan had not presented an opportunity to rule on the legality of military commissions, the Supreme Court might never have been able to clarify the meaning of the Geneva Conventions, and the government could continue declaring that the inhuman treatment of suspected Al Qaeda and Taliban members is permitted by international law. The story of the *Hamdan* case is a powerful reminder of the need to protect basic human rights through the domestic incorporation of international human rights obligations.

One purpose of the Military Commissions Act, passed by Congress at the administration's behest in October 2006, was to block the courts from ever again applying the Geneva Conventions in support of individual rights claims. The Act, which as we have seen immunized officials for various forms of inhumane treatment formerly punishable under the War Crimes Act and (in a provision later overturned by the Supreme Court) deprived "enemy combatants" of the right to habeas corpus, further stated that "the President has the authority for the United States to interpret the meaning and application of the Geneva Conventions,"[122] that "no person may invoke the Geneva Conventions . . . as a source of rights in any court of the United States or its States or territories,"[123] and that "no foreign or international source of law shall supply a basis for a rule of decision . . . in interpreting" grave breaches of Common Article 3.[124] Had these provisions been enacted a year earlier, the

Supreme Court would have been statutorily barred from issuing the *Hamdan* decision. The 2006 MCA was revenge for *Hamdan* in more than one sense. At the time *Hamdan* was handed down, the points of access to international human rights and humanitarian law were few and precarious. They have been dramatically reduced since then.[125]

The 2006 MCA gave the president exclusive authority to interpret the requirements of Common Article 3, an authority Bradbury used in his July 20, 2007, memo to claim that techniques such as 1,000-calorie-a-day diets, prolonged sleep deprivation, shackling, slapping, and diapering did not violate the Common Article 3 prohibition of cruel or inhumane treatment, "outrages on personal dignity," and "humiliating and degrading treatment." On the same day that Bradbury signed his memo, President Bush issued an executive order that set out in general terms the meaning of Common Article 3 as applied to the CIA interrogation program. In a familiar maneuver, he used the pretense of *clarifying* U.S. international obligations for the actual purpose of *narrowing* them. The Common Article 3 prohibition of "outrages upon human dignity, in particular humiliating and degrading treatment" was rendered as a prohibition of

> willful and outrageous acts of personal abuse done for the purpose of humiliating or degrading the individual in a manner so serious that any reasonable person, considering the circumstances, would deem the acts to be beyond the bounds of human decency, such as sexual or sexually indecent acts undertaken for the purpose of humiliation, forcing the individual to perform sexual acts or to pose sexually, threatening the individual with sexual mutilation, or using the individual as a human shield; [and a prohibition of] acts intended to denigrate the religion, religious practices, or religious objects of the individual.[126]

President Obama rescinded this order (and Bradbury's companion memo) in his first days of office. It remains to be seen how future presidents will interpret Common Article 3.

The 2006 MCA thus functioned as a belated non-self-executing declaration for the Geneva Conventions. In the 2008 case of *Medellín v. Texas*,[127] the Supreme Court raised a potential new obstacle to the judicial enforcement of human rights treaties. José Ernesto Medellín, a Mexican national convicted and sentenced to death for the rape and murder of two teenage girls, had not been informed by Texas authorities of his right to inform Mexican consular officials of his detention, a right established in the Vienna Convention on Consular Relations, which the United States had ratified along with the Convention's Optional Protocol in 1969. Under the Optional Protocol, the United States accepted the compulsory jurisdiction of the International Court of Justice (ICJ) in interstate disputes arising from the Convention, and in 2004 the ICJ ruled, in a case brought by Mexico, that Medellín was entitled to review and reconsideration of his case in light of the treaty violation. Given the United States' ratification of the Optional Protocol and the Supremacy Clause of the U.S. Constitution, several scholars believed that U.S. courts were clearly authorized to enforce the ICJ ruling. However, the Supreme Court ruled that the relevant treaty provisions were not self-executing, because they were not intended to have "domestic legal effect" in the absence of implementing legislation. The ruling was highly controversial,[128] but it may be construed by lower courts (and future majorities on the Supreme Court) as a message that international treaties should be presumed to be non-self-executing unless their terms clearly indicate otherwise.[129] Medellín was put to death a few months after the Supreme Court decision.

After *Medellín*, Congress might still choose to authorize judicial enforcement of human rights treaties by enacting implementing legislation. However, some judges are now placing in doubt Congress' power to do so. In the 2014 case of *Bond v. United States*, Justice Scalia wrote a concurring opinion, joined by Justices Thomas and Alito, claiming that Congress may not enact treaty-implementing legislation on matters otherwise reserved to the states. This position, if adopted by the majority of the Court, could prevent Congress from requiring states to comply with international human rights treaties. Although the Fourteenth Amendment authorizes Congress to pass legislation requiring states to respect rights to life, liberty, and property and to uphold equal protection of the laws, the Supreme Court ruled in *City of Boerne v. Flores* (1997) that Congress must limit such legislation to the Supreme Court's previous interpretation of those rights.[130] The three concurring justices in *Bond* made clear that in their view congressional legislation applying human rights treaties to the states would violate the Constitution.[131] The same justices went even further in a concurring opinion by Justice Thomas that implied that human rights treaties are constitutionally invalid (and therefore binding neither on federal nor state officials), because "the Treaty Power can be used to arrange intercourse with other nations, but not to regulate purely domestic affairs."[132] This startling position, though not presently commanding a majority of the court, signals potential dangers ahead. It is psychologically facilitated (though not legally justified) by the absence of international human rights law in American jurisprudence, an absence that was the intended result of actions taken by the executive, legislative, and judicial branches over several decades.

Having discussed the marginalization of international human rights treaties, whether by "reservations, understandings, and declarations" or by separate congressional and judicial action, I shall now examine two additional features of the American self-exemption policy that facilitated the U.S. use of torture after 9/11: (1) executive and judicial doctrine limiting the authority of customary international law, and (2) the U.S. decision not to join the International Criminal Court.

The U.S. Self-Exemption Policy and Its Consequences: Customary International Law

Customary international law (CIL) "results from a general and consistent practice of states followed by them from a sense of legal obligation."[133] Treaty and custom are the two primary (but not exclusive) sources of international law.[134]

CIL forms a substantial part of international human rights law and international humanitarian law. As we have seen, it establishes a universal prohibition of torture and ill-treatment, and this prohibition is not subject to any of the gaps that Bush administration lawyers claimed to find in treaty law.[135] As a federal appeals court stated in the 1980 case of *Filártiga v. Peña-Irala*, "the torturer has become like the pirate and slave trader before him *hostis humani generis*, an enemy of all mankind."[136] In a classic example of CIL reasoning, the *Filártiga* court drew this conclusion from numerous official sources: the UN Charter; the Universal Declaration of Human Rights; the 1975 UN Declaration on Torture and Other Cruel, Inhuman or Degrading Treatment or Punishment (which like the UDHR was adopted without dissent by the UN General Assembly); numerous international treaties; the universal rejection of torture in domestic law; its prohibition in over fifty-five national constitutions; and the absence of assertions "by any contemporaneous state of a right to torture its own or another nation's citizens."

The nation's founders venerated CIL, then referred to as "the law of nations." Edwin Dickinson observes: "With the achievement of independence, there was as little doubt among men of legal learning in America as in England that the Law of Nations was adopted in its full extent as part of the law of the land and that it was the responsibility of courts to apply it like any other law when the appropriate case was presented."[137] The Constitution grants Congress the power to define and punish "offenses against the law of nations," and the first Congress gave federal district courts original jurisdiction over civil actions by aliens for torts committed "in violation of the law of nations or a treaty of the United States." The assumption that U.S. courts would have authority to enforce the law of nations is explicit in Jay's and Hamilton's contributions to *The Federalist*.[138] In the nation's early years, the Supreme Court often applied the law of nations in its rulings, sometimes even in domestic disputes, and affirmed that the law of nations is "part of the law of the land."[139] In *Murray v. The Charming Betsy* (1804), it established the doctrine, still in effect, that whenever possible congressional statutes should be interpreted so as not to violate the law of nations.[140]

The Bush administration's enhanced interrogation techniques were an obvious violation of CIL. The OLC dealt with this problem by declaring in a January 9, 2002, memo written by John Yoo and Robert Delahunty that "customary international law cannot bind the executive branch under the Constitution."[141] In consequence, CIL was ignored in all the interrogation memos to follow. The legal determination was crucial, because it allowed the OLC to rely on alleged gaps in the coverage of the treaty-based prohibition of torture and ill-treatment and to ignore the plentiful CIL sources on the meaning of torture and cruel, inhuman, or degrading treatment. As José Alvarez writes,

> This dismissal of non-treaty sources allows the memoranda's authors to ignore considerable evidence of what constitutes torture as well as degrading treatment under customary law that is at odds with their restrictive interpretation of the "plain meaning" of the Torture Convention. It means that these memoranda dismiss the Universal Declaration of Human Rights, relevant General Assembly resolutions, and influential treaties that the United States has not ratified such as the American Convention on Human Rights or the First Additional Protocol to the Geneva Conventions, as simply "not binding on the United States" and only "instruments [that] may inform the views of other nations."[142]

The OLC's dismissal of CIL earned the forceful protest of State

Department legal advisor William H. Taft IV, and was soundly condemned by several scholars.[143] But it is less novel than one might think. In the leading contemporary case, the Eleventh Circuit Court of Appeals ruled in *Garcia-Mir v. Meese* (1986) that under U.S. law a policy decision by the president or a cabinet-level official is sufficient to override CIL.[144] In a 1989 opinion, never since withdrawn, the OLC used *Garcia-Mir* to support its finding that the executive branch has the authority under U.S. law to override CIL.[145] The OLC opinion appeared not to regard CIL as a source of legal obligation, treating its observance as a "political issue rather than a legal one."[146] The opinion was prominently invoked in the Yoo-Delahunty Memo's claim that CIL did not constrain the president's policies regarding Al Qaeda and Taliban detainees.

Legal scholars in the New Sovereigntist movement have waged a concerted campaign against CIL, with increasing support from the courts. The seminal work is a 1997 *Harvard Law Review* article by Curtis Bradley and Jack Goldsmith, prominently cited in the Yoo-Delahunty Memo.[147] Bradley and Goldsmith argue that CIL is not federal law and that because of this it may not be enforced by the courts; they argue further that the president has the domestic legal authority to violate CIL.[148] The authors, though dutifully stating that CIL is binding on the international plane, do not regard this as a source of strong legal obligation, for they state that in their view the executive branch and Congress "would have the primary role in deciding *when* and how the United States carried out its international obligations" (emphasis added).[149]

Bradley and Goldsmith's arguments sweep more broadly than their ostensible conclusions. Beyond challenging the justiciability of CIL in U.S. courts, the authors question its legitimacy as law:

> the modern position that CIL is federal common law is in tension with basic notions of American representative democracy. When a federal court applies CIL as federal common law, it is not applying law generated by U.S. lawmaking processes. Rather, it is applying law derived from the views and practices of the international community. The foreign governments and other non-U.S. participants in this process "are neither representative of the American political community nor responsive to it."[150]

If courts should not apply CIL because of its allegedly undemocratic character, then presumably no one else should either; CIL (on this logic) should not be recognized as law binding on the United States. The authors note with disapproval that "under modern conceptions of CIL, CIL rules may be created *and bind the United States* without any express support for the rules from the U.S. political branches" (emphasis added).[151] In 2007, Goldsmith explained that his scholarship "decried developments in 'customary international law' that purported to bind the United States to international rules to which the nation's political leaders had not consented."[152] Bradley and Goldsmith's "democratic" critique of CIL, ostensibly limited to the justiciability of CIL but directed to CIL itself, is echoed in the climax of Justice Scalia's concurring opinion in *Sosa v. Alvarez-Machain* (2004):

> We Americans have a method for making the laws that are over us. We elect representatives to two Houses of Congress, each of which must enact the new law and present it for the approval of a President, whom we also elect. For over two decades now, unelected federal judges have been usurping this lawmaking power by converting what they regard as norms of international law into American law.... American law—the law made by the people's democratically elected representatives—does not recognize a category of activity that is so universally disapproved by other nations that it is automatically unlawful here, and automatically gives rise to a private action for money damages in federal court.[153]

The logic that underlies Scalia's words is breathtakingly radical, for it implies that the United States need not and indeed should not recognize any law but its own—that it should not recognize any international *legal* constraint on its behavior at home or abroad. If the United States were to embark on aggressive, predatory, or otherwise outrageous conduct—if, for example, Congress or the president considered (and an amended Constitution permitted) the formation of raiding parties to harvest human organs in foreign countries—no international law (on this view) should legally inhibit it. (In *Sosa*, the Supreme Court blocked the lawsuit of a Mexican citizen who argued that U.S. government agents violated CIL when they abducted him on Mexican soil without the consent of the Mexican government in order to have him stand trial in a U.S. court.) Scalia implicitly denies the right of the international community to create binding rules necessary for peace, justice, and the common good.

The doctrine that customary international law is not part of U.S. law may be gaining ground in the courts. In *Hamdi v. Rumsfeld* (2004), Justice O'Connor applied international law of war principles to limit the president's detention authority in the "War on Terror." However, Judge Janice Rogers Brown, writing for a three-judge panel of the D.C. Circuit Court of Appeals in *Al-Bihani v. Obama* (2010), held that the international laws of war "are not a source of authority for U.S. courts."[154] When Al-Bihani petitioned for en banc review, the Obama administration dissociated itself from Judge Brown's holding about international law,[155] and seven of nine judges voted against a rehearing, explaining that discussion of the international law question was unnecessary to dispose of the merits of the case.[156] Their statement appears to cancel the precedential value of Judge Brown's holding, but she continued to insist it had "binding authority,"[157] and she was supported by a lengthy opinion from Judge Brett Kavanaugh arguing that customary international law norms "are not part of domestic U.S. law."[158] This view is contradicted by the Supreme Court's 2004 observation in *Sosa* that "For two centuries we have affirmed that the domestic law of the United States recognizes the law of nations." Kavanaugh invoked the argument made in Bradley and Goldsmith's 1997 article but rejected by the *Sosa* majority that the 1938 case of *Erie Railroad Co. v. Tompkins* had the effect of displacing the law of nations from U.S. domestic law.[159] James Pohl, the chief presiding officer for the military commissions in Guantanamo Bay, relied on Kavanaugh's opinion when announcing that he would not apply customary international law norms, including the *jus cogens* prohibition of torture. He used this argument to dismiss claims by detainees that the government order forbidding them to publicly discuss their torture by U.S. officials was a violation of *jus cogens*.[160]

Nonratification of the International Criminal Court Treaty

"What unites many countries in the world," Charles Simic writes, "both the ones that don't give a fig about human rights and the ones that profess they do, is their unwillingness to punish their war criminals."[161] Recognition of this problem was the main impetus for the creation of an International Criminal Court, empowered to prosecute individuals responsible for war crimes, crimes against humanity, and genocide.[162] The ICC rests on the principle that atrocities are properly prosecuted by the governments whose officials perpetrate them or on whose territories they take place. Only if those governments fail to take action will the ICC launch judicial proceedings. The hope is that governments, fearing ICC intervention, will enforce their own criminal laws, and that would-be perpetrators, aware of this fact, will abstain from committing crimes in the first place.

The Rome Statute of the International Criminal Court was opened for signature July 17, 1998, and came into force July 1, 2002. A total of 123 countries have ratified the Rome Statute, and several of them have incorporated its provisions into domestic law, empowering national courts to prosecute ICC crimes. Torture and ill-treatment are crimes under the Rome Statute. In armed conflicts of an international character, war crimes include torture, inhuman treatment, and "willfully causing great suffering" when inflicted on persons protected by the Geneva Conventions (art. 8(2)(a)(ii) and (iii)), and "outrages upon personal dignity, in particular humiliating and degrading treatment," whether or not the victims are protected by the Geneva Conventions (art. 8(2)(b)(xxi)). In armed conflicts of a non-international character, war crimes include torture, cruel treatment, and "outrages upon personal dignity, in particular humiliating and degrading treatment" (art. 8(2)(c)(i) and (ii)). Crimes against humanity include torture, rape, and "other inhumane acts of a similar character intentionally causing great suffering, or serious injury to body or to mental or physical health" when they are "committed as part of a widespread or systematic attack directed against any civilian population" (art. 7(1) and 7(1)(f), (g), and (k)).

The United States has not ratified the Rome Statute, much less incorporated its provisions into domestic law. President Clinton signed the Statute in December 2000, but stated that his successor should not ratify the treaty until "fundamental concerns" were satisfied. In May 2002, the Bush administration announced that it had no intention to seek ratification, a declaration commonly described as "unsigning," because it freed the United States, under Article 18 of the Vienna Convention on the Law of Treaties, to act contrary to the object and purpose of the ICC. In explaining its action, the Bush administration emphasized the danger of politicized prosecutions, but made no objections to the substantive law of the Rome Statute. It asserted that the United States would continue to support "accountability for war crimes and other serious violations of international humanitarian law" and that "the armed forces of the United States will obey the law of war, while our international policies are and will remain completely consistent with these norms."[163]

In fact, nonratification and nonincorporation of the Rome Statute would prove crucial to the Bush administration torture policy, because the Rome Statute refuses to recognize the various legal loopholes the United States carved out with respect to its treatment of "War on Terror" detainees. As we have seen, the Bush administration determined that torturing such detainees would not violate the War Crimes Act, because the detainees neither enjoyed the status of protected persons under the Geneva Conventions nor were covered by Common Article 3. When the Supreme Court ruled in *Hamdan* (2006) that Al Qaeda detainees were indeed covered by Common Article 3, Congress responded by using the 2006 Military Commissions Act to amend the War Crimes Act so that "outrages upon personal dignity" were no longer included, "torture" was defined by the narrow terms of the U.S. Torture Statute, and the meaning of "cruel or inhuman treatment" was limited to the most extreme acts. The 2005 McCain Amendment, though it banned ill-treatment abroad, appended no criminal penalty, and in fact extended criminal and civil immunity for detention and interrogation practices "that were officially authorized and determined to be lawful at the time they were committed," so long as the agent "did not know" and "a person of ordinary sense and understanding would not know" that "the practices were unlawful."

These maneuvers occurred far from the shadow of international criminal law. They are incompatible with the Rome Statute, which does not adopt the United States' eccentrically narrow definition of torture and "cruel or inhuman treatment," criminalizes outrages upon human dignity in all international and non-international armed conflicts, and bars numerous fanciful arguments made in the Bush administration interrogation memos.[164]

Contrasts with Europe

In Chapter 3, I argued that international human rights institutions in Europe have prevented much torture and ill-treatment that would otherwise have occurred. In the past two chapters, I have argued that the marginalization of international human rights law by the United States facilitated much torture and ill-treatment that otherwise might *not* have occurred. I make no attempt to draw a global comparison of the extent or gravity of torture and ill-treatment in the United States versus Europe. Instead I have looked at each case separately, to try to observe the effects resulting from the presence or absence of a meaningful international human rights regime.

Four differences are worth emphasizing. Unlike the United States, Europe (1) abstained from adding loopholes to the international legal prohibition of torture and ill-treatment; (2) established judicial oversight of its international human rights commitments at both the international and domestic levels; (3) adopted an international inspection regime to monitor compliance with the international prohibition of torture and ill-treatment; and (4) committed itself firmly to the criminalization of torture and other war crimes.

Loopholes

None of the 47 states parties to the European Convention on Human Rights (ECHR) attached a reservation or understanding to the Article 3 prohibition of torture or inhuman or degrading treatment or punishment. Nor has any European country attached reservations or understandings to the nearly identical Article 7 of the ICCPR, or attached reservations and understandings to the Torture Convention comparable in significance to those attached by the United States. In effect, Europe and the United States adopted different laws. In Europe, therefore, we have not seen elaborate efforts to reclassify torture as "psychological techniques," nor efforts to brush aside the prohibition of inhuman or degrading treatment, nor creative arguments to ignore the non-derogable character of the prohibition of torture and ill-treatment, enshrined in Article 15 of the European Convention, Article 4 of the ICCPR, and Article 2 of the Torture Convention. The 1978 affirmation in *Ireland v. UK* that the non-derogable prohibition of ill-treatment including torture applies even in the struggle against terrorism remains a bedrock of European law.

This is not to deny that European states have sometimes devised legal arguments that seek to circumvent or even chip away at the international legal prohibition of torture and ill-treatment. The UK has tried to loosen the prohibition against the deportation of individuals to countries where they face a real risk of torture or ill-treatment. Though the European Court of Human Rights unanimously rejected the UK position in *Saadi v. Italy* (2006), it may have tacitly ceded some ground in *Ahmad and Others v. UK* (2012) (see Chapter 3).[165] To evade the prohibition, some European governments have invoked "diplomatic assurances" by the receiving country that the deported individual will not be subjected to ill-treatment, notwithstanding notorious patterns of torture in the countries concerned. The European Court of Human Rights has generally taken a firm line against this tactic, but has not succeeded in stamping out the practice.[166] European governments have often used various legal arguments to impede civil and criminal prosecution of officials associated with the U.S. torture program.[167] Though European countries have not succeeded in creating anything like U.S.-style loopholes, the abovementioned practices demonstrate the need for continued vigilance.

Judicial Oversight

Because the ECHR places member states under the compulsory jurisdiction of the European Court of Human Rights and because the ECHR is now incorporated into the domestic law of all member states (though in some cases incorporation is more nominal than real), judicial oversight of international human rights commitments is established at both the international and national level.[168] The scene in the United States is altogether different. Compliance with the ICCPR and Torture Convention, as spelled out in the treaty texts, is overseen by two part-time committees, the Human Rights Committee and the Committee Against Torture, whose views are not legally binding. The United States did not accept the optional provisions granting individuals the right to submit complaints to the committees. It accepted the provisions permitting inter-state complaints, but there has not been a single inter-state complaint in the forty-year history of the UN-based human rights treaty system. This reduces the committees' role to that of questioning and commenting on the U.S. periodic reports on national compliance (theoretically due every five years, but often delayed). The committees have voiced increasingly stern criticisms, which the United States has felt free to reject. Nor does the United States view itself bound by the general comments periodically issued by the committees on general questions of treaty interpretation. And as we have seen, the United States has precluded oversight of its international human rights commitments by domestic courts. Because the human rights treaties enshrine the right to a remedy for the violation of one's rights, the U.S. self-exemption policy has weakened the ability of human rights victims to seek justice not only under international but also under domestic constitutional and statutory law.

A striking manifestation of the lack of judicial oversight in the United States is the fact that every lawsuit brought against U.S. officials for employing torture or extraordinary rendition in the "War on Terror" has been blocked from going to trial. Though Khaled El-Masri, Al Nashiri, and Abu Zubaydah were tortured by the United States, it was only in Europe that they could seek and obtain civil remedies (see Chapter 3). It was European, not American, judges who affirmed that "enhanced interrogation techniques" are torture, that U.S. officials broke the law by subjecting these men to torture and extraordinary rendition, that torture and ill-treatment are forbidden under all circumstances, that governments are legally obligated to investigate and prosecute torture and ill-treatment, and that extraordinary rendition is forbidden "as anathema to the rule of law." The absence of a U.S. counterpart to the *El-Masri*, *Al Nashiri*, and *Abu Zubaydah* rulings is as startling as it is significant.

International Inspection

In Chapter 3, we examined the regional monitoring regime established by the European Convention for the Prevention of Torture and Inhuman or Degrading Treatment or Punishment. Unlike Europe, the United States has not welcomed international inspection of its detention practices. It has neither signed nor ratified the Optional Protocol to the Torture Convention. (Most European countries have ratified the Optional Protocol in addition to the European Convention for the Prevention of Torture.) Judicial oversight of prison conditions was weakened by the 1996 Prison Litigation Reform Act. The Bush administration did not act on the blistering reports by the International Committee of the Red Cross (ICRC) on the ill-treatment, including torture, of prisoners in Guantanamo Bay, Iraq, and Afghanistan. It moreover adopted various stratagems to conceal its most brutal practices from the ICRC, and kept some detainees, the so-called "ghost prisoners," entirely hidden. (Shortly after assuming office, President Obama guaranteed ICRC access to all detainees in U.S. military custody.)

Criminalization

The 123 countries that have ratified the ICC Treaty include all 28 EU member states and 40 of the 47 countries in the Council of Europe. Several of these countries have incorporated its provisions into national law. Participation in the ICC system rendered impossible the kind of creative redefinition of international criminal law and international humanitarian law found in the Bush administration's interrogation memos and executive orders and enshrined in U.S. law by the 2006 Military Commissions Act. The torture memos reveal both that U.S. officials were highly motivated to avoid prosecution and that the specter of prosecution could be dispelled. The memos and the 2006 MCA accomplished their intended purpose of furnishing a "golden shield" to those implicated in the controversial techniques. When the Department of Justice under Obama announced a "preliminary review" to consider criminal investigation into Bush-era abuses, it excluded actions that complied with the memos' legal advice. None of the architects of the torture program have been the subject of U.S. criminal investigation, much less prosecution.

Conclusion

The incorporation of international human rights obligations into U.S. domestic law would contribute significantly to the prevention of torture. I do not claim that international human rights law is a panacea. Determined resistance by powerful officials can defeat any legal system, however well designed. Moreover, the protection afforded by international human rights law against torture is incomplete, sometimes because of gaps and sometimes because of generally worded obligations that require further specification. For example, the ICCPR obligates member states to institute adequate civil remedies for human rights violations, but leaves open the precise means of implementing such remedies, no doubt to accommodate the varying legal systems of different countries. The United States should strengthen national protections of human rights in ways that go beyond the requirements of international law. The ideal is a process of "circular reinforcement" in which national and international institutions prod each other toward improved protection of human rights.[169]

That said, the incorporation of international human rights law is a necessary step, and a substantial one. The traditional justification for not taking this step is that human rights already enjoy full protection under U.S. law. The post 9/11 torture policy of the U.S. government exposes the fallacy of this argument. As I have argued, the Bush administration would have found it significantly more difficult to institute a policy of torture if the United States had not previously loosened the restraints of international human rights law.

Since to a large extent international human rights law recapitulates promises found in the U.S. Constitution, it may strike some people as redundant. But it is a mistake to believe that because international human rights law is redundant it is also unnecessary. Human rights require multiple, overlapping protections. Against the power of the state, individuals need all the protection they can get. Additional rights guarantees are not mere exercises in repetition, but strengthen the protections that already exist. The United States, its individual rights tradition notwithstanding, can benefit from the incorporation of international human rights law.

Americans generally take great pride in their legal system, believing that it surpasses others in shielding individual liberties from governmental abuse. But pride in our legal institutions has turned into a trap, blocking the adoption of needed reforms. Recent events prove that the U.S. legal system has permitted widespread and systematic human rights abuses, and in fact genuine atrocities. We need international human rights law to reinforce, supplement, and complete the rights promised in our Constitution.

Humility, not pride, is the principle of constitutional government. Recognition of our limitations counsels adoption of checks and balances, a system of mutual oversight to guard against moral error. Madison noted the "many errors and follies" that America would have avoided "if the justice and propriety of her measures had, in every instance, been previously tried by the light in which they would probably appear to the unbiased part of mankind" (*Fed.* 63, p. 369). His argument for domestic checks and balances extends to the transnational sphere. American exceptionalism is a betrayal of human rights and a betrayal of the Founders' constitutional vision. The United States is not so pure that it can place itself above international human rights law. These lessons, though seemingly obvious, have not been absorbed.

Chapter 6

The Democratic Legitimacy of International Human Rights Law

International human rights law is sometimes criticized as antidemocratic. The complaint is that it improperly limits the public policies that the people might otherwise choose to adopt—it restricts the people's will. The democracy objection (as I shall call it) is a staple of New Sovereigntist discourse, but it receives a sympathetic hearing in many quarters, on the left as well as on the right.[1]

The objection rests on two broad arguments, not always distinguished. The first is that international human rights law is insufficiently responsive to popular opinion. Critics charge that the treaty-drafting process is cut off from the input of ordinary citizens and that too much power is placed in the hands of international judges. They also lament the indeterminate character of customary international law, which, they argue, leaves too much discretion to judges and too much influence to legal scholars. In sum, international human rights law is said to bypass the democratic processes that, at least ideally, guide the formation of domestic law.

Whether and to what extent international human rights law excludes popular input is a matter for debate. As Oona Hathaway points out, the ratification of treaties in most countries follows a procedural path similar to that of domestic legislation,[2] so popular control over the adoption of treaty law varies according to the democratic attributes of individual states.[3] International courts owe their authority to treaties, and thus (at least in democratic countries) to the consent of the people's representatives.[4] Customary international law rests ultimately on the practices and statements of public officials, who, in democracies, owe their position to the democratic process.

A second argument for the democracy objection, however, is invulnerable to such observations. This is the belief that the nation-state is the necessary locus of democracy. International human rights law allows outsiders to participate in decisions that (on this view) should be left only to us, members of the nation-state. The problem, therefore, resides in the very premise of international human rights law: the idea of a supranational human rights legal code that can be applied across national jurisdictions and should constrain national laws and policies. In the critics' view, this idea is a standing affront to the democratic right of nation-states to choose their own laws and policies.

These two arguments, woven together, find expression in a 2004 article by Yale Law School professor Jed Rubenfeld. "The entire contemporary discourse of 'international human rights,'" he writes, "is predicated on the idea that there exists an identifiable body of universal law, everywhere binding, requiring no democratic provenance. In this sense, contemporary international law is deeply antidemocratic."[5] Kenneth Anderson, a law professor at American University, finds in international human rights law a lack of popular consent and democratic legitimacy and asks rhetorically, "We count democratic legitimacy to be the *sine qua non* of legitimacy of the sovereign national state, but why, I wonder, do we suddenly jettison it when it comes to the international system[?]"[6] He describes the effort to empower international human rights law as "international legal imperialism," because it seeks "the establishment of an international system that is genuinely constitutionally supreme with respect to both nation states and the people that, in the best of cases, they democratically represent."[7]

In this chapter I defend international human rights law against the democracy objection.[8] International human rights law is not antidemocratic, I argue, because it leaves ample room for popular government. The policies it bars are policies that governments should not consider anyway, so their removal from legislative consideration represents no loss for democracy. There is no "democratic" right for legislatures to enact or even consider policies that violate human rights. The only democracy worthy of the name is constitutional democracy, in which popular government is limited by human rights. International human rights law, by upholding this limit, bolsters democracy. (Note that my argument applies only to international human rights law, not to international law in general.)

Exponents of the democracy objection, aware of this argument, typically respond that it ignores the problem of disagreement. There is no use saying that human rights should limit popular government, they claim, if people disagree about the meaning of human rights. Such disagreement should be settled by the people, through the procedures that define popular government. This usually means the legislative process of democratic states, though we might recommend various reforms to make the legislative process more reflective of the popular will.

Because of this rejoinder, I address the heart of my discussion to the problem of disagreement. I do not deny disagreement about human rights, nor that it is a problem. But I argue that the fact of disagreement is not a reason to reject international human rights law. The constitutionalization of human rights through domestic and international law, backed by judicial review, offers the best known method for responding to disagreements about human rights.

The democracy objection vis-à-vis international human rights law recalls familiar criticisms of judicial review, which I shall define as the judicial correction of legislative and executive conduct deemed to violate constitutionally mandated human rights.[9] In both cases, the complaint is that the popular will is thwarted, because certain important decisions are placed outside the ordinary legislative process.[10] (Even when judicial constitutional review is applied to the executive rather than the legislature, the complaint is that courts act without the legislature's bidding.)[11] Though some critics of international human rights law do not extend their objections to domestic judicial review,[12] the arguments against both institutions are often similar.[13] In this chapter I seek to defend both institutions against the charge of being antidemocratic.

Let us use the term "political constitutionalism" for the view that international human rights law and constitutional bills of rights should not limit the decision-making power of elected legislatures.[14] The underlying problem with this view is that it grants human rights insufficient priority. Scholars have documented the role of courts in curbing some of the worst legislative and executive abuses in the "War on Terror." Fiona de Londras concludes in her study of the UK and the United States:

> no other organ of the state than the judiciary has shown itself to be better at insisting upon a rights-protecting balance being struck in relation to counter-terrorist detention in the context of the terrorism-related crisis that has prevailed since the autumn of 2001 and to which no end is yet in sight. The executives in the US and the UK have advocated extremely repressive laws and policies and, to bolster the case, created "folk devils" in this endeavor; the legislatures, forced by *Realpolitik* not

to "endanger security," have largely facilitated the executive's desired actions; and "the people" have supported politicians and administrations that have pursued repressive approaches.[15]

Jonathan Hafetz concludes in his study of the United States:

> The most significant resistance to extrajudicial detention, military commissions, and abusive interrogations came from the courts. Congress, after finally awakening from its post-9/11 slumber, repeatedly showed its willingness to ratify if not expand on the sweeping claims of executive power asserted by President Bush and to deprive the courts of any meaningful role. . . . The federal judiciary remained the one branch in which law and facts mattered, even if they did not matter enough, in which the incarceration of human beings was not reduced to sloganeering or partisan gamesmanship, and in which decisions could be rendered with at least some immunity from the fear, hysteria, and irrationality that had so thoroughly infected the public debate over national security.[16]

By eliminating judicial oversight of human rights obligations enshrined in constitutional and international law, political constitutionalism endangers human rights.

Human rights require a form of legal entrenchment deeper than legislative statute. Consider the absolute prohibition of torture. Political constitutionalists might argue that legislatures can be depended on to uphold this prohibition. This seems doubtful, as indicated by loopholes in the 1994 U.S. Torture Statute and 2006 U.S. Military Commissions Act, and by post-9/11 attempts of the UK government to chip away at Article 3 of the European Convention of Human Rights. But imagine for the sake of argument that a legislature empowered to rescind the absolute prohibition of torture would never in fact do so. In that case, we should still say that the right not to be tortured deserves something more. Legislators should be *legally forbidden* to rescind the absolute prohibition of torture. A just political community is one that permanently renounces such a power. The absolute prohibition of torture is a higher law, and its status as higher law should be recognized in law.

There is nothing antidemocratic about this position, or so I intend to show in the following discussion. I shall first argue that we find a strong basis in linguistic usage, constitutional tradition, and political theory for a conception of democracy with a built-in commitment to human rights. I shall then argue that this is the conception of democracy that we ought, morally, to adopt. I am especially interested in showing that persistent disagreement about human rights is no reason for rejecting either international human rights law or judicial review.

The Harmony of Human Rights and Democracy

My argument, in brief, is that neither international human rights law nor judicial review conflicts with democracy, because democracy properly understood involves a commitment to popular government limited by human rights. (Democracy may entail additional limits on popular government, but I leave that question aside.) Before I argue that this represents a sound understanding of democracy, let me briefly explain what I mean by "popular government limited by human rights."

The prevailing contemporary form of popular government is the creation of laws by the people's elected representatives—the legislature. This system (barring extreme corruption) allows laws to be shaped by a process of deliberation involving legislators, rival candidates for legislative office, and the public at large—a process I shall call *political deliberation*. When I claim that under democracy popular government is limited by human rights, I mean, first, that the legislature (as well as the executive) should be *under an obligation* to adhere to human rights, and second, that it should be *institutionally constrained* to do so. The obligation is properly formalized by adoption of a bill of rights and ratification of international human rights treaties (such as the International Covenant on Civil and Political Rights, Torture Convention, and European Convention on Human Rights). The institutional constraint may take various forms, but should include some version of judicial review and a number of supervisory mechanisms, operating at both the international and domestic level, to ensure compliance with international human rights law. (In Chapter 3, we examined what some of these mechanisms might look like.)

The underlying principle, as discussed in Chapter 2, is concurrent responsibility. Different institutional actors share an obligation to adhere to human rights, and each should ensure that the others fulfill this obligation. It is a mistake to think that judicial review elevates the judiciary over the legislature. Under a system of judicial review, both the legislature and judiciary can and should block laws that violate human rights. When the legislature rejects a law on these grounds, that is the end of the matter: the courts can no more resurrect a law rejected by the legislature than the legislature can restore a law struck down by the courts.[17] As Richard Fallon writes, the best case for judicial review rests on the idea that "legislatures and courts should both be enlisted in protecting fundamental rights, and . . . both should have veto powers over legislation that might reasonably be thought to violate such rights."[18]

Legislatures play a crucial role. They have an obligation to reject laws that violate human rights—recall the oath taken by U.S. members of Congress to uphold the Constitution. They have a further affirmative obligation to pass laws necessary for the protection of human rights. States parties to the International Covenant on Civil and Political Rights, for example, are obligated "to adopt such legislative or other measures as may be necessary to give effect to the rights recognized in the present Covenant" (art. 2(2)). Legislatures should approve ratification of well-drafted human rights treaties and incorporate their provisions into domestic law; they should enact constitutional amendments that strengthen human rights; and they should pass rights-protective laws beyond those required by the national constitution and international treaties.

Judicial review is a check—a means of ensuring that the legislature honors its already existing obligation to reject laws that violate human rights. History has proven that judicial review can strengthen human rights. There is broad agreement that human rights have benefited from judicial review exercised by the European Court of Human Rights[19] and by domestic constitutional courts in continental Europe.[20] Judicial review has strengthened respect for human rights in much of Latin America,[21] and in countries such as South Africa,[22] India,[23] Taiwan,[24] Mongolia,[25] South Korea,[26] Canada,[27] New Zealand,[28] and the UK.[29] The United States is a thornier example. On notorious occasions, the Supreme Court has struck down as unconstitutional valuable legislation that did not violate human rights and in some cases greatly advanced human rights.[30] I believe most of these decisions resulted from judicial doctrines (concerning federalism, enumerated powers, and state action) that are peculiarities of the U.S. constitutional tradition and not inherent to judicial review. The *Lochner*-era cases resulted from an extreme laissez-faire ideology that is corrected by modern human rights law (and subsequent changes in U.S. Supreme Court jurisprudence). Meanwhile, U.S. courts exercising judicial review have made dramatic and lasting contributions to freedom of speech and religion, the rights of criminal defendants, prisoners' rights, freedom from police abuse, sexual and reproductive freedoms, and freedom from discrimination. The U.S. system of judicial review has been marked by serious flaws,[31] and we must avoid the error of thinking that judicial review must take the U.S. form.[32] But even the U.S. experience, carefully examined, proves the value of judicial review.

Judicial review is not risk-free. One danger is that courts will strike down laws that ought to be upheld. To avoid this danger, we should promote adoption of the right constitutional and international human rights code and foster judicial doctrines that interpret it correctly. We should improve rather than reject judicial review, on the plausible assumption that the evil of underenforcement of rights that would occur in the absence of judicial review is greater than the evil of overenforcement of rights that would occur in a well-designed but achievable system of judicial review.[33] Another danger is that legislatures will neglect their duty to reject laws that violate human rights, believing that this is the exclusive responsibility of courts.[34] We should do all we can to combat this attitude, one possible measure being the establishment of parliamentary committees (such as the UK Joint Committee on Human Rights) to carry out preenactment human rights review of proposed legislation.[35]

This, then, is what I have in mind by "popular government limited by human rights." My claim (to repeat) is that this constitutes an appropriate definition of democracy. For convenience, I shall sometimes refer to this as the "compound conception of democracy" (not to be confused with Madison's notion of a "compound republic"). In Chapter 2, I presented one defense of the compound conception, arguing that democracy is properly understood as a shared project of holding one another accountable for the promotion of justice and the common good, where human rights figure as a core component of justice. Popular government is a necessary but insufficient element of democracy, because additional devices are needed to prevent the misuse and abuse of political power, and these include the judicial and international protection of human rights.[36] In the following remarks, I will not rely on this argument, however, because I want to show that the compound conception can be supported by several alternative arguments. It does not depend on the particular theoretical account of democracy presented in Chapter 2.

The first thing to say is that the compound conception is not particularly exotic. "Majority rule plus individual rights" is a familiar shorthand for democracy. Political scientists who study democracy in comparative perspective not infrequently include both components in their definition of the term.[37] It is striking that one of the measures of democracy most frequently used by comparative politics scholars is the Freedom House ranking of countries as "free, partly free, or not free"—a ranking based in equal measure on political rights and civil liberties. The former refer to rights of political participation, while the latter refer to individual rights that face possible violation by governments, even popularly elected ones.

So the compound conception of democracy does not depart notably from existing usage. The main revision is that it refers to "human rights" rather than "civil liberties." If human rights are thought to include social and economic rights as well as civil and political rights, the revision may seem significant. I have argued in Chapter 1 that human rights *should* include social and economic rights, such as economic subsistence, education, and dignified conditions of work. But the revision does not make a big difference to the argument presented in this chapter, because contemporary international human rights law (like domestic constitutional law) is predominantly concerned with civil and political rights, and critics generally have such rights in mind when voicing the democracy objection. Readers who are skeptical about social and economic rights but are otherwise persuaded by my argument can still believe in the democratic legitimacy of international laws protecting civil and political rights.

The compound conception of democracy resembles the theory of political legitimacy expressed in the celebrated human rights declarations of the eighteenth century, including the founding documents of the American republic. The declarations asserted that human rights are primary and that the only legitimate form of government is one that respects human rights. They demanded representative government, with separation of powers, as the political system best suited to the defense of human rights and the realization of the people's will, but they took the precaution of itemizing certain individual rights that their elected representatives must not transgress. The declarations combine a desire for representative government with a commitment to human rights. Madison wrote in *The Federalist*: "To secure the public good and private rights against the danger of [majority] faction, and at the same time to preserve the spirit and the form of popular government, is . . . the great object to which our inquiries are directed."[38] The compound conception of democracy is that which is most faithful to the political vision of the American founders.

Those who challenge international human rights law in the name of the American tradition of democracy confront the embarrassing fact of the

Founders' belief in a set of natural rights that limit legitimate government activity. To avoid this embarrassment, scholars sometimes resort to questionable historical narrative. Thus, Jed Rubenfeld distinguishes between what he calls European and American understandings of constitutionalism. Europeans are drawn to "international constitutionalism," which "is based on the idea of universal rights and principles that derive their authority from sources outside of or prior to national democratic processes."[39] Eighteenth-century America, Rubenfeld tells us, rejected this understanding, inventing an alternative conception of "democratic constitutionalism" to take its place.[40] Under democratic constitutionalism, constitutional rights "represent the nation's self-given law."[41] He elaborates:

> This is the reason why it is much less typical for Americans (as compared to Europeans) to speak of "human rights." The American Constitution does not claim the authority of universal law. It claims rather the authority of democracy—of law made by "the People," of self-given law. "Human Rights" are natural rights. Constitutional rights are man-made.[42]

This view is not supported by the text of the U.S. Constitution or its well-known antecedents, the Declaration of Independence and the Virginia Declaration of Rights. The Declaration of Independence states, "We hold these truths to be self-evident, that all men are created equal, that they are endowed by their Creator with certain unalienable Rights, that among these are Life, Liberty and the pursuit of Happiness." The Virginia Declaration of Rights, appearing only a few weeks earlier, opens with the following words: "That all men are by nature equally free and independent, and have certain inherent rights, of which, when they enter into a state of society, they cannot, by any compact, deprive or divest their posterity." Did the signers of the Declaration of Independence forget their belief in natural rights in eleven short years? The text of the Constitution suggests not, for the Ninth Amendment states as plainly as one could imagine that the Constitution is not the source of our rights: "The enumeration in the Constitution, of certain rights, shall not be construed to deny or disparage others retained by the people." Madison drafted the Bill of Rights in fulfillment of a promise to his fellow Virginians, many of whom had opposed the original Constitution because such a bill was lacking.[43] His earlier ambivalence about adding a Bill of Rights reflected a fear that it would imply the nonexistence of rights not mentioned;[44] the purpose of the Ninth Amendment was to prevent any such implication.[45] The wording of other clauses suggests that the Constitution recognizes rights that exist independently of its authority.[46] Jefferson, for his part, maintained his belief in the universal underpinnings of constitutional rights. Writing to Madison in December 1787, the primary author of the Declaration of Independence had this to say: "Let me add that a bill of rights is what the people are entitled to against every government on earth, general or particular, and what no just government should refuse, or rest on inference."[47]

It is true that the Constitution was ratified by the people's representatives, and that it permits amendments when approved by a supermajority of state legislatures and members of Congress. But this is no reason to infer any belief on the framers' part that the U.S. government was unconstrained by natural rights or that the Constitution would remain legitimate if it were amended to authorize the violation of natural rights.[48] The Virginia Declaration of Rights, the Declaration of Independence, and the Ninth Amendment plainly tell us the contrary.[49]

The double commitment of the American founders to human rights and popular government found permanent expression in the U.S. Constitution and survives in current understandings of the term "democracy." Moreover, as I shall now discuss, these two values are not independent of each other. In the view of most theorists who have turned their attention to the matter, human rights and popular government are strongly connected. The upshot is that we do not need to choose between them. If we embrace one, we should embrace the other, too.

The connection has been drawn in different ways. One view holds that popular government is impossible, even unintelligible, unless the people enjoy all the rights and liberties necessary to form and express opinions about public policy.[50] These rights assume even greater importance if one associates popular government not with the expression of people's preexisting preferences, but with informed public deliberation.[51] The rights needed to maintain popular government include, at a minimum, freedom of thought and discussion and freedom of association and assembly. There is disagreement on how many rights are required: all human rights, or only civil and political rights?[52] All civil and political rights, or only some? Another question is whether popular government requires respect for the human rights of foreigners. What is agreed is that it requires many (if not all) human rights. In a nutshell: "If you want popular government, you need human rights."

Another view holds that popular government is necessary to make human rights secure.[53] Popular election of legislative and executive officials is among the devices needed to prevent government's abuse or culpable neglect of the people. Citizens have enough enlightened self-interest and empathy to exert a salutary watch on government's activities. So important is the role of representative institutions in preventing government misconduct that some thinkers classify popular government as a human right in itself. In brief: "If you want human rights, you need popular government." (I present one version of this argument in Chapter 2.)

A third view holds that the values that underlie one of these two principles (human rights or popular government) underlie the other as well. Often the argument is posed in terms of autonomy. We value popular government (the argument runs) because we value autonomy—being able to exercise some control over the direction of our lives. Popular government is an important dimension of autonomy, but not the only one. Autonomy depends on a complete package of human rights.[54] Or (to run the argument in the other direction) we value human rights because of the importance we attach to autonomy. But we ought to recognize that popular government is a crucial dimension of autonomy.[55] In sum: "If you want popular government, you already want human rights (or vice versa)."

This broad sketch ignores the different versions of each type of argument. Moreover, there are other ways of connecting popular government and human rights not captured in this three-part scheme.[56] *How* one connects these values matters for the practical implications of one's view; those who perceive a connection often argue with each other how it should be drawn.

Here I will not enter into the details of this debate (my own view is developed in Chapter 2), but will content myself with the assertion that each of the three kinds of argument contains a substantial degree of truth. (This is not to endorse every version of each argument.) Popular government becomes meaningless unless citizens are free to express and advocate their views without fear. Representative institutions provide an important check on government abuse. Autonomy, offered as a reason for popular government, is an argument for human rights also, and vice versa. All of these arguments give us a reason to adopt the compound conception of democracy.

Theorists who draw a connection between human rights and popular government often refer to the latter as "democracy."[57] I find no compelling reason for this practice. Perhaps theorists tacitly assume that a single concept must refer to a single idea. This assumption is unwarranted: a single concept can (and in this case should) refer to two (or more) ideas in combination. We should avoid the assumption that because the compound conception defines democracy as *bounded popular government*, the conception itself is *less democratic*. The mistake of thinking so has played havoc with our understanding of democracy and human rights. Consider the analogy with liberty. As Locke plausibly observed, our liberty is not diminished by laws that prohibit morally criminal acts such as murder, because liberty *never included* permission to commit such acts.[58] In the same way, prohibitions on human rights violations are no limitation of democracy, because democracy never included permission to violate human rights. As George Kateb writes, speaking of the judicial protection of human rights, "What judicial review may take away from the majority, the majority could never claim. The legitimate will of the majority is the constitutional will, the constitutionally restricted will of the majority."[59] Democracy is not group license.

To sum up, the compound conception of democracy (popular government limited by human rights) draws support from linguistic usage, constitutional tradition, and political theory. Of course I cannot compel readers to adopt this definition; people may use terms as they choose. But I have sought to show that this definition has certain virtues, and that, at the very least, it is neither eccentric nor self-contradictory. It should not be ignored. I continue to defend this conception of democracy in the remainder of this chapter. To avoid dogmatism, I shall refer to it as "constitutional democracy." I believe that democracy *is* constitutional democracy, but I realize that not everyone agrees.

In Defense of Constitutional Democracy

The obvious attraction of constitutional democracy is its entrenchment of human rights. Despite this, it faces continuing theoretical resistance. Some of the criticisms have almost obtained the status of conventional wisdom. Even thinkers who assert the primacy of human rights sometimes question the legitimacy of institutional arrangements traditionally (and I believe correctly) associated with constitutional democracy. Jeremy Waldron, an eloquent champion of human rights, has argued that courts should not have the power to strike down legislation on human rights grounds. He defends this view in the name of a right to participation, which he calls "the right of rights."[60]

Constitutional democracy requires both domestic and international safeguards. In this chapter, I defend it from a common set of "pro-democratic" objections directed against both domestic-level judicial review (on the one hand) and international human rights law (on the other). I note up front that not all "pro-democratic" critics of international human rights law extend their objections to domestic-level judicial review. Rubenfeld claims that American-style judicial review meets the criteria of "democratic constitutionalism" because the Constitution and its amendments were ratified by a supermajority of Congress and the states.[61] The weakness of this argument is that, given the difficulty of amending the Constitution, the American public has little ability to rewrite constitutional rights clauses. If citizens want to alter these provisions, a minority favoring the status quo can "undemocratically" defeat a majority favoring constitutional change. Not surprisingly, such attempts rarely get far and almost never succeed. Thus Rubenfeld's arguments against international human rights law undermine judicial review as well: when the people's elected representatives deliberate over policy, constitutional restrictions created by earlier generations of citizens would seem (by the criteria of "democratic constitutionalism") no less problematic than the constraints of international human rights law.[62]

What could the objection to constitutional democracy be? The now-familiar objection is that it limits public autonomy. This does not seem plausible. There is no limitation of public autonomy worth complaining about if we insist, in advance of political deliberation, that people have the right to be free from religious persecution, censorship, arbitrary imprisonment, unfair trials, capital punishment, slavery, and cruel and degrading treatment, especially torture; and that they have the right to education, economic subsistence, health care, and dignified conditions of labor. Public autonomy is not enhanced by permission to violate human rights. A legislative debate on the merits of reintroducing slavery or torture, for example, would degrade the political discourse without contributing anything to public autonomy.

Some people may object that the last example is misleading. We now agree that slavery and torture are wrong, but not everyone agrees that capital punishment or the denial of health care or primary education is a violation of human rights. It is precisely because we disagree about the content of certain portions of the human rights catalog (it is argued) that we should let the content of human rights be determined through political deliberation, unconstrained by constitutional and international human rights codes.

The bulk of my discussion will be devoted to answering this objection, but I want to begin by suggesting that it does less work than advertised. If we look hard enough, we will find citizens who support the reintroduction of slavery or the use of torture. (And we don't have to look that hard. Polls reveal that a growing percentage of Americans support the occasional use of torture to combat terrorism, an unsurprising outcome of the Republican Party leadership's support for "enhanced interrogation techniques," torture in all but name, a position in turn encouraged by the earlier U.S. loosening of international human rights law constraints.) Surely that is no reason to open the legislative process to the possible adoption of these practices. It is not because we *agree* about the wrongness of slavery and torture that such proposals should be kept off the legislative table. It is because they constitute an unacceptable assault on human dignity. That, however, is a feature shared with all other human rights violations. The reason why slavery and torture should be kept off the legislative table is the same reason why other human rights violations should be kept off the legislative table.

Moreover, the example of slavery and torture is far from irrelevant in the context of international human rights law since several treaties (not to mention rules of customary international law) are specifically directed to prohibiting these kinds of extreme human rights violations. Such treaties include the Slavery Convention, the Torture Convention, the Genocide Convention, the Human Trafficking Convention, the Consent to Marriage Convention, the Enforced Disappearance Convention, and the treaty creating the International Criminal Court, authorized to punish individuals guilty of genocide, war crimes, crimes against humanity, and aggressive war. Prohibitions against torture, slavery, and extrajudicial killing are also built into other treaties, such as the International Covenant on Civil and Political Rights, the European Convention on Human Rights, the African Charter on Human and Peoples' Rights, and the Inter-American Convention on Human Rights.

Is Disagreement About Human Rights a Reason to Reject Constitutional Democracy?

Insistence on respect for those rights that *truly are* human rights does not limit public autonomy in any objectionable way. The problem is that we do not agree about the content of human rights. Political deliberation, it is suggested, is the right way to resolve such disagreement. Human rights legitimately constrain normal democratic politics, it is argued, if and only if they are endorsed by the people, as represented by the electoral and deliberative mechanisms of the ordinary legislative process.

The argument from disagreement (as we might call it) is widespread. Referring to the Declaration of Independence, Rubenfeld writes:

> the truth about self-evident truths is that they cannot govern, not by themselves. If Enlightenment principles are to be made into governing law, it must be done by real human beings, who will disagree with one another, perhaps radically, about what the principles are or how to interpret them or how to apply them in real life. How are these disagreements to be resolved? The American answer was: . . . by the people themselves, through democratic deliberation and consent.[63]

Disagreement about rights is Waldron's underlying argument for opposing judicial review. He puts the word "disagreement" in the title of his book-length presentation of this argument.[64] Disagreement is a central argument in Richard Bellamy's case for the superiority of "political constitutionalism" over "legal constitutionalism."[65]

The argument may seem plausible, but it is, I shall argue, misleading. One significant problem is that it leaves noncitizens out in the cold. Though noncitizens generally cannot vote,[66] their lives are continually affected by legislative decisions. To say that the definition of human rights should be left to the free disposition of elected legislatures means that the human rights of one group of people (noncitizens) may be defined by a *different* group of people (citizens). Sensitivity to the problem of disagreement curiously disappears where the rights of noncitizens are concerned. Leaving all human rights questions to the free disposition of elected legislatures does not benefit the public autonomy of noncitizens, but on the contrary places them in a more vulnerable position. The severe liabilities imposed on noncitizens in the "War on Terror" powerfully illustrate the danger.

Even if we imagined a world without noncitizens, the invocation of disagreement is not the decisive argument many imagine it to be. Frailties appear when we stop to ask *why* disagreement about human rights is a problem. Three possible reasons may be distinguished:

1. *The legitimacy problem.* It is wrong to impose a conception of human rights on someone who disagrees with it.
2. *The fallibility problem.* Disagreement about human rights shows that someone has an incorrect view, and it might be us.

3. *The political weakness problem.* When too many people disagree with the *correct* understanding of human rights, human rights are imperiled.

As I shall argue, the first of these is a false problem, while the second and third, though genuine problems, are not resolved by leaving questions about rights solely to the ordinary legislative process, unconstrained by constitutional and international law. Moral disagreement poses a less formidable objection to international human rights law and judicial review than critics have supposed.

The Legitimacy Problem

The thought is that it is wrong to impose one's conception of human rights on those who do not share it. As Michael Ignatieff writes, "If human rights principles exist to validate individual agency and collective rights of self-rule, then human rights practice is obliged to seek consent for its norms and to abstain from interference when consent is not freely given."[67]

But this view is wrong. Human rights do not require consent. That they do not is part of their point. Human rights allow us to take certain actions regardless of other people's opinions, just as they place obligations on other people whether or not the other people agree.

This point may be illustrated by means of a primal example. If you form a desire to kill me, I have a right to defend myself. When you raise your weapon to strike me, I may knock it from your hand. It does not matter whether you or anyone else agrees, because my right to life does not depend on anyone's agreement. There is nothing wrong with the imposition of my conception of human rights on you when I knock the weapon from your hand.

Of course, my right to life extends beyond permission to defend myself in situations of immediate peril. Just as I may knock the weapon from your hand, I may demand institutional arrangements that provide me with a reasonable degree of safety. I have a right to general protection by a police force of some kind, and to a socially maintained threat that people attempting to kill me will be punished. I also have a right to institutional devices that protect me from being killed by government agencies (including the police). To say that my right to these things requires general consent is a gratuitous and impertinent demand. It raises an illegitimate hurdle to the fulfillment of my rights.

My right to life is not the only human right that I have. Just as I may insist on my right to life, I may insist on the essentials of a dignified existence—on a right to food, shelter, clothing, decent working conditions, freedom of speech, freedom of religion, freedom from abuse, and the right to a fair trial. These rights do not depend on consent. To say that they do is to make my dignity hostage to other people's opinions.

It makes all the difference in the world whether human rights precede or derive from public deliberation. Imagine we are speaking to a young West African girl who is being threatened with forced early marriage.[68] If we believe that human rights precede public deliberation, we may say, "You have the right to an education; to health training and basic medical care; to be trained in an occupation of your choice; to be spared the severe pain and danger of genital cutting and attendant loss of sexual pleasure; to choose your own spouse; to be free from domestic violence; to refuse sex; to decide whether to have children, and, if so, how many; and to have an equal voice in the conduct of your marriage and your community." (These are all rights that the practice of forced early marriage denies.)

However, if we believe that human rights are derived from public deliberation we must instead say something like the following: "You have the right (perhaps not now, but at least when you become an adult) to participate equally with all the other members of your community in determining what rights you have. We cannot guarantee that you have a right to an education, etc., because that will depend on what your community ends up deciding." And further: "If your father wants to force you into marriage with a much older (and perhaps polygamous) man of his choosing, you have the right (or will have it, when you are an adult, after your forced marriage) to engage your father in a dialogue about whether you have a right to refuse. But if your father is not persuaded that you have such a right, it would be wrong to refuse his demand in the name of your human rights."

I submit that the first message does far more good than the second. It does more to help girls take control of their future, and makes a greater ultimate contribution to the creation of communities built on equal respect for the dignity and agency of all their members. Deriving human rights from public deliberation is the death of human rights. Human rights are the precondition of any healthy form of public deliberation.[69]

Confusion about consent bedevils discussions of international human rights law. Anderson writes that in today's world authority must "be perceived to be legitimate by those over whom [it] is exercised."[70] This is untrue: a law prohibiting murder does not require the consent of the would-be murderer. Some American critics of the International Criminal Court have invoked the principle of consent to protest the Court's jurisdiction over war crimes, crimes against humanity, and genocide committed on the territory of a state party by citizens of a non-state party.[71] Such jurisdiction is illegitimate, the critics complain, because the state whose citizens stand accused has not given its consent. This argument denies the right of vulnerable states to invoke the assistance of an international court in defending their inhabitants from foreign-perpetrated atrocities. Arguments like this abuse the notion of consent. It is a mistake to suppose that, until an individual or a state grants its consent, no rules apply.[72] We might call this the law of the jungle, but it is not a view we should associate with democracy.

The Declaration of Independence states that governments "deriv[e] their just powers from the consent of the governed." It is a mistake, I have argued, to suppose that human rights themselves require our consent, and the Declaration of Independence certainly expresses no such view.[73] Indeed one can go further and argue that the very idea of "government by consent" implies a government constrained by human rights not derived from consent. The argument proceeds as follows.

Suppose that "government by consent" means that no one may be governed without his or her consent. This sets a high bar: laws must receive consent not from the majority but from everyone. Of course no law can literally satisfy such a requirement. But we may say that a legitimate government is one that comes as close as possible to meeting this requirement. It does not apply laws that receive literally every person's consent—that is impossible—but instead laws that are *capable* of receiving every person's consent, in the sense that everyone has reason to accept them. Now, there are some laws that *cannot* receive everyone's consent. Let us call them "unreasonable" laws. Laws that permit or authorize human rights violations fall under this category. Such laws impose unacceptable costs on their victims. Because there is no possible justification for these laws, we will not attempt to justify them. For this reason, government by consent excludes human rights violations from legislative consideration.

One benefit of construing "government by consent" in this manner is that it can (at least partly) accommodate the legitimate claims of noncitizens. Given that noncitizens usually cannot vote (directly or indirectly) on the public policies that affect them, how can government honor their right not to be governed without their consent? The least it can do is to refrain from policies to which they could not reasonably consent, and this means, at a minimum, acting in accord with their human rights.[74]

The Fallibility Problem

I have argued that the authority of human rights does not depend on consent. But how do we know that our conception of human rights is the right one? Other people may disagree, and if so, their disagreement shows that we may be mistaken.

This is a serious problem, but notice that the problem is the possibility of error rather than disagreement itself. We could all agree and all be mistaken. Disagreement is not the problem, but rather a sign of the problem. Nor does it always signify a problem. When you raise your weapon to kill me, I may be reasonably sure, despite your apparent disagreement, that I have a right to defend myself. It is clear in this situation that I am right and you are wrong.

But not all cases are this clear-cut. The possibility of error grows when we try to draw up a complete human rights code and apply it in practice. How to prevent such error is a vast question demanding our full attention. I do not pretend to offer a full answer, but hope to show that an intelligent response to the problem does not entail the rejection of international human rights law or judicial review.

The mistake to be avoided here is an all-embracing skepticism from which political deliberation (meaning the set of debates among legislators, political candidates, and an engaged public that culminate in laws passed by a legislative majority) is thought to be the only outlet. The reasoning to be avoided goes like this: "Ultimately, we do not know how to prevent error about human rights. To prevent such error, we would need a standard that distinguishes truth from error, but our very fallibility places such a standard out of reach. Our views are shrouded in doubt, as are the methods needed to resolve such doubt. Under these circumstances, the only reasonable policy is to let the people decide, through ongoing political deliberation, which human rights we do and do not have."

Such skepticism is excessive. We are confident that such practices as torture, slavery, extrajudicial execution, race and sex discrimination, and the denial of due process are wrong. Centuries of experience and reflection have nourished and reinforced these convictions, and have generated theoretical insights into the nature, basis, and content of our human rights. We don't have to start from scratch; we may retain our reasonable convictions, and use them to test new arguments and theories, and to assess the reliability of alternative procedures for formulating and applying human rights codes.

John Rawls coined the term "reflective equilibrium" to describe such reasoning.[75] The idea has been further refined, with particular reference to human rights, in recent work by William Talbott.[76] The goal is to avoid skepticism on the one hand and epistemic complacency on the other. On Talbott's account, we improve the reliability of our moral judgments when we strive to adopt an impartial perspective informed by empathic understanding of the needs and interests of others. To avoid error, we must stand guard against, and endeavor to correct, the distorting influence that self-interest and social pressure can exert on our beliefs. When we take these steps, we can form reasonably reliable, though not infallible, moral judgments about particular kinds of acts. These moral judgments in turn justify broader moral principles that make sense of our beliefs as a whole and that in some instances cause us to reexamine and revise our particular moral judgments. The more we bring our particular moral judgments and moral principles into equilibrium, and the more we test our moral beliefs against other people's reasonable arguments and against the known facts about human nature and human society, the more reliable our moral beliefs become.

Debate is essential to this process. It exposes faulty reasoning and the operation of influences (such as self-interest and social pressure) likely to produce error. It contributes new information and ideas. Therefore, we need to guarantee the communicative and associative freedoms and minimum welfare provisions that give all persons a voice and permit them to hear what others have to say. We also need to promote universal education, an independent media, and a vigorous civil society. If debate is to promote understanding rather than error, however, we need to lay a foundation of public support for and understanding of basic human rights values. Knowledge of human rights law and the values on which it rests should be a required element of everyone's education.[77] Such education does not prevent citizens from revising their views about human rights through further reflection and debate. Of course, the pedagogic effect of human rights law itself must not be underestimated.[78]

Human rights education, freedom of thought and discussion, and mutual encouragement to engage in equilibrium moral reasoning help foster trustworthy views about human rights in the general public. We still face the question of which system to adopt for formulating and applying an enforceable human rights code. While this task should be informed by debate, the debate must be properly *structured* in order to generate good outcomes. It would be unwise to let legislators enact laws without the constraint of a domestic or international rights charter and without judicial review, in the belief that the resulting deliberations will lead to improved understanding and more conscientious guardianship of human rights. The likelier outcome is that human rights will often become lost in a sea of other issues, especially given the frequent inattention to human rights by the voting public. Unless human rights are constitutionally entrenched, we can expect them to be eroded by inattention, majority pressure, legislative patterns of logrolling and scapegoating, and the competitive bidding of legislators seeking to prove their toughness on hot-button issues like crime, terrorism, and immigration.

We need to distinguish between the adoption and application of a human rights code. As to the former, the task of drafting human rights provisions in domestic constitutions and international treaties is sensibly entrusted to learned and intelligent people who have demonstrated a sincere commitment to and sophisticated understanding of human rights, and who collectively represent, either through personal experience or acquired knowledge, a reasonable cross-section of social interests.[79] There are different ways of selecting such people, and political constraints will often dictate which method is adopted. But we should strive to prevent uncommitted or unqualified people from playing too great a role. A common danger at the domestic level is the influence of those seeking to preserve or restore authoritarian forms of rule. A common danger at the international treaty level is the influence of delegates seeking to undermine rather than strengthen the protection of human rights.

Human rights nongovernmental organizations (NGOs) play an invaluable role in both settings.[80] Though not given voting powers, they remind delegates of relevant precedents in international law and domestic bills of rights. They share lessons learned from the history of human rights abuses and give voice to the victims of those abuses. They mobilize pressure from a broader constituency of human rights supporters. They provide logistical and technical assistance to delegates in the pro-human rights camp. Their vigilance deters maneuvers to undermine human rights. Though not popularly elected, NGO leaders are evaluated by peers who are passionately committed to the cause of human rights. They have been tested by the discipline of producing factual reports whose every detail must survive microscopic examination and by the experience of challenging hostile governments in highly charged settings. Their contributions to human rights law are difficult to overstate. Contrary to the claims of some scholars, their participation in the treaty-drafting process is vital to the legitimacy of international human rights law.[81]

Submission of constitutional bills of rights and international human rights treaties to legislative approval or popular referendum does not alter the fact that the actual work of drafting tends, for practical reasons, to be handled by a relatively small number of people. The point is to choose individuals who are fit for the task. In objection to this view, some might point to the South African Constitution, claiming that it shows how to involve the public more directly in the drafting process. The Constitutional Assembly, its members chosen by direct or indirect popular election, made extensive use of talk radio, television, mailings, and the Internet to inform citizens about the drafting process and to solicit their input.[82] Citizens responded with millions of "petitions, comments, objections, and proposals."[83] Passage of the Constitution required approval by two-thirds of the Assembly. I am persuaded that, among its other virtues, this process succeeded in instilling in the public a deeper loyalty to and understanding of the final Bill of Rights. However, what must be remembered is that public deliberations occurred within clear boundaries, demarcated in advance. The Constitutional Court was assigned the duty of rejecting any constitutional provisions in conflict with the Constitutional Principles in the Interim Constitution, one of which stated that "Everyone shall enjoy all universally accepted fundamental rights, freedoms and civil liberties, which shall be provided for and protected by entrenched and justiciable provisions in the Constitution." In other words, the people were free to develop and expand, but not water down, internationally recognized human rights.[84]

When a sound human rights code is adopted, it should be scrupulously followed by each branch of government, with each monitoring the others for compliance. The executive, given its ample powers, requires energetic oversight by legislators and judges, while judicial review of legislation is a sensible means of ensuring that legislators do not violate human rights by statute. When courts invalidate a statute on human rights grounds, it may be asked why judicial interpretation of the human rights code should supersede that of the people's elected representatives in the legislature. The reasons are as follows. (1) Even if the legislature conscientiously examines whether a proposed statute complies with human rights law, it may erroneously (though honestly) arrive at a false affirmative answer, and a second examination of the question by an independent branch of government lowers the risk that a rights-violating statute will remain in effect. Given the primacy of human rights, we want to block rights-violating statutes, even if the unavoidable cost is the erroneous judicial veto of some statutes that do not violate rights. (But everything should be done to minimize this cost, and if it grows too high, the case for judicial review is undermined.) (2) We should realistically expect that legislators often will *not* conscientiously examine a proposed statute for its compliance with human rights law. Legislators have too many policy issues to address and are too vulnerable to electoral pressure to keep the question of human rights always squarely in view. (And citizens sometimes elect legislators who are ideologically opposed to human rights, at least in part.) While we should implement mechanisms, such as mandatory preenactment human rights review, that redirect legislative attention to human rights criteria, judicial review offers added protection in case such mechanisms fall short.[85] (3) By virtue of their mandate, vocation, preparation, selection, and methodology, judges can bring special qualifications to the task of human rights review. The sole task of judges is to uphold the law, including constitutional and human rights law. (In constitutional and human rights courts, their task narrows to upholding these particular kinds of law.) Therefore, they face fewer distractions, and the general expectation is that they are personally committed to the rule of law, thoroughly educated in law (including rights law), and chosen for the quality and integrity of their legal reasoning. In addition, they must defend their rulings with published opinions open to general scrutiny. These norms are not always followed, but often they are; a healthy system of judicial review applies these norms in order to strengthen human rights (and the rule of law in general).

Mattias Kumm has illuminated the epistemic contributions of judicial review. As he argues, courts exercising judicial review act as a gadfly by refocusing the attention of public authorities on human rights constraints. Like Socrates (in Plato's early dialogues), they improve political discourse and policy outcomes, not by delivering oracular insights into the nature of justice, but by asking the right kind of questions.[86] This "legal institutionalisation of Socratic contestation," in Kumm's words,

> helps keep alive the idea that acts by public authorities must be understandable as reasonable collective judgments about what justice and good policy require to be legitimate. This is likely to have a disciplining effect on public authorities and help foster an attitude of civilian confidence among citizens. Such contestation helps correct certain political pathologies to which legislatures are vulnerable.

Kumm identifies these as, first, "the vice of thoughtlessness based on tradition, convention or preference" that can perpetuate injustice; second, "illegitimate reasons relating to the good, which do not respect the limits of public reason"; and third, ideological thinking that rallies the nation against a purported threat, characterized as such "without much attention to relevant detail and . . . immunised from serious scrutiny either by put-downs, threats or claims of secrecy." [87] As noted above, the value of judicial review has been demonstrated in practice: it has strengthened respect for human rights in several democratic countries.[88]

Constructive debate does not end with the adoption of human rights codes and mechanisms for their implementation. The codes become available for public inspection and criticism. Judges charged with their interpretation and enforcement must defend their opinions against collegial criticism, and such disagreements stimulate (and respond to) a debate in the public at large. Citizens and legislatures can register satisfaction or dissatisfaction with judicial rulings. The debate extends across national borders. Increasingly, judges test their own reasoning against human rights arguments made by foreign courts.[89] International courts, such as the European Court of Human Rights, listen carefully to the domestic courts of member states, but sometimes find reasons to contradict their rulings. Differences in the way particular treaties and constitutions define human rights force us to evaluate and compare. Why is this human right defined differently here than there? Which definition is better and why?

Debate does not merely shape the judicial interpretation and application of human rights codes. It may also illuminate defects in the codes themselves, thereby encouraging their revision. Such revisions can be accomplished in different ways: through ordinary legislation (when not prohibited by constitutional law), constitutional amendment, adoption of a new constitution, ratification of a human rights treaty, domestic incorporation of treaty law through legislation or constitutional amendment, negotiation of a new human rights treaty, or the amendment of an existing human rights treaty. This process is most advanced in Europe, where concerted and continuing dialogue among numerous domestic and international actors has led to profound changes in the human rights provisions of domestic statutory and constitutional and international treaty law.[90] A similar, if less accelerated, process can be observed elsewhere in the world—for example, in the domestic constitutional and legislative reforms prompted by ratification of the Rome Statute of the International Criminal Court.[91]

Domestic legislatures can make constructive contributions to domestic and international debates over human rights. They can add human rights protections to those already existing under the constitution, ratify human rights treaties and incorporate their provisions into domestic law, and seek to amend their national constitutions. Sometimes the constructive contribution will take the form of "talking back" to international human rights law. If domestic legislatures are presented with a defective human rights treaty, they can refuse to approve ratification or add substantive reservations to correct the flawed provisions. In the extreme case, a legislature might seek the country's withdrawal from the treaty (an action permitted by some treaties, but not others) or pass legislation in direct conflict with previous treaty commitments. (Such laws, though invalid under international law,[92] are sometimes upheld by domestic courts.)[93]

Is legislative resistance to international human rights law morally legitimate? It may be so (making allowances for various practical considerations) if the law being resisted is not genuinely required by human rights, or indeed undermines genuine human rights.[94] What if there is disagreement on this very point? Then, at the very least, a national legislature should present a credible good-faith argument that its resistance does not subvert, or is indeed necessitated by, human rights. As Kumm observes, widely ratified human rights treaties are entitled to a certain measure of deference, given that they "establish a common point of reference negotiated by a large number of states across cultures" and therefore overcome "limitations connected to national parochialism."[95] This does not mean that such treaties are 100 percent correct, but it does mean that at a minimum national legislatures should give human rights-based reasons when seeking exemption from specific treaty provisions. Such reasons have the potential to persuade other members of the international community. Just as national legislatures can learn from international human rights law, so international human rights law can learn from national legislatures. When legislatures resist certain aspects of international human rights law and claim that their resistance is guided by human rights considerations, we must ultimately judge the legitimacy of their resistance by reference to the quality of the arguments put forward.

The United States provides an example of what not to do. As discussed in Chapter 5, its routine practice when ratifying human rights treaties is to exempt itself from all obligations not already enshrined in U.S. law. There is no discussion whether U.S. law would be improved by assuming new obligations—no discussion whether these obligations remedy a failure of existing U.S. law to protect genuine human rights. By refusing to reevaluate its laws and policies in light of international human rights law, the United States demonstrates a dangerous oblivion to its own fallibility.

Disagreement about human rights is troubling because it points out the possibility that our conception of human rights is mistaken. Deliberation is needed to minimize the possibility of error. But the necessary deliberation is compatible with, and indeed requires, the constitutionalization of human rights through domestic and international law, backed by judicial review. International human rights treaties and domestic bills of rights encourage disciplined inquiry into the meaning of human rights. They foster constructive debate. There is little reason to believe—and much reason to doubt—that the fallibility problem is properly addressed by leaving human rights controversies to the sole purview of the legislative process. Therefore, we have not yet encountered a good argument for rejecting international human rights law or judicial review.

The Political Weakness Problem

Finally, disagreement poses the risk of political weakness. Suppose a court rules that a legislative statute or executive policy violates a human rights obligation enshrined in constitutional or international law. Suppose the ruling is correct: the human right is a genuine human right and the violation a genuine violation. However, a substantial portion of the public disagrees with the ruling. The broader and more intense the disagreement, the more vulnerable the ruling becomes. If the disagreement turns into resistance, and if the resistance targets an entire category of human rights, or targets the court's authority to block legislative and executive conduct found to violate human rights, the threat to human rights expands.

Here the question is not about legitimacy or fallibility, but strategy. We assume for the sake of argument that international and constitutional human rights law and the courts charged with interpreting it have a correct understanding of human rights, and that it is legitimate to enforce such law despite disagreement. We worry, however, that disagreement may imperil the realization of human rights.

Disagreement threatening to human rights is a problem, but the solution to this problem is not the replacement of international human rights law and judicial review by political constitutionalism. We should avoid thinking as follows: "Disagreement about human rights may weaken human rights. The best way to handle such disagreement is to refer it to the people's elected representatives for debate leading to a vote, not subject to judicial review. The outcome of this process will command general respect, and the political weakness problem will thereby be resolved." Such thinking loses sight of the ball: it tries to fix one problem (lack of support for the correct conception of human rights) by introducing another, potentially worse one (easier legislative suppression of human rights). The question is which institutional arrangement provides the best overall protection of human rights, and the likeliest answer, for reasons previously discussed, is a checks and balances system that includes judicial review and international human rights law.[96]

Thinking strategically, we can identify three objectives:

1. an institutional arrangement that yields decisions providing maximum protection for human rights;

2. popular support for human rights, correctly understood; and

3. popular support for an institutional arrangement that maximally protects human rights.

These three objectives fit together, and the second and third exist largely for the sake of the first. However, the second objective should not be confused with "popular support for any conception of human rights, regardless of its correctness," and the third objective should not be confused with "popular support for any institutional arrangement claiming to protect human rights, regardless of its effectiveness in doing so." Human rights and effective human rights institutions depend on popular support; however, it is a requirement of an effective human rights regime that it be prepared to render unpopular decisions. The bottom line is that we need to use a variety of means to cultivate and maintain the people's support for a sound conception of human rights and for the constitutional architecture necessary to improve understanding and protection of human rights, where it is understood that such a regime occasionally renders decisions the people dislike.

In support of political constitutionalism, it might be claimed that citizens will feel greater connection to, identification with, or ownership of human rights if their elected representatives are made responsible for protecting human rights. This is probably right, but it is not a reason to choose political constitutionalism over constitutional democracy. The key distinction is between shared responsibility and exclusive authority. Legislative guardianship is (to repeat) essential: legislatures must enact laws necessary to protect human rights, reject and repeal laws that violate human rights, adopt well-drafted human rights treaties, block the executive from violating human rights, find ways without disrupting the constitution to resist and oppose judicial action harmful to human rights, and support constitutional amendments to strengthen the protection of human rights. This is different, however, from saying that legislatures should have final or exclusive say over what human rights require. Because the people and their elected representatives are susceptible to passion and bias, a checks and balances system is necessary for the mutual correction of error. Therefore, if the people and their elected representatives want to give human rights maximum protection, they should support a checks and balances system with domestic and international courts exercising rights-based review of legislative and executive conduct. To proceed otherwise is to exhibit a foolish and arrogant trust in their own infallibility.

If the people (or a substantial portion of them) nonetheless prefer political constitutionalism to constitutional democracy, the likeliest explanation is *not* that they mistakenly believe that political constitutionalism is more favorable to human rights. The human rights benefits of a checks and balances system are not difficult to understand. The likeliest explanation is a belief that human rights should sometimes be subordinated to other considerations and that the people's representatives should be authorized to make such determinations. In this case, the goal is not to strengthen but rather to weaken human rights.

Someone might argue: "The most we can expect from the people is support for a second-best system of human rights protection. If we try to establish the best system, the people will revolt, and will not only block that system but retreat all the way to a third-best system. So we should cut our losses and establish the second-best system if it can garner significantly greater popular support than the best system." If this scenario were accurate, I agree that it would require an adjustment of strategy. But we need evidence that it is accurate, and offhand that seems unlikely. In general, we should seek to establish the best system, and if popular opposition makes that impossible despite our best efforts at persuasion, we should remind the people that they should still prefer the second-best system to the third.

To think through these issues, it may help to consider the case of the United Kingdom. In recent years, the European Convention on Human Rights has come under attack from powerful media outlets and from Conservative and UK Independence Party leaders. Polls show rising popular opposition.[97] The antipathy reflects some misunderstanding of the Convention,[98] but also disagreement about the scope and priority of human rights.

Condemnation has focused on Strasbourg rulings in favor of suspected terrorists and prisoners, notably the *Othman v. United Kingdom* (2012) judgment that blocked the deportation of a Jordanian citizen (Abu Qatada) in order to protect him from a criminal trial based on torture-elicited testimony, and the *Hirst v. United Kingdom* (2005) judgment that opposed a UK law denying all prisoners, without exception, the right to vote.[99]

At various times, the Conservative, Labour, and Liberal Democratic parties have called for adoption of a domestic bill of rights.[100] An argument often made is that this would create greater popular "ownership" of and therefore support for human rights.[101] The Labour and Liberal Democratic parties do not recommend withdrawal from the Convention or repeal of the Human Rights Act; a domestic bill of rights is intended to reinforce rather than replace these instruments. By contrast, the Conservative Party now urges repeal of the Human Rights Act and either a loosening of the Strasbourg Court's authority over the UK or UK withdrawal from the Convention altogether. The avowed purpose of these proposals is to shield the UK from future judgments like *Hirst* and *Othman*. (The UK Independence Party advocates repeal of the Human Rights Act and withdrawal from the Convention, while the Scottish National Party supports both the HRA and continued membership in the Convention.)

The UK experience suggests that political constitutionalism is not beneficial to human rights. It has plausibly been suggested that the popular backlash to the European Convention is partly the result of the lack of a domestic tradition of judicial review prior to the 1998 Human Rights Act.[102] We can also imagine what would happen if the UK dismantled or weakened institutions of judicial review. To begin with the most extreme case, consider the likely result if the UK repealed the Human Rights Act, left the Convention, and did not adopt a domestic bill of rights. Over the decades, Strasbourg judgments applied to the UK have affirmed the absolute prohibition of torture and ill-treatment and the prohibition of slavery and strengthened privacy rights, due process rights, rights to freedom of the press and freedom of religion, rights against unreasonable searches and obtrusive government surveillance, and the rights of children, homosexuals, transgender people, immigrants, mentally ill people, Iraqi civilians, and Iraqi detainees in British custody.[103] If the UK left the Convention, it would lose the benefit of a similar pattern of judgments in the future. As a matter of international law, the UK would still be bound by Strasbourg judgments concerning violations committed prior to withdrawal,[104] but it is not clear that any court would have authority to enforce those judgments. As we have seen in Chapter 3, the Convention as applied by the Strasbourg Court and domestic judges has placed a significant check on repressive policies adopted by the UK government in the "War on Terror."

Consider now the likely result of adopting Conservative proposals to replace the Human Rights Act with a domestic (as yet undrafted) "Bill of Rights and Responsibilities," to free UK judges from the obligation to consider Strasbourg precedent in their rulings, and to declare that adverse judgments of the European Court of Human Rights do not require changes in UK law, a move that party leaders acknowledge might lead to the UK's withdrawal from the Convention.[105] Conservatives have stated that the purpose of the proposed changes is to liberate the UK from what they regard as the Strasbourg Court's overly strict interpretation of the Convention. The new Bill of Rights and Responsibilities would "clarify the Convention rights, to reflect a proper balance between rights and responsibilities." It would define "degrading treatment or punishment" more narrowly than the Strasbourg Court, limit the prohibition of deportations that pose a "real risk" of torture or ill-treatment, and block judicial application of human rights law to UK military actions abroad.[106] Under the proposed changes, we should expect domestic courts to become more timid in their rulings, especially if the UK withdraws from the Convention altogether. A panel of legal experts recently concluded that "a plausible effect of the Bill of Rights is a limitation of existing rights" and that withdrawal from the ECHR would cause "a substantial reduction of human rights protection, in particular for minority and vulnerable groups."[107] In addition, UK distancing or withdrawal from the Convention could encourage other European countries to follow suit, weakening the protection of human rights across the region, and even threatening the Convention system with collapse.[108]

We can encourage popular dedication to human rights without dismantling judicial and international guarantees. Citizens and their elected representatives should become more involved in the protection of human rights; their efforts will be enhanced by the simultaneous involvement of courts and international institutions. Legislatures and courts, domestic and international institutions, should work together for a common goal.

Conclusion

International human rights law is not antidemocratic in any objectionable sense. It bars policies that governments should not undertake anyway. Some readers may object that a flawed conception of human rights could lead international human rights law to exclude policies that are in fact blameless, and that such exclusions would constitute a regrettable restriction of democracy. This danger should not be exaggerated, however; nor should the corresponding benefit be overlooked. Since the vast majority of international human rights obligations are morally justified (most uncontroversially so in the realm of civil and political rights, where international human rights law enjoys its greatest leverage), the danger of excluding some blameless policy options pales next to the gain for human rights.

No system of human rights protection is infallible. If we are serious about protecting human rights, we cannot wait for an infallible system that will never come. The proper response to mistaken provisions in international human rights law is not the removal of a "democratic deficit"; it is the correction of the mistaken provisions. As I have argued, there are important resources within international human rights law itself for making the necessary corrections. These resources include the recognizably democratic practices of dialogue, debate, and persuasion.

To say that international human rights law subverts democracy is to adopt an unworthy conception of democracy. On the best conception of democracy, there is no conflict. Indeed, international human rights law strengthens democracy. The main problem with international human rights protections is not their antidemocratic character but their inadequate development. Rather than criticize international human rights law as antidemocratic, we should study how human rights may be more effectively promoted through international law.

Conclusion

In the preceding chapters I have argued that countries committed to the principles of constitutional democracy should incorporate international human rights law into their domestic legal system and accept international oversight of their human rights obligations. Such measures are necessary for the protection of human rights, harmonious with democracy, and consistent with wise principles of constitutional design, such as those articulated by the founders of the United States. They help prevent the misuse and abuse of political power by extending and reinforcing domestic checks and balances and by enlisting external as well as internal guardians against state misconduct.

International Human Rights Law and Sovereignty

Readers may ask how the position defended in this book stands in relation to the norm of state sovereignty. (1) Does it conflict with state sovereignty, and (2) if so, is this cause for regret? A clear answer to the first question is impeded by the presence of widely varying definitions of "sovereignty," to the point that one sometimes finds supporters and critics of "sovereignty" defending the same substantive position. I limit myself to the claim that international human rights law rules out certain *conceptions* of sovereignty. If we distinguish between moderate and expansive understandings of the term, the latter but not necessarily the former conflict with international human rights law, and since expansive conceptions of sovereignty represent a false political ideal, rejection of such conceptions is no cause for regret.

Sovereignty is a polarizing word. Many human rights advocates view it with distrust, because governments have invoked it to rebuff external criticism of human rights violations and to reject international oversight mechanisms for the protection of human rights. But for others, sovereignty is what is threatened by the objectionable intrusiveness of certain international laws and institutions, including, some feel, international human rights law. The term's critics are troubled by its unsavory pedigree, its historical association with the untethered will of absolute monarchs. The term's defenders connect it to the self-determination of independent communities, and therefore regard it as a precondition of democracy. Critics recall the nineteenth-century doctrine that sovereignty includes the right of a state to wage war as an instrument of national policy. Defenders (or most of them) argue that the "sovereign equality" principle enshrined in the UN Charter (art. 2(1)) signifies a transformation of the sovereignty norm. States are now forbidden to threaten or use force "against the territorial integrity or political independence" of other states (art. 2(4)); force may be used only in self-defense in response to an armed attack (art. 51) or when authorized by the Security Council as necessary for international peace and security (art. 42). In other words, the UN Charter clarifies that the sovereignty of each state is limited, at a minimum, by respect for the sovereignty of other states.

That the meaning of sovereignty has moderated over time is generally conceded.[1] Some New Sovereigntists dissent, because they chafe at international legal restraints on the right to wage war.[2] Under the doctrine of preemptive self-defense, the Bush administration sought to broaden the legal grounds for the unilateral use of force, a position that in the eyes of some commentators moved it closer to an old-fashioned conception of sovereignty.[3] It is a curious feature of some New Sovereigntist writings that only international institutions, not powerful states, are represented as posing a threat to national sovereignty, and that the role of international institutions in protecting weak state sovereignty against strong state aggression is overlooked. At times, New Sovereigntists can sound like the big bad wolf encouraging the little pig to liberate himself from his brick house.[4] But although New Sovereigntists represent an extreme, it is generally assumed that sovereignty gives states a general right to chart their own foreign policy—to choose their own ambassadors, for example, and to represent their interests before foreign states and international institutions.[5] That this right is more limited than the corresponding right to chart domestic policy is a reminder that sovereignty is not a simple concept, but incorporates multiple normative considerations.

Legal and political theorists disagree whether the sovereignty norm should be retained.[6] Critics recognize that the norm is often invoked for legitimate purposes—for example, to condemn territorial conquests or predatory invasions and interventions—but they worry that it lends itself to illegitimate purposes as well, and they wish for a more discriminating norm or set of norms to take its place.[7] The concept figures prominently in debates over the legitimacy of humanitarian intervention (military force used by foreign states in the attempt to stop domestic human rights atrocities). Brad Roth has argued that we need the concept of sovereignty to affirm a general (though not absolute) prohibition of humanitarian intervention in the absence of UN Security Council authorization, since otherwise powerful states will be led (for either sincere or cynical reasons) into unjust and unwise interventions, entailing a dangerous and counterproductive escalation of violence.[8] The important topic of humanitarian intervention lies outside the scope of this book.

Let us say that in contemporary legal and political discourse, sovereignty implies the right of a state *in general* to determine its own political system, choose its own domestic and foreign policy, and participate as an equal with other states in the making of international law. Hence our question: Is sovereignty compatible with limits placed by international human rights law on a state's choice of its political system and domestic and foreign policy? Some leading theorists of sovereignty answer yes. Brad Roth writes: "States do not diminish their sovereignty by binding themselves to international legal obligations, even in respect of internal public order."[9] Jean Cohen writes: "It is perfectly conceivable that a state can give up the *jus belli* [right to wage war], accept that all states are bound by enforceable human rights norms, and open up its territory to jurisdiction by a functionally delimited supranational legal order and still be sovereign."[10] New Sovereigntists disagree. Representative is the claim by David Rivkin and Lee Casey that contemporary international human rights law, because it "purports to govern the relationship of citizens to their governments," is a "frontal assault on sovereignty." They add that "any attack upon the principle of sovereignty threatens the very foundation of American democracy."[11]

The arguments laid out in previous chapters (especially 2 and 6) support the view that a legitimate conception of sovereignty is compatible with international human rights law. International human rights law leaves plenty of room for self-determination. Extending what I called the "Madisonian" definition of democracy, we can conceptualize sovereignty as a norm that provides states the space to examine and select policies necessary to uphold justice—policies that may include the adoption of international oversight mechanisms. Self-determination rightly understood does not include permission to violate human rights or hinder institutional arrangements necessary for the protection of human rights. On a moderate conception of sovereignty, therefore, there is no necessary conflict with international human rights law, and the values of democracy and constitutionalism do not require, or indeed permit, anything more than a moderate conception of sovereignty.

If some people are attracted to a stronger conception of sovereignty, the reason, I suggest, is that they associate sovereignty with the will of the political community and view any restrictions on the collective will (at least as regards domestic policy, but perhaps foreign policy as well) as intrinsically regrettable (even if not regrettable all things considered). This outlook need not pose a challenge to the legitimacy of *domestic* constitutional restraints on popular government, since those restraints may be interpreted as an expression of the community's deeper will. But external restraints cannot be so regarded, and must therefore be viewed with some measure of regret. This outlook finds a home in the classical or "Westphalian" conception of sovereignty, especially as articulated in the political theory of Jean-Jacques Rousseau.

A little background first. Writing a century before Rousseau, Hobbes (1588–1679) had made sovereignty the organizing principle of his absolutist political theory.[12] (His theory of sovereignty is partly anticipated by that of Jean Bodin [1530–96].)[13] He meant to defend the legitimacy of monarchical rule, while purifying it of medieval restrictions. Order would collapse, he argued, unless the final authority to declare, interpret, and enforce the law was vested in the same person or group of persons. John Locke (1632–1704) and Montesquieu (1689–1755) were among those who insisted to the contrary that public order, not to mention individual freedom, was best secured by the division of authority among different branches of government, each operating in accordance with clearly established rules and procedures (and, Locke added, legally obligated to respect human rights).[14] Centuries of experience have proven Hobbes wrong and Locke and Montesquieu right about the relative merits of autocracy on the one hand and constitutional government on the other. If constitutional democracies leave some legal controversies unresolved (because there is no sovereign to issue a final determination), they have shown themselves well able to live with the resulting ambiguity. Quite obviously, political order does not depend on our having a clear answer to every dispute.[15] Perhaps not having the answer to some disputes is a *necessary condition* of order—because it lowers the risk of definite but wrong answers; because it develops our skills in cooperation, coexistence, and dialogue; and because it checks authoritarian or servile attitudes that may come from over-reliance on rules.

Rousseau (1712–78) memorably yoked the concept of sovereignty to a theory of popular rule. Hobbes had acknowledged that sovereignty could be vested in the people as a whole, but argued that democracy (as he called this arrangement) was woefully inferior to monarchy. Rousseau differed from Hobbes (and Bodin) in insisting that sovereignty can reside *only* in the people. Unlike Hobbes also, he separated the executive function from the tasks of the sovereign, though the sovereign preserves ultimate control by choosing the form of the executive branch and the people who staff it. But like Hobbes, Rousseau insisted that sovereignty is illimitable, indivisible, and inalienable.[16] He "accomplished for the people what Hobbes had done for the ruler."[17] If anything, he made sovereignty purer, more monolithic and unyielding, because he gave it a prestige unattainable in Hobbes's account. In Hobbes, the value of sovereignty, though overwhelming, is clearly instrumental: sovereignty is the indispensable condition of political order. In Rousseau, sovereignty is something we, as its possessors, actually enjoy. We all get to be king. Sovereignty is no longer a cold necessity of political life, but an intrinsic good.

Rousseau made a triple identification of popular sovereignty, collective freedom, and individual freedom. The general will is the will of the collective and the (true) will of each citizen, so that in obeying the sovereign, each citizen obeys him or herself alone. Given this convergence of ideals, it is not surprising that Rousseau shed limitations that even Hobbes had placed on the sovereign. Hobbes gave the sovereign a moral obligation to obey natural law, although to be sure subjects had no right to enforce the sovereign's compliance. According to Rousseau, the sovereign is unconstrained by natural law, since the sovereign cannot err, and cannot even harm any subject. Whether we find this reassuring will depend in large degree on whether we accept Rousseau's claim that the general will is constrained by its formal properties to adhere strictly to justice. On one point, Hobbes and Rousseau were agreed. Though all law emanates from the sovereign, the sovereign itself is not tied down by law. Hobbes made it clear that the sovereign may replace any law he finds irksome. Rousseau wrote, referring to the sovereign, that "it is absurd for the will to bind itself for the future."[18] Law requires a lawmaker unbound by law.

Rousseau's conceptual alchemy, identifying sovereignty with freedom and vice versa, raised the stakes over sovereignty. To be free is to be supreme, to have no external tie on one's conduct, no rule but that of one's own will. Gone is the view of Locke and Montesquieu that freedom means only a choice among morally permissible actions.[19] Obviously, Rousseau did not intend to license immorality in the name of freedom. He was groping for the argument that Immanuel Kant later articulated: namely, that an autonomous will is a moral will because immoral actions come only from heteronomous impulses external to the will.[20] The danger in adopting this line is that if we do not subscribe to Kant's theory of freedom—a theory that raises controversy even among trained philosophers and is not, to put it gently, deeply internalized in the world of international politics—then we are left only with the view that freedom equals an untethered will.

As a metaphor for personal independence, sovereignty is hard to resist. "Over himself, over his own body and mind, the individual is sovereign" is John Stuart Mill's memorable line.[21] Individual freedom must be surrounded with the same awe and respect once reserved for kings and queens. The modern belief in personal freedom has encouraged the metaphor of the sovereign individual. And when refracted through nationalism (another modern idea), it has led, in circular motion, to renewed support for state sovereignty, now a metaphor no longer. If I as an individual am entitled to be free, to live my life as I choose without external dictation, then the nation, which is my larger self, is entitled to no less a degree of freedom. My nation's dignity, and therefore my own, is attacked when outsiders interfere in its domestic life. (The nation exercises its sovereignty through the state it already has or else seeks to acquire.) If in analogy to Mill's harm principle we restrict sovereignty to self-regarding actions, then only interference in a nation's domestic affairs is forbidden. But if we allow *sovereignty* itself to become our guiding concept, then any constraint may be resented.

Against the celebration of sovereignty, understood as the empowerment of the individual or collective will, Hannah Arendt mounted a potent critique. She argued that sovereignty (in this sense) is not the basis of freedom and order, but rather tyranny and chaos. It trades on the fantasy of being alone in the world, or of being the only person whose wishes shall prevail. It cannot accommodate the reality of other people: "If it were true that sovereignty and freedom are the same, then indeed no man could be free, because sovereignty, the ideal of uncompromising self-sufficiency and mastership, is contradictory to the very condition of plurality. No man can be sovereign because not one man, but men, inhabit the earth."[22] Elsewhere she declares: "If men wish to be free, it is precisely sovereignty they must renounce."[23] Arendt suggests that sovereignty answers morally dubious yearnings: to stay in charge, to be boss, not to bend or adjust for others.

Nor is sovereignty conducive to order. Subjectivist in logic, it purchases unity and determinacy at the price of inconstancy and unpredictability, both domestically and internationally:

> Rousseau took his metaphor of a general will seriously and literally enough to conceive of the nation as a body driven by one will, like an individual, which also can change direction at any time without losing its identity. . . . [He] therefore insisted that it would "be absurd for the will to bind itself for the future," thus anticipating the fateful instability and faithlessness of revolutionary governments as well as justifying the old fateful conviction of the nation-state that treaties are binding only so long as they serve the so-called national interest.[24]

Thus "a community founded on this sovereign will would be built not on sand but on quicksand."[25] The problem is familiar to any reader of Hobbes's *Leviathan*, where the authority of the law seems rather undermined by the fact that it changes at the sovereign's pleasure.

The genius of the American Revolution, in Arendt's view, was that it refused to associate power with sovereignty: 150 years of effective self-rule as nominal British subjects had taught the colonists that sovereignty was unnecessary to the exercise of power.[26] In townships, counties, and colonial legislatures, they managed their collective affairs without claiming that authority derived from their own will. Not construing their power in terms of sovereignty, they never sought to liberate power from law.[27] Governing experience and reverence for the law prepared them for the task of making state constitutions in 1776, and for creating a federal Constitution in the following decade:

> Those who received the power to constitute, to frame constitutions, were duly elected delegates of constituted bodies; they received their authority from below, and when they held fast to the Roman principle that the seat of power lay in the people, they did not think in terms of a fiction and an absolute, the nation above all authority and absolved from all laws, but in terms of a working reality, the organized multitude whose power was exerted in accordance with laws and limited by them.[28]

The Founders were clear that although the people are the original source of power, the power originally held by them is not unlimited. The 1776 Virginia

Declaration of Rights, in a formula widely echoed by other states, held both that "all power is vested in, and consequently derived from, the people" and that "all men are by nature equally free and independent and have certain inherent rights, of which, when they enter into a state of society, they cannot, by any compact, deprive or divest their posterity."[29]

Freedom, according to Arendt, resides in our capacity to form and keep promises, and such capacity is the only viable foundation of order: "All political business is, and always has been, transacted within an elaborate framework of ties and bonds for the future—such as laws and constitutions, treaties and alliances—all of which derive in the last instance from the faculty to promise and to keep promises in the face of the essential uncertainties of the future."[30] Reaching agreement with others, not amalgamating all preferences and perspectives into a single will; being held to our mutual promises, not asserting a sovereign prerogative to alter course at any time—this is the key to stability. Consequently, federation rather than sovereignty is the proper basis of politics, and what Arendt called "the greatest revolutionary innovation" was "Madison's discovery of the federal principle for the foundation of large republics," although the discovery was indebted to the earlier American experience of combining powers through institutions of popular government.[31]

Arendt helps move us from an expansive to a moderate conception of sovereignty. If we conceive political action not as an effort to empower the will of the political community, but as the forging of mutual pledges among equals, then the limitation of domestic and foreign policy by salutary international law (such as international human rights law) entails no loss of legitimacy or power. The creation and improvement of such law may be seen as an expression rather than a curtailment of political agency.[32] A recent application of the federal principle is found in Jean Cohen's theorization of a transnational federal union of states, in which states retain their independence while granting certain decision-making powers to the union and allowing some jurisdictional overlap of state and federal authority within each state's territory.[33] (Cohen is thinking among other things of the European Union.) The purpose of such a scheme is to solve collective problems and promote good governance while preserving spaces for democratic citizenship that have been achieved within the nation-state. Cohen notes the Madisonian virtues of the arrangement: "The elective affinity between republican and federal structures is due to the similarity in constitutional logic: both establish, separate, and divide power; both set up counter-powers so as to expand the power of the whole while preserving liberty of the parts."[34] The Arendtian logic is evident here, though Cohen stands by the principle of state sovereignty and criticizes Arendt for not recognizing that sovereignty can take a moderate form.[35]

One of the lessons taught by *The Federalist* is that rigid conceptions of sovereignty are best avoided. Interestingly, it is a lesson learned by the authors in the course of writing the essays. In essays 15 through 20, Hamilton and Madison strenuously argue that individual states cannot retain sovereignty as part of a viable union.[36] "A sovereignty over sovereigns . . . as it is a solecism in theory, so in practice it is subversive of the order and ends of civil polity," writes Madison in *Federalist* 20 (p. 172). But in later essays they find it simpler to say the individual states preserve considerable albeit limited sovereignty.[37] Because Madison and Hamilton learn to be comfortable with the idea of limited and disaggregated sovereignty, they leave the door open to systems of mutual oversight among nations (though since no such systems had yet been devised they do not develop the possibility). If the states forming the American republic can remain sovereign even though the Constitution forbids them to pass bills of attainder, enact ex post facto laws, grant titles of nobility, or abandon a republican form of government (art. 1, §10; art. 4, §4),[38] and even though the central government is explicitly directed to enforce the last of these prohibitions (art. 4, §4), it would seem that the national republic can retain its sovereignty even while integrating itself into a strong international human rights regime.

Noteworthy, too, is the long passage in *Federalist* 45 (p. 293) in which Madison pleads with his readers to relax their devotion to sovereignty as a political ideal. The Revolution was fought to secure "peace, liberty, and safety," not to array the states "with certain dignities and attributes of sovereignty." To sacrifice public happiness to the preservation of sovereignty would be to revive in a new form "the impious doctrine of the old world that the people were made for kings, not kings for the people." Though the immediate reference is to the sovereignty of the individual states, the argument extends more broadly. Madison reminds us that sovereignty (traditionally an attribute of kings) is valuable only insofar as it contributes to the public happiness, and that whether and to what extent and in what manner it does so is an empirical question on which we should preserve an open mind.[39]

In the preceding remarks I have tried to show that only an expansive conception of sovereignty is in conflict with international human rights law, and that such a conception is not worthy of our support. But we should note the argument that even moderate conceptions of state sovereignty, depending on how they are defined, may pose an obstacle to justice. If sovereignty implies that states are (rebuttably) presumed not to be obligated without their consent,[40] then it potentially licenses the use of national vetoes to block necessary solutions to transnational problems such as pollution, climate change, nuclear proliferation, global inequality, and economic policies of developed countries harmful to developing countries. Acquiescence to these evils threatens (or indeed violates) human rights, which is why compelling arguments have been made that human rights require a radical restructuring of the international order and a significant reduction of national sovereignty.[41] Even a moderate conception of sovereignty may encourage the view that states are permitted to assert national self-interest at the expense of impartial justice. David Held has observed that the contemporary understanding of sovereignty, which incorporates significant restrictions rooted in human rights and democracy, tames the arrogance of rulers in some respects but compounds it in others. "Democratic princes," unlike their monarchical antecedents, "derive their support from that most virtuous source of power— the demos" and "can energetically pursue public policies—whether in security, trade, technology, or welfare—because they feel, and to a large degree are, mandated to do so."[42] I have argued (in Chapter 3 and elsewhere) that the international protection of civil and political rights (such as those promised in the European Convention on Human Rights) succeeds best when it takes a decentralized form, but other transnational problems may require more centralized forms of integration. These reflections prompt the thought that sovereignty should perhaps be disaggregated—upheld in some domains but transferred or relinquished in others, a notion that ought to be familiar to readers of *The Federalist*.[43]

A Final Word

When it comes to human rights, transnational cooperation furnishes protections that a single country cannot provide on its own. Participation in a strong international human rights regime grants other countries the power to judge the adequacy of one's record. One's policies must satisfy a higher standard of justification, because they are judged by other countries not sharing one's biases and blind spots (at least not to the same extent). But the other countries cannot judge in an arbitrary or capricious manner, since the standards they apply to others will be applied to themselves. If the parties do not really care about human rights, the regime will sink into a meaningless exercise (or worse). But if they begin with a measure of genuine commitment, the regime can hold each party to its professed ideals. Mutual oversight and collective decision making, when sincerely undertaken in the service of human rights, can raise the standard of minimally acceptable behavior and generate improved means of enforcement.

There is nothing to stop the United States from integrating itself more fully into existing international human rights laws and institutions. It can withdraw the reservations, understandings, and declarations that dilute the impact of ratified human rights treaties. It can implement its human rights treaty obligations through domestic legislation. It can ratify the Optional Protocol to the Torture Convention and the Rome Statute of the International Criminal Court. It can grant individuals the right to submit complaints to the UN committees that oversee its compliance with treaties like the ICCPR and the Torture Convention. It can ratify the Inter-American Convention on Human Rights and accept the jurisdiction of the Inter-American Court of Human Rights. Most important, it can increase the power of domestic judges to enforce its human rights obligations under international (not to mention domestic) law. Only the will, not the opportunity, has been lacking.

To reject participation in a strong international human rights regime is to make oneself judge in one's own case. Such a posture (compounded when a state enjoys hegemonic power in the international system) encourages the arrogance and blindness that Locke diagnosed as the incurable condition of absolute monarchies. The dismissal of international human rights law is anti-constitutional, because it is opposed to fundamental constitutional principles of checks and balances, impartial adjudication, and a guaranteed remedy for the violation of individual rights. In the case of the United States, it has severely undermined the protection of human rights. The United States, if it is serious about respecting human rights, must no longer seek exemption from the international human rights regime. Other countries claiming the title of constitutional democracy should forswear such exemptions as well.

Notes

Introduction

1. I substitute "human beings" for the problematic and ambiguous "men" in the original document.

2. See Michael Ignatieff, ed., *American Exceptionalism and Human Rights* (Princeton, N.J.: Princeton University Press, 2005).

3. Natalie Hevener Kaufman, *Human Rights Treaties and the Senate: A History of Opposition* (Chapel Hill: University of North Carolina Press, 1990). No doubt, the United States' great power status has been a major source of this resistance, as it encourages a certain impatience toward international legal restraint in general.

4. The term was coined by Peter J. Spiro in "The New Sovereigntists: American Exceptionalism and Its False Prophets," *Foreign Affairs* 79 (November/December 2000): 9–15.

5. Examples include Jeremy Rabkin, *Law Without Nations? Why Constitutional Government Requires Sovereign States* (Princeton, N.J.: Princeton University Press, 2005); Jack Goldsmith, "Should International Human Rights Law Trump U.S. Domestic Law?," *Chicago Journal of International Law* 1 (2000): 327–39; Lee A. Casey and David B. Rivkin, Jr., "The Rocky Shoals of International Law," *National Interest* 62 (2000–2001): 35–46; and Robert H. Bork, *Coercing Virtue: The Worldwide Rule of Judges* (Washington, D.C.: AEI Press, 2003). Ignatieff, ed., *American Exceptionalism and Human Rights*, offers important rejoinders to defenders of the self-exemption policy.

6. I discuss examples in Chapter 5.

7. For example, Jed Rubenfeld, "Unilateralism and Constitutionalism," *New York University Law Review* 79 (2004): 1971–2028; and Richard Bellamy, *Political Constitutionalism* (Cambridge: Cambridge University Press, 2007).

8. Especially in the United Kingdom. See, for example, Michael Pinto-Duschinsky, "Bringing Rights Back Home: Making Human Rights Compatible with Parliamentary Democracy in the UK," *Policy Exchange*, February 2011.

9. For a discussion of ways in which international law can support democracy at the domestic level, see Robert O. Keohane, Stephen Macedo, and Andrew Moravcsik, "Democracy-Enhancing Multilateralism," *International Organization* 63 (2009): 1–31. For discussions showing how international law can sometimes undermine both human rights and democracy, see Angelina Snodgrass Godoy, *Of Medicines and Markets: Intellectual Property and Human Rights in the Free Trade Era*

(Stanford, Calif.: Stanford University Press, 2013); and Kim Lane Scheppele, "The Migration of Anti-Constitutional Ideas: The Post-9/11 Globalization of Public Law and the International State of Emergency," in *The Migration of Constitutional Ideas*, ed. Sujit Choudhry (Cambridge: Cambridge University Press, 2006).

10. The process, characterized by blatant bias and selectivity, has understandably fueled cynicism about international human rights institutions. But the resolutions system should not be conflated with the Council as a whole, much less international human rights institutions in general. The Council, along with the Commission it replaced in 2006, has contributed to the development of human rights norms, especially by overseeing the drafting of human rights treaties; fostered dialogue and information-sharing; and carried out comprehensive thematic and country-specific investigations. More recently, the Council has encouraged states to promise human rights improvements under the rubric of the Universal Periodic Review. Rosa Freedman's mixed verdict is that the Council has contributed to the *promotion* of human rights but failed when it comes to the *protection* of human rights. Freedman, *Failing to Protect: The UN and the Politicisation of Human Rights* (Oxford: Oxford University Press, 2015), p. 140. See also Rosa Freedman, *The United Nations Human Rights Council: A Critique and Early Assessment* (New York: Routledge, 2013); Bertrand G. Ramcharan, *The UN Human Rights Council* (London: Routledge, 2011); and Hilary Charlesworth and Emma Larking, eds., *Human Rights and the Universal Periodic Review: Rituals and Ritualism* (Cambridge: Cambridge University Press, 2014). I do not examine the Human Rights Council in this book.

11. As one example, the Organization of Islamic Cooperation a few years ago persuaded the UN Human Rights Council to pass a series of resolutions calling on governments to combat "defamation of religion," a measure that could be construed to lend support to anti-blasphemy legislation. After the ensuing controversy, these resolutions have been dropped in favor of more reasonable resolutions condemning discrimination and incitement against persons based on religion. See Turan Kayaoglu and Marie Juul Petersen, "Will the Istanbul Process Relieve the Tension Between the Muslim World and the West?," *Washington Review of Turkish and Eurasian Affairs* (October 2013). As another example, Russia has successfully lobbied the Human Rights Council to pass resolutions upholding the role of "traditional values" in promoting human rights. The initiative is rightly condemned by human rights organizations as a strategy for undermining the rights of sexual minorities in the name of tradition. See Michael Blake, "'Traditional Values' and Human Rights: Whose Traditions? Which Rights?," *Cicero Foundation*, December 2013. I thank Michael Blake for urging me to address this problem.

12. See the essays in Marie Juul Petersen and Turan Kayaoglu, eds., *The Organisation of Islamic Cooperation and Human Rights* (Philadelphia: University of Pennsylvania Press, 2019): Anthony Tirado Chase, "Setting the Scene"; Turan Kayaoglu, "The OIC's Human Rights Regime"; and Ann Elizabeth Mayer, "The OIC's Human Rights Policies in the UN: A Problem of Coherence."

13. This discussion is indebted to Chase, "The Organization of Islamic Cooperation."

14. Martin Luther King, Jr., warned against the "Western arrogance of feeling that it has everything to teach others and nothing to learn from them." King, "Why I Am Opposed to the War in Vietnam," Riverside Church, New York, April 30, 1967.

15. The arguments made in this book lend support to the view that the United States should deepen its ties to the Inter-American human rights regime. As a member of the Organization of American States, the United States falls under the oversight of the Inter-American Commission on Human Rights, but it has not ratified the Inter-American Convention on Human Rights, and therefore does not fall under the jurisdiction of the Inter-American Court of Human Rights. The

Inter-American regime has made a decisive and at times heroic contribution to the protection of human rights. It has produced authoritative investigative reports, interceded for victims, and raised the legal standard of acceptable human rights practices. The jurisprudence of the Inter--American Court has influenced the domestic law of several member states. See Tom Farer, "The Rise of the Inter-American Human Rights Regime: No Longer a Unicorn, Not Yet an Ox," *Human Rights Quarterly* 19 (1997): 510–46; Juan E. Méndez, "The Inter-American System of Protection: Its Contributions to the International Law of Human Rights," in *Realizing Human Rights*, ed. Samantha Power and Graham Allison (New York: St. Martin's, 2000); and the symposium on "The Future of the Inter-American System of Human Rights," *Human Rights Brief* 20 (2013): 2–45.

16. This book does not examine two other policies of the United States in the "War on Terror" that breach long-recognized moral and political norms protective of fundamental human rights: the use of drones outside conflict zones to conduct "targeted" killings, causing heavy infliction of civilian casualties, and mass surveillance of telephone and email communications. For a discussion of connections between the torture and targeted killing policies, see Lisa Hajjar, "Anatomy of the US Targeted Killing Policy," *Middle East Research and Information Project*, Fall 2012.

17. The best overview of the U.S. torture policy is *The Report of the Constitution Project's Task Force on Detainee Treatment*, 2013 (Washington, D.C.: The Constitution Project, 2013) (hereafter *Constitution Project Report*). For harrowing details of the CIA torture program, see *The Senate Intelligence Committee Report on Torture* (Brooklyn, N.Y.: Melville, 2014) (hereafter *Senate Torture Report*). The U.S. military also practiced torture.

18. Hima Shamsi, *Command's Responsibility: Detainee Deaths in U.S. Custody in Iraq and Afghanistan*, ed. Deborah Pearlstein, Human Rights First, February 2006.

19. For an example of victim testimonies, see International Committee of the Red Cross, *ICRC Report on the Treatment of Fourteen "High Value Detainees" in CIA Custody*, February 2007 (hereafter *ICRC Report*). For the government's internal communications, see *Senate Torture Report*.

20. *Constitution Project Report*, pp. 261–62.

21. Robert A. Pape, "Review," *H-Diplo/ISSF Forum (no. 5) on the Senate Select Committee on Intelligence (SSCI) and the United States' Post-9/11 Policy on Torture* (February 16, 2005): 18–42; Thérèse Postel, "How Guantanamo Bay's Existence Helps Al-Qaeda Recruit More Terrorists," *Atlantic*, April 12, 2013; Matthew Alexander, "I'm Still Tortured by What I Saw in Iraq," *Washington Post*, November 30, 2008.

22. The leaders of the campaign include former Vice President Dick Cheney and his entourage and current and former CIA officials. See David Jackson, "Cheney Again Defends Interrogation Techniques," *U.S.A. Today*, December 14, 2014; Kevin Gosztola, "CIA Had Propaganda Campaign Which Involved Leaking Classified Information to Sell Torture," *The Dissenter*, December 10, 2014. The *Senate Torture Report* documents a pattern of CIA lying to Congress, the Department of Justice, and the public about the effectiveness of torture. Notoriously, the CIA took part in scripting the narrative of the popular Hollywood movie *Zero Dark Thirty*, suggesting that CIA torture techniques helped disclose the location of Osama bin Laden, an account the *Senate Torture Report* has confirmed is a near-total fabrication. Charlie Savage and James Risen, "Senate Report Rejects Claim on Hunt for Bin Laden," *New York Times*, December 9, 2014. For an insightful discussion, see Robert Crawford, "Torture and the Ideology of National Security," *Global Dialogue* 12 (Winter/Spring 2010).

23. Mark Mazzetti and Carl Hulse, "Inquiry by C.I.A. Affirms It Spied on Senate Panel," *New York Times*, July 31, 2014.

24. Military Commissions Act of 2006 (discussed in Chapter 4).

25. See Katherine R. Hawkins, "The Promises of Torturers: Diplomatic Assurances and the Legality of 'Rendition,'" *Georgetown Immigration Law Journal* 20 (2006): 213–68; Jane Mayer, *The Dark Side: The Inside Story of How The War on Terror Turned into a War on American Ideals* (New York: Doubleday, 2008), pp. 129–34.

26. *Arar v. Ashcroft*, 585 F.3d 559 (2nd Circ. 2009).

27. Murat Kurnaz, *Five Years of My Life: An Innocent Man in Guantanamo* (New York: Palgrave Macmillan, 2007); Carol D. Leonnig, "Panel Ignored Evidence on Detainee: U.S. Military Intelligence, German Authorities Found No Ties to Terrorists," *Washington Post*, March 27, 2005; Carol D. Leonnig, "Evidence of Innocence Rejected at Guantanamo," *Washington Post*, December 5, 2007.

28. Marc Perelman, "From Sarajevo to Guantanamo: The Strange Case of the Algerian Six," *Mother Jones*, December 4, 2007; Seema Jilani, "Algerians, Freed from Guantanamo, Still Paying the Price," *McClatchy*, September 9, 2009; Lakhdar Boumediene, "My Guantánamo Nightmare," *New York Times*, January 7, 2012; *Boumediene v. Bush*, 579 F. Supp. 2d 191 (D.C. Circ. 2008).

29. Motion to Dismiss for Outrageous Government Conduct, *U.S.A. v. Padilla*, U.S. District Court, Southern District of Florida, October 4, 2006, http://www.discourse.net/archives/docs/Padilla_Outrageous_Government_Conduct.pdf.

30. The government provided as its main evidence an application form he allegedly completed in 2000 to attend an Al Qaeda training camp in Afghanistan. Peter Whoriskey, "Jury Convicts Jose Padilla of Terror Charges," *Washington Post*, August 17, 2007.

31. *Padilla v. Yoo*, 678 F.3d 748 (9th Circ. 2012); *Lebron v. Rumsfeld*, 670 F.3d 540 (4th Circ. 2012).

32. George W. Bush, Address to the Nation, June 6, 2002; George W. Bush, Remarks by the President at Thaddeus McCotter for Congress Dinner, October 14, 2002.

33. *Senate Torture Report*, 32–57; *ICRC Report*; Jason Leopold, "Torture Diaries, Drawings and the Special Prosecutor," *Truthout*, March 29, 2010; Scott Shane, "Waterboarding Used 266 Times on 2 Suspects," *New York Times*, April 19, 2009.

34. Larry Siems, *The Torture Report* (New York: OR Books, 2011), p. 214, quoting U.S. government filings in Abu Zubaydah's habeas corpus case, "Respondent's Memorandum of Points and Authorities in Opposition to Petitioner's Motion for Discovery and Petitioner's Motion for Sanctions," *Husayn v. Gates*, 08-cv-1360 (D.D.C. Oct. 27, 2009). For the earlier claim that Zubaydah helped plan the 9/11 attacks, see Jay S. Bybee, "Memorandum for John Rizzo: Interrogation of al Qaeda Operative," August 1, 2002, in *The Torture Memos*, ed. David Cole (New York: New Press, 2009), p. 113. See also Jason Leopold, "U.S. Recants Claims on 'High-Value' Detainee Abu Zubaydah," *Truthout*, March 30, 2010.

35. Joseph Margulies, "Abu Zubaydah's Suffering," op-ed, *Los Angeles Times*, April 30, 2009.

36. A few studies include the *Constitution Project Report*; *Senate Torture Report*; U.S Senate Committee on Armed Services, Inquiry into the Treatment of Detainees in U.S. Custody, November 20, 2008; Jonathan Hafetz, *Habeas Corpus After 9/11* (New York: New York University Press, 2011); Lisa Hajjar, *Torture: A Sociology of Violence and Human Rights* (New York: Routledge, 2013); David Luban, *Torture, Power, and Law* (Cambridge: Cambridge University Press, 2014); Joseph Margulies, *Guantánamo and the Abuse of Presidential Power* (New York: Simon and Schuster, 2007); Mayer, *The Dark Side*; Alfred W. McCoy, *A Question of Torture: CIA Interrogation, from the Cold War to the War on Terror* (New York: Metropolitan Books, 2006); John T. Parry, *Understanding Torture* (Ann Arbor: University of Michigan Press, 2010); Joshua E. S. Phillips, *None of Us Were*

like This Before: American Soldiers and Torture (London: Verso, 2012); Philippe Sands, *Torture Team* (New York: Palgrave Macmillan, 2008); and Siems, *Torture Report.*

37. "Bush: 'I Have Never Ordered Torture,'" *CNN.com*, June 22, 2004.

38. See Peter Beinart, "Torture Is Who We Are," *Atlantic*, December 11, 2014. For examination of the larger problem, see Jeanne Morefield, *Empires Without Imperialism: Anglo-American Decline and the Politics of Deflection* (Oxford: Oxford University Press, 2014).

39. U.S. Senate Committee on Armed Services, *Inquiry into the Treatment of Detainees in U.S. Custody*, November 20, 2008, p. xii.

40. In June 2015, the Senate adopted an amendment requiring all U.S. personnel to adhere to the strict anti-torture guidelines of the U.S. Army Field Manual and requiring International Committee of the Red Cross access to wartime detainees in U.S. custody. The proposal may be interpreted as a partial retreat from the self-exemption policy. If enacted, it would inhibit the return of "enhanced interrogation techniques," but its deterrent impact would be greatly strengthened if the United States incorporated other international human rights law provisions, such as those requiring additional preventive measures, mandating civil remedies for the victims of torture, and enhancing judicial enforcement powers, and if it withdrew loopholes from its ratification of various human rights treaties.

41. Linda Camp Keith, "The United Nations International Covenant on Civil and Political Rights: Does It Make a Difference in Human Rights Behavior?" *Journal of Peace Research* 36 (1999): 95–118; Oona Hathaway, "Do Human Rights Treaties Make a Difference?" *Yale Law Journal* 111 (2002): 1935–2042; and Emilie M. Hafner-Burton and Kiyoteru Tsutsui, "Human Rights in a Globalizing World: The Paradox of Empty Promises," *American Journal of Sociology* 110 (2005): 1373–1411.

42. Eric Posner cites the skeptical studies to claim that "the overall picture at the aggregate level . . . is that human rights treaties do not systematically improve human rights outcomes." Eric A. Posner, *The Twilight of Human Rights Law* (Oxford: Oxford University Press, 2014), p. 77. See also Posner, *The Perils of Global Legalism* (Chicago: University of Chicago Press, 2009), p. 68; and Jeremy A. Rabkin, *The Case for Sovereignty: Why the World Should Welcome American Independence* (Washington, D.C.: AEI Press, 2004), pp. 107–8.

43. Beth A. Simmons, *Mobilizing for Human Rights* (Cambridge: Cambridge University Press, 2009). Other studies reporting a statistical correlation between human rights treaty ratification and improved human rights performance under certain conditions include Eric Neumayer, "Do International Human Rights Treaties Improve Respect for Human Rights?," *Journal of Conflict Resolution* 49 (2005): 925–53; Wade M. Cole, "Human Rights Treaties as Myth and Ceremony? Reevaluating the Effectiveness of Human Rights Treaties, 1981–2007," *American Journal of Sociology* 117 (2012): 1131–71; and Ann Marie Clark, "The Normative Context of Human Rights Criticism: Treaty Ratification and UN Mechanisms," in *The Persistent Power of Human Rights*, ed. Thomas Risse, Stephen C. Ropp, and Kathryn Sikkink (Cambridge: Cambridge University Press, 2013).

44. Neumayer, "Do International Human Rights Treaties Improve Respect for Human Rights?"

45. That's because, over time, any given level of *actual* human rights violations will correspond to a worse human rights *score*. For convincing evidence of this pattern, see Ann Marie Clark and Kathryn Sikkink, "Information Effects and Human Rights Data: Is the Good News About Increased Human Rights Information Bad News for Human Rights Measures?," *Human Rights Quarterly* 35 (2013): 539–68; Bridget Marchesi and Kathryn Sikkink, "The Effectiveness of the International Human Rights Legal Regime: What Do We Know and How Do We Know It?" (unpublished paper); Christopher J. Fariss, "Respect for Human Rights Has Improved Over Time: Modeling the Changing Standard of Accountability," *American Political Science Review* 108 (2014): 297–318; and Ryan

Goodman and Derek Jinks, "Measuring the Effects of Human Rights Treaties," *European Journal of International Law* 14 (2003): 171–83.

The datasets contain other distortions. See Clark and Sikkink, "Information Effects and Human Rights Data." It should be emphasized that the primary sources (e.g., Amnesty International and State Department reports) are not produced with the intention of providing social scientists comparative measures of human rights violations valid across countries and across time.

46. Goodman and Jinks, "Measuring the Effects of Human Rights Treaties," pp. 175–78.

47. Fariss, "Respect for Human Rights Has Improved over Time."

48. Ibid.; Fariss, "The Changing Standard of Accountability and the Positive Relationship Between Human Rights Treaty Ratification and Compliance," *British Journal of Political Science* 48 (2018): 239–71. Fariss examines the six principal UN-based human rights treaties: the Covenant on Civil and Political Rights; the Covenant on Economic, Social and Cultural Rights; the Torture Convention; the Convention to Eliminate Racial Discrimination; the Convention to Eliminate Discrimination Against Women; and the Children's Rights Convention.

49. See also Goodman and Jinks, "Measuring the Effects of Human Rights Treaties," pp. 173–74.

50. For the increasing role played by national human rights institutions, see Julie A. Mertus, *Human Rights Matters: Local Politics and National Human Rights Institutions* (Stanford, Calif.: Stanford University Press, 2009), and Sonia Cardenas, *Chains of Justice: The Global Rise of State Institutions for Human Rights* (Philadelphia: University of Pennsylvania Press, 2014).

51. This is a central theme of Simmons, *Mobilizing for Human Rights.*

52. Zachary Elkins, Tom Ginsburg, and Beth Simmons, "Getting to Rights: Treaty Ratification, Constitutional Convergence, and Human Rights Practice," *Harvard International Law Journal* 54 (2013): 61–95; Hurst Hannum, "The Status of the Universal Declaration of Human Rights in National and International Law," *Georgia Journal of International and Comparative Law* 25 (1995/96): 287–397, pp. 312–15. As Elkins et al. show, the timing of the constitutional rights provisions leaves no doubt that many were inspired by the international charters. The language of the constitutional provisions is sometimes taken verbatim from the international charters, and several national constitutions refer to the Universal Declaration of Human Rights by name.

53. Elkins et al., "Getting to Rights."

54. Harold Hongju Koh, "How Is International Human Rights Law Enforced?" *Indiana Law Journal* 74 (1999): 1397–1417, pp. 1413–16.

55. For example, Helen Keller and Alec Stone Sweet, eds. *A Europe of Rights: The Impact of the ECHR on National Legal Systems* (Oxford: Oxford University Press, 2008).

56. This is another central theme of Simmons, *Mobilizing for Human Rights.*

57. Geoff Dancy and Christopher J. Fariss, "Rescuing Human Rights Law from International Legalism and Its Critics," *Human Rights Quarterly* 39 (2017): 1–36, p.4.

58. I have earlier developed this thesis with reference to the International Criminal Court (ICC), arguing that the ICC helps consolidate democracy, and that democratic member states are needed to enhance the Court's integrity and effectiveness. For a long version of the argument, see Jamie Mayerfeld, "The Mutual Dependence of External and Internal Justice: The Democratic Achievement of the International Criminal Court," *Finnish Yearbook of International Law* 12 (2001): 71–107. For a shorter version, see Mayerfeld, "The Democratic Legacy of the International Criminal Court," *Fletcher Forum of World Affairs* 28 (2004): 147–56.

59. See generally Luis Cabrera, "World Government: Renewed Debate, Persistent Challenges," *European Journal of International Relations* 16 (2010): 511–30; and Peter Singer, *One World: The*

Ethics of Globalization, 2nd ed. (New Haven, Conn.: Yale University Press, 2004), pp. 196–201. On nuclear proliferation, see Campbell Craig, *Glimmer of a New Leviathan: Total War in the Realism of Niebuhr, Morgenthau, and Waltz* (New York: Columbia University Press, 2003), pp. 166–72; and Daniel Deudney, *Bounding Power: Republican Security Theory from the Polis to the Global Village* (Princeton, N.J.: Princeton University Press, 2007), chap. 9. On global climate change, see Peter Haas, "Addressing the Global Governance Deficit," *Global Environmental Politics* 4, (2004): 1–15. On world poverty, see Luis Cabrera, *Political Theory of Global Justice* (Abingdon: Routledge, 2004), and Thomas Pogge, *World Poverty and Human Rights*, 2nd ed. (Cambridge: Polity, 2008).

Chapter 1. Human Rights

1. For cogent arguments that human rights should not be reduced to legal rights, see Amartya Sen, "Elements of a Theory of Human Rights," *Philosophy and Public Affairs* 32 (2004): 315–56, p. 345; and John Tasioulas, "Exiting the Hall of Mirrors: Morality and the Law in Human Rights," in *Political and Legal Approaches to Human Rights*, ed. Tom Campbell and Kylie Bourne (London: Routledge, 2017).

2. To be sure, human rights require the creation of particular legal arrangements, some of which are themselves human rights (see the discussion below in "The Right to Have Rights"). But my point is that we have a human right to the creation of those legal arrangements, whether or not they exist in fact.

3. Here and throughout, I use the term "human rights" to mean what Allen Buchanan calls "moral human rights" (rights we have because we are human, whether or not they are recognized in law). Buchanan, *The Heart of Human Rights* (Oxford: Oxford University Press, 2013). This is the meaning of the term implied in the introductory passages of the Universal Declaration of Human Rights and subsequent human rights treaties, and I believe it still prevails in the human rights movement at large. Like Buchanan, I believe there is a strong *moral* justification for a legal human rights regime. Unlike Buchanan, I believe it makes sense to say that most of the entitlements that deserve the status of legal human rights are moral human rights.

Buchanan denies this because of his austere conception of moral rights. He argues that human rights such as (full) legal due process, health care, and democracy are not moral rights, because they require the creation and preservation of large-scale social arrangements and I would not be justified in demanding such arrangements for my benefit alone (ibid., pp. 58–64). But I don't think we should restrict moral rights to those I would possess if I were the sole beneficiary of the requisite social arrangements. It so happens that the social coordination required to deliver the benefits of due process, health care, and democracy to one person will deliver similar benefits to other people. This is a deep fact about our world, and one that profoundly shapes our thinking about individual rights. (Perhaps I would still have a moral right to legal due process, etc., if I were the sole beneficiary of the requisite social arrangements—I am more sympathetic to the idea than Buchanan—but settling this question is unnecessary.) Consider the assertion in the Universal Declaration of Human Rights that "everyone is entitled to a social and international order in which the rights and freedoms set forth in this Declaration can be fully realized" (art. 28). Given that such an order benefits everyone, we each have a right to its creation and a right not to be excluded from it. The solidaristic aspect of moral human rights is an old theme, traceable at least as far back as Locke's *Two Treatises of Government* (where individual rights are linked to a general duty to preserve mankind).

The arguments Buchanan uses to justify legal human rights are arguments that, in my view, establish their credentials as moral human rights. He states that the underlying purpose of legal human rights is to provide individuals the opportunities for a "minimally good or decent life" and to affirm and protect "the basic equal status of each individual" (p. 87). What bars the conclusion that the resulting legal rights are also moral rights is Buchanan's stipulation that moral rights must be those which I could still claim if only I and no one else benefitted from the requisite social arrangements. To repeat, I think this stipulation is unwarranted. It is clearer to say that the fundamental set of universal, morally compulsory human entitlements necessary for the protection of basic interests and the recognition of equal status are moral human rights. Buchanan's claim that many or most legal human rights are not moral human rights is one that (in my view) may invite confusion, and I fear that it could take some wind out of the sails of the human rights movement.

4. Maurice Cranston compares the Declaration unfavorably to the European Convention on Human Rights, but the latter is patterned closely on equivalent provisions in the Declaration. Cranston, "Human Rights, Real and Supposed," in *Political Theory and the Rights of Man*, ed. D. D. Raphael (Bloomington: Indiana University Press, 1967).

5. As sentient, emotional, task-oriented, and social beings, animals share some of the same morally significant interests that underlie human rights. (The case is stronger still for the great apes, with their more advanced cognitive abilities.) And once recognition of animal rights frees us from an anthropocentric perspective, we may become open to other domains of value, including nature—we may come to perceive a morally deep world.

6. Stuart Hampshire, *Innocence and Experience* (Cambridge, Mass.: Harvard University Press, 1990), p. 90.

7. What I call autonomy is related to James Griffin's concept of "normative agency," defined as "our capacity to choose and to pursue our conception of a worthwhile life." Griffin, *On Human Rights* (Oxford: Oxford University Press, 2008), p. 45. Normative agency is the basis of Griffin's theory of human rights. See also Alan Gewirth, "The Epistemology of Human Rights," *Social Philosophy and Policy* 1 (1984): 1–24.

8. Children, too, have a right to autonomy, though one that is more limited in scope.

9. For a thorough philosophical defense, see F. M. Kamm, *Morality, Mortality*, vol. 2, *Rights, Duties, and Status* (New York: Oxford University Press, 1996). For a helpful discussion, see Thomas Nagel, "Personal Rights and Public Space," *Philosophy and Public Affairs* 25 (1995): 83–107.

10. For an eloquent discussion of the right to equal standing, see Elizabeth S. Anderson, "What Is the Point of Equality?" *Ethics* 109 (1999): 287–337.

11. The inspiration is John Rawls's idea of a "political conception of justice." Rawls, *Political Liberalism* (New York: Columbia University Press, 1993). (I here leave aside Rawls's discussion of human rights in *The Law of Peoples* [Cambridge, Mass.: Harvard University Press, 1999].) My sense is similar to Rawls's, but I want to avoid the suggestion, present in Rawls's discussion, that such a conception applies only to political institutions and policies as normally understood. As I argue later, a public conception of human rights can and should apply to interpersonal relations outside the political domain (as normally understood).

12. Other theorists have argued that belief in human rights is now supported by an overlapping consensus of diverse religious and philosophical views. See, for example, Jack Donnelly, *International Human Rights*, 4th ed. (Boulder, Colo.: Westview, 2012), chap. 3; Ari Kohen, *In Defense of Human Rights* (Abingdon: Routledge, 2007), chap. 6; and Charles Taylor, "A World Consensus on Human Rights?" *Dissent* 43 (Summer 1996): 15–21. I emphasize that an overlapping consensus supports not only human rights themselves, but the principles underlying them.

13. Rawls originated the term in *Political Liberalism*. I use it to recognize a broad though not universal consensus in favor of human rights principles. For an argument that philosophical defenses of universal human rights should not lean too much on the existence of an overlapping consensus, see Eun-Jung Katherine Kim, "Justifying Human Rights: Does Consensus Matter?," *Human Rights Review* 13 (2012): 261–78.

14. Ronald Dworkin, *Taking Rights Seriously* (Cambridge, Mass.: Harvard University Press, 1978), p. 272.

15. George Kateb, *The Inner Ocean: Individualism and Democratic Culture* (Ithaca: Cornell University Press, 1992), p. 5. For a similar (though not identical) perspective, see John Tasioulas, "Towards a Philosophy of Human Rights," *Current Legal Problems* 65 (2012): 1–30.

16. Here I depart from some of Rawls's views in *Political Liberalism*, because I draw a less sharp distinction between public and philosophical reason.

17. In the category of "philosophical conceptions," I include religious conceptions that can be translated into nonsectarian terms.

18. My preceding paragraph is misleading inasmuch as it adopts this practice.

19. A classic example is the 1947 American Anthropological Association "Statement on Human Rights," *American Anthropologist* 49 (1947): 539–43.

20. Contemporary anthropologists underscore the point. In the words of Sally Engle Merry, "Cultures consist of repertoires of ideas and practices that are not homogeneous but continually changing because of contradictions among them or because new ideas and institutions are adopted by members. They typically incorporate contested values and practices." Merry, *Human Rights and Gender Violence* (Chicago: University of Chicago Press, 2006), p. 11.

21. There is an American counterpart to such thinking: human rights as alien because they came from the outside (the United Nations).

22. For an argument that belief in universal human rights need not entail moral imperialism, see William J. Talbott, *Which Rights Should Be Universal?* (Oxford: Oxford University Press, 2005).

23. There are exceptions. For example, children may be obligated to attend school.

24. It is true that the defense of human rights sometimes means imposing the value of human rights on those who threaten or oppose them (as when a court orders a public official to desist from a rights violation). But since the human rights idea privileges respect for autonomy, it honors everyone's right to form and act on their own nontyrannical values. In that deeper sense, it is not about imposing some people's values on others.

25. For a general discussion, see Eva Brems, ed., *Conflicts Between Fundamental Rights* (Cambridge: Intersentia, 2008).

26. The distinction between prima facie and all-things-considered duties derives from W. D. Ross, *The Right and the Good* (Oxford: Clarendon, 1930).

27. I do not deny that life presents us with difficult moral dilemmas, cases in which it is difficult to know which action is right. We can argue about how such cases are best understood: whether there is a right answer, though it is difficult for us to know what it is, or whether there is no right answer. These matters need not detain us, since this is not a book about resolving difficult moral dilemmas, but rather about the prevention of human rights violations, most of which are not or should not be viewed as morally controversial.

28. See Michael Ignatieff, *Human Rights as Politics and Idolatry*, ed. Amy Gutmann (Princeton, N.J.: Princeton University Press, 2001), pp. 20–22.

29. See Henry Shue, *Basic Rights* (Princeton, N.J.: Princeton University Press, 1980);

Amartya Sen, *Development as Freedom* (New York: Random House, 1999); Jeremy Waldron, "Liberal Rights: Two Sides of the Coin," in Waldron, *Liberal Rights* (Cambridge: Cambridge University Press, 1993); and James Nickel, *Making Sense of Human Rights*, 2nd ed. (Malden, Mass.: Blackwell, 2007), chap. 9. See also Charles Beitz, *The Idea of Human Rights* (Oxford: Oxford University Press, 2009), pp. 161–74; Talbott, *Which Rights Should Be Universal?*, pp. 178–80; Allen Buchanan, *Justice, Legitimacy, and Self-Determination* (Oxford: Oxford University Press, 2004), pp. 195–200. The political philosophy of Rawls and Dworkin can also be read as an argument for socioeconomic rights.

30. An example is the lynching of African Americans, permitted by the U.S. federal and state governments over several decades.

31. Stephen Holmes and Cass R. Sunstein, *The Cost of Rights: Why Liberty Depends on Taxes* (New York: Norton, 2000), p. 1.

32. See Anna Reid, *Leningrad: The Epic Siege of World War II, 1941–44* (New York: Walker, 2011); Robert Conquest, *The Harvest of Sorrow: Soviet Collectivization and the Terror-Famine* (Oxford: Oxford University Press, 1986); Timothy Snyder, "Stalin and Hitler: Mass Murder by Starvation," *New York Review of Books*, June 21, 2012 (Snyder writes: "In the decade between 1932 and 1942 some eleven million people in the Soviet Union starved to death, first as a result of Soviet policy, then as a result of German policy"); Paula Mitchell Marks, *In a Barren Land: American Indian Dispossession and Survival* (New York: William Morrow, 1998); Frank Dikötter, *Mao's Great Famine* (New York: Walker, 2011); Mike Davis, *Late Victorian Holocausts* (London: Verso, 2001); Alex De Waal, *Famine Crimes: Politics and the Disaster Relief Industry in Africa* (Bloomington: Indiana University Press, 1997).

33. See UN Commission on Human Rights, *Forced Evictions*, December 7, 1993 (ECN.4/1994/20).

34. See Vandana Shiva, *Water Wars: Privatization, Pollution, and Profit* (Cambridge, Mass.: South End, 2002); John Bulloch and Adel Darwish, *Water Wars: Coming Conflicts in the Middle East* (London: Victor Gollancz, 1993); Amnesty International, *Troubled Waters: Palestinians Denied Fair Access to Water*, October 2009.

35. See Corey Brettschneider's argument that since the right to private property entails coercion, it must be justified on terms acceptable to all, and therefore must accommodate a right to welfare. Brettschneider, *Democratic Rights* (Princeton, N.J.: Princeton University Press, 2007), chap. 6.

36. Sen, *Development as Freedom*, chaps. 7 and 9.

37. See Thomas Pogge, *World Poverty and Human Rights*, 2nd ed. (Cambridge: Polity, 2008).

38. Shue, *Basic Rights*, p. 17.

39. See Kim Lane Scheppele, "Social Rights in Constitutional Courts: Strategies of Articulation and Strategies of Enforcement," address at the Annual Meeting of the Association of American Law Schools, 2009; Varun Gauri and Daniel M. Brinks, eds., *Courting Social Justice: Judicial Enforcement of Social and Economic Rights in the Developing World* (Cambridge: Cambridge University Press, 2008); Limburg Principles on the Implementation of the International Covenant on Economic, Social and Cultural Rights, 1987; Maastricht Guidelines on Violations of Economic, Social and Cultural Rights, 1997. For a sophisticated analysis of socioeconomic rights jurisprudence, showing the real support it can lend to economically vulnerable populations and its potential to buttress democracy, see Kim Lane Scheppele, "A Realpolitik Defense of Social Rights," *Texas Law Review* 82 (2004): 1921-61.

40. Among philosophers, Thomas Pogge has taken the lead in clarifying these duties.

41. John Locke, *Two Treatises of Government*, ed. Peter Laslett (Cambridge: Cambridge University Press, 1988 [1689]), II, paras. 33, 37; I, para. 42.

42. George Kateb, "The Night Watchman State," *American Scholar* 56 (1975–76): 816–26, pp. 824–25.

43. In Thomas Paine's words, "Separate an individual from society, and give him an island or a continent to possess, and he cannot acquire personal property. He cannot be rich. . . . All accumulation, therefore, of personal property, beyond what a man's own hands produce, is derived to him by living in society; and he owes on every principle of justice, of gratitude, and of civilization, a part of that accumulation back again to society from whence the whole came." Thomas Paine, *Agrarian Justice* (1797), in Paine, *Rights of Man, Common Sense and Other Political Writings*, ed. Mark Philp (Oxford: Oxford University Press, 1998), p. 428.

44. Stuart White, "Social Rights and the Social Contract: Political Theory and the New Welfare Politics," *British Journal of Political Science* 30 (2000): 507–32, p. 510.

45. Scheppele, "Social Rights in Constitutional Courts."

46. The state-centric conception is prevalent in legal scholarship, but common in theoretical treatments as well. See, for example, Kateb, *The Inner Ocean*, pp. 1–3; Talbott., *Which Rights Should Be Universal?*, p. 3; Beitz, *The Idea of Human Rights*, p. 13.

47. Defenses of the broad institutional conception include Cristina Lafont, "Accountability and Global Governance: Challenging the State-Centric Conception of Human Rights," *Ethics and Global Politics* 3 (2010): 193–215; and Pogge, *World Poverty and Human Rights*, pp. 57–58, 169–78. Lafont argues for the superiority of a broad institutional conception over the state-centric conception, while Pogge argues for its superiority over interpersonal accounts. Long ago, John Stuart Mill emphasized the threat to individual liberty from social institutions other than the state. Mill, *On Liberty*, ed. Elizabeth Rapaport (Indianapolis: Hackett, 1978 [1859]), pp. 4–5.

48. Brian Orend defends this conception in *Human Rights: Concept and Context* (Peterborough, Ont.: Broadview, 2002), pp. 129–36.

49. Remarks delivered at presentation of the human rights booklet *In Your Hands* to the United Nations Commission on Human Rights, New York, March 27, 1958.

50. Tasioulas, "Towards a Philosophy of Human Rights," p. 25.

51. See the discussion of Tostan in Nicholas D. Kristof and Sheryl WuDunn, *Half the Sky* (New York: Random House, 2009), chap. 13.

52. Note the oddity of saying that a man who beats his wife violates her human rights (because he becomes thereby an agent of patriarchy), whereas a woman who beats her husband does not violate his human rights.

53. That is not their only value. See George Kateb, "Punishment and the Spirit of Democracy," *Social Research* 74 (2007): 269–306, p. 279.

54. For an excellent restatement of Locke's argument, see Shue, *Basic Rights*, pp. 78–82.

55. Hannah Arendt, "The Decline of the Nation-State and the End of the Rights of Man," in *The Origins of Totalitarianism* (Cleveland: Meridian, 1958), p. 296. Arendt's chapter is sometimes invoked to criticize the purportedly nonpolitical character of the human rights movement (a criticism partly encouraged by Arendt). But the "right to have rights" is embedded in the Universal Declaration of Human Rights, and subsequent international human rights law has built on this principle. For illuminating commentary, see Seyla Benhabib, *The Rights of Others* (Cambridge: Cambridge University Press, 2004), chap. 2.

56. For an overview of the international human rights regime, see Donnelly, *International Human Rights*.

Chapter 2. Madison's Compound Republic and the Logic of Checks and Balances

1. Parenthetical references are to James Madison, Alexander Hamilton, and John Jay, *The Federalist Papers*, ed. Isaac Kramnick (London: Penguin, 1987 [1787–88]). Unless otherwise noted (as here), all essays cited are written by Madison.

2. I leave aside the debate whether, past improvements notwithstanding, the Constitution remains deeply flawed. For criticisms, see Robert A. Dahl, *How Democratic Is the American Constitution?*, 2nd ed. (New Haven, Conn.: Yale University Press, 2003); and Sanford Levinson, *Our Undemocratic Constitution* (Oxford: Oxford University Press, 2006).

3. Contemporary versions of this view may be found in Daniel H. Deudney, *Bounding Power* (Princeton, N.J.: Princeton University Press, 2007); Martin S. Flaherty, "Judicial Globalization in the Service of Self-Government," *Ethics and International Affairs* 20 (2006): 477–503; Michael Goodhart, *Democracy as Human Rights* (New York: Routledge, 2005); and Thomas Pogge, *World Poverty and Human Rights*, 2nd ed. (Cambridge: Polity, 2008).

4. The conclusions defended below share elements of David Watkins's analysis of democracy in "Reconceptualizing Democracy in a Global Era," Ph.D. dissertation, Department of Political Science, University of Washington, 2008. I am indebted to Watkins's original and insightful arguments.

5. Manin, *The Principles of Representative Government* (Cambridge: Cambridge University Press, 1997), p. 3.

6. See Lance Banning, *The Sacred Fire of Liberty: James Madison and the Founding of the Federal Republic* (Ithaca, N.Y.: Cornell University Press, 1995); Colleen A. Sheehan, *James Madison and the Spirit of Republican Self-Government* (Cambridge: Cambridge University Press, 2009).

7. Madison's anti-Federalist opponents, whom we now credit with democratic sentiments, did not call themselves democrats either. All parties to the ratification debates claimed the title of republicans.

8. In the 1820s he wrote: "It is . . . certain, that there are various ways in which the rich may oppress the poor; in which property may oppress liberty; and that the world is filled with examples. It is necessary that the poor should have a defence against the danger." Madison, "Notes on Suffrage," 1821-1829, in *Letters and Other Writings of James Madison* (Philadelphia: J.B. Lippincott, 1865), 4: p. 22. In *Fed.* 62, p. 368, he writes that one effect of public instability (which the Senate helps prevent) "is the unreasonable advantage it gives to the sagacious, the enterprising, and the moneyed few over the industrious and uninformed mass of the people. Every new regulation concerning commerce or revenue, or in any manner affecting the value of the different species of property, presents a new harvest to those who watch the change, and can trace its consequences; a harvest, reared not by themselves, but by the toils and cares of the great body of their fellow-citizens. This is a state of things in which it may be said with some truth that laws are made for the *few*, not for the *many*."

9. Though some commentators portray his outlook as aristocratic, it is not a description he applies to himself. See his comment on the need to defend republican government from "aristocratic or monarchical innovations," *Fed.* 43, p. 281.

10. Later he writes of the members of the House of Representatives that "they can make no law which will not have its full operation on themselves and their friends, as well as on the great mass of the society. This has always been deemed one of the strongest bonds by which human policy can connect the rulers and the people together. It creates between them that communion of interests

and sympathy of sentiments of which few governments have furnished examples; but without which every government degenerates into tyranny," *Fed.* 57, p. 345.

11. Repeatedly in the *Federalist*, Madison invokes popular vigilance as the ultimate and most potent check against government tyranny. See *Fed.* 44, p. 290; *Fed.* 46, pp. 299, 302; *Fed.* 54, p. 337; *Fed.* 63, p. 373.

12. In his contributions to the *National Gazette* in 1791–92 and his 1800 *Report on the Alien and Sedition Acts*, Madison emphasizes the need for free public discourse and a free press to check the abuse of power.

13. Though some scholars have denied that the original Constitution implied a judicial power to declare laws unconstitutional, the power is well established in practice.

14. "Thoughts on Government" (1776), in *The Portable John Adams*, ed. John Patrick Diggins (New York: Penguin, 2004), p. 240. He continues: "which causes good humor, sociability, good manners, and good morals to be general."

15. See John MacKenzie, *Absolute Power: How the Unitary Executive Theory Is Undermining the Constitution* (New York: Century Foundation Press, 2008); Charlie Savage, *Takeover: The Return of the Imperial Presidency and the Subversion of American Democracy* (New York: Little, Brown, 2007). A version of the unitary executive theory is asserted by Justice Scalia in his dissent to *Morrison v. Olson*, 487 U.S. 654, p. 697 (1988). My following remarks provide reasons to reject his argument, including his claim that "A system of separate and coordinate powers necessarily involves an acceptance of exclusive power that can theoretically be abused" (p. 710).

16. This is equivalent to what M. J. C. Vile calls the "pure doctrine" of the separation of powers, according to which "each branch of the government must be confined to the exercise of its own function and not allowed to encroach upon the functions of the other branches." Vile, *Constitutionalism and the Separation of Powers* (Oxford: Clarendon, 1967), p. 13.

17. John Ferejohn, "Madisonian Separation of Powers," in *James Madison: The Theory and Practice of Republican Government*, ed. Samuel Kernell (Stanford, Calif.: Stanford University Press, 2003).

18. Observations on the "Draught of a Constitution for Virginia," in Madison, *Writings*, ed. Jack Rakove (New York: Modern Library, 1999), p. 417.

19. John Locke, *Two Treatises of Government*, ed. Peter Laslett (Cambridge: Cambridge University Press, 1988 [1689]), II, para. 143. Baron de Montesquieu, *The Spirit of the Laws*, trans. Thomas Nugent (New York: Hafner, 1949 [1748]), book XI, chap. 6, pp. 151–52.

20. David Hume, "Of the Independence of Parliament," in *David Hume's Political Essays*, ed. Charles W. Hendel (New York: Liberal Arts Press, 1953), p. 68. Kant later echoed Hume: "The problem of organizing a state, however hard it may seem, can be solved even for a race of devils, if only they are intelligent." Immanuel Kant, *Perpetual Peace*, ed. and trans. Lewis White Beck (New York: Liberal Arts Press, 1957 [1795]), p. 30. This is emphatically not Madison's view.

21. Montesquieu, *Spirit of the Laws*, book III, chaps. 3 and 4.

22. Madison, *Writings*, p. 398.

23. Banning, *Sacred Fire of Liberty*, p. 95.

24. Madison, "Parties," *National Gazette*, January 23, 1792, in Madison, *Writings*, p. 504. Madison did not believe in automatic deference to the market. In 1790 he fought against Hamilton's plan to reimburse the holders of public notes at full face value, because he believed it would reward speculators over the original note-holders, most of them former revolutionary soldiers, who resold the notes at a lower value because of the government's earlier failure to repay. Instead of Hamilton's plan, "Madison suggested paying secondary holders the highest value that certificates had reached

on private money markets, subtracting that amount from the certificates' face value, and returning the remainder to the citizens to whom the notes had been originally issued." Lance Banning, *Jefferson and Madison: Three Conversations from the Founding* (Lanham, Md.: Madison House, 1995), p. 42. He defended his proposal "on the great and fundamental principles of justice" (congressional speech of February 18, 1790, quoted in ibid.). Banning writes: "I think it no exaggeration to suggest that Madison's discrimination plan was probably the era's clearest instance of a scheme that would have taken property from some and given it to others on considerations that were plainly redistributive in their intent," *Three Conversations*, p. 42.

For more evidence that Madison favored measures to moderate economic inequality, see Eric Nelson, *The Greek Tradition in Republican Thought* (Cambridge: Cambridge University Press, 2004), pp. 206–9. John F. Hart has shown through comprehensive research that Madison adopted a rather more moderate conception of the right to private property than has generally been supposed. He helped lead the fight in Virginia to abolish entail, which was thought to favor aristocracy, and supported a range of laws that regulated land use without compensation. John F. Hart, " 'A Less Proportion of Idle Proprietors': Madison, Property Rights, and the Abolition of Fee Tail," *Washington and Lee Review* 58 (2001): 167-94; Hart, "Fish, Dams, and James Madison: Eighteenth-Century Species Protection and the Original Understanding of the Takings Clause," *Maryland Law Review* 63 (2004): 287-319; Hart, "Land Use Law in the Early Republic and the Original Meaning of the Takings Clause," *Northwestern University Law Review* 94 (2000): 1099-1156. Madison's fear of stark economic inequality was connected to republican concerns about virtue. He noted, for example, that the "habits and manners of the people" in colonial Virginia had been tainted by "the too unequal distribution of property favored by laws derived from the British code." Letter to Robert Walsh, March 2, 1819, in Madison, *Writings*, p. 724.

25. Drew R. McCoy, *The Last of the Fathers: James Madison and the Republican Legacy* (Cambridge: Cambridge University Press, 1989), chap. 7.

26. I borrow from Víctor Ferreres Comella, *Constitutional Courts and Democratic Values* (New Haven, Conn.: Yale University Press, 2009), p. 32.

27. *Lawrence v. Texas*, 539 U.S. 558 (2003), pp. 578–79.

28. See especially *Fed.* 10; and *Vices of the Political System of the United States*, in Madison, *Writings*, esp. pp. 75–79.

29. *Fed.* 10, p. 124; and *Vices*, in Madison, *Writings*, p. 76.

30. *Fed.* 37 anticipates Rawls's well-known discussion of the "burdens of judgment" in *Political Liberalism* (New York: Columbia University Press, 1993).

31. Speech to the Virginia Ratifying Convention, Madison, *Writings*, p. 398.

32. The phrase comes from an 1888 speech by James Russell Lowell, criticizing the attitude it conveys. Michael G. Kammen, *A Machine That Would Go of Itself: The Constitution in American Culture* (New York: Knopf, 1986), p. 18. As Kammen reports, others used the machine metaphor with admiring intent.

33. Charles Babington and Jonathan Weisman, "Senate Approves Detainee Bill Backed by Bush," *Washington Post*, September 29, 2006. Specter's strategy was reckless on its own terms. The Supreme Court originally refused to hear a challenge to the law. It later changed its mind, but overturned the habeas corpus-stripping provisions by a vote of only five to four. *Boumediene v. Bush*, 553 U.S. 723 (2008).

34. Madison, "Notes on Suffrage," pp. 21–30.

35. See John Stuart Mill's observation that "such phrases as 'self-government,' and 'the power of the people over themselves,' do not express the true state of the case. . . . [T]he 'self-government'

spoken of is not the government of each by himself, but of each by all the rest." Mill, *On Liberty*, ed. Elizabeth Rapaport (Indianapolis: Hackett, 1978 [1859]), pp. 3–4.

36. Madison is not innocent of this practice. See, for example, *Fed.* 51, p. 322.

37. I say more about the challenge of moral disagreement, in particular disagreement about human rights, in Chapter 6.

38. It is not clear, however, that the institutions Madison proposes would have overcome Socrates's pessimism about politics.

39. *Vices*, in Madison, *Writings*, p. 77.

40. Arend Lijphart is the leading theorist of this model. See Lijphart, *Patterns of Democracy*, 2nd ed. (New Haven, Conn.: Yale University Press, 2012).

41. Deudney, *Bounding Power*, chap. 6; James Brown Scott, *James Madison's Notes of Debates in the Federal Convention of 1787 and Their Relation to a More Perfect Society of Nations* (Oxford: Oxford University Press, 1918); John Tomasi, "Governance Beyond the Nation State: James Madison on Foreign Policy and 'Universal Peace,'" in *James Madison and the Future of Limited Government*, ed. John Samples (Washington, D.C.: Cato, 2002).

42. However, the Jay Treaty concluded between the U.S. and Britain in 1794 established Anglo-American commissions to settle disputes between the two nations, an innovation that has been described as "the birth of modern international arbitration." Richard B. Lillich, "The Jay Treaty Commissions," *St. John's Law Review* 37 (1963): 260-83, p. 282.

43. Letter to George Washington, April 16, 1787, in Madison, *Writings*, p. 81.

44. *Fletcher v. Peck* 10 U.S. (6 Cranch) 87 (1810), p. 138.

45. "[I]t is this circumstance principally which renders factious combinations less to be dreaded in [republican than democratic government]." *Fed.* 10, p. 127.

46. See Flaherty, "Judicial Globalization in the Service of Self-Government."

47. Madison, *Writings*, pp. 69–80.

48. *Vices*, in Madison, *Writings*, p. 77.

49. Madison, *Writings*, p. 81.

50. Mark Weston Janis, *America and the Law of Nations 1776-1939* (Oxford: Oxford University Press, 2010), chap. 2; Edwin D. Dickinson, "The Law of Nations as Part of the National Law of the United States," *University of Pennsylvania Law Review* 101 (1952): 26–56, p. 35; See also Stewart Jay, "The Status of the Law of Nations in Early American Law," *Vanderbilt Law Review* 42 (1989): 819-50.

51. James Madison, *Notes of Debates in the Federal Convention of 1787* (Athens, OH: Ohio University Press, 1966 [1840]), p. 29 (May 29, 1787).

52. Ibid., p. 142 (June 19, 1787).

53. We should recall that upon declaring independence, the Founders professed "a decent respect to the opinions of mankind."

54. Kant, *Perpetual Peace*, pp. 7, 11–20.

55. Daniel Deudney argues that the founding of the United States was itself a kind of international compact, the creation of a "Philadelphian system" that contrasted to the "Westphalian system" of Europe. Deudney, *Bounding Power*, chap. 6.

Chapter 3. Europe and the Virtues of International Constitutionalism

1. This chapter echoes the argument in Andrew Moravcsik's influential article "The Origins of Human Rights Regimes: Democratic Delegation in Postwar Europe," *International Organization* 54

(2000): 217–52. Moravcsik shows that in the early postwar period, support for a strong regional human rights regime came largely from new and fragile democracies, seeking protection against domestic antidemocratic forces.

2. Madison's attitude toward a national bill of rights evolved from ambivalence to firm support. On his early ambivalence, see the letter to Thomas Jefferson, October 17, 1788, in James Madison, *Writings*, ed. Jack Rakove (New York: Library of America, 1999), pp. 418–23. On his later support, see the essay on "Public Opinion" in the *National Gazette*, December 19, 1791, in Madison, *Writings*, pp. 500–501. He had always championed the Virginia Declaration of Rights. See the peroration of the "The Memorial and Remonstrance Against Religious Assessments," in Madison, *Writings*, pp. 35–36.

3. *Federalist* 51, p. 322 (see chap. 2, n. 1).

4. *Vices of the Political System of the United States*, in Madison, *Writings*, p. 69; Letter to George Washington, April 15, 1787, in Madison, *Writings*, p. 81.

5. See Jamie Mayerfeld, "The Mutual Dependence of External and Internal Justice: The Democratic Achievement of the International Criminal Court," *Finnish Yearbook of International Law* 12 (2001): 71–107.

6. Alexis de Tocqueville, *Democracy in America*, trans. Arthur Goldhammer (New York: Library of America, 2004 [1840]), pp. 595–99; and John Stuart Mill, *On Liberty*, ed. Elizabeth Rapaport (Indianapolis: Hackett, 1978 [1859]), pp. 110–11.

7. As Rousseau says in the *Social Contract*, "The first man to propose [a new] law is only giving voice to what everyone already feels." Jean-Jacques Rousseau, *The Social Contract*, trans. and ed. Maurice Cranston (London: Penguin, 1968 [1762]), book IV, chap. i, p. 149.

8. Aristotle, *Politics*, trans. Ernest Barker, ed. R. F. Stalley (Oxford: Oxford University Press, 1995), book II, chap. 5, pp. 46–47; Mancur Olson, *The Logic of Collective Action* (Cambridge, Mass.: Harvard University Press, 1971).

9. It appears difficult to introduce accountability in the polling booth, which is one reason why the actual practice of voting falls short of Rousseau's ideal (see note 7). And yet the ancient Athenians sought to make voting an accountable act, not only by holding votes in public but also by penalizing, through the *graphê paranomôn*, the proposal of unlawful decrees—a reminder that the original democrats viewed citizen accountability as a defining feature of their political system. See Josiah Ober, *Mass and Elite in Democratic Athens* (Princeton, N.J.: Princeton University Press, 1989), p. 109, and Bernard Manin, *The Principles of Representative Government* (Cambridge: Cambridge University Press, 1997), pp. 19–23.

10. A point emphasized by Steven Greer, *The European Convention on Human Rights* (Cambridge: Cambridge University Press, 2006).

11. As revised and strengthened by the Lisbon Treaty, which entered into force in December 2009, the relevant treaty provision states: "The Union is founded on the values of respect for human dignity, freedom, democracy, equality, the rule of law and respect for human rights, including the rights of persons belonging to minorities. These values are common to the Member States in a society in which pluralism, non-discrimination, tolerance, justice, solidarity and equality between women and men prevail" (Treaty on European Union, art. 2).

12. Jason Coppel and Aidan O'Neill, "The European Court of Justice: Taking Rights Seriously?," *Legal Studies* 12 (1992): 227–45, p. 228. The ECJ was renamed the Court of Justice of the European Union in 2009.

13. See Rachel A. Cichowski, *The European Court and Civil Society* (Cambridge: Cambridge University Press, 2007).

14. Andrew Williams, *EU Human Rights Policies: A Study in Irony* (Oxford: Oxford University Press, 2004), pp. 98–102.

15. Williams, *EU Human Rights Policies*, chap. 2; Lorand Bartels, *Human Rights Conditionality in the EU's International Agreements* (Oxford: Oxford University Press, 2005).

16. Michael Newman, "The European Union," in *A Force Profonde: The Power, Politics, and Promise of Human Rights*, ed. Edward A. Kolodziej (Philadelphia: University of Pennsylvania Press, 2003), p. 186.

17. Williams, *EU Human Rights Policies*, pp. 73–77.

18. See the discussion and sources listed in Frank Schimmelfennig, "European Regional Organizations, Political Conditionality, and Democratic Transformation in Eastern Europe," *East European Politics & Societies* 21 (2007): 126–41.

19. Williams, *EU Human Rights Policies*.

20. Kim Lane Scheppele, "Other People's Patriot Acts: Europe's Response to September 11," *Loyola Law Review* 50 (2004): 89–148, pp. 93–97.

21. Coppel and O'Neill, "The European Court of Justice," p. 228.

22. Frank Schimmelfennig, Stefan Engert, and Heiko Knobel, *International Socialization in Europe* (Houndmills: Palgrave/Macmillan, 2006), p. 29.

23. Dick Marty, *Secret Detentions and Illegal Transfers of Detainees Involving Council of Europe Member States*, Second Report to the Parliamentary Assembly of the Council of Europe, June 7, 2007.

24. Daniel Thomas, *The Helsinki Effect* (Princeton, N.J.: Princeton University Press, 2001).

25. On the work of the OSCE, see Janne Haaland Matláry, *Intervention for Human Rights in Europe* (Houndmills: Palgrave, 2002), chap. 6. See also the organization's website, http://www.osce.org/.

26. Matláry, *Intervention for Human Rights in Europe*, p. 142.

27. This language appears in the 2005 Factsheet of OSCE High Commissioner on National Minorities and is restated in a speech by High Commissioner Knut Vollebaek at Cardozo Law School, March 10, 2008, www.osce.org/hcnm/31082?download=true.

28. Ibid.

29. See Matláry, *Intervention for Human Rights in Europe*, pp. 141, 156–57.

30. Ibid., pp. 156–57.

31. A. W. Brian Simpson, "Britain and the European Convention," *Cornell International Law Journal* 34 (2001): 523–54, pp. 523–24.

32. On the human rights contributions of these and other COE bodies, see generally Matláry, *Intervention for Human Rights in Europe*, chap. 5.

33. Ibid., 119–21; Schimmelfennig, Engert, and Knobel, *International Socialization in Europe*, p. 35.

34. Greer, *European Convention on Human Rights*, p. 26.

35. On Turkey, see Ihsan Dagi, "Democratic Transition in Turkey, 1980–83: The Impact of European Diplomacy," *Middle Eastern Studies* 32 (1996): 124–41; and Leo Zwaak, "Turkey and the European Convention on Human Rights," in *The Role of the Nation-State in the 21st Century: Human Rights, International Organisations and Foreign Policy*, ed. Monique Castermans-Holleman, Fried van Hoof, and Jacqueline Smith (The Hague: Kluwer, 1998), p. 209. On Russia, see Michael D. Goldhaber, *A People's History of the European Court of Human Rights* (New Brunswick, N.J.: Rutgers University Press, 2007), p. 158. In April 2014 the Council of Europe suspended Russia's voting rights in the Parliamentary Assembly because of its intervention in Ukraine.

36. Greer, *European Convention on Human Rights*, p. 17.

37. There is a large literature on the Convention and its impact. Major studies include Dia

Anagnostou, ed., *The European Court of Human Rights: Implementing Strasbourg's Judgments on Domestic Policy* (Edinburgh: Edinburgh University Press, 2013); Ed Bates, *The Evolution of the European Convention on Human Rights* (Oxford: Oxford University Press, 2010); Robert Blackburn and Jörg Polakiewicz, eds., *Fundamental Rights in Europe: The ECHR and Its Member States, 1950–2000* (Oxford: Oxford University Press, 2001); Goldhaber, *People's History* (see note 35); Greer, *European Convention on Human Rights*; and Helen Keller and Alec Stone Sweet, eds., *A Europe of Rights: The Impact of the ECHR on National Legal Systems* (Oxford: Oxford University Press, 2008). For a philosophical analysis of the Convention and the jurisprudence of its Court, see George Letsas, *A Theory of Interpretation of the European Convention on Human Rights* (Oxford: Oxford University Press, 2007).

38. Jochen Frowein, "European Integration Through Fundamental Rights," *University of Michigan Journal of Law Reform* 18 (1984): 5–27, p. 8.

39. Goldhaber, *People's History*, p. 6; Dia Anagnostou, "Politics, Courts and Society in the National Implementation and Practice of European Court of Human Rights Case Law," in *European Court of Human Rights*, ed. Anagnostou, p. 212.

40. Helen Keller and Alec Stone Sweet, "Assessing the Impact of the ECHR on National Legal Systems," in *A Europe of Rights*, ed. Keller and Stone Sweet, p. 688.

41. David J. Harris, Michael O'Boyle, and Colin Warbrick, *Law of the European Convention on Human Rights* (London: Butterworths, 1995), p. 31.

42. See Greer, *European Convention on Human Rights*, chap. 2.

43. Human Rights Watch, "Chechnya: Research Shows Widespread and Systematic Use of Torture," November 13, 2006.

44. The recent upsurge of repression targets urban protestors, independent journalists, and certain members of the political opposition (including Kurdish activists). Violence between the state and the Kurdish insurgency had declined, until a renewal of hostilities in July 2015.

45. Elizabeth Lambert Abdelgawad and Anne Weber, "The Reception Process in France and Germany," in *A Europe of Rights*, ed. Keller and Stone Sweet.

46. Goldhaber, *People's History*, p. 2.

47. Laurence R. Helfer, "Redesigning the European Court of Human Rights: Embeddedness as a Deep Structural Principle of the European Human Rights Regime," *European Journal of International Law* 19 (2008): 125–59, p. 126.

48. Their role is vividly described in Goldhaber, *People's History*. See also Rachel Cichowski, "Civil Society and the European Court of Human Rights," in *The European Court of Human Rights between Law and Politics*, ed. Jonas Christoffersen and Mikael Rask Madsen (Oxford: Oxford University Press, 2011).

49. For the contribution of human rights NGOs throughout the world, see William Korey, "Human Rights NGOs: The Power of Persuasion," *Ethics and International Affairs* 13 (1999): 151–74.

50. Rachel A. Cichowski, "Courts, Rights and Democratic Participation," *Comparative Political Studies* 39 (2006): 50–75; Cichowski, *The European Court and Civil Society*.

51. See Cichowski, "Courts, Rights and Democratic Participation," p. 69; and David Jacobson and Galya Benarieh Ruffer, "Courts Across Borders: The Implications of Judicial Agency for Human Rights and Democracy," *Human Rights Quarterly* 25 (2003): 74–92, p. 75.

52. Keller and Stone Sweet, "Assessing the Impact of the ECHR on National Legal Systems," pp. 686–87.

53. Greer, *European Convention on Human Rights*, pp. 126–31. Keller and Stone Sweet ("Assessing the Impact of the ECHR on National Legal Systems") offer a more upbeat overall assessment, though not when it comes to Russia.

54. Keller and Stone Sweet, "Assessing the Impact of the ECHR on National Legal Systems," p. 694.

55. Ibid., pp. 677, 687–88, 695–701, 710.

56. Fionnuala Ní Aoláin, "The European Convention on Human Rights and Its Prohibition on Torture," in *Torture: A Collection*, ed. Sanford Levinson (Oxford: Oxford University Press, 2004), p. 219.

57. Stephen L. Gardbaum, *The New Commonwealth Model of Constitutionalism* (Cambridge: Cambridge University Press, 2013), pp. 174–75.

58. *A and Others v. Secretary of State for the Home Department* [2004] UKHL 56.

59. *A and Others v. the United Kingdom* [GC], no. 3455/05, ECHR 2009.

60. Laura K. Donohue, *The Cost of Counterterrorism* (Cambridge: Cambridge University Press, 2008), pp. 57–71; Clive Walker, "Keeping Control of Terrorists Without Losing Control of Constitutionalism," *Stanford Law Review* 59 (2007): 1395–1463; Fiona de Londras, *Detention in the "War on Terror": Can Human Rights Fight Back?* (Cambridge: Cambridge University Press, 2011), pp. 263–67.

61. As of August 2013, nine men were under TPIM surveillance.

62. *Al-Skeini v. Secretary of State for Defence* [2007] UKHL 26.

63. *Al-Skeini and Others v. the United Kingdom* [GC], no. 55721/07, ECHR 2011; *Al-Jedda v. the United Kingdom* [GC], no. 27021/08, ECHR 2011.

64. *AS and DD (Libya) v. Secretary of State for the Home Department* [2008] EWCA Civ 289.

65. *A v. Secretary of State for the Home Department* [2005] UKHL 71. However, the HRA did not stop Parliament in 2013 from enacting the Justice and Security Act, heavily criticized by human rights organizations for permitting judges on national security grounds to limit the access of nongovernmental parties to trial evidence relevant to civil proceedings involving the government. It remains to be seen whether the Act will survive legal challenge under the Convention.

66. Helen Fenwick, "Recalibrating ECHR Rights, and the Role of the Human Rights Act Post 9/11: Reasserting International Human Rights Norms in the 'War on Terror'?," *Current Legal Problems* 63 (2010): 153–234; K. D. Ewing and Joo-Cheong Tham, "The Continuing Futility of the Human Rights Act," *Public Law* (2008): 668–93.

67. Gardbaum, *The New Commonwealth Model of Constitutionalism*, p. 182–83. See also David Bonner: "in this HRA era, United Kingdom courts have begun to undertake an enhanced level of scrutiny in an area they once characterized as too sensitive for judicial involvement and in which they exercised undue restraint in the face of the marked impact of the powers on the rights and freedoms of individuals." Bonner, *Executive Measures, Terrorism and National Security* (London: Ashgate, 2007), pp. ix–x.

68. De Londras, *Detention in the "War on Terror"*.

69. Nicholas Watt, "Michael Gove to Proceed with Tories' Plans to Scrap Human Rights Act," *Guardian*, May 10, 2015.

70. "Protecting Human Rights in the UK: The Conservatives' Proposals for Changing Britain's Human Rights Laws," October 3, 2014.

71. Ibid.

72. Ed Bates et al., "The Legal Implications of a Repeal of the Human Rights Act 1998 and Withdrawal from the European Convention on Human Rights," ed. Kanstantsin Dzehtsiarou and Tobias Lock, May 12, 2015, pp. 24, 33.

73. David Allen Green, "Why Repealing the Human Rights Act Is Not Going to Be Easy," *Financial Times*, May 12, 2015.

74. This is a theme in Schimmelfennig, Engert, and Knobel, *International Socialization in Europe;* as well as Judith G. Kelley, *Ethnic Politics in Europe: The Power of Norms and Incentives* (Princeton, N.J.: Princeton University Press, 2004).

75. The following discussion is drawn from Kelley, *Ethnic Politics in Europe,* pp. 1–2, 12–13, 17–18, 73–77, 84–93.

76. *Human Rights Watch World Report 2015* provides a good update on these trends.

77. Ibid., pp. 444–52.

78. Ibid., pp. 547–54.

79. Ibid., pp. 229–51.

80. Alec Stone Sweet and Helen Keller, "The Reception of the ECHR in National Legal Orders," in *A Europe of Rights,* ed. Keller and Stone Sweet, p. 12.

81. As Ed Bates writes, the backlog "threatens to make the right of individual petition illusory in the sense that applications may be regarded as ineffective because they simply take far too long to achieve an outcome." Bates, *Evolution of the European Convention on Human Rights,* p. 480.

82. "Pending Applications Allocated to a Judicial Formation," European Court of Human Rights website, December 31, 2014, http://www.echr.coe.int/Documents/Stats_pending_month _2014_BIL.pdf.

83. Bates, *Evolution of the European Convention on Human Rights,* p. 489. See, for example, *Ananyev and Others v. Russia,* nos. 42525/07, 60800/08, ECHR 2012, in which the Russian government is directed to "produce, in co-operation with the Committee of Ministers, within six months from the date on which this judgment becomes final, a binding time frame in which to make available a combination of effective remedies having preventive and compensatory effects and complying with the requirements set out in the present judgment."

84. Bates, *Evolution of the European Convention on Human Rights,* p. 490.

85. Alice Donald, "Backlog, Backlash and Beyond: Debating the Long Term Future of Human Rights Protection in Europe," *UK Human Rights Blog,* April 14, 2014 (with automatically updated figures).

86. Laurence R. Helfer, "The Burdens and Benefits of Brighton," *European Society of International Law* 1, 1 (June 8, 2012), http://www.esil-sedi.eu/node/138.

87. On the history of modern torture in Europe, see Edward Peters, *Torture,* expanded ed. (Philadelphia: University of Pennsylvania Press, 1996); and Darius Rejali, *Torture and Democracy* (Princeton, N.J.: Princeton University Press, 2007).

88. Rejali, *Torture and Democracy,* chaps. 3–5.

89. *Yearbook of the European Convention on Human Rights (European Commission of Human Rights: Documents and Decisions) 1955–1956–1957* (The Hague: Nijhoff, 1959), p. 51.

90. Ibid., pp. 46–47.

91. A. W. Brian Simpson, *Human Rights and the End of Empire: Britain and the Genesis of the Convention* (Oxford: Oxford University Press, 2001), p. 1099.

92. The 1972 Parker Report on use of the "Five Techniques" in Northern Ireland revealed that similar techniques had been used in Palestine, Malaya, Kenya, Cyprus, the Cameroons, Brunei, Guyana, Aden, Borneo, and the Persian Gulf. For discussion of UK torture in Kenya, Aden, and Cyprus, see Ian Cobain, *Cruel Britannia: A Secret History of Torture* (London: Portobello, 2013), chap. 3.

93. Simpson, *Human Rights and the End of Empire,* chaps. 18 and 19; Cobain, *Cruel Britannia,* p. 98.

94. On the historic significance of the Commission report, see Kathryn Sikkink, *The Justice Cascade* (New York: Norton, 2011), pp. 38–40.

95. *Ireland v. United Kingdom* (Plenary), no. 5310/71, ECHR 1978, Series A no. 25.

96. See John Conroy, *Unspeakable Acts, Ordinary People: The Dynamics of Torture* (Berkeley: University of California Press, 2001).

97. *Selmouni v. France* [GC], no. 25803/94, ECHR 1999-V.

98. Fiona de Londras, "Revisiting the Five Techniques in the European Court of Human Rights," *EJIL: Talk!*, December 12, 2014.

99. Amnesty International, *Torture in the Eighties*, 1984; Amnesty International, *Turkey Testimony on Torture*, 1985; Goldhaber, *People's History*, p. 132.

100. *Aksoy v. Turkey*, no. 21987/93, ECHR Reports 1996-VI.

101. Thomas W. Smith, "Leveraging Norms: The ECHR and Turkey's Human Rights Reforms," in *Human Rights in Turkey*, ed. Zehra F. Kabasakal Arat (Philadelphia: University of Pennsylvania Press, 2007), p. 268.

102. The following information is taken from Smith, "Leveraging Norms"; Goldhaber, *People's History*, pp. 131–32; Schimmelfennig, Engert, and Knobel, *International Socialization in Europe*, chap. 7; Dan Gardner, "An End to Torture," *Ottawa Citizen*, February 5, 2004; *Amnesty International Annual Report 2007*: Turkey.

103. Amnesty International, *Russian Federation: Torture and Forced "Confessions" in Detention*, November 2006. See also Andrew E. Kramer, "Amnesty Says Russian Police Torture Suspects," *New York Times*, November 22, 2006.

104. Human Rights Watch, "Chechnya: Research Shows Widespread and Systematic Use of Torture," November 13, 2006; Human Rights Watch, *"Who Will Tell Me What Happened to My Son?" Russia's Implementation of European Court of Human Rights Judgments on Chechnya*, September 2009.

105. Clare Ovey and Robin C. A. White, *Jacobs and White, The European Convention on Human Rights*, 4th ed. (Oxford: Oxford University Press, 2006), chap. 5.

106. *Assenov and Others v. Bulgaria*, no. 24760/94, ECHR 1998-VIII.

107. *Chahal v. the United Kingdom*, no. 22414/93, ECHR 1996-V.

108. *A v. the United Kingdom*, no. 25599/94, ECHR 1998-VI.

109. The exceptions are Andorra, Denmark, Iceland, Liechtenstein, Luxembourg, Monaco, Norway, Portugal, and San Marino. European Court of Human Rights, "Violations by Article and by State, 1959–2014," http://www.echr.coe.int/Documents/Stats_violation_1959_2014_ENG.pdf.

110. Jim Murdoch, *The Treatment of Prisoners: European Standards* (Strasbourg: Council of Europe, 2006), pp. 219–20.

111. Ibid., pp. 46–51, 220–21.

112. *Kalashnikov v. Russia*, no. 47095/99, ECHR 2002-VI; *Dougoz v. Greece*, no. 40907/98, ECHR 2001-II. See also Antonio Cassese, *Inhuman States: Imprisonment, Detention and Torture in Europe Today*, trans. Jennifer Greensleaves (Cambridge: Polity, 1996).

113. For a gripping insider account of the work of the Committee, see Cassese, *Inhuman States*. Other works include Malcolm D. Evans and Rod Morgan, *Preventing Torture: A Study of the European Convention for the Prevention of Torture and Inhuman or Degrading Treatment or Punishment* (Oxford: Oxford University Press, 1998); Rod Morgan and Malcolm Evans, *Combating Torture in Europe* (Strasbourg: Council of Europe, 2001); and Jim Murdoch, "Tackling Ill-Treatment in Places of Detention: The Work of the Council of Europe's 'Torture Committee,'" *European Journal of Criminal Policy Research* 12 (2006): 121–42.

114. Council of Europe, *A Visit by the CPT—What's It All About? 15 Questions and Answers for the Police* (Geneva: Council of Europe, 1999).

115. Murdoch, "Tackling Ill-Treatment in Places of Detention," p. 140.

116. Ibid., pp. 138–42.

117. Ibid., pp. 134–38.

118. Murdoch, *Treatment of Prisoners*, p. 52.

119. Amnesty International, *Partners in Crime: Europe's Role in US Renditions*, June 2006.

120. Florian Geyer, "Fruit of the Poisonous Tree: Member States' Indirect Use of Extraordinary Rendition and the EU Counter-Terrorism Strategy," Center for European Policy Studies Working Document No. 263, April 3, 2007.

121. Jane Mayer, *The Dark Side* (New York: Doubleday, 2008), pp. 275–77; *The Report of the Constitution Project's Task Force on Detainee Treatment*, 2013, pp. 182–92; Amnesty International, *Europe: Breaking the Conspiracy of Silence: USA's European "Partners in Crime" Must Act After Senate Torture Report*, January 2015.

122. For a discussion of how global security networks have found ways to roll back international human rights protections, see Kim Lane Scheppele, "The Migration of Anti-Constitutional Ideas: The Post-9/11 Globalization of Public Law and the International State of Emergency," in *The Migration of Constitutional Ideas*, ed. Sujit Choudhry (New York: Cambridge University Press, 2006).

123. Dick Marty, *Secret Detentions and Illegal Transfers of Detainees Involving Council of Europe Member States*, Second Report to the Parliamentary Assembly of the Council of Europe, June 7, 2007.

124. Amnesty International, *Partners in Crime*.

125. Human Rights Watch, *Cruel Britannia: British Complicity in the Torture and Ill-Treatment of Terror Suspects in Pakistan,* November 2009; Cobain, *Cruel Britannia*, pp. 239–54, 257–62.

126. Amnesty International, *Partners in Crime*; European Center for Constitutional and Human Rights, *CIA "Extraordinary Rendition" Flights, Torture and Accountability—A European Approach*, 2nd ed. January 2009; Cobain, *Cruel Britannia*, p. 220.

127. David Rose, "How MI5 Colluded in My Torture: Binyam Mohamed Claims British Agents Fed Moroccan Torturers Their Questions," *Daily Mail*, March 7, 2009.

128. Cobain, *Cruel Britannia*, chap. 8.

129. Ibid., pp. 271–75, 312.

130. "Agency Policy on Liaison with Overseas Security and Intelligence Services in Relation to Detainees Who May Be Subject to Mistreatment," esp. paragraphs 26–38. The directive was made public by Ian Cobain in "UK's Secret Policy on Torture Revealed," *Guardian*, August 4, 2011.

131. Cobain, *Cruel Britannia*, pp. 310–14; Patrick Wintour, "Guantánamo Bay Detainees to Be Paid Compensation by UK Government," *Guardian*, November 15, 2010.

132. Joint NGO Letter to the Solicitor to the Detainee Inquiry, August 3, 2011, https://www.amnesty.org/en/documents/EUR45/010/2011/en/.

133. Amnesty International, *Europe: Breaking the Conspiracy of Silence*, p. 19.

134. Most of the following information is taken from Cobain, *Cruel Britannia*, chap. 9.

135. Sir William Gage, *Report of the Baha Mousa Inquiry*, September 2011.

136. Ian Cobain, "Police Reinvestigate Baha Mousa Death," *Guardian*, September 10, 2013; Rajeev Syal, "MoD Criticised for Limiting Inquests into Civilian Deaths in Military Custody," *Guardian*, December 6, 2013.

137. European Center for Constitutional and Human Rights and Public Interest Lawyers, "The

Responsibility of Officials of the United Kingdom for War Crimes Involving Systematic Detainee Abuse in Iraq from 2003–2008," Communication to the Office of the Prosecutor of the International Criminal Court, January 10, 2014.

138. *Chahal v. the United Kingdom*, no. 22414/93, ECHR 1996-V.

139. *Saadi v. Italy* [GC], no. 37201/06, ECHR 2008.

140. See European Court of Human Rights, "Factsheet—Expulsions and Extraditions," July 2013, at http://www.echr.coe.int/Documents/FS_Expulsions_Extraditions_ENG.pdf.

141. *Al-Skeini and Others v. the United Kingdom* [GC], no. 55721/07, ECHR 2011; *Al-Jedda v. the United Kingdom* [GC], no. 27021/08, ECHR 2011.

142. Dana Priest, "Wrongful Imprisonment: Anatomy of a CIA Mistake," *Washington Post*, December 4, 2005.

143. *El-Masri v. US*, 479 F. 3d 296 (4th Circ. 2007); Linda Greenhouse, "Supreme Court Refuses to Hear Torture Appeal," *New York Times*, October 9, 2007.

144. *El-Masri v. the Former Yugoslav Republic of Macedonia* [GC], no. 39630/09, ECHR 2012.

145. *Al Nashiri v. Poland*, no. 28761/11, ECHR 2014; and *Husayn (Abu Zubaydah) v. Poland*, no. 7511/13, ECHR 2014.

146. *Ahmad and Others v. the United Kingdom*, nos. 24027/07, 24027/07, 11949/08, 36742/08, 66911/09, 67354/09, ECHR 2012.

147. *Vinter and Others v. the United Kingdom*, nos. 66069/09 130/10 3896/10, ECHR 2013.

148. Helen Fenwick, "An Appeasement Approach in the European Court of Human Rights?," *UK Human Rights Blog*, April 15, 2012. See also Fenwick, "Post 9/11 UK Counter-Terrorism Cases in the European Court of Human Rights: A 'Dialogic' Approach to Rights Protection or Appeasement of National Authorities?," in *Critical Debates on Counter-Terrorism Judicial Review*, ed. Fergal Davis and Fiona de Londras (Cambridge: Cambridge University Press, 2014).

149. *Jones and Others v. the United Kingdom*, nos. 34356/06 and 40528/06, ECHR 2014.

150. The controversy found its most famous symbol in Abu Qatada, a radical Muslim preacher and alleged terrorist from Jordan, whom the British government placed in indefinite detention in 2002, and then sought to deport after the *Belmarsh* ruling led to repeal of the indefinite detention law. His deportation was initially blocked, first by a British appeals court and subsequently the ECtHR, which ruled that he was at risk of being tried and convicted with evidence from torture. His eventual deportation in July 2013 became possible only after the UK and Jordan ratified a treaty guaranteeing a fair trial and humane treatment. Ian Patel and Sajid Suleman, "Appealing Against Torture: Deportation, the UK, and Human Rights," *Al Jazeera*, August 21, 2013.

151. "Protecting Human Rights in the UK: The Conservatives' Proposals for Changing Britain's Human Rights Laws," October 3, 2014. The Conservatives did not present a draft of the proposed bill.

152. However, UK proposals to repeal the Human Rights Act and possibly even leave the ECHR threaten to weaken the regional human rights system.

153. My claims are restricted to multilateral *human rights* regimes. Other multilateral regimes—for example, those dedicated to military cooperation or counterterrorism—may sometimes act to the detriment of human rights. See Scheppele, "Migration of Anti-Constitutional Ideas."

154. Here I mean citizens in the moral rather than legal sense. I include residents without formal citizenship status, because governments are bound to respect their human rights also, and because they (the noncitizen residents) have a duty to respect the human rights of others.

155. This dynamic emerges powerfully in Goldhaber's stories in *People's History* of the individual plaintiffs behind the landmark cases of the European Court of Human Rights.

156. Simpson, "Britain and the European Convention," p. 553; Jonas Christoffersen and Mikael Rask Madsen, "Denmark and the Europeanization of Human Rights: From Export Business to Domestic Battleground," in *International Constitutional Law*, ed. Luca Mezzetti (Turin: Giappichelli, 2014), p. 31.

157. Stone Sweet and Keller, "The Reception of the ECHR in National Legal Orders," p. 19.

158. See Floribert H. Baudet "The Netherlands and the Rank of Denmark: Prestige as Stimulus for Human Rights Policies," in *Les droits de l'homme en Europe depuis 1945/Human Rights in Europe Since 1945*, ed. Carole Fink (Bern: Peter Lang, 2003).

159. Cassese, *Inhuman States*, p. 7.

160. Baron de Montesquieu, *The Spirit of the Laws*, trans. Thomas Nugent (New York: Hafner, 1949 [1748]), book IX, chap. 1, p. 127. The passage is quoted at length by Alexander Hamilton in *Federalist* 9.

161. My remarks echo Kathryn Sikkink's observation of the emergence across the world of a "decentralized but interactive system of accountability for violations of core political rights." Sikkink, *The Justice Cascade: How Human Rights Prosecutions Are Changing World Politics* (New York: Norton, 2011), p. 18.

162. Jason Coppel and Aidan O'Neill, "The European Court of Justice: Taking Rights Seriously?," *Legal Studies* 12 (1992): 227–49, p. 228.

Chapter 4. American Exceptionalism and the Betrayal of Human Rights, Part I: The Torture Memos

1. Reprinted in Karen J. Greenberg and Joshua L. Dratel, eds., *The Torture Papers: The Road to Abu Ghraib* (Cambridge: Cambridge University Press, 2005), pp. 619–21. The letter is incorrectly dated 2004.

2. Letter from William J. Haynes to Senator Patrick Leahy, June 25, 2003; reprinted in *The Torture Papers*, ed. Greenberg and Dratel, pp. 628–29.

3. Jack Goldsmith, *The Terror Presidency: Law and Judgment Inside the Bush Administration* (New York: Norton, 2007), pp. 22–23. The other members were David Addington, counsel to the vice president; John Yoo, deputy assistant attorney general; Alberto Gonzales, White House counsel; and Timothy Flanigan, deputy White House counsel.

4. Colin Powell, Commencement Address, Wake Forest University, May 17, 2004.

5. Madison himself emphasized that no constitutional system could protect individual rights if public officials were lacking in virtue. See James Madison, Alexander Hamilton, and John Jay, *The Federalist Papers*, ed. Isaac Kramnick (London: Penguin, 1987 [1787-88]), no. 55, p. 339. I develop this point in Chapter 2.

6. On the latter point, see George Kateb, "A Life of Fear," in Kateb, *Patriotism and Other Mistakes* (New Haven, Conn.: Yale University Press, 2006); and Richard Falk, "Encroaching on the Rule of Law: Post-9/11 Policies Within the United States," in *National Insecurity and Human Rights*, ed. Alison Brysk and Gershon Shafir (Berkeley: University of California Press, 2007).

7. Carol Anderson, *Eyes Off the Prize: The United Nations and the African American Struggle for Human Rights, 1944-55* (Cambridge: Cambridge University Press, 2003). For my discussion of American exceptionalism, I am indebted to Natalia Gubbioni, "The Enforcement of International Human Rights Law in U.S. Courts," master's thesis, University of Bologna, Forlì, 2010.

8. Natalie Hevener Kaufman, *Human Rights Treaties and the Senate: A History of Opposition* (Chapel Hill: University of North Carolina Press, 1990).

9. Louis Henkin, "U.S. Ratification of Human Rights Conventions: The Ghost of Senator Bricker," *American Journal of International Law* 89 (1995): 341–50.

10. Peter J. Spiro, "The New Sovereigntists: American Exceptionalism and Its False Prophets," *Foreign Affairs* 79 (November/December 2000): 9–15. For a penetrating discussion of this school of thought and its influence on Bush administration detention and interrogation policies, see also M. Cherif Bassiouni, *The Institutionalization of Torture by the Bush Administration* (Antwerp: Intersentia, 2010), pp. 31–37.

11. Jack L. Goldsmith, "Should International Human Rights Law Trump U.S. Domestic Law?," *Chicago Journal of International Law* 1 (2000): 327–39, p. 338.

12. Ibid., p. 333: "There is a powerful case to be made that human rights treaties, which do not involve reciprocal obligations, and which only regulate domestic relations between a nation and its citizens are beyond the scope of the treaty power."

13. Jeremy Rabkin, *Law Without Nations? Why Constitutional Government Requires Sovereign States* (Princeton, N.J.: Princeton University Press, 2005), p. 267.

14. David B. Rivkin, Jr., and Lee A. Casey, "The Rocky Shoals of International Law," *National Interest* 62 (2000–2001): 35–46, pp. 35, 38.

15. Samantha Power, "Boltonism," *New Yorker*, March 21, 2005, p. 23.

16. Jack L. Goldsmith and Eric A. Posner, *The Limits of International Law* (Oxford: Oxford University Press, 2005). For a penetrating critique of this book, see Paul Schiff Berman, "Seeing Beyond the Limits of International Law," *Texas Law Review* 84 (2006): 1265–1306.

17. For the conclusion that states are not inhibited by a sense of legal obligation with respect to international law, see Goldsmith and Posner, *Limits of International Law*, pp. 39–40, 90–91. For the argument that there is no moral obligation to obey international law, see chap. 7.

18. Thus legal scholar John Rogers writes: "The protective power of U.S. human rights law is enormous. It is perhaps what we treasure most about our Nation." John M. Rogers, *International Law and United States Law* (Aldershot: Ashgate, 1999), p. 208. Even those critical of the U.S. self-declared exceptions sometimes give voice to this belief, when they ask in puzzlement why a country with such a strong commitment to protecting rights would resist the incorporation of international human rights law. This sentiment appears in a number of the essays in Michael Ignatieff, ed., *American Exceptionalism and Human Rights* (Princeton, N.J.: Princeton University Press, 2005).

19. United States Initial Report to the Human Rights Committee, July 29, 1994, para. 8.

20. Jack Goldsmith, "International Human Rights Law and the United States Double Standard," *Green Bag* 1 (1998): 365–73, pp. 371, 373. Elsewhere he writes: "The United States has a vigorous, and successful method for human rights protection." It is a "flourishing constitutional democracy with a powerful tradition of domestic human rights protection." Goldsmith, "Should International Human Rights Law Trump U.S. Domestic Law?," p. 335.

21. See Alfred W. McCoy, *A Question of Torture: CIA Interrogation, from the Cold War to the War on Terror* (New York: Metropolitan Books, 2006); John T. Parry, *Understanding Torture* (Ann Arbor: University of Michigan Press, 2010), chap. 6.

22. See Jerome H. Skolnick, "American Interrogation: From Torture to Trickery," in *Torture: A Collection*, ed. Sanford Levinson (Oxford: Oxford University Press, 2004). As late as the 1960s, inmates in Arkansas prisons were being whipped, having their knuckles cracked by pliers, and receiving electric shocks to their genitals. Malcolm M. Feeley and Edward L. Rubin, *Judicial Policy Making and the Modern State: How the Courts Reformed America's Prisons* (Cambridge: Cambridge University Press, 1998), p. 79. Police torture was largely curtailed in response to the 1931

Wickersham Report on Lawlessness in Law Enforcement. See Jerome H. Skolnick and James J. Fyfe, *Above the Law: Police and the Excessive Use of Force* (New York: Free Press, 1993), chap. 3. However, in the 1970s and 1980s, dozens of detainees in the Area 2 Police Station in Chicago were subjected to beatings, burnings, electric shocks, suffocation, and mock execution. John Conroy, *Unspeakable Acts, Ordinary People: The Dynamics of Torture* (Berkeley: University of California Press, 2001), chaps. 3, 7, 11, 15. Interrogational torture has not been eliminated. Spencer Ackerman, "The Disappeared: Chicago Police Detain Americans at Abuse-Laden 'Black Site,'" *Guardian*, February 24, 2015.

23. See Stuart Creighton Miller, *"Benevolent Assimilation": The American Conquest of the Philippines, 1899–1903* (New Haven, Conn.: Yale University Press, 1982), pp. 213, 225–26; Evan Wallach, "Drop by Drop: Forgetting the History of Water Torture in U.S. Courts," *Columbia Journal of Transnational Law* 45 (2007): 468–507.

24. Conroy, *Unspeakable Acts, Ordinary People*, pp. 113–20; McCoy, *A Question of Torture*, pp. 60–71; Nick Turse, *Kill Anything That Moves: The Real American War in Vietnam* (New York: Picador, 2013), pp. 171–91; Jennifer Van Bergen and Douglas Valentine, "The Dangerous World of Indefinite Detentions: Vietnam to Abu Ghraib," *Case Western Reserve Journal of International Law* 37 (2006): 449–508, p. 460. Turse adds, "The brutality regularly exhibited by interrogators behind closed doors at U.S. bases was also frequent among troops in the field. American soldiers in the countryside regularly beat, slapped, punched, and kicked civilian detainees and captured prisoners." Turse, *Kill Anything That Moves*, pp. 187–88. Rape by U.S. soldiers was widespread (pp. 164-71). Torture was used in the massive capture and assassination campaign known as the Phoenix Program.

25. Jennifer K. Harbury, *Truth, Torture and the American Way* (Boston: Beacon, 2005), chaps. 2–3.

26. McCoy, *Question of Torture*, chap. 2.

27. Central Intelligence Agency, *Kubark Counterintelligence Interrogation* (1963), p. 8, http://www2.gwu.edu/~nsarchiv/NSAEBB/NSAEBB122/index.htm.

28. Ibid., p. 41.

29. Ibid., p. 85. The manual seems to recognize few outer limits on interrogation techniques. One paragraph mentions the possibility of obtaining headquarters approval for techniques that involve infliction of "bodily harm" or the use of "medical, chemical, or electrical methods or materials" (p. 8).

30. Ibid., p. 89; CIA, Human Resource Exploitation Training Manual—1983, http://www.gwu.edu/%7Ensarchiv/NSAEBB/NSAEBB122/index.htm#hre.

31. James LeMoyne, "Testifying to Torture," *New York Times Magazine*, June 5, 1988, p. 45.

32. See Gary Cohn and Ginger Thompson, "Unearthed: Fatal Secrets," *Baltimore Sun*, June 11, 1995.

33. M. Gregg Bloche, *The Hippocratic Myth* (New York: Palgrave Macmillan, 2011), p. 128.

34. Ibid., pp. 128–41.

35. The best single overview of the U.S. torture program is *The Report of the Constitution Project's Task Force on Detainee Treatment*, 2013 (Washington, D.C.: The Constitution Project, 2013) (hereafter *Constitution Project Report*).

36. American Civil Liberties Union, *Enduring Abuse: Torture and Cruel Treatment by the United States at Home and Abroad*, April 2006, p. 1.

37. Jane Mayer, *The Dark Side: The Inside Story of the How the War on Terror Turned into a War on American Ideals* (New York: Doubleday, 2008), pp. 125–38; Amnesty International, *Below the Radar: Secret Flights to Torture and "Disappearance"*, April 2006.

38. Center for Human Rights and Global Justice, *Fate and Whereabouts Unknown: Detainees in the "War on Terror"*, December 2005.

39. Human Rights Watch, *"No Blood, No Foul": Soldiers' Accounts of Detainee Abuse in Iraq*, July 2006, p. 11.

40. Mark Danner, *Torture and Truth: America, Abu Ghraib, and the War on Terror* (New York: New York Review of Books, 2004), p. 227.

41. David Rose, "MI6 and CIA 'Sent Student to Morocco to Be Tortured': An Ethiopian Claims That His Confession to al-Qaeda Bomb Plot Was Signed After Beatings," *Observer*, December 11, 2005.

42. Mohamedou Ould Slahi, *Guantánamo Diary*, ed. Larry Siems (New York: Little, Brown, 2015), p. 259.

43. In February 2006, Human Rights First reported that nearly one hundred detainees had died in U.S. custody, and that nearly half of these cases were confirmed or suspected homicides. It concluded that eight detainees had been "tortured to death," but gave reasons to believe that the actual number of detainees who died as a result of torture or ill-treatment was significantly higher. For example, several detainees are known to have been subjected to torture or ill-treatment shortly before their deaths for "undetermined causes." A pattern of "grossly inadequate reporting, investigation, and follow-through" has obscured the actual number of wrongful deaths. Human Rights First, *Command's Responsibility: Detainee Deaths in U.S. Custody in Iraq and Afghanistan*, February 2006. See also John Sifton, "The Bush Administration Homicides," *Daily Beast*, May 5, 2009.

44. *Senate Torture Report*, pp. 61–63; Adam Goldman and Kathy Gannon, "Death Shed Light on CIA 'Salt Pit' Near Kabul," *Associated Press*, March 28, 2010.

45. *Constitution Project Report*, pp. 95–97; Jane Mayer, "A Deadly Interrogation," *New Yorker*, November 14, 2005.

46. *Constitution Project Report*, pp. 97–99.

47. Ibid., pp. 68–72. Several of these cases are also discussed in Human Rights First, *Command's Responsibility*.

48. For examples of spontaneous abuse, see Joshua Phillips, *None of Us Were like This Before: American Soldiers and Torture* (New York: Verso, 2010). Human rights investigator John Sifton observed that detainee abuse in Iraq was "widespread, but that doesn't mean it's all the same. There's been spontaneous abuse at the troops' level; there's been more authorized abuse; there's been overlap—a sort of combination of authorized and unauthorized. And you have abuse that passed around like a virus; abuse that started because one unit was approved to use it, and then another unit which wasn't started copying them." Quoted in Joshua E. S. Phillips and Michael Montgomery, "What Killed Sergeant Gray?," *American Radio Works* (January 2010), http://americanradioworks.publicradio.org/features/vets/transcriptb.html. Quoted in *Constitution Project Report*, p. 109.

49. President George W. Bush, "President Discusses Creation of Military Commissions to Try Suspected Terrorists," September 6, 2006, http://www.whitehouse.gov/news/releases/2006/09/2006 0906-3.html.

50. See Adam Hochschild, "What's in a Word? Torture," *New York Times*, May 23, 2004; Tom Malinowski, "Call Cruelty What It Is," *Washington Post*, September 18, 2006; Dan Eggen, "Cheney's Remarks Fuel Torture Debate: Critics Say He Backed Waterboarding," *Washington Post*, October 27, 2006.

51. In Jordan, for example, the State Department has observed that "the most frequently alleged methods of torture are sleep deprivation, beatings, and extended solitary confinement." Department of State, *1999 Country Reports on Human Rights Practices: Jordan* (2000). In State

Department reports on other countries, sleep deprivation, waterboarding, forced standing, hypothermia, blindfolding, and deprivation of food and water were specifically referred to as torture. See the 1999 State Department human rights reports on Iran, Libya, and Tunisia, and the 2005 report on Egypt. For a comprehensive discussion, see *Constitution Project Report*, pp. 359–60.

52. *Constitution Project Report*, p. 3. This finding is defended on pp. 347–69.

53. President George W. Bush, News Conference at Sea Island, Georgia (June 10, 2004), quoted in Danner, *Torture and Truth*, pp. 45–46.

54. "Bush: 'I Have Never Ordered Torture,'" CNN, June 22, 2004.

55. Ibid.

56. Larry Siems, *The Torture Report: What the Documents Say About America's Post-9/11 Torture Program* (New York: OR Books, 2011), pp. 6–7.

57. *Constitution Project Report*, p. 334. On the record of the Obama administration, see chap. 10, from which most of the following is drawn.

58. Ibid., p. 19; see also pp. 227–33.

59. Jamie Mayerfeld, "In Defense of the Absolute Prohibition of Torture," *Public Affairs Quarterly* 22 (2008): 109–28.

60. The ineffectiveness of torture as a counterterrorist method is comprehensively demonstrated by Darius Rejali, *Torture and Democracy* (Princeton, N.J.: Princeton University Press, 2007), pp. 446–536. For an insightful discussion of torture's ineffectiveness as an intelligence-gathering tool, see William d'Ambruoso, "Norms, Perverse Effects, and Torture," *International Theory* 7 (2015): 33–60, pp. 58–60. For a firsthand account that separates myth from fact about interrogation, see Matthew Alexander, *How to Break a Terrorist: The U.S. Interrogators Who Used Brains, Not Brutality, to Take Down the Deadliest Man in Iraq* (New York: Free Press, 2008). For evidence of the huge strategic costs of torture in the U.S. "War on Terror," see Robert A. Pape, "Review," *H-Diplo/ISSF Forum (no. 5) on the Senate Select Committee on Intelligence (SSCI) and the United States' Post-9/11 Policy on Torture* (February 16, 2005): 18–42. For examination of claims that U.S. torture assisted the U.S. struggle against terror, see *Constitution Project Report*, pp. 243–66. An exhaustive investigation of CIA torture by the Senate Select Committee on Intelligence concluded that "The CIA's use of its enhanced interrogation techniques was not an effective means of acquiring intelligence or gaining cooperation from detainees." *Senate Torture Report*, p. 3. This fact has not been fully absorbed by the public, largely because, as the Senate Committee also demonstrated, the CIA claimed false intelligence gains from enhanced interrogation in its communications to Congress, the executive branch, and the media. Ibid., pp. 4–5, 12, 153–331, 340–59. An internal 1,000-page CIA review corroborated the Senate Committee finding that enhanced interrogation techniques were not an effective intelligence-gathering method. Mark Mazzetti, "CIA Report Found Value of Brutal Interrogation Was Inflated," *New York Times*, January 20, 2015.

61. *U.S. Senate Committee on Armed Services, Inquiry into the Treatment of Detainees in U.S. Custody*, November 30, 2008 (hereafter *SASC Report*), p. xii.

62. For a well-documented argument that the Constitution prohibits torture, see Seth F. Kreimer, "Too Close to the Rack and the Screw: Constitutional Constraints on Torture in the War on Terror," *University of Pennsylvania Journal of Constitutional Law* 6 (2003): 278–325.

63. Regarding the Eighth Amendment, see *Hudson v. McMillian*, 503 U.S. 1 (1992). Regarding the Due Process Clause of the Fifth Amendment, see *Rochin v. California*, 342 U.S. 165 (1952).

64. 538 U.S. 760 (2003), p. 796 (Kennedy concurring in part and dissenting in part). Martinez had been severely wounded in a confrontation with police. As he was receiving emergency medical

care, he was questioned by police officer Chavez over his protests, while in great pain, in fear of dying, and under the apparent (albeit mistaken) belief that care would be withheld until he answered Chavez's questions. The case produced six opinions, none commanding a majority. Kennedy's opinion was joined by Justices Stevens and Ginsburg. Justice Stevens wrote a separate opinion stating that the "attempt to obtain an involuntary confession from a prisoner by torturous methods" was a violation of the Due Process Clause (pp. 784–85), and two additional justices, Souter and Breyer, signaled that they were inclined toward Stevens's opinion, though they believed that this particular case should be remanded to the lower courts for final judgment (pp. 779–80). None of the other opinions contested Kennedy's or Stevens's statement that torture violated the Constitution. Justice Thomas's opinion, the relevant part of which was joined by Justices Rehnquist and Scalia, denied that Chavez's conduct was "egregious" or "conscience-shocking," because Chavez did not delay Martinez's treatment or exacerbate his injuries and because police had a legitimate government interest in gathering information from Martinez (p. 775). When rehearing the case, the court of appeals unanimously ruled that the alleged conduct was a violation of the Due Process Clause. *Martinez v. City of Oxnard*, 337 F.3rd 1091 (9th Circ. 2003).

65. Charter of the Nuremberg Tribunal (1945), art. 6(b), (c); Charter of the Tokyo Tribunal (1946), art. 5(c); Geneva Convention I for the Amelioration of the Condition of the Wounded and Sick in Armed Forces in the Field (1949) (hereafter GC I), arts. 3, 12, 49–50; Geneva Convention II for the Amelioration of the Condition of Wounded, Sick and Shipwrecked Members of Armed Forces (1949) (hereafter GC II), arts. 3, 12, 50–51; Geneva Convention III Relative to the Treatment of Prisoners of War (1949) (hereafter GC III), arts. 3, 13, 129–30; Geneva Convention IV Relative to the Protection of Civilian Persons in Time of War (1949) (hereafter GC IV), arts. 3, 5, 27, 31, 32, 37, 146–47.

66. Johannes Morsink, *The Universal Declaration of Human Rights: Origins, Drafting, and Intent* (Philadelphia: University of Pennsylvania Press, 1999), pp. 42–43.

67. European Convention on Human Rights (1950), art. 3; African Charter on Human and Peoples' Rights (1981), art. 5; American Convention on Human Rights (1969), art. 5(2).

68. ICCPR, art. 4; Torture Convention, art. 2; European Convention of Human Rights, art. 15; Inter-American Convention on Human Rights, art. 27.

69. Declaration on the Protection of All Persons from Being Subjected to Torture and Other Cruel, Inhuman or Degrading Treatment or Punishment, G.A. Res. 3542 (XXX) (hereafter UN Torture Declaration).

70. *R v. Bow Street Metropolitan Stipendiary Magistrate*, ex parte *Pinochet Ugarte*, 2 W.L.R. 827 (H.L. 1999). In the same year, the Israeli Supreme Court barred security services from engaging in torture or any other form of cruel, inhuman, or degrading treatment or punishment, even for the purpose of combating terrorism. H.C. 5100/94 *Public Committee Against Torture in Israel v. The State of Israel*, 53 (4) PD 817 (1999), excerpted in *Torture: A Collection*, ed. Levinson. The Court held that ill-treatment was always contrary to law, but added that a plea of necessity of the "ticking time bomb" variety could in exceptional and unpredictable cases furnish the possible basis of criminal defense; see paras. 33–38.

71. Statute of the International Criminal Tribunal for Rwanda (ICTR Statute), (1994) arts. 3, 4; Statute of the International Criminal Tribunal for the Former Yugoslavia (ICTY Statute), (1993), arts. 2, 5; Rome Statute of the International Criminal Court (1998), arts. 7(1)(f), 8(2)(a)(ii), 8(2)(b)(xxi), 8(2)(c)(i).

72. *Siderman de Blake v. Republic of Argentina*, 965 F.2d 699 (9th Cir. 1992), p. 717.

73. I shall follow the U.N. Committee Against Torture in using "ill-treatment" as a shorthand

for cruel, inhuman, or degrading treatment or punishment. (Note that the European Court of Human Rights does not generally use the term "ill-treatment" this way.)

74. See *De Sanchez v. Banco Central de Nicaragua*, 770 F.2d 1385 (5th Cir. 1985), p. 1397; American Law Institute, *Restatement (Third) of the Foreign Relations Law of the United States*, vol. 2 (Saint Paul: American Law Institute, 1987), § 702, pp. 161, 164, 169–71; Jean-Marie Henckaerts and Louise Doswald-Beck, *International Committee of the Red Cross: Customary International Humanitarian Law*, vol. 1 (Cambridge: Cambridge University Press, 2005), p. 306 (Rule 87); *Public Committee Against Torture v. Israel*, paras. 23–32. See also the numerous judgments of the ICTY and other national and international courts cited in Jordan J. Paust, "Executive Plans and Authorizations to Violate International Law Concerning Treatment and Interrogation of Detainees," *Columbia Journal of Transnational Law* 43 (2005): 811–63, pp. 816 n.17, 821 n.40. Reprinted in revised form as chapter 1 of Jordan J. Paust, *Beyond the Law: The Bush Administration's Unlawful Responses in the "War" on Terror* (Cambridge: Cambridge University Press, 2007), n.17 on pp. 136–37, n.40 on p. 141–43. In its 1999 judgment, the Israeli Supreme Court declined to determine which of the coercive interrogation techniques of the security services rose to the level of torture, instead ruling that as violations of the non-derogable prohibition of cruel, inhuman, or degrading treatment, they constituted impermissible offenses against human dignity.

75. ICCPR, art. 4(2); European Convention of Human Rights, art. 15(2); American Convention on Human Rights; art. 27(2); U.N. Torture Declaration, art. 3.

76. United Nations Committee Against Torture, General Comment No. 2, Implementation of Article 2 by States Parties, January 24, 2008, paragraph 3.

77. Nuremberg Charter, art. 6(b)-(c); Tokyo Charter, art. 5(c).

78. See GC I, arts. 3, 12, 49–50; GC II, arts. 3, 12, 50–51; GC III, arts. 3, 13, 89, 129–30; GC IV, arts. 3, 5, 27, 31–32, 37, 146–47. Moreover, the prohibition of inhuman treatment is the premise of most other articles. See also Geneva Protocol I Relating to the Protection of Victims of International Armed Conflicts (1977), art. 75; Geneva Protocol II Relating to the Protection of Victims of Non-International Armed Conflicts (1977), art. 4; ICTY Statute, arts. 2, 5; ICTR Statute, arts. 3, 4; and Rome Statute of the International Criminal Court (1998), arts. 7(1)(k), 8(2)(a)(ii), 8(2)(b)(xxi), 8(2)(c)(ii).

79. Brief for Law Professors et al. as Amici Curiae Supporting Respondents, pp. 12–13 & n.19, *Rasul v. Bush*, 542 U.S. 466 (2004) (Nos. 03–334, 03–343).

80. See Lisa Hajjar, "Universal Jurisdiction as Praxis: An Option to Pursue Legal Accountability for Superpower Torturers," in *When Governments Break the Law: The Rule of Law and the Prosecution of the Bush Administration*, ed. Austin Sarat and Nasser Hussain (New York: New York University Press, 2010).

81. I read Article 16 to extend all these provisions to ill-treatment as well as torture. See Committee Against Torture, General Comment No. 2, paragraph 3.

82. Nuremberg Charter, arts. 7–8; Rome Statute of the International Criminal Court, arts. 27–28, 33.

83. *Constitution Project Report*, p. 119. Jack Goldsmith, who directed the Office of Legal Counsel from September 2003 until July 2004, later wrote that lawyers played a "surprisingly central and sometimes unfortunate role" in "determining counterterrorism policy." Goldsmith, *The Terror Presidency*, p. 12.

84. Mayer, *The Dark Side*, p. 66.

85. See the indispensable analysis of Stuart Streichler, "Mad About Yoo, or, Why Worry about the Next Unconstitutional War?" *Journal of Law and Politics* 24 (2008): 93–128.

86. David Johnston, "Senate Democrats Revive Demand for Classified Data," *New York Times,* November 24, 2006; Scott Shane, David Johnston, and James Risen, "Secret U.S. Endorsement of Severe Interrogations," *New York Times,* October 4, 2007.

87. *Senate Torture Report,* p. 28.

88. *SASC Report,* pp. 3–7; *Constitution Project Report,* pp. 205-06.

89. U.S. officials sometimes divided extreme techniques between "standard" and "enhanced" techniques. "Standard" as distinct from "enhanced" techniques were said to include "sleep deprivation up to 72 hours, reduced caloric intake, use of loud music, isolation, and the use of diapers 'generally not to exceed 72 hours'" *Senate Torture Report,* p. 69. I use the term "enhanced interrogation techniques" to designate the entire range of extreme techniques.

90. *Constitution Project Report,* pp. 132–33.

91. Memorandum from John C. Yoo, Deputy Assistant Attorney General, to Timothy Flanigan, Deputy Counsel to the President, *Re: The President's Constitutional Authority to Conduct Military Operations Against Terrorists and Nations Supporting Them,* September 25, 2001. Reprinted in *The Torture Papers: The Road to Abu Ghraib,* ed. Karen J. Greenberg and Joshua L. Dratel (Cambridge: Cambridge University Press, 2005), p. 24.

92. *Constitution Project Report,* p. 133.

93. Memorandum from John C. Yoo, Deputy Assistant Attorney General, and Robert J. Delahunty, Special Counsel, to William J. Haynes II, General Counsel, Department of Defense, *Re: Application of Treaties and Laws to al Qaeda and Taliban Detainees,* January 9, 2002, Reprinted in *The Torture Papers,* ed. Greenberg and Dratel (hereafter Yoo-Delahunty Memo).

94. Ibid., pp. 28, 34–39.

95. Memorandum from William H. Taft, Legal Adviser, Department of State, to John C. Yoo, Deputy Assistant Attorney General, *Re: Your Draft Memorandum of January 9,* January 11, 2002, http://nsarchive.gwu.edu/torturingdemocracy/documents/20020111.pdf (hereafter Taft Memo). For additional criticisms, see José E. Alvarez, "Torturing the Law," *Case Western Reserve Journal of International Law* 37 (2006): 175–223, p. 180 n.15; and Paust, *Beyond the Law,* pp. 9–11.

96. *Constitution Project Report,* pp. 134–38, 372.

97. Memorandum from President George W. Bush to the Vice President, the Secretary of State, the Secretary of Defense, the Attorney General, Chief of Staff to the President, Director of Central Intelligence, Assistant to the President for National Security Affairs, and Chairman of the Joint Chiefs of Staff, *Re: Humane Treatment of al Qaeda and Taliban Detainees,* February 7, 2002. The memo was not released to the public until June 2004. Stephen Henderson, Shannon McCaffrey, and Jonathan F. Landay, "Memos on Detainees Released," *Philadelphia Inquirer,* June 23, 2004.

98. Those delivering this message included John Yoo, David Addington, and Alberto Gonzales. In a February 2003 memo, for instance, CIA General Counsel Scott Muller records that he had been reassured by John Yoo two months previously that the February 2002 memo "had been deliberately limited to be binding only on 'the Armed Forces' which did not include the CIA." See David Cole, "'New Torture Files': Declassified Memos Detail Roles of Bush White House and DOJ Officials Who Conspired to Approve Torture," *Just Security,* March 2, 2015. See also the revealing self-correction by attorney general nominee Alberto Gonzales in January 2005: "It has always been the case that everyone should be treated—that the military would treat detainees humanely, consistent with the president's February order." Confirmation Hearing on the Nomination of Alberto R. Gonzales to Be Attorney General of the United States: Hearing Before the Senate Committee on the Judiciary, Senate Judiciary Committee, January 6, 2005.

99. In his Senate confirmation hearing, Alberto Gonzales reported that in the president's view "we should do everything that we can to win this war on terror, so long as we are meeting our legal obligations" (Confirmation Hearing). In 2005, CIA director Michael Hayden stated, "My spikes will have chalk on them. . . . We're pretty aggressive within the law. As a professional, I'm troubled if I'm not using the full authority allowed by law" (Dana Priest, "Covert CIA Program Withstands New Furor," *Washington Post*, December 30, 2005). Jack Goldsmith wrote that his job as OLC director in 2003–2004 "was to make sure the President could act right up to the chalk line of legality." Goldsmith, *The Terror Presidency*, p. 78.

100. Department of State, International Information Programs, "Charges of Guantanamo Detainee Torture Unfounded, General Says," July 14, 2005.

101. Memorandum from Jay S. Bybee, Assistant Attorney General, for William J. Haynes, II, General Counsel, Department of Defense, *Re: The President's Power as Commander in Chief to Transfer Captured Terrorists to the Control and Custody of Foreign Nations*, March 13, 2002, http://nsarchive.gwu.edu/torturingdemocracy/documents/20020313.pdf (hereafter OLC Detainee Transfer Memo).

102. The Bush administration maintained this argument in public, telling the Committee Against Torture that "Article 3 of the [Torture Convention] does not impose obligations on the United States with respect to an individual who is outside the territory of the United States." Response of the United States to the U.N. Committee Against Torture, List of Issues to be Considered During the Examination of the Second Periodic Report of the United States of America, May 5, 2006. The Obama administration has not renounced this position. See *Constitution Project Report*, p. 320.

103. OLC Detainee Transfer Memo, p. 6.

104. International Committee of the Red Cross, *ICRC Report on the Treatment of Fourteen "High Value Detainees" in CIA Custody*, February 2007, pp. 28–30.

105. *Senate Torture Report*, pp. 51–54. See also Ali H. Soufan, *The Black Banners: The Inside Story of 9/11 and the War Against al-Qaeda* (New York: Norton, 2011), pp. 373–435; Siems, *Torture Report*, chap. 1; Mayer, *The Dark Side*, chap. 7; Peter Finn and Joby Warrick, "Detainee's Harsh Treatment Foiled No Plots," *Washington Post*, March 29, 2009; and Jason Leopold, "Torture Diaries, Drawings and the Special Prosecutor," *Truthout*, March 29, 2010.

106. Peter Taylor, " 'Vomiting and Screaming' in Destroyed Waterboarding Tapes," *BBC News*, May 9, 2012; Siems, *Torture Report*, pp. 72–86.

107. *Senate Torture Report*, p. 49. Six days into the twenty-day torture session, interrogators told CIA headquarters it was unlikely that he was withholding actionable information, yet the torture continued (p. 53).

108. Ibid., p. 298.

109. Soufan, *Black Banners*, p. 399.

110. Siems, *Torture Report*, p. 214, quoting U.S. government filings in Abu Zubaydah's habeas corpus case, "Respondent's Memorandum of Points and Authorities in Opposition to Petitioner's Motion for Discovery and Petitioner's Motion for Sanctions," *Husayn v. Gates*, 08-cv-1360 (D.D.C. Oct. 27, 2009).

111. *Senate Torture Report*, pp. 46–49.

112. George W. Bush, *Decision Points* (New York: Random House, 2010), p. 169. His claim is challenged by the *Senate Torture Report*, pp. 50–51. For a discussion of the controversy, see Peter Baker, "Bush Team Approved C.I.A. Tactics, But Was Kept in Dark on Details, Report Says," *New York Times*, December 9, 2014.

113. R. Jeffrey Smith and Peter Finn, "Harsh Methods Approved as Early as Summer 2002," *Washington Post*, April 23, 2009.

114. Memorandum from Jay S. Bybee, Assistant Attorney General, Office of Legal Counsel, for Alberto R. Gonzales, Counsel to the President, *Re: Standards of Conduct for Interrogation under 18 U.S.C. §§ 2340-2340A*, August 1, 2002, reprinted in *The Torture Memos: Rationalizing the Unthinkable*, ed. David Cole (New York: New Press, 2009) (hereafter Bybee-Yoo Torture Memo).

115. Memorandum from Jay S. Bybee, Assistant Attorney General, Office of Legal Counsel, for John Rizzo, Acting General Counsel, Central Intelligence Agency, *Re: Interrogation of al Qaeda Operative*, August 1, 2002, reprinted in *The Torture Memos: Rationalizing the Unthinkable*, ed. David Cole (New York: New Press, 2009) (hereafter Bybee-Yoo Techniques Memo).

116. One veteran of SERE waterboarding reports: "Contrary to popular opinion, it is not a simulation of drowning – it is drowning. In my case, the technique was so fast and professional that I didn't know what was happening until the water entered my nose and throat. It then pushes down into the trachea and starts the process of respiratory degradation. It is an overwhelming experience that induces horror and triggers frantic survival instinct. As the event unfolded, I was fully conscious of what was happening – I was being tortured." Malcolm W. Nance, "Waterboarding Is Not Simulated Drowning—It Is Drowning," *Salon*, November 9, 2007. See also Mark Benjamin, "Waterboarding for Dummies," *Salon*, March 9, 2010.

117. Ryan Pollyea, "Mancow Waterboarded, Admits It's Torture," *NBC Chicago*, May 22, 2009.

118. Bloche, *Hippocratic Myth*, pp. 129–30.

119. See *SASC Report*, p. xx.

120. Central Intelligence Agency, Office of the Inspector General, *Counterterrorism Detention and Interrogation Activities (September 2001–October 2003)*, May 7, 2004 (hereafter CIA IG Report), pp. 22–23 n.26, p. 37.

121. *Senate Torture Report*, p. 54.

122. Bloche, *Hippocratic Myth*, p. 140; *Constitution Project Report*, pp. 205–7.

123. Scott Shane, "Waterboarding Used 266 Times on 2 Suspects," *New York Times*, April 19, 2009.

124. "Counter Resistance Strategy Meeting Minutes," October 2, 2002, reproduced in *SASC Report*, Supporting Documents (hereafter Counter Resistance Minutes); Memorandum from Diane Beaver, Staff Judge Advocate, Department of Defense, JTF 170, for General James T. Hill, Commander, Joint Task Force 170, *Re: Legal Review of Aggressive Interrogation Techniques*, October 11, 2002. Reprinted in *The Torture Papers*, ed. Greenberg and Dratel (hereafter Beaver Memo).

125. Rumsfeld's order stated that approval of three techniques (death threats, exposure to cold temperature and cold water, and waterboarding) "is not warranted at this time," but noted that even these techniques "may be legally available." This was the order to which he added the infamous handwritten comment, "However, I stand for 8-10 hours a day. Why is standing limited to 4 hours?" General Action Memo for Secretary of Defense Donald Rumsfeld, Re: Counter-Resistance Techniques, approved December 2, 2002.

126. *SASC Report*, pp. xviii–xx.

127. Ibid., pp. xxii–xxiv.

128. Memorandum from John C. Yoo, Deputy Assistant Attorney General, for William J. Haynes II, General Counsel of the Department of Defense, *Re: Military Interrogation of Alien Unlawful Combatants Held Outside the United States*, March 14, 2003, nsarchive.gwu.edu/torturingdemocracy/documents/20030314.pdf (hereafter Yoo Military Interrogation Memo).

129. Working Group Report on Detainee Interrogations in the Global War on Terrorism, April

4, 2003, reprinted in *The Torture Papers*, ed. Greenberg and Dratel (hereafter Pentagon Interrogation Working Group Report).

130. Siems, *Torture Report*, pp. 366–68.

131. Ibid., pp. 345–56.

132. *SASC Report*, pp. 190–200.

133. *SASC Report* entire.

134. Goldsmith, *The Terror Presidency*, pp. 153–54.

135. Ibid., pp. 161-62.

136. Ibid., pp. 155–56. Goldsmith himself wrote a March 19, 2004, draft memo arguing that, appearances notwithstanding, Article 49 of the Fourth Geneva Convention permitted U.S. forces in Iraq to transfer protected civilians against their will across international boundaries. Memorandum from Jack L. Goldsmith, III, Assistant Attorney General, for Alberto O. Gonzales, Counsel to the President, *Re: Permissibility of Relocating Certain 'Protected Persons' from Occupied Iraq*, March 19, 2004, reprinted in *The Torture Papers*, ed. Greenberg and Dratel. Critics allege that the draft memo was meant to enable the sort of practices that sent detainees to Guantanamo, CIA black sites, and foreign interrogation centers. For criticism of the memo, see Alvarez, "Torturing the Law," pp. 198–221.

137. Memorandum from Daniel Levin, Acting Assistant Attorney General, Office of Legal Counsel, for James B. Comey, Deputy Attorney General, *Re: Legal Standards Applicable under 18 U.S.C. §§ 2340-2340A*, December 30, 2004, reprinted in *The Torture Memos*, ed. Cole (hereafter Levin Memo).

138. Memorandum from Steven G. Bradbury, Principal Deputy Assistant Attorney General, Office of Legal Counsel, for James A. Rizzo, Senior Deputy General Counsel, Central Intelligence Agency, *Re: Application of 18 U.S.C. §§ 2340-2340A to Certain Techniques That May Be Used in the Interrogation of a High Value al Qaeda Detainee*, May 10, 2005, excerpted in *The Torture Memos*, ed. Cole (hereafter Bradbury Techniques Memo).

139. Memorandum from Steven G. Bradbury, Principal Deputy Assistant Attorney General, Office of Legal Counsel, for James A. Rizzo, Senior Deputy General Counsel, Central Intelligence Agency, *Re: Application of 18 U.S.C. §§ 2340-2340A to the Combined Use of Certain Techniques in the Interrogation of High Value al Qaeda Detainees*, May 10, 2005, excerpted in *The Torture Memos*, ed. Cole (hereafter Bradbury Combined Use Memo).

140. Memorandum from Steven G. Bradbury, Principal Deputy Assistant Attorney General, Office of Legal Counsel, for James A. Rizzo, Senior Deputy General Counsel, Central Intelligence Agency, *Re: Application of United States Obligations Under Article 16 of the Convention Against Torture to Certain Techniques That May Be Used in the Interrogation of High Value al Qaeda Detainees*, May 30, 2005, reprinted in *The Torture Memos*, ed. Cole (hereafter Bradbury Article 16 Memo).

141. Bradbury's memos dropped one technique approved in the Bybee-Yoo Techniques Memo (cramped confinement with insect) but added four new ones (dietary manipulation, nudity, abdominal slap, and water dousing).

142. For details of the legislative battle, see Jamie Mayerfeld, "Playing by Our Own Rules: How U.S. Marginalization of International Human Rights Law Led to Torture," *Harvard Human Rights Journal* 20 (2007): 89–140, pp. 103–4.

143. Detainee Treatment Act §1004.

144. Detainee Treatment Act §1005.

145. See Josh White and Carol D. Leonnig, "U.S. Cites Exception in Torture Ban," *Washington*

Post, March 3, 2006. The complaint was filed by Mohammed Bawazir, a Guantanamo Bay detainee who had been subjected to forced feeding as a result of his hunger strike. Officials had strapped him in a chair, forced a thick feeding tube down his nose, and left him to sit in his own feces.

146. President George W. Bush, President's Statement on Signing of H.R. 2863, December 30, 2005.

147. *Hamdan v. Rumsfeld*, 548 U.S. 557 (2006), pp. 629–31.

148. Military Commissions Act of 2006, Pub. L. No. 109–366 § 6(b), 120 Stat. 2600 (2006) (codified in Chapter 47A of Title 10 of U.S.C.).

149. "Cruel or inhuman treatment" is defined to mean either (a) mental torture according to the very narrow definition in the U.S. Torture Statute (to be discussed in Chapter 5), though after 2006 the mental harm intentionally inflicted on the victim by means of the specified techniques need not be "prolonged," but only "serious and non-transitory"; (b) physical torture; or (c) "bodily injury that involves (i) a substantial risk of death; (ii) extreme physical pain; (iii) a burn or physical disfigurement of a serious nature (other than cuts, abrasions, or bruises); or (iv) significant loss or impairment of the function of a bodily member, organ, or mental faculty."

150. Senator John McCain, who supported the final version of the act, said that most of these acts were indeed federal crimes. Administration officials insisted they were not. See R. Jeffrey Smith, "McCain Names Practices Detainee Bill Would Bar: Senator Says 3 Interrogation Methods Are Among the 'Extreme Measures' the Plan Would Outlaw," *Washington Post*, September 25, 2006; R. Jeffrey Smith and Charles Babington, "White House, Senators Near Pact on Interrogation Rules: President Would Have a Voice in How Detainees Are Questioned," *Washington Post*, September 22, 2006.

151. Military Commissions Act § 5(a).

152. Military Commissions Act § 7(a).

153. Ibid.

154. *Boumediene v. Bush*, 553 U.S. 723 (2008).

155. More recently, however, a federal appeals court ruled that Guantanamo detainees may challenge their conditions of confinement by means of habeas corpus petitions. *Aamer v. Obama*, 742 F.3d 1023 (D.C. Cir. 2014).

156. Memorandum from Steven G. Bradbury, Principal Deputy Assistant Attorney General, Office of Legal Counsel, for John A. Rizzo, Acting General Counsel, Central Intelligence Agency, *Re: Application of the War Crimes Act, the Detainee Treatment Act, and Common Article 3 of the Geneva Conventions to Certain Techniques That May Be Used by the CIA in the Interrogation of High Value al Qaeda Detainees*, July 20, 2007, www.justice.gov/sites/default/files/olc/legacy/2009/08/24/memo-warcrimesact.pdf (hereafter Bradbury July 2007 Memo). The memo did not discuss waterboarding, wall-slamming, or cramped confinement, techniques for which the CIA was no longer seeking legal authorization. The memo authorized continuous sleep deprivation up to ninety-six hours (four days).

157. Deborah Pearlstein has aptly compared this memo to "one of those dizzying Escher paintings, where one's eyes try in vain to follow a staircase to its logical conclusion, and yet keep being tricked when it turns out the staircase turns back upon itself, or otherwise enters into a parallel and upside down universe in which no rules of gravity, logic, or meaning apply." Pearlstein, "In the Flooded Zone," *Opinio Juris* (blog), September 3, 2009. The techniques approved in Bradbury's memo were promptly applied to Muhammad Rahim from July 21 to mid-September and November 2 to December 9, during which time he was subjected to eight extensive sleep deprivation sessions, usually while diapered and shackled to the ceiling. His interrogation yielded "no intelligence."

Senate Torture Report, pp. 146–49. See Katherine Hawkins, "And the Last Detainee," *Guardian*, December 9, 2014.

158. Executive Order 13491—Ensuring Lawful Interrogations, January 22, 2009.

159. This point is vividly conveyed in Stuart Streichler, "The War Crimes Trial That Never Was: An Inquiry into the War on Terrorism, the Laws of War, and Presidential Accountability," *University of San Francisco Law Review* 45 (2011): 959–1004.

160. I steal this formulation from Stuart Streichler.

161. Among the many devastating critiques, see Office of Professional Responsibility, Department of Justice, *Investigation into the Office of Legal Counsel's Memoranda Concerning Issues Relating to the Central Intelligence Agency's Use of "Enhanced Interrogation Techniques" on Suspected Terrorists*, July 29, 2009 (*OPR Report*); Alvarez, "Torturing the Law"; Bassiouni, *The Institutionalization of Torture by the Bush Administration*; David Cole, "Introductory Commentary: Torture Law," in *The Torture Memos*, ed. Cole; Harold Hongju Koh, "A World Without Torture," *Columbia Journal of Transnational Law* 43 (2005): 641–61; David Luban, "Liberalism, Torture, and the Ticking Bomb," in *The Torture Debate in America*, ed. Karen J. Greenberg (Cambridge: Cambridge University Press, 2006); David Luban, *Torture, Power, and Law* (Cambridge: Cambridge University Press, 2014), chaps. 8, 9; Paust, *Beyond the Law*; Jeremy Waldron, "Torture and Positive Law: Jurisprudence for the White House," *Columbia Law Review* 105 (2005): 1681–1750, republished as chap. 7 of Waldron, *Torture, Terror, and Trade-Offs* (Oxford: Oxford University Press, 2010).

162. *OPR Report*, p. 11.

163. Ibid., pp. 242–49.

164. David Margolis, Memorandum of Decision Regarding the Objections to the Findings of Professional Misconduct in the Office of Professional Responsibility's Report of Investigation into the Office of Legal Counsel's Memoranda Concerning Issues Relating to the Central Intelligence Agency's Use of "Enhanced Interrogation Techniques" on Suspected Terrorists, January 5, 2010.

165. See David Luban, "David Margolis Is Wrong," *Slate*, February 22, 2010; Dahlia Lithwick, "Torture Bored," *Slate*, February 22, 2010.

166. Counter Resistance Minutes (see n. 124), p. 3.

167. *OPR Report*, pp. 51, 131, 142, 144.

168. Ibid., pp. 220–22.

169. Ben Emmerson, the UN Special Rapporteur on Counter Terrorism and Human Rights, has called the U.S. torture program an "international conspiracy of crime." Spencer Ackerman, "U.N.'s Drone Inquisitor: CIA Torture Was an 'International Conspiracy of Crime,'" *Wired*, March 5, 2013.

170. *Senate Torture Report*; *CIA IG Report*.

171. Mark Mazzetti and Matt Apuzzo, "C.I.A. Director Defends Use of Interrogation Tactics, Avoiding Issue of Torture," *New York Times*, December 11, 2014.

172. Bradbury approved nudity, dietary manipulation, the abdominal slap, water dousing, and diapering after the CIA began using these techniques. *Senate Torture Report*, pp. 16, 69; Bradbury Techniques Memo; Bradbury July 2007 Memo.

173. *Senate Torture Report*, pp. 4–8, 297–317, emphasizes that the OLC memos relied on factual assertions by the CIA that the CIA knew to be untrue. Yet the OLC reliance on those assertions gives an impression of insincerity. By the time Steven Bradbury wrote his 2005 and 2007 interrogation memos, he had ample evidence of past CIA misrepresentations, yet continued to take CIA assertions at face value. *OPR Report*, pp. 242–29. The reliance of the Bybee-Yoo Techniques Memo on CIA assertions exhibits a similar insincerity (pp. 235–36).

174. Notoriously, it spied on and threatened criminal charges against Senate committee staff

investigating the interrogation program. Mark Mazzetti and Carl Hulse, "Inquiry by C.I.A. Affirms It Spied on Senate Panel," *New York Times*, July 31, 2014; Katherine Hawkins, "Torture and the CIA's Unaccountability Boards," *Just Security*, February 5, 2015; Rob Crawford, "The CIA, the President, and the Senate's Torture Report," *Counterpunch*, September 26–28, 2014.

175. On the organized effort of the CIA to cultivate popular support for its interrogation program, see *Senate Torture Report*, pp. 12, 290–96. The effort went hand in hand with CIA misrepresentations to Congress and the executive branch regarding the effectiveness of enhanced interrogation. Ibid., pp. 4–5, 12, 153–331, 340–59. The most famous example of the CIA's public relations campaign was its role in shaping the narrative of *Zero Dark Thirty*, a 2012 Hollywood film implying that enhanced interrogation helped U.S. officials discover the location of Osama bin Laden. The Senate Intelligence Committee investigation confirms that the movie's narrative is a near-total fabrication. Charlie Savage and James Risen, "Senate Report Rejects Claim on Hunt for Bin Laden," *New York Times*, December 9, 2014.

Chapter 5. American Exceptionalism and the Betrayal of Human Rights, Part II: Enabling Torture

1. In June 2015 the Senate adopted an amendment requiring all U.S. personnel, including CIA officials, to abide by the strict anti-torture guidelines of the U.S. Army Field Manual. As this book goes to press, the law's passage is still pending. The measure, which could be interpreted as a partial retreat from the self-exemption policy, would inhibit the resumption of torture, but full incorporation of international human rights law would greatly strengthen that inhibition.

2. The ICCPR had previously been signed and submitted to the Senate by President Jimmy Carter and the Torture Convention by President Ronald Reagan. For a detailed historical account of the ratification of these two treaties, see John T. Parry, *Understanding Torture* (Ann Arbor: University of Michigan Press, 2010), pp. 55–60; Duane W. Krohnke, "U.S. Ratification of the Multilateral Treaty Against Torture," December 1, 2011, http://dwkcommentaries.com/2011/12/01/; and Krohnke, "U.S. Ratification of the International Covenant on Civil and Political Rights," February 5, 2013, http://dwkcommentaries.com/2013/02/05.

3. See Kenneth Roth, "The Charade of U.S. Ratification of International Human Rights Treaties," *Chicago Journal of International Law* 1 (2000): 347–53. The Human Rights Committee of the ICCPR had countries like the United States in mind when it criticized the intentional use of reservations to avoid any changes in national law. Human Rights Committee, General Comment 24 regarding reservations (1994), §12. The Comment suggests that such reservations defeat the object and purpose of the Covenant and may therefore be invalid under international law.

4. See Natalie Hevener Kaufman, *Human Rights Treaties and the Senate: A History of Opposition* (Chapel Hill: University of North Carolina Press, 1990), chap. 6.

5. International Covenant on Civil and Political Rights: Hearing Before the Senate Committee on Foreign Relations, 101st Congress, November 21, 1991 (hereafter ICCPR Senate Hearing), Prepared Statement of Richard Schifter, Assistant Secretary of State for Human Rights and Humanitarian Affairs, p. 18.

6. In *Stanford v. Kentucky*, 492 U.S. 361 (1989), the Supreme Court had upheld the constitutionality of the death penalty for murders committed by children aged sixteen and seventeen. Not until 2005, in *Roper v. Simmons*, 543 U.S. 551, did the Supreme Court declare the juvenile death penalty unconstitutional.

7. *Sosa v. Alvarez-Machain*, 542 U.S. 692 (2004), pp. 734–35.

8. See David Sloss, "The Domestication of International Human Rights: Non-Self-Executing Declarations and Human Rights Treaties," *Yale Journal of International Law* 24 (1999): 129–221. The non-self-executing declarations could mean (1) that individuals may not use treaties as a private cause of action, or (2) that courts are altogether barred from direct enforcement of the treaties, or (3) that the treaties do not acquire the status of domestic law. Sloss argues in favor of the first interpretation. The Supreme Court in *Sosa v. Alvarez-Machain* indicated support for the second (treaties accompanied by non-self-executing declarations do not by themselves "create obligations enforceable in the federal courts," pp. 734–35). The Supreme Court in *Medellín v. Texas* 128 S.Ct. 1346 (2008) sometimes implied support for the third (non-self-executing treaties "do not by themselves function as binding federal law," p. 1356).

9. Sloss, "Domestication of International Human Rights," pp. 196–203.

10. Vienna Convention on the Law of Treaties (1969), art. 26.

11. Mark W. Janis, *An Introduction to International Law*, 4th ed. (New York: Aspen, 2003), pp. 97–102.

12. Leading cases are *Foster v. Neilson*, 27 U.S. 253 (1829); *Whitney v. Robertson*, 124 U.S. 190 (1888); and *Medellín v. Texas* 128 S.Ct. 1346 (2008).

13. *Trop v. Dulles*, 356 U.S. 86 (1958).

14. For similar provisions in the Torture Convention, see arts. 1(2) and 16(2).

15. ICCPR Article 5(2) does not cancel obligations contained in the treaty that, like Article 20, arguably weaken rights. To handle such provisions, a reservation is necessary.

16. Convention Against Torture: Hearing Before the Senate Committee on Foreign Relations, 101st Congress, January 30, 1990 (hereafter Torture Convention Senate Hearing), p. 5.

17. The identical passage appears in Human Rights Watch statements submitted to the Torture Convention and ICCPR hearings. Torture Convention Senate Hearing, p. 96; ICCPR Senate Hearing, p. 184.

18. The latter is an allusion to the conditions of "death row," judged by the European Court of Human Rights to fall into the category of inhuman or degrading treatment. On these grounds, in the case of *Soering v. UK* (1989), the ECtHR blocked extradition of a murder suspect to Virginia. *Soering v. the United Kingdom* (Plenary), no. 14038/88, ECHR 1989, Series A no. 161.

19. Whereas Article 3 of the Convention prohibits deportation "where there are substantial grounds for believing" in such danger, the U.S. understanding clarifies that the prohibition applies "if it is more likely than not that [the individual] would be tortured."

20. For criticisms of these restrictions, see the prepared statement of Human Rights Watch in Torture Convention Senate Hearing, pp. 94–95.

21. Some commentators have argued that "understandings," unlike "reservations," do not modify the U.S. international obligations, but only govern the domestic interpretation of a treaty. See Office of Professional Responsibility, Department of Justice, *Investigation into the Office of Legal Counsel's Memoranda Concerning Issues Relating to the Central Intelligence Agency's Use of "Enhanced Interrogation Techniques" on Suspected Terrorists*, July 29, 2009 (hereafter *OPR Report*), p. 239. However, as Brad R. Roth notes, the term "understanding" has "no specified significance in international law; thus, whether qualifications under [this heading] amount to reservations is a question of intent." Brad R. Roth, "Understanding the 'Understanding': Federalism Constraints on Human Rights Implementation," *Wayne Law Review* 47 (2001–2002): 891–910, p. 891 n.2. The text and legislative history of the Torture Convention and ICCPR RUDs suggest that understandings no less than reservations were intended to modify the United States' international obligations, a view

reflected in U.S. communications with the two treaties' international monitoring bodies, the Committee Against Torture and the Human Rights Committee. See the statement by the United States to the former body that "The United States . . . conditioned its ratification on two reservations and a number of interpretive understandings." United States Initial Report to the Committee Against Torture, October 15, 1999, para. 3.

22. There are minor differences. The Torture Victim Protection Act does not replace "intentionally inflicted" with "specifically intended," but otherwise follows the U.S. understanding. The Torture Statute changes a few words not generally thought to carry practical significance. (But see Kate Riggs, Richard Blakeley, and Jasmine Marwaha, "Prolonged Mental Harm: The Torturous Reasoning Behind a New Standard for Psychological Abuse," *Harvard Human Rights Journal* 20 [2007]: 263–92, arguing for the significance of these changes.) The Foreign Affairs Reform and Restructuring Act provision makes no changes to the definition in the U.S. understanding. The 2006 MCA uses the Torture Statute definition.

23. Bradbury Techniques Memo (see chap. 4, n. 138), pp. 153–54.

24. Whereas the Convention defines torture as "any act by which severe pain or suffering, whether physical or mental, is *intentionally* inflicted," the U.S. understanding states that "in order to constitute torture, an act must be *specifically intended* to inflict severe physical pain or suffering" (emphasis added).

25. Torture Convention Senate Hearing, pp. 10 and 17 (prepared statements of Abraham Sofaer, State Department legal advisor, and Mark Richard, deputy attorney general, Criminal Division).

26. Wayne R. LaFave, *Criminal Law*, 4th ed. (St. Paul: West, 2003), pp. 252–54. LaFave notes that the Model Penal Code drops the terminology of specific and general intent, declaring it "an abiding source of confusion and ambiguity in the penal law." Model Penal Code § 2.02.

27. *United States v. Bailey*, 444 U.S. 394 (1980).

28. *United States v. Neiswender*, 590 F.2d 1269 (4th Cir. 1979).

29. I obviously exclude medical or rescue situations in which, by seeking to help someone, we may knowingly though regretfully subject them to pain.

30. Bybee-Yoo Torture Memo (see chap. 4, n. 114), p. 63.

31. Ibid., pp. 44–45.

32. *OPR Report*, pp. 168–69.

33. Levin Memo (see chap. 4, n. 137), p. 150.

34. Bybee-Yoo Techniques Memo (see chap. 4, n. 115), p. 124.

35. See also the letter from John Yoo to John Rizzo, July 13, 2002, http://www.aclu.org/files/torturefoia/released/082409/olcremand/2004olc1.pdf; and the bullet points discussing "Legal Principles Applicable to CIA Detention and Interrogation of Captured Al-Qa'ida Personnel," June 16, 2003, https://www.aclu.org/sites/default/files/torturefoia/released/082409/olcremand/2004olc17.pdf.

36. Bybee-Yoo Techniques Memo, p. 125; Bradbury Techniques Memo, pp. 172, 174–77; Bradbury Combined Use Memo (see chap. 4, n. 139), pp. 206, 210; Bradbury Article 16 Memo (see chap. 4, n. 140), p. 235.

37. Jack Goldsmith heard the term "golden shield" used by a CIA official. Jack Goldsmith, *The Terror Presidency: Law and Judgment Inside the Bush Administration* (New York: Norton, 2007), p. 144.

38. Counter Resistance Minutes (see chap. 4, n. 124), p. 3.

39. Maureen E. Mahoney and Everett C. Johnson, "Classified Response to the U.S. Department of Justice Office of Professional Responsibility Classified Report Dated July 29, 2009, Submitted on

268   Notes to Pages 154–159

Behalf of Judge Jay S. Bybee," October 9, 2009, at https://www.fas.org/irp/agency/doj/opr-by
beefinal.pdf, 29 n.28. See the discussion in Siems, *Torture Report*, pp. 100–101. Rahman was captured on October 29, 2002, and died three weeks later. His family learned his fate for the first time
in February 2010, and then only because a redaction error left Rahman's name intact in the publication of Bybee's response to the Department of Justice OPR investigation.

40. *Pierre v. Attorney General of U.S.*, 528 F. 3d 180 (3rd Circ. 2008), pp. 189–90.

41. In Yoo's view, the *Pierre* holding proved his analysis "manifestly *correct*." Miguel A. Estrada,
"Response to the U.S. Department of Justice Office of Professional Responsibility Final Report
Dated July 29, 2009, Submitted on Behalf of John C. Yoo," October 9, 2009, http://www.aclu.org
/files/pdfs/natsec/opr20100219/YooResponse091009.pdf, pp. 38–42.

42. For example, the OLC provided a reasonable interpretation of the Torture Statute when it
asserted, with regard to mental pain or suffering, that "if a defendant has a good faith belief that his
actions will not result in prolonged mental harm, he lacks the mental state necessary for his actions
to constitute torture." Bybee-Yoo Torture Memo, p. 51. The memo's sections on "Prolonged Mental
Harm" and "Harm Caused By Or Resulting From Predicate Acts" offer a mostly (if not entirely)
unproblematic interpretation of the Statute.

43. Torture Convention Hearing, p. 17.

44. Ibid., pp. 12–14.

45. David Luban and Henry Shue, "Mental Torture: A Critique of Erasures in U.S. Law,"
Georgetown Law Journal 100 (2012): 823–63. This article is republished as chap. 7 of Luban, *Torture,
Power, and Law* (Cambridge: Cambridge University Press, 2014).

46. Ibid. This argument is outlined on p. 825, and developed on pp. 840–55.

47. Ibid, p. 849.

48. See Almerindo E. Ojeda, "What Is Psychological Torture?," in *The Trauma of Psychological
Torture*, ed. Almerindo E. Ojeda (Westport, Conn.: Praeger, 2008), pp. 1–3, cited in Luban and
Shue, "Mental Torture."

49. Torture Convention Hearing, p. 94.

50. This was to be accomplished, the CIA explained, by demonstrating to the detainee "that he
has no control over basic needs." *The Report of the Constitution Project's Task Force on Detainee
Treatment*, 2013 (Washington, D.C.: The Constitution Project, 2013) (hereafter *Constitution Project
Report*), p. 206, quoting a fax from the CIA to OLC director Daniel Levin, December 30, 2004.
Note, however, that by seeking to induce learned helplessness, the CIA program presses against the
limits of the Torture Statute, since learned helplessness could constitute "prolonged mental harm."

51. *Constitution Project Report*, chap. 6; James Risen, "Outside Psychologists Shielded U.S. Torture Program, Report Finds," *New York Times*, July 10, 2015.

52. "A 'Tortured' Debate," editorial, *Wall Street Journal*, November 12, 2005.

53. Luban and Shue, "Mental Torture," pp. 856, 862.

54. Charter of the Nuremberg Tribunal (1945), art. 6(b), (c); Charter of the Tokyo Tribunal
(1946), art. 5 (c); Geneva Convention I for the Amelioration of the Condition of the Wounded and
Sick in Armed Forces in the Field (1949), arts. 49–50; Geneva Convention II for the Amelioration
of the Condition of Wounded, Sick and Shipwrecked Members of Armed Forces (1949), arts. 50–51;
Geneva Convention III Relative to the Treatment of Prisoners of War (1949), arts. 129–30; Geneva
Convention IV Relative to the Protection of Civilian Persons in Time of War (1949), arts. 146–47.

55. *Filártiga v. Peña-Irala*, 630 F.2d 876 (2d Cir. 1980).

56. A *jus cogens* rule is a peremptory norm of international law from which no derogation is
permitted. Torture has long been recognized as a *jus cogens* violation.

57. For an argument that America's harsh system of criminal punishment is a betrayal of the Constitution, see George Kateb, "Punishment and the Spirit of Democracy," *Social Research* 74 (2007): 269–306.

58. Torture Convention Senate Hearing, p. 3.

59. "The formulation used by Article 16 [of the Torture Convention] is ambiguous, particularly in its reference to 'degrading treatment.' . . . [B]ecause the Constitution of the United States directly addresses this area of the law, and because of the ambiguity of the phrase 'degrading,' we would limit our obligations under this Convention to the proscriptions already covered in our Constitution" (ibid., p. 11). This language was echoed in the U.S. initial report to the Committee Against Torture: "In the view of the United States, it was necessary to limit United States undertakings under [Art. 16] primarily because the meaning of the term 'degrading treatment' is at best vague and ambiguous." U.S. Initial Report to the Committee Against Torture, October 15, 1999, para. 303.

60. See *Whitley v. Albers*, 475 U.S. 312 (1986).

61. Torture Convention Senate Hearing, p. 11.

62. Ibid.

63. James Q. Whitman, *Harsh Justice: Criminal Punishment and the Widening Divide Between America and Europe* (Oxford: Oxford University Press, 2003).

64. James Forman, Jr., "Exporting Harshness: How the War on Crime Has Made the War on Terror Possible," *New York University Review of Law and Social Change* 33 (2009): 331–74.

65. Ibid.; and American Civil Liberties Union, *Enduring Abuse: Torture and Cruel Treatment by the United States at Home and Abroad*, April 2006. In 2005 the American Civil Liberties Union (ACLU) brought a suit on behalf of 1,000 prisoners in a Mississippi supermax facility who "are confined twenty-three to twenty-four hours a day in total isolation and complete monotony, . . . constantly exposed to pervasive filth and stench, malfunctioning plumbing, human excrement, lethal extremes of heat and humidity, grossly inadequate physical and mental care, and the constant pandemonium created by severely mentally ill prisoners housed in adjoining cells without treatment, who scream, rave, and hallucinate. . . . They are deprived of any meaningful review of their placement in, or indefinite confinement to, the supermax, and they have no opportunity to earn their way into less-restrictive housing." ACLU, *Enduring Abuse*, p. 54. Mississippi agreed to close the facility in 2010. However, grave abuses in Mississippi prisons persist. See Erica Goode, "Seeing Squalor and Unconcern in a Mississippi Jail," *New York Times*, June 7, 2014.

66. David Kaiser and Lovisa Stannow, "The Shame of Our Prisons: New Evidence," *New York Review of Books*, October 24, 2013.

67. Forman, "Exporting Harshness," p. 355.

68. See Amnesty International, *Entombed: Isolation in the US Federal Prison System*, July 2014; Lorna Rhodes, *Total Confinement: Madness and Reason in the Maximum Security Prison* (Berkeley: University of California Press, 2004); and Jules Lobel, "Prolonged Solitary Confinement and the Constitution," *University of Pennsylvania Journal of Constitutional Law* 11 (2008): 115–38. My understanding of this practice is indebted to two senior honors theses by Law, Societies & Justice students at the University of Washington: Joshua Hansen-King, "Human Rights and Solitary Confinement: The American Story," 2009; and Reed Klein and Laura Martin, "Out of Sight and Out of Reach: The Challenge of Reforming Solitary Confinement Through the Courts," 2015.

69. Atul Gawande, "Hellhole: Is Solitary Confinement Torture?" *New Yorker*, March 30, 2009; Tracy Hresko, "In the Cellars of the Hollow Men: Use of Solitary Confinement in U.S. Prisons and Its Implications Under International Laws Against Torture," *Pace International Law Review* 18 (2006): 1–27, pp. 19–24.

70. See the powerful arguments of Forman, "Exporting Harshness"; Morris B. Kaplan, "'Criminal Justice' and the Politics of Punishment," lecture to the Greater Philadelphia Philosophy Consortium, April 12, 2008; and Colin Dayan, *The Story of Cruel and Unusual* (Cambridge, Mass.: MIT Press, 2007).

71. Malcolm M. Feeley and Edward L. Rubin, *Judicial Policy Making and the Modern State: How the Courts Reformed America's Prisons* (Cambridge: Cambridge University Press, 1998).

72. *Brown v. Plata*, 131 S. Ct. 1910 (2011).

73. *Wilson v. Seiter*, 501 U.S. 294 (1991), p. 296. For a strong critique of this requirement, see the concurring opinion of Justice Blackmun in *Farmer v. Brennan*, 511 U.S. 825 (1994).

74. *Wilson v. Seiter*, pp. 299, 305.

75. Ibid., p. 302.

76. *Hudson v. McMillian*, 503 U.S. 1 (1992), pp. 6–7. On the practical implications of this turn in Eighth Amendment jurisprudence, see Dayan, *The Story of Cruel and Unusual*. John Parry observes that in recent years, as "public policy approaches to crime have turned increasingly punitive, the trend of court decisions has run against prisoner claims." Parry, *Understanding Torture*, p. 155.

77. Human Rights Watch and American Civil Liberties Union, *Human Rights Violations in the United States*, December 1993, p. 99.

78. ACLU, *Enduring Abuse*, p. 85.

79. Counter Resistance Minutes (see chap. 4, n. 124), p. 4.

80. Beaver Memo (see chap. 4, n. 124), p. 233. In *Hudson v. McMillian* (pp. 6–7) the Supreme Court held that "whenever prison officials stand accused of using excessive physical force in violation of the Cruel and Unusual Punishments Clause, the core judicial inquiry is . . . whether force was applied in a good-faith effort to maintain or restore discipline, or maliciously and sadistically to cause harm." Beaver's argument seems to have been that the interrogation methods were constitutional because they were not malicious or sadistic. However, one can argue that the interrogation methods failed the *Hudson* standard, because they were not "applied in a good-faith effort to maintain or restore discipline."

81. Yoo Military Interrogation Memo (see chap. 4, n. 128), pp. 9–10. The administration was making these arguments in public by April 2005. See letter from William E. Moschella, assistant attorney general, to Senator Patrick Leahy, April 4, 2005, http://www.scotusblog.com/movabletype/archives/CAT%20Article%2016.Leahy-Feinstein-Feingold%20Letters.pdf, 3.

82. Ibid. Abraham Sofaer, the former George H. W. Bush official who shepherded ratification of the Torture Convention and helped draft the RUDs, vigorously rejected the view that either the jurisdictional language of Article 16 or the U.S. reservation confined U.S. obligations within its own borders. Abraham Sofaer, "No Exceptions," *Wall Street Journal*, November 26, 2005.

83. Bradbury Article 16 Memo.

84. "[No person] shall be compelled *in any criminal case* to be a witness against himself" (emphasis added). The Supreme Court has not extended this right beyond the criminal justice context.

85. So a 5-4 majority held in *Ingraham v. Wright*, 430 U.S. 651 (1977). In his dissenting opinion, Justice White objected: "the fact that the Framers did not choose to insert the word 'criminal' into the language of the Eighth Amendment is strong evidence that the Amendment was designed to prohibit all inhumane or barbaric punishments, no matter what the nature of the offense for which the punishment is imposed" (p. 685).

86. The Supreme Court has held that government conduct shocking to the conscience is a violation of the Due Process Clause. See *Rochin v. California*, 342 U.S. 165 (1952).

87. Some of these are discussed by David Cole in *The Torture Memos*, "Introductory Commentary," pp. 30–34. Bradbury stretches credulity when he claims that the enhanced interrogation techniques do not clash with "understanding of traditional executive behavior, of contemporary practice, and of the standards of blame generally applied to them" (quoting *County of Sacramento v. Lewis*, 523 U.S. 833 [1998], p. 847 n.8). His efforts to deem irrelevant the State Department's condemnation of torture by other governments and the categorical prohibition of torture and inhuman treatment in the 1992 Army Field Manual on Intelligence Interrogation are notably unpersuasive. See Bradbury Article 16 Memo, pp. 228 ff.

88. Amnesty International, "Law and Executive Disorder: President Gives Green Light to Secret Detention Program," August 17, 2007. Although the Bradbury Article 16 Memo had not yet been released to the public, Amnesty International correctly surmised the "shocks the conscience" justification of torture from other official documents.

89. U.S. Initial Report to the Human Rights Committee (HRC), July 29, 1994, para. 8.

90. U.S. Initial Report to the Committee Against Torture (CAT), October 15, 1999, para. 60.

91. U.S. Initial Report to the HRC, para. 8.

92. See the penetrating critique by David Heffernan, in "America the Cruel and Unusual? An Analysis of the Eighth Amendment Under International Law," *Catholic University Law Review* 45 (1996): 481–560.

93. Statement of Conrad Harper, State Department Legal Advisor, to Human Rights Committee, Human Rights Committee, 53rd Session, 1405th meeting, March 31, 1995. This has been the consistent position of the United States since 1995, against which the Human Rights Committee has consistently held the contrary. See Margaret L. Satterthwaite, "Rendered Meaningless: Extraordinary Rendition and the Rule of Law," *George Washington Law Review* 75 (2007): 1333–1420, pp. 1358–65.

94. Satterthwaite, "Rendered Meaningless."

95. See ibid., pp. 1358–65; and Parry, *Understanding Torture*, pp. 31–32.

96. See Pentagon Interrogation Working Group Report (see chap. 4, n. 129), p. 290. The ICCPR would still apply to individuals subjected to torture and abuse inside the United States, such as Jose Padilla, Yaser Hamdi, and Ali al-Marri.

97. The Statute applies only to torture committed "outside the United States." Originally, the "United States" was defined to include the U.S. Special Maritime and Territorial Jurisdiction (SMTJ), which in the October 2001 PATRIOT Act was expanded to cover crimes by or against U.S. nationals in overseas U.S. military, diplomatic, and other facilities. Following an October 2004 amendment to the Torture Statute, the definition of the "United States" no longer mentioned the SMTJ and instead became "the several States of the United States, the District of Columbia, and the commonwealths, territories, and possessions of the United States." See Yoo Military Interrogation Memo, pp. 34–36; and Pentagon Interrogation Working Group Report, p. 291.

98. U.S. Initial Report to the CAT, para. 178.

99. The legislation partially incorporated art. 7 of the ICCPR as well as art. 16 of the Torture Convention.

100. As Gerald L. Neuman writes, "the Supreme Court has reason to examine international human rights norms and decisions interpreting them for the normative and functional insights that they may provide on analogous issues of constitutional right." Neuman, "The Uses of International Law in Constitutional Interpretation," *American Journal of International Law* 98 (2004): 82–90, p. 88.

101. As we have seen, the same refusal to view the treaties as an opportunity to reflect on

constitutional rights may be seen in several of the treaty reservations and understandings. The treaty prohibition of ill-treatment is one example, but there are others. Where, for example, the ICCPR affirms the rights of criminal defendants to receive legal assistance and summon witnesses and not to suffer double jeopardy, and does so in terms that are potentially more generous than U.S. Supreme Court interpretations of the corresponding constitutional rights, the U.S. understandings stipulate limits that match the Supreme Court's stingier readings of the Constitution. Why not consider that the (potentially) more generous interpretations found in the international treaties may provide the correct reading of U.S. constitutional rights?

102. Article 14, enshrining a right to civil remedies, is partly incorporated by the Torture Victim Protection Act, but this Act does not cover torture committed by the U.S. government.

103. *Constitution Project Report*, pp. 330–31.

104. John Couwels, "Ex-Liberian President's Son Convicted of Torture," *CNN*, October 30, 2008.

105. *Arar v. Ashcroft*, 585 F.3d 559 (2nd Circ. 2009); *Padilla v. Yoo*, 678 F.3d 748 (9th Circ. 2012); *Lebron v. Rumsfeld*, 670 F.3d 540 (4th Circ. 2012); *El-Masri v. U.S.*, 479 F.3d 296 (4th Circ. 2007); *Al-Zahrani v. Rodriguez*, 669 F.3d 315 (D.C. Circ. 2012); *Rasul v. Myers*, 512 F.3d 644 (D.C. Cir. 2008); *Janko v. Gates*, 741 F. 3d 136 (D.C. Circ. 2014).

106. Jonathan Stempel, "Abu Ghraib Torture Lawsuit Revived by U.S. Appeals Court," *Reuters*, June 30, 2014. The case is *Al-Shimari v. CACI* (4th Circ. 2014).

107. *Mohamed v. Jeppesen Dataplan*, 614 F.3d 1070 (9th Cir. 2010) (en banc).

108. Charlie Savage, *Takeover: The Return of the Imperial Presidency and the Subversion of American Democracy* (New York: Little, Brown, 2008).

109. Gwynne L. Skinner, "Roadblocks to Remedies: Recently Developed Barriers to Relief for Aliens Injured by U.S. Officials, Contrary to the Founders' Intent," *University of Richmond Law Review* 47 (2013): 555–629; Denise Gilman, "Calling the United States' Bluff: How Sovereign Immunity Undermines the United States' Claim to an Effective Domestic Human Rights System," *Georgetown Law Journal* 95 (2007): 591–652; Jeffrey Davis, *Justice Across Borders: The Struggle for Human Rights in U.S. Courts* (Cambridge: Cambridge University Press, 2008).

110. Martin S. Flaherty, "Judicial Globalization in the Service of Self-Government," *Ethics and International Affairs* 20 (2006): 477–503.

111. Goldsmith, *The Terror Presidency*, pp. 32–33.

112. Ibid., p. 33.

113. *OPR Report*, p. 17.

114. Trevor Morrison, "Constitutional Alarmism," *Harvard Law Review* 124 (2011): 1688–1749, pp. 1716–17.

115. Bradbury Article 16 Memo, pp. 272–74.

116. Judge James L. Pohl, *U.S.A v. Mohammed et al.*, Order AE 200 II, To Defense Motion to Dismiss Because *Amended* Protective Order #1 Violates the Convention Against Torture, December, 16, 2013, http://justsecurity.org/wp-content/uploads/2013/12/AE-200II.pohl_.pdf. However, Judge Pohl later ordered the government to provide defense lawyers with detailed information about CIA black site interrogations, a decision now being appealed by the prosecution. Carol Rosenberg, "Prosecution to Guantánamo Judge: Take Back Your CIA Ruling," *Miami Herald*, May 9, 2014.

117. Katherine Hawkins, "The GTMO Military Commissions Are Starting to Move Away from Censorship," *Classified Section*, February 9, 2015.

118. Noting that the Senate did not adopt a non-self-executing declaration when approving

ratification of the Conventions, the court stated that "United States courts are bound to give effect to international law and to international agreements of the United States unless such agreements are 'non-self-executing.'" *Hamdan v. Rumsfeld*, 344 F. Supp. 2d 152 (D.D.C. 2004), pp. 164–65.

119. The appeals court invoked a footnote from a World War II-era Supreme Court opinion (*Johnson v. Eisentrager*, 339 U.S. 763 [1950]), which stated that U.S. judges were not authorized to enforce the Geneva Conventions of 1929, the precursor to the 1949 Conventions. *Hamdan v. Rumsfeld*, 415 F.3d 33, 38–40 (D.C. Cir. 2005), pp. 38–40.

120. *Hamdan v. Rumsfeld*, 548 U.S. 557 (2006), p. 628.

121. Ibid., pp. 629–31.

122. Military Commissions Act § 6(a)(3)(a).

123. Military Commissions Act § 5(a).

124. Military Commissions Act § 6(a)(2).

125. After passage of the Military Commissions Act, members of the administration became less guarded. In an interview on October 24, 2006, Vice President Cheney supported the use of waterboarding in the fight against terror, calling it a "no-brainer." Interview by Scott Hennen with Richard Cheney, vice president, in Washington, D.C. (October 24, 2006), http://www.whitehouse.gov/news/releases/2006/10/20061024-7.html. He seemed to say, too, that waterboarding is not torture and that it is not a violation of international treaties. These claims are not plausible, but after the passage of the Military Commissions Act there was little if anything the courts could do to stop the executive branch from acting on them.

126. Executive Order 13440 of July 20, 2007. See Bradbury July 2007 Memo (see chap. 4, n. 156), pp. 76–78.

127. *Medellín v. Texas*, 128 S.Ct. 1346 (2008).

128. See the forceful dissent by Justice Breyer. See also Lori F. Damrosch, "*Medellín* and *Sanchez-Llamas*: Treaties from John Jay to John Roberts," and David Sloss, "*Medellín* and the Passive Vices," in *International Law in the U.S. Supreme Court*, ed. David L. Sloss, Michael D. Ramsey, and William S. Dodge (Cambridge: Cambridge University Press, 2011).

129. For an argument that this presumption is incorrect and that *Medellín* should not be read to endorse it, see Carlos Manuel Vázquez, "Treaties as Law of the Land: The Supremacy Clause and the Judicial Enforcement of Treaties," *Harvard Law Review* 122 (2008): 599–695.

130. *City of Boerne v. Flores*, 521 U.S. 507 (1997). The majority opinion, written by Justice Kennedy, denied that "Congress has the power to decree the substance of the Fourteenth Amendment's restrictions on the States" (p. 519). On the significance of *City of Boerne* for congressional implementation of human rights treaty law, see Brad R. Roth, "Understanding the 'Understanding': Federalism Constraints on Human Rights Implementation," *Wayne Law Review* 47 (2001–2002): 891–910.

131. *Bond v. United States*, 134 S. Ct. 2077 (2014), pp. 2098–2102.

132. Ibid., p. 2103. When Thomas observes that "a number of recent treaties . . . regulat[e] what appear to be purely domestic affairs" (p. 2103), he is clearly referring to human rights treaties. The opinion was joined by Justices Scalia and Alito.

133. American Law Institute, *Restatement of the Law (Third): The Foreign Relations Law of the United States*, vol. 1 (Saint Paul: American Law Institute, 1987), §102, p. 24.

134. Statute of the International Court of Justice, art. 38.

135. But the Bush administration's claim that the United States' treaty obligations did not prohibit the U.S. government from subjecting members of Al Qaeda and Taliban to ill-treatment does not survive a straightforward reading of the Torture Convention and ICCPR (even with U.S.

RUDs), the Geneva Prisoner of War Convention, the Geneva Civilian Convention, and Common Article 3 of the Geneva Conventions.

136. *Filártiga v. Peña-Irala*, 630 F.2d 876 (2nd Cir. 1980), p. 890.

137. Dickinson, "The Law of Nations as Part of the National Law of the United States," *University of Pennsylvania Law Review* 101 (1952): 26–56, p. 34.

138. *Fed.* 3, p. 90; *Fed.* 80, p. 446. (See chap. 2, n. 1.)

139. *The Nereide*, 13 U.S. 388 (1815), p. 423. See David L. Sloss, Michael D. Ramsey, and William S. Dodge, "International Law in the Supreme Court to 1860," in *International Law in the U.S. Supreme Court*, ed. Sloss, Ramsey, and Dodge (Cambridge: Cambridge University Press, 2011), pp. 23–37; and Jordan J. Paust, *International Law as Law of the United States*, 2nd ed. (Durham, N.C.: Carolina Academic Press, 2003), chap. 1.

140. *Murray v. The Charming Betsy*, 6 U.S. (2 Cranch) 64 (1804).

141. Yoo-Delahunty Memo (see chap. 4, n. 93), pp. 70–76. The assertion reappears in the nearly identical Memorandum from Jay S. Bybee, Assistant Attorney General, for Alberto R. Gonzales, Counsel to the President, and William J. Hayes, II, General Counsel, Department of Defense, *Re: Application of Treaties and Laws to al Qaeda and Taliban Detainees*, January 22, 2002, reprinted in *The Torture Papers*, ed. Greenberg and Dratel, pp. 111–16; and in the Yoo Military Interrogation Memo, pp. 73–74.

142. José E. Alvarez, "Torturing the Law," *Case Western Reserve Journal of International Law* 37 (2006): 175–223, pp. 187–88.

143. Taft Memo (see chap. 4, n. 95), pp. 31–36; Alvarez, "Torturing the Law," pp. 186–89; Jordan J. Paust, *Beyond the Law: The Bush Administration's Unlawful Responses in the "War" on Terror* (Cambridge: Cambridge University Press, 2007), pp. 20–23.

144. *Garcia-Mir v. Meese*, 788 F. 2d 1446 (11th Cir. 1986), pp. 1453–55.

145. Department of Justice, Office of Legal Counsel, *Authority of the Federal Bureau of Investigation to Override International Law in Extraterritorial Law Enforcement Activities*, 13 Op. O.L.C. 163 (1989), p. 168.

146. Ibid., pp. 178–79 and n. 26.

147. Curtis A. Bradley and Jack L. Goldsmith, "Customary International Law as Federal Common Law: A Critique of the Modern Position," *Harvard Law Review* 110 (1997): 815–76. José Alvarez comments that the Yoo-Delahunty Memo "is written as a brief in favor of the controversial Bradley-Goldsmith position." Alvarez, "Torturing the Law," p. 187 n.43.

148. Bradley and Goldsmith, "Customary International Law as Federal Law," pp. 870, 844–46. For criticisms of the article, see Gerald L. Neuman, "Sense and Nonsense About Customary International Law: A Response to Professors Bradley and Goldsmith," *Fordham Law Review* 66 (1997): 371–92; Ryan Goodman and Derek Jinks, "*Filártiga's* Firm Footing: International Human Rights and Federal Common Law," *Fordham Law Review* 66 (1997): 463–529; and Carlos Vázquez, "Customary International Law as U.S. Law: A Critique of the Revisionist and Intermediate Positions and a Defense of the Modern Position," *Notre Dame Law Review* 86 (2011): 1495–1634.

149. Bradley and Goldsmith, "Customary International Law as Federal Law," p. 871. The acknowledgment that CIL is binding on the international plane sometimes disappears in the discussion, for example in the apparent denial on p. 846 that "CIL binds the President."

150. Ibid., p. 857. The quotation is from Phillip R. Trimble, "A Revisionist View of Customary International Law," *UCLA Law Review* 33 (1986): 665–732, p. 721.

151. Bradley and Goldsmith, "Customary International Law as Federal Law," p. 857.

152. Goldsmith, *The Terror Presidency*, p. 21.

153. *Sosa v. Alvarez-Machain*, 542 U.S. 692 (2004), p. 751.

154. *Al-Bihani v. Obama*, 590 F.3d 866 (D.C. Cir. 2010), p. 871. My discussion is indebted to David Luban, "Opting Out of the Law of War: Comments on 'Withdrawing from International Custom,'" *Yale Law Journal (Online)* 120 (2010): 151–67, pp. 152–53.

155. *Al-Bihani v. Obama*, 619 F.3d 1 (D.C. Cir 2010), where Judge Brown notes the "government's eager concession that international law does in fact limit the AUMF" (p. 3).

156. Ibid., p. 1.

157. Ibid., p. 3.

158. Ibid., p. 16.

159. *Sosa v. Alvarez-Machain*, p. 729; *Erie Railroad Co. v. Tompkins*, 304 U.S. 64 (1938).

160. Pohl, *U.S.A v. Mohammed et al.*, Order AE 200 II, n. 11.

161. Charles Simic, "Connoisseurs of Cruelty," *New York Review of Books*, March 12, 2009.

162. Starting in 2017, the ICC will also have authority to prosecute the crime of aggression, but only on a highly limited basis.

163. Marc Grossman, U.S. Under Secretary of State, "American Foreign Policy and the International Criminal Court, Address to the Center for Strategic and International Studies," May 6, 2002.

164. John Yoo made a remarkable misreading of the Rome Statute when he assured CIA and Pentagon officials that Article 8, defining war crimes, "applies only to those protected by the Geneva Conventions." In fact, the list of war crimes in Article 8(2) extends over four sections. Section (a) is limited to acts against persons or property protected by the Geneva Conventions, but sections (b), (c), and (e) enumerate a long list of war crimes in international and non-international armed conflict not subject to this limitation. It appears that Yoo did not read beyond section (a) of Article 8(2). His misreading appears in his six-page letter to Alberto Gonzales regarding the Torture Convention and the ICC, August 1, 2002, https://nsarchive.gwu.edu/~nsarchiv/NSAEBB/NSAEBB127/020801.pdf (pp. 5–6), is restated in the Yoo Military Interrogation Memo of March 14, 2003 (p. 48 n.53), and reappears in the Pentagon Interrogation Working Group Report (p. 339).

165. See also Helen Fenwick, "Post 9/11 UK Counter-Terrorism Cases in the European Court of Human Rights: A 'Dialogic' Approach to Rights Protection or Appeasement of National Authorities?," in *Critical Debates on Counter-Terrorism Judicial Review*, ed. Fergal Davis and Fiona de Londras (Cambridge: Cambridge University Press, 2014).

166. Human Rights Watch, *Still at Risk: Diplomatic Assurances No Safeguard Against Torture*, April 2005; European Court of Human Rights, "Fact Sheet on Terrorism and the European Convention on Human Rights," February 2015, http://www.echr.coe.int/Pages/home.aspx?p=press/factsheets.

167. European Center for Constitutional and Human Rights, *CIA "Extraordinary Rendition" Flights, Torture and Accountability—A European Approach*, 2nd ed., January 2009.

168. This is not to deny persistent efforts to impede judicial supervision. Among such efforts, we may include the recent enactment in the UK of the Justice and Security Act, expanding the use of secret hearings in civil lawsuits deemed to raise national security concerns.

169. Fionnuala Ní Aoláin, "The European Convention on Human Rights and Its Prohibition on Torture," in *Torture: A Collection*, ed. Sanford Levinson (Oxford: Oxford University Press, 2004), p. 219 (as discussed in Chapter 3).

Chapter 6. The Democratic Legitimacy of International Human Rights Law

1. For examples of New Sovereigntist works that raise the democracy objection, see Jeremy A. Rabkin, *Law Without Nations? Why Constitutional Government Requires Sovereign States* (Princeton, N.J.: Princeton University Press, 2005); Jack L. Goldsmith, "Should International Human Rights Law Trump U.S. Domestic Law?," *Chicago Journal of International Law* 1 (2000): 327–39; David B. Rivkin, Jr., and Lee A. Casey, "The Rocky Shoals of International Law," *National Interest* 62 (2000–2001): 35–46; Robert H. Bork, *Coercing Virtue: The Worldwide Rule of Judges* (Washington, D.C.: AEI Press, 2003); and Eric Posner, *The Perils of Global Legalism* (Chicago: University of Chicago Press, 2009), p. 227. Writings outside the New Sovereigntist school that raise the democracy objection include Jed Rubenfeld, "Unilateralism and Constitutionalism," *New York University Law Review* 79 (2004): 1971–2028; Kenneth Anderson, "The Ottawa Convention Banning Landmines, the Role of International Non-Governmental Organizations and the Idea of International Civil Society," *European Journal of International Law* 11 (2000): 91–120; Richard Bellamy, *Political Constitutionalism: A Republican Defence of the Constitutionality of Democracy* (Cambridge: Cambridge University Press, 2007); and Madeline Morris, "The Disturbing Democratic Defect of the International Criminal Court," *Finnish Yearbook of International Law* 12 (2001): 109–18. I concentrate the analysis in this chapter on the arguments of Rubenfeld and Anderson.

Rubenfeld and Bellamy are among those who present the democratic objection from a liberal or left-leaning perspective. Bellamy's 2007 book *Political Constitutionalism* is critical of the 1998 UK Human Rights Act, which incorporated the European Convention on Human Rights into domestic law (see pp. 46–48). More recently, Bellamy has expressed support for the Human Rights Act, noting that it institutes a "weak" form of judicial review under which Parliament retains the formal power to affirm legislation that domestic courts declare to be incompatible with the European Convention. Bellamy, "The Democratic Legitimacy of International Human Rights Conventions: Political Constitutionalism and the Hirst Case," in *The Legitimacy of International Human Rights Regimes*, ed. Andreas Føllesdal, Johan Karlsson Schaffer, and Geir Ulfstein (Cambridge: Cambridge University Press, 2014). In both the 2007 book and the 2014 paper, however, Bellamy's theory of political constitutionalism challenges the proposition that an international human rights treaty legitimately restricts the decision-making powers of national legislatures.

In the UK, the democracy objection is often raised against the European Convention on Human Rights. Justice secretary Chris Grayling, objecting to the judicial oversight of the European Court of Human Rights, declared: "I do not believe decisions about the way this country is governed—we are a democracy after all—should be taken elsewhere." Quoted in "Tories May Propose Leaving European Convention On Human Rights," *Huffington Post UK*, December 30, 2013.

2. Oona A. Hathaway, "International Delegation and State Sovereignty," *Law and Contemporary Problems* 71 (2007): 115–49, pp. 115, 125 n.33.

3. This observation is in turn subject to at least two qualifications. First, treaties are usually presented to legislatures on a take-it-or-leave-it basis without opportunities for amendment, except to the extent that reservations, understandings, and declarations are permitted. Note, however, that in democracies the people exercise ultimate control over the selection of delegates charged with drafting treaties. Moreover, refusal to ratify can lead to a renegotiation of the terms of the treaty, a recurrent pattern in the evolution of the EU. The second qualification is that powerful states may sometimes use strong-arm tactics to make weaker states ratify (or not ratify) treaties. But powerful states have also pressured weaker states when it comes to the passage of ordinary legislation. No

simple contrast distinguishes the extent of popular control over domestic versus international law. See generally, Hathaway, "International Delegation and State Sovereignty"; and Andrew Moravcsik, "In Defence of the Democratic Deficit: Reassessing Legitimacy in the European Union," *Journal of Common Market Studies* 40 (2002): 603–24.

4. Some critics argue that the International Criminal Court (ICC) deviates from this rule, because it enjoys limited jurisdiction over non-party nationals. As indicated below, I do not regard the ICC as an antidemocratic institution.

5. Rubenfeld, "Unilateralism and Constitutionalism," p. 1976.

6. Anderson, "Ottawa Convention," p. 103.

7. Ibid., p. 104. Here Anderson speaks of "international law" in general, but the examples used in his article are two human rights treaties: the Ottawa Convention to Ban Landmines and, secondarily, the Rome Statute of the International Criminal Court.

8. For an excellent response to the democracy objection, see also Michael Goodhart, "Human Rights and Global Democracy," *Ethics and International Affairs* 22 (2008): 395–420.

9. Many of these criticisms take their cue from Alexander Bickel's observation of what he called the "countermajoritarian difficulty." *See* Alexander Bickel, *The Least Dangerous Branch* (Indianapolis: Bobbs-Merrill, 1962), pp. 16–17. For an excellent rebuttal of the countermajoritarian critique, see Scott E. Lemieux and David J. Watkins, "Beyond the 'Countermajoritarian Difficulty': Lessons from Contemporary Democratic Theory," *Polity* 41 (2009): 30–62; and David Watkins and Scott Lemieux, "Compared to What? Judicial Review and Other Veto Points in Contemporary Democratic Theory," *Perspectives on Politics* 13 (2015): 312–26.

10. Some critics of judicial review make clear that their objection is directed only toward judicial review of legislation, not judicial review of executive acts. See Jeremy Waldron, "The Core of the Case Against Judicial Review," *Yale Law Journal* 115 (2006): 1346–1406, p. 1353.

11. It is worth noting that under a broad system of judicial review, the review of executive conduct sets limits on permissible legislative conduct and vice versa.

12. For example, Rubenfeld, "Unilateralism and Constitutionalism," pp. 1993–99. However, Robert Bork in *Coercing Virtue* decries what he sees as a similar pattern of judicial activism in both international human rights law and judicial review.

13. For example, Rubenfeld's arguments bear a striking resemblance to Jeremy Waldron's critique of judicial review. See Waldron, "A Right-Based Critique of Constitutional Rights," *Oxford Journal of Legal Studies* 13 (1993): 18–51; and Waldron, *Law and Disagreement* (Oxford: Oxford University Press, 1999).

14. I take the term from Bellamy, *Political Constitutionalism*.

15. Fiona de Londras, *Detention in the "War on Terror": Can Human Rights Fight Back?* (Cambridge: Cambridge University Press, 2011), p. 283. One exception is the McCain Amendment, prohibiting U.S. infliction of cruel, inhuman, or degrading treatment outside U.S. territory, but as we have seen in Chapters 4 and 5, even this legislation was undercut by damaging qualifications.

16. Jonathan Hafetz, *Habeas Corpus after 9/11: Confronting America's New Global Detention System* (New York: New York University Press, 2011), p. 256. After these words were written, the DC Circuit Court of Appeals began to issue a series of rulings that weakened the right of habeas corpus by implementing a low standard of justification for the continued detention of Guantanamo detainees. However, Hafetz's comparative assessment of the behavior of the judiciary and political (legislative and executive) branches still stands.

17. In my remarks, I often characterize "judicial review" as a system in which courts are empowered to strike down or invalidate statutes that violate rights enshrined in a domestic or

international charter. Strictly speaking, this is "strong" or "strong-form judicial review." Some countries (such as the UK and New Zealand) have adopted a system of "weak-form judicial review," in which domestic courts lack the power to strike down or invalidate legislation, but (as in both the UK and New Zealand) may interpret it, within reason, to comply with the rights charter, or (as in the UK) declare its incompatibility with the rights charter. For an in-depth discussion, see Stephen Gardbaum, *The New Commonwealth Model of Constitutionalism* (Cambridge: Cambridge University Press, 2013). I do not want to engage the debate over the comparative merits of strong-form and weak-form judicial review. My aim is to defend the democratic legitimacy of judicial review in general. If the standard "pro-democratic" objections fail as a critique of strong-form judicial review, they also fail with regard to weak-form judicial review.

18. Richard H. Fallon, Jr., "The Core of an Uneasy Case for Judicial Review," *Harvard Law Review* 121 (2008): 1693–1736, p. 1695.

19. "Through both dynamic interpretation and enforcement, the ECtHR has over time substantially upgraded and expanded human rights standards across established European democracies, and also vis-à-vis the democratizing states of the ex-communist world." Dia Anagnostou, Introduction to *The European Court of Human Rights*, ed. Dia Anagnostou (Edinburgh: Edinburgh University Press, 2013), p. 1. "It is no exaggeration to state that the Convention and its growing and diverse body of case law have transformed Europe's legal and political landscape." Laurence R. Helfer, "Redesigning the European Court of Human Rights: Embeddedness as a Deep Structural Principle of the European Human Rights Regime," *European Journal of International Law* 19 (2008): 125–59, p. 126. For a collection of similar verdicts, see Michael D. Goldhaber, *A People's History of the European Court of Human Rights* (New Brunswick, N.J.: Rutgers University Press, 2007), p. 2.

20. "In the European context, the liberal consensus is clearly supportive of the role of constitutional courts. Even scholars who are otherwise critical of judicial review on democratic grounds share the generalized opinion that, by and large, those courts have served the cause of rights, even if they have sometimes missed opportunities to overturn objectionable laws or have struck down laws that were perfectly acceptable or even commendable." Victor Ferreres Comella, *Constitutional Courts and Democratic Values: A European Perspective* (New Haven, Conn.: Yale University Press, 2009), p. 35. See also Alec Stone Sweet, *Governing with Judges: Constitutional Politics in Europe* (Oxford: Oxford University Press, 2000); and Herman Schwartz, *The Struggle for Constitutional Justice in Post-Communist Europe* (Chicago: University of Chicago Press, 2000).

21. Rachel Sieder, Line Schjolden, and Alan Angell, eds., *The Judicialization of Politics in Latin America* (New York: Palgrave Macmillan, 2005).

22. Mark S. Kende, *Constitutional Rights in Two Worlds: South Africa and the United States* (Cambridge: Cambridge University Press, 2009).

23. S. P. Sathe, "Judicial Activism: The Indian Experience," *Washington University Journal of Law and Policy* 6 (2001): 29–107.

24. Tom Ginsburg, *Judicial Review in New Democracies* (New York: Cambridge University Press, 2003), chap. 5.

25. Ibid., chap. 6; Munkhsaikhan Odonkhuu, *Towards Better Protection of Fundamental Rights in Mongolia* (Nagoya: CALE Books, 2014).

26. Ginsburg, *Judicial Review in New Democracies*, chap.7.

27. Gardbaum, *The New Commonwealth Model of Constitutionalism*, pp. 104–6, 121–22.

28. Ibid., pp. 135–36, 141, 147–50.

29. Ibid., pp. 182–83. See also my discussion of the UK Human Rights Act in Chapter 3.

30. Iconic examples include the *Civil Rights Cases* (1883), which struck down federal legislation

prohibiting racial discrimination in public facilities, and the *Lochner*-era cases from the early twentieth century, which struck down legislation limiting workers' hours, regulating child labor, and establishing a minimum wage. A further problem with the *Civil Rights Cases* is that they denied Congress's explicit constitutional mandate to enforce equal protection of the laws.

31. Flaws include the influence of detrimental judicial doctrines, a highly partisan appointments process, rules that limit individual access to the courts, and, perhaps most important, an incomplete and underspecified bill of rights. Mattias Kumm warns against overgeneralizing from the U.S. experience: "The rich literature on judicial review generated by U.S. scholars that generally addresses U.S. Constitutional practice does not capture some central features of European Constitutional practice. It does not fit that practice and therefore does little to illuminate it." Kumm, "Institutionalising Socratic Contestation: The Rationalist Human Rights Paradigm, Legitimate Authority and the Point of Judicial Review," *European Journal of Legal Studies* 1 (2007): 1–32, p. 3.

32. Distinctive features of U.S.-style judicial review include its application by diffuse all-purpose courts. For an argument for the superiority of European-style judicial review (applied by a single specialized "constitutional court"), see Ferreres Comella, *Constitutional Courts and Democratic Values*. For an argument for the superiority of the "New Commonwealth Model of Constitutionalism" (featuring mandatory preenactment political rights review and weak-form judicial review), see Gardbaum, *New Model Commonwealth of Constitutionalism*.

33. Fallon, "The Core of an Uneasy Case for Judicial Review," p. 1709. U.S. Supreme Court cases overturning campaign finance reform on free speech grounds (e.g., *Citizens United v. FEC*, 130 S.Ct. 876 [2010]) and affirmative action and desegregation policies on antidiscrimination grounds (e.g., *Parents Involved v. Seattle Schools*, 127 S.Ct. 2738 [2007]) place this assumption under strain. Arguably worse are cases like the *Civil Rights Cases* and *Shelby County v. Holder*, 133 S.Ct. 2612 (2013), in which the Supreme Court struck down rights-protective legislation without even claiming that countervailing rights were threatened. (I still believe that, even in the United States, the benefits of judicial review outweigh the costs.)

34. James B. Thayer worried about this danger in "The Origin and Scope of the American Doctrine of Constitutional Law," *Harvard Law Review* 7 (1893): 129–56, pp. 155–56.

35. For discussion of the Joint Committee on Human Rights, see Gardbaum, *The New Commonwealth Model of Constitutionalism*, pp. 165–69. For discussion of similar practices elsewhere in Europe, see Helen Keller and Alec Stone Sweet, "Assessing the Impact of the ECHR on National Legal Systems," in *A Europe of Rights: The Impact of the ECHR on National Legal Systems*, ed. Keller and Stone Sweet (Oxford: Oxford University Press, 2008), pp. 686–87.

36. For the argument that this arrangement is properly called "democracy," see in particular the section on "Madisonian Democracy."

37. For example: "A democratic system . . . requires (1) *government accountability* achieved through elections (and other political processes) open to the participation of virtually all adults, and (2) *respect for individual and group rights* guaranteed through legal processes and constitutional structures." Mary Ellen Fischer, Introduction to *Establishing Democracies*, ed. Mary Ellen Fischer (Boulder, Colo.: Westview, 1996), p. 4. "In mature democracies, government policy, including foreign and military policy, is made by officials chosen through free, fair, and periodic elections in which a substantial proportion of the adult population can vote; the actions of officials are constrained by constitutional provisions and commitments to civil liberties; and government candidates sometimes lose elections and leave office when they do." Jack Snyder, *From Voting to Violence* (New York: Norton, 2000), pp. 25–26.

38. James Madison, Alexander Hamilton, and John Jay, *The Federalist Papers*, ed. Isaac Kramnick (London: Penguin, 1987 [1787-88]), no. 10, p. 125.

39. Rubenfeld, "Unilateralism and Constitutionalism," p. 1999.

40. Ibid., p. 2001.

41. Ibid., p. 1994.

42. Ibid., pp. 2000–2001.

43. Jack N. Rakove, *James Madison and the Creation of the American Republic*, 3rd ed. (New York: Pearson/Longman, 2006), pp. 88–92.

44. Letter to Thomas Jefferson, October 17, 1788, in James Madison, *Writings*, ed. Jack Rakove (New York: Library of America, 1999), p. 420.

45. Madison, "Speech in Congress Proposing Constitutional Amendments," June 8, 1789, in *Writings*, pp. 448–49. Madison's belief in inalienable rights that no government has authority to infringe is forcefully proclaimed in the peroration to his 1785 "Memorial and Remonstrance Against Religious Assessment." Madison, *Writings*, pp. 35–36.

46. Consider the language of the Fourth Amendment: "The right of the people to be secure in their persons, houses, papers, and effects, against unreasonable searches and seizures, shall not be violated." And the Suspension Clause (art. 1, sec. 9): "The privilege of the Writ of Habeas Corpus shall not be suspended, unless when in Cases of Rebellion or Invasion the public Safety may require it." The wording implies that rights to personal security and habeas corpus would still bind the government even if the Constitution never mentioned it.

47. December 20, 1787, in *The Portable Thomas Jefferson*, ed. Merrill D. Peterson (New York: Viking, 1975), p. 430. Jefferson identified the rights that he believed should be included: "freedom of religion, freedom of the press, protection against standing armies, restriction against monopolies, the eternal and unremitting force of the habeas corpus laws, and trials by jury in all matters of fact triable by the laws of the land and not by the Law of Nations" (p. 429).

48. The truth is that the *original* Constitution was illegitimate because of provisions that supported slavery. It was (if one may say so) illegitimate on its own terms. Note that one cannot lean on the slavery provisions of the original Constitution to deny that it expressed a commitment to natural rights and simultaneously assert that it expressed a commitment to democracy. Slaves did not "ordain and establish" the Constitution. Neither did women.

49. See Miriam Galston and William A. Galston, "Reason, Consent, and the U.S. Constitution: Bruce Ackerman's *We the People*," *Ethics* 104 (1994): 446–66, pp. 452–59.

50. See Robert A. Dahl, *Polyarchy* (New Haven, Conn.: Yale University Press, 1971), pp. 1–16; David Beetham, *Democracy and Human Rights* (Cambridge: Polity, 1999), chap. 5.

51. See Stephen Holmes, "Constitutionalism," in *The Encyclopedia of Democracy*, ed. Seymour Martin Lipset (Washington, D.C.: Congressional Quarterly, 1995).

52. For the argument that it requires all human rights, including social and economic rights, see Beetham, *Democracy and Human Rights*.

53. Henry Shue, *Basic Rights*, 2nd ed. (Princeton, N.J.: Princeton University Press, 1996), chap. 3; Amartya Sen, *Development as Freedom* (New York: Knopf, 1999), chap.6; William J. Talbott, *Which Rights Should Be Universal?* (New York: Oxford University Press, 2005), chaps. 6–7.

54. See Jack Turner, *Awakening to Race* (Chicago: University of Chicago Press, 2012), p. 134 n.52: "The normative force of the idea that the people should rule is grounded in the right of individuals to self-determination." See also Turner, "The Constitution of Radical Democracy," *Polity* 47 (2015): 558–65; Michael Goodhart, *Democracy as Human Rights* (New York: Routledge, 2005); Goodhart, "Human Rights and Global Democracy"; and Carol C. Gould, *Globalizing Democracy*

and Human Rights (New York: Cambridge University Press, 2004). For a similar view, see Corey Brettschneider, *Democratic Rights* (Princeton, N.J.: Princeton University Press, 2007). George Kateb proposes that the common underlying value is equal respect for persons. See Kateb, "Remarks on Robert B. McKay, 'Judicial Review in a Liberal Democracy,'" in *Liberal Democracy*, NOMOS XXV, ed. J. Roland Pennock and John W. Chapman (New York: New York University Press, 1983), pp. 145, 149.

55. Waldron, *Law and Disagreement*, chaps. 10–11.

56. For example, Ronald Dworkin, "Introduction: The Moral Reading and the Majoritarian Premise," in Dworkin, *Freedom's Law* (Cambridge, Mass.: Harvard University Press, 1996). Habermas's argument for the co-originality of public and private autonomy combines elements of all three types of argument. See Jürgen Habermas, *Between Facts and Norms*, trans. William Rehg (Cambridge, Mass.: MIT Press, 1996), chap. 3.

57. One exception is Goodhart, *Democracy as Human Rights*.

58. "Though [the state of nature] be a *state of liberty*, yet *it is not a state of licence*. . . . The *state of nature* has a law of nature to govern it, which obliges every one: and reason, which is that law, teaches all mankind who will but consult it, that being all *equal and independent*, no one ought to harm another in his life, health, liberty, or possessions." *Second Treatise of Government*, para. 6.

59. "Remarks on McKay," pp. 148–49.

60. See Waldron, "A Right-Based Critique of Constitutional Rights" (1993); *Law and Disagreement* (1999), chaps. 10–13. Waldron's position has moderated over time. In his 2006 article, "The Core of the Case Against Judicial Review," he states that judicial review may sometimes be legitimate in countries whose people lack a strong commitment to human rights. He has dropped his earlier opposition to constitutional bills of rights, though he argues that (in countries most of whose citizens have a strong commitment to human rights) courts should not have authority to strike down legislation for violating constitutional rights and that legislators should be able to "pose [rights-disagreements] for themselves if they like without reference to the Bill of Rights' formulations" (p. 1381). He exempts the UK Human Rights Act from his critique, regarding it as an acceptably "weak" form of judicial review, because Parliament retains the formal power to uphold statutes that domestic courts declare to be incompatible with the European Convention (pp. 1354–55). These clarifications notwithstanding, he still invokes "the right to participate" as his fundamental objection to (strong) judicial review (p. 1375).

61. Rubenfeld, "Unilateralism and Constitutionalism," p. 1994. He is influenced by the arguments of Bruce Ackerman regarding the dualist character of U.S. law. See Ackerman, *We the People*, vol. 1, *Foundations* (Cambridge, Mass.: Harvard University Press, 1991). Rubenfeld ("Unilateralism and Constitutionalism," pp. 1995, 1998) says that another reason for associating American judicial review with democratic constitutionalism is that the process of appointing judges is highly politicized: the people shape the content of constitutional rights inasmuch as they can influence the selection of judges whose task it is to interpret those rights. One can take this argument only so far, however, since judges must frame their interpretations within limits set by the constitutional text.

62. One suspects that Rubenfeld's conception of "democratic constitutionalism" rests in part on a nationalist identification with earlier generations of American citizens who got to make the decisions. Their constitutional decisions are ours also, because we imagine them as ourselves. Stanley N. Katz argues convincingly that a certain kind of reverence for the Constitution has raised psychological though not legal obstacles to the domestic incorporation of international human rights. Katz, "A New American Dilemma? U.S. Constitutionalism vs. International Human Rights," *University of Miami Law Review* 58 (2003): 323–45.

63. Rubenfeld, "Unilateralism and Constitutionalism," p. 2001.

64. Waldron, *Law and Disagreement*.

65. Bellamy, *Political Constitutionalism*, pp. 3, 8, 16, 53, 93, 147–49, 219. See also the pointed remarks of Rabkin, *Law Without Nations?*, p. 163.

66. A few jurisdictions grant resident aliens the right to vote, but usually on a limited basis. The right of resident aliens to vote remains the exception, and of course does not extend to aliens living abroad. See David C. Earnest, "Neither Citizen nor Stranger: Why States Enfranchise Resident Aliens," *World Politics* 58 (2006): 242-75, p. 259.

67. Michael Ignatieff, *Human Rights as Politics and Idolatry*, ed. Amy Gutmann (Princeton, N.J.: Princeton University Press 2001), p. 18. Ignatieff's position is more nuanced than this excerpt suggests, but I quote it as representative of a common pattern of thought.

68. I draw instruction from the work of human rights NGO Tostan, whose courses on human rights have helped persuade hundreds of villages in Senegal to collectively renounce female genital cutting and early marriage. See "Tostan: Community-Led Successes," http://www.tostan.org.

69. My remarks are therefore not directed against discourse theoretic accounts of human rights that make human rights a constitutive feature of fair processes of justification. For examples of such accounts, see Seyla Benhabib, "Reason-Giving and Rights-Bearing: Constructing the Subject of Rights," *Constellations* 20 (2013): 38–50; and Rainer Forst, "The Justification of Human Rights and the Basic Right to Justification: A Reflexive Approach," *Ethics* 120 (2010): 711–40.

70. Anderson, "Ottawa Convention," p. 113.

71. See Lee A. Casey and David B. Rivkin, Jr., "The International Criminal Court vs. the American People," The Heritage Foundation Backgrounder #1249, http://www.heritage.org/Research/InternationalOrganizations/BG1249.cfm-pgfId=1018109. See also Morris, "The Disturbing Democratic Defect of the International Criminal Court."

72. See Jamie Mayerfeld, "The Democratic Legacy of the International Criminal Court," *Fletcher Forum of World Affairs* 28 (2004): 147–56, p. 153.

73. See Galston and Galston, "Reason, Consent, and the U.S. Constitution," pp. 454–55.

74. The position of noncitizens continues to haunt the theoretical literature on democracy. For an indispensable discussion, see Goodhart, *Democracy as Human Rights*, chaps. 6–7.

75. John Rawls, *A Theory of Justice* (Cambridge, Mass.: Harvard University Press, 1971), p. 20.

76. Talbott, *Which Rights Should Be Universal?*, chaps. 2–4.

77. "Education shall be directed to the full development of the human personality and to the strengthening of respect for human rights and fundamental freedoms." Universal Declaration of Human Rights, art. 26(1).

78. Compare Madison: "In proportion as government is influenced by opinion, it must be so, by whatever influences opinion. This decides the question concerning a *Constitutional Declaration of Rights*, which requires an influence on government, by becoming a part of the public opinion." Madison, *Writings*, p. 501.

79. For an illuminating discussion of the institutional processes favoring the adoption of legitimate human rights codes, see Allen E. Buchanan, "Human Rights and the Legitimacy of the International Order," *Legal Theory* 14 (2008): 39–70, pp. 61–65.

80. See William Korey, *NGOs and the Universal Declaration of Human Rights: "A Curious Grapevine"* (New York: St. Martin's, 1998).

81. Anderson, "Ottawa Convention," pp. 113–14.

82. See Albie Sachs, "The Creation of South Africa's Constitution," *New York Law School Law*

Review 41 (1997): 669–83; and Christina Murray, "A Constitutional Beginning: Making South Africa's Final Constitution," *University of Arkansas at Little Rock Law Review* 23 (2001): 809–38.

83. Sachs, "The Creation of South Africa's Constitution," p. 675.

84. Moreover, the Constitutional Court acted on its duty, ruling that the 1996 Constitution made amendment of the Bill of Rights too easy and therefore left human rights inadequately entrenched. The Final Constitution of 1997 made the requisite alteration.

85. Preenactment rights review tends not to be legally binding, and it can be politically co-opted.

86. Kumm's argument is made partly in response to the complaint of political constitutionalists like Waldron and Bellamy that judicial review causes rights debates to become excessively legalistic, concerned with technical issues of precedent, textual construction, and standing, when attention should instead be focused on the moral issues at the heart of a rights claim. Kumm argues that this problem is less pronounced in Europe than in the United States (see Ferreres Comella, *Constitutional Courts and Democratic Values*, for a similar argument) and that its significance even in the United States may be exaggerated (Kumm, "Institutionalising Socratic Contestation," p. 18). Even if the political constitutionalists' complaint were accurate, however, it would not negate the plausible claim that judicial review makes a net contribution to the protection of human rights. (Let me note that I am not interested in mounting a general defense of U.S. constitutional practice. I believe it can be improved in several ways, one being the domestic incorporation of international human rights law.)

87. Ibid., pp. 20, 21.

88. My argument is a defense of "judicial supremacy," where that means the power of courts to strike down legislation that violates constitutional or human rights. I do not support the holding of the U.S. Supreme Court in *City of Boerne v. Flores*, 521 U.S. 507 (1997), that Congress's explicit constitutional authority to enforce individual rights in the states is limited by judicial interpretation of those rights. Judicial review, properly understood, means that courts may block laws that violate rights, not laws that interpret rights more generously than the judiciary. The *Boerne* ruling rested on a particular (and in my view mistaken) understanding of U.S. federalism, particularly with regard to the meaning of the Tenth Amendment and Section 5 of the Fourteenth Amendment.

89. See Anne-Marie Slaughter, *A New World Order* (Princeton, N.J.: Princeton University Press, 2004), pp. 79–82.

90. See Chapter 3 and the sources cited therein, especially Robert Blackburn and Jörg Polakiewicz, eds., *Fundamental Rights in Europe: The ECHR and Its Member States, 1950–2000* (Oxford: Oxford University Press, 2001); Helen Keller and Alec Stone Sweet, eds., *A Europe of Rights: The Impact of the ECHR on National Legal Systems* (Oxford: Oxford University Press, 2008); Steven Greer, *The European Convention on Human Rights: Achievements, Problems and Prospects* (Cambridge: Cambridge University Press, 2006); Michael D. Goldhaber, *A People's History of the European Court of Human Rights* (New Brunswick, N.J.: Rutgers University Press, 2007); Frank Schimmelfennig, Stefan Engert, and Heiko Knobel, *International Socialization in Europe: European Organizations, Political Conditionality and Democratic Change* (New York: Palgrave, 2006); and Janne Haaland Matláry, *Intervention for Human Rights in Europe* (New York: Palgrave, 2002).

91. William A. Schabas, *An Introduction to the International Criminal Court*, 2nd ed. (Cambridge: Cambridge University Press, 2004), p. 20.

92. Vienna Convention on the Law of Treaties, art. 27.

93. Anthony Aust, *Handbook of International Law* (Cambridge: Cambridge University Press), p. 81.

94. Here I address the reception of human rights treaties, rather than the response to judicial rulings in an established international human rights regime. In the latter case, resistance may threaten the effectiveness of the regime as a whole, a factor that should weigh heavily in our assessment of the legitimacy and wisdom of the resistance.

95. Mattias Kumm, "Democratic Constitutionalism Encounters International Law: Terms of Engagement," in *The Migration of Constitutional Ideas*, ed. Sujit Choudhry (Cambridge: Cambridge University Press, 2006).

96. In the domestic context, it is noteworthy that courts tend to be more popular than legislatures. See Vanessa A. Baird, "Building Institutional Legitimacy: The Role of Procedural Justice," *Political Research Quarterly* 54 (2001): 333–54; and John R. Hibbing and Elizabeth Theiss-Morse, *Congress as Public Enemy: Public Attitudes Toward American Political Institutions* (Cambridge: Cambridge University Press, 1995). See also Kim Lane Scheppele, "Democracy by Judiciary: Or, Why Courts Can Be More Democratic than Parliaments," in *Rethinking the Rule of Law After Communism*, ed. Adam Czarnota, Martin Krygier, and Wojciech Sadurski (Budapest: Central European University Press, 2005). This would seem to challenge the view that human rights would receive more popular support if they were defined by legislatures rather than courts. However, popular support for courts does not always extend to international courts, as I note below with regard to the attitudes of the British public to the European Court of Human Rights.

97. In a YouGov/*Sunday Times* survey conducted in February 2011, only 24 percent of respondents said the UK should remain in the European Convention on Human Rights, while 55 percent said the UK should leave the Convention and adopt in its stead a UK Bill of Rights with the UK Supreme Court serving as the highest court of appeal.

98. See the discussion in the UK government's Commission on a Bill of Rights, *A UK Bill of Rights? The Choice Before Us*, December 2012, chap. 10, "Promoting a Better Understanding of the UK's Obligations under the Convention"; Adam Wagner, "The Monstering of Human Rights," Speech at University of Liverpool, September 19, 2014.

99. *Othman (Abu Qatada) v. the United Kingdom*, no. 8139/09, ECHR 2012; *Hirst v. the United Kingdom (No. 2)* [GC], no. 74025/01, ECHR 2005-IX.

100. Commission on a Bill of Rights, *A UK Bill of Rights?*, p.12.

101. This is a principal theme in the favorable recommendation made by a majority of the government-appointed Commission on a Bill of Rights (ibid., p. 80).

102. See ibid., p. 17; and Jon Henley, "Why Is the European Court of Human Rights Hated by the UK Right?," *Guardian*, December 22, 2013.

103. For a powerful defense of the legitimacy of the Strasbourg Court's jurisprudence, see George Letsas, "The ECHR as a Living Instrument: Its Meaning and Legitimacy," in *Constituting Europe: The European Court of Human Rights in a National, European and Global Context*, ed. Andreas Føllesdal, Birgit Peters, and Geir Ulfstein (Cambridge: Cambridge University Press, 2013). See also George Letsas, *A Theory of Interpretation of the European Convention on Human Rights* (Oxford: Oxford University Press, 2009).

104. Ed Bates et al., "The Legal Implications of a Repeal of the Human Rights Act 1998 and Withdrawal from the European Convention on Human Rights," ed. Kanstantsin Dzehtsiarou and Tobias Lock, May 12, 2015, pp. 28–29, citing ECHR, Article 58(2).

105. "Human Rights in the UK: The Conservatives' Proposals for Changing Britain's Human Rights Laws," October 3, 2014.

106. Ibid.

107. Bates et al., "The Legal Implications of a Repeal of the Human Rights Act 1998," pp. 24, 33.
108. Ibid., p. 28.

Conclusion

1. See David Held, *Global Covenant* (Cambridge: Polity, 2004), chaps. 8–9; and Jean L. Cohen, *Globalization and Sovereignty* (Cambridge: Cambridge University Press, 2012).

2. See, in particular, Jeremy Rabkin, *The Case for Sovereignty* (Washington, D.C.: AEI, 2004), pp. 1–4; and Rabkin, *Law Without Nations? Why Constitutional Government Requires Sovereign States* (Princeton, N.J.: Princeton University Press, 2005), pp. 2–3, 20.

3. See Antony Anghie, "Rethinking Sovereignty in International Law," *Annual Review of Law and Social Science* 5 (2009): 291–310.

4. Note the complete title of Rabkin's 2004 book: *The Case for Sovereignty: Why the World Should Welcome American Independence*. His opening example of sovereignty besieged is the international criticism of the United States for its 2003 invasion of Iraq without Security Council authorization (pp. 1–4). See also Rabkin, *Law Without Nations?* pp. 2–3.

5. For this reason, I believe that the familiar definition of sovereignty as "supreme authority within a territory" is somewhat imprecise.

6. Besides Hannah Arendt, discussed below, theorists who advocate rejection of the sovereignty norm include Harold J. Laski, *Studies in the Problem of Sovereignty* (New Haven, Conn.: Yale University Press, 1917); Jacques Maritain, *Man and the State* (Chicago: University of Chicago Press, 1951); and Bertrand de Jouvenel, *Sovereignty* (Chicago: University of Chicago Press, 1957).

7. Louis Henkin, "The Mythology of Sovereignty," *ASIL Newsletter*, March–May 1993.

8. Brad R. Roth, *Sovereign Equality and Moral Disagreement* (Oxford: Oxford University Press, 2011), esp. chap. 7. There is a vast literature on sovereignty and humanitarian intervention. An influential contribution to the debate is the work of the International Commission on Intervention and State Sovereignty (ICISS), defending the legitimacy of humanitarian intervention in limited circumstances, and arguing that the concept of sovereignty should be defined in terms of responsibility rather than control. ICISS, *The Responsibility to Protect* (Ottawa: International Development Research Centre, 2001).

9. Roth, *Sovereign Equality and Moral Disagreement*, p. 61. Roth also recognizes that states may be obligated by customary international human rights norms to which they do not individually consent, or from which they subsequently withdraw consent, and by human rights obligations that constitute "peremptory norms" (*jus cogens*) of international law (pp. 68, 71).

10. Cohen, *Globalization and Sovereignty*, p. 68.

11. David B. Rivkin, Jr., and Lee A. Casey, "The Rocky Shoals of International Law," *National Interest* 62 (2000–2001): 35–46, pp. 35, 37, 38.

12. Thomas Hobbes, *Leviathan*, ed. Edwin Curley (Indianapolis: Hackett, 1994 [1651]).

13. Jean Bodin, *Six Books of the Commonwealth*, excerpted in *Bodin on Sovereignty*, ed. Julian Franklin (Cambridge: Cambridge University Press, 1992 [1583]).

14. John Locke, *Two Treatises of Government*, ed. Peter Laslett (Cambridge: Cambridge University Press, 1988 [1689]); Baron de Montesquieu, *The Spirit of the Laws*, trans. Thomas Nugent (New York: Hafner, 1949 [1748]).

15. As Allen Buchanan writes, "It is a tautology that unless there is a supreme lawmaker, there

is the possibility of a conflict of laws for which there is no authoritative resolution. But why assume that a legal system cannot exist unless the *possibility* of conflict is ruled out?" Buchanan, *Justice, Legitimacy, and Self-Determination* (Oxford: Oxford University Press, 2004), p. 47.

16. Jean-Jacques Rousseau, *The Social Contract*, trans. Maurice Cranston (London: Penguin, 1968 [1762]), book II, chaps. 1–4.

17. Charles E. Merriam, Jr., *History of the Theory of Sovereignty since Rousseau* (New York: Garland, 1972 [1900]), p. 35.

18. Rousseau, *Social Contract*, book II, chap. 1. I use the more accurate G.D.H. Cole translation.

19. Locke: "Though [the state of nature] be a *state of liberty*, yet *it is not a state of licence*. . . . The *state of nature* has a law of nature to govern it, which obliges every one: and reason, which is that law, teaches all mankind who will but consult it, that being all *equal and independent*, no one ought to harm another in his life, health, liberty, or possessions" (*Second Treatise of Government*, para. 6). Montesquieu: "In governments, that is, in societies directed by laws, liberty can consist only in the power of doing what we ought to will, and in not being constrained to do what we ought not to will" (*The Spirit of the Laws*, book XI, chap. 3).

20. Immanuel Kant, *Foundations of the Metaphysics of Morals*, trans. Lewis White Beck (Indianapolis: Bobbs-Merrill, 1959 [1785]).

21. John Stuart Mill, *On Liberty*, ed. Elizabeth Rapaport (Indianapolis: Hackett, 1978 [1859]), p. 9.

22. Hannah Arendt, *The Human Condition*, 2nd ed. (Chicago: University of Chicago Press, 1998), p. 234.

23. Hannah Arendt, "What Is Freedom?" in Arendt, *Between Past and Future* (New York: Viking, 1968), p. 165.

24. Hannah Arendt, *On Revolution* (Middlesex: Penguin, 1965), pp. 76–77.

25. Arendt, "What Is Freedom?," p. 164.

26. Arendt, *On Revolution*, p. 168.

27. Arendt makes the point (perhaps confusingly) by stating that the American Revolution rested on a "radical separation of law and power, with clearly recognized different origins, different legitimations, and different spheres of application." *On Revolution*, p. 166.

28. Ibid.

29. For the wide acceptance of this view, see the documents accompanying ratification of the U.S. Constitution by North Carolina, New York, and Rhode Island, http://avalon.law.yale.edu/subject_menus/18th.asp.

30. Arendt, "What Is Freedom?" p. 164.

31. Arendt, *On Revolution*, p. 168.

32. In their important book, Abram and Antonia Chayes defend a conception of sovereignty as "status—the vindication of the state's existence as a member of the international system." They argue that "in today's setting, the only way most states [all but a few isolated nations] can realize and express their sovereignty is through participation in the various regimes that regulate and order the international system." Abram Chayes and Antonia Handler Chayes, *The New Sovereignty: Compliance with International Regulatory Agreements* (Cambridge, Mass.: Harvard University Press, 1996), p. 27.

33. Cohen, *Globalization and Sovereignty*, chap. 2.

34. Ibid., p. 96.

35. See Andrew Arato and Jean L. Cohen, "Banishing the Sovereign? Internal and External Sovereignty in Arendt," *Constellations* 16 (2009): 307–30. Whereas Arendt advocates a wholesale

rejection of sovereignty, Arato and Cohen argue that only the absolutist conception of sovereignty should be rejected. I shall not try to adjudicate between these positions. The dispute, which is partly though not entirely terminological, should not obscure the considerable overlap between Cohen's and Arendt's substantive views.

36. In James Madison, Alexander Hamilton, and John Jay, *The Federalist Papers*, ed. Isaac Kramnick (London: Penguin, 1987 [1787-88]). The six essays, which include extended historical illustrations, form a unified argument for this proposition. Essays 15 through 17 are generally attributed to Hamilton and essays 18 through 20 to Madison, though the essays show signs of collaboration.

37. Hamilton in *Fed.* 32: "the State governments would clearly retain all the rights of sovereignty which they before had, and which were not, by [the Constitution], *exclusively* delegated to the United States" (p. 220). Madison in *Fed.* 39: The jurisdiction of the central government "extends to certain enumerated objects only, and leaves to the several States a residuary and inviolable sovereignty over all other objects" (p. 258). Madison in *Fed.* 45: "the States will retain, under the proposed Constitution, a very extensive portion of active sovereignty" (pp. 293–94). See the illuminating notes of J. R. Pole in Alexander Hamilton, James Madison, and John Jay, *The Federalist*, ed. J. R. Pole (Indianapolis: Hackett, 2005), pp. 45–47, 168–69, 210.

38. Madison discusses these provisions in *Federalist* 43.

39. *The Federalist* takes it for granted that the United States should be sovereign on the international plane, but the idea is neither examined nor defended. Sovereignty receives theoretical attention only as it pertains to the relative authority of the union and the states. (Note that although the Federalists believed that power derives from the people, the term "popular sovereignty" does not appear in *The Federalist*.)

40. Roth, *Sovereign Equality and Moral Disagreement*, p. 67.

41. Luis Cabrera, *Political Theory of Global Justice* (London: Routledge, 2004), pp. 77–84; Thomas Pogge, *World Poverty and Human Rights*, 2nd ed. (Cambridge: Polity, 2008), chap. 7.

42. Held, *Global Covenant*, p. 140.

43. For one argument along these lines, see Pogge, *World Poverty and Human Rights*, chap. 7.

Index

Acknowledgments

In the many years I have worked on this book, friends and colleagues set aside valuable time to ask questions, make suggestions, share expertise, improve arguments, and save me from innumerable mistakes. Their contributions shaped this book in ways large and small, and I am deeply grateful.

Bruce Kochis first encouraged me to make human rights the subject of my scholarly research. Early conversations with George Kateb, Morris Kaplan, Chandra Sriram, and Stanley Katz steered me to the arguments at the heart of this book. At the University of Washington, the Department of Political Science; Law, Societies & Justice program; and Center for Human Rights have provided an ideal environment in which to develop my ideas. I have benefited enormously from the critical engagement of faculty colleagues and graduate and undergraduate students.

My greatest debt is to William Talbott and Jack Turner. Bill and Chip read multiple chapter drafts, helped me puzzle through difficult questions, and encouraged me toward greater clarity and rigor. Their inspired advice and extraordinary generosity helped me every step of the way. I owe another huge debt to George Lovell and Michael McCann, who each read several chapter drafts, and whose penetrating challenges and questions spurred revisions that made the book much stronger. My colleagues Robert Crawford, Christine Di Stefano, Angelina Godoy, Peter May, Cynthia Steele, and Susan Whiting provided steadfast support and encouragement.

I thank all those who commented on individual chapter drafts. I cannot name them all here, but would like to recognize (besides those previously mentioned) Joyce Appleby, Laura Back, Katherine Beckett, Charles Beitz, Paul Schiff Berman, Michael Blake, Barbara Buckinx, Luis Cabrera, Mary Anne Case, Rachel Cichowski, William d'Ambruoso, Fiona de Londras, Laura Dickinson, Michael Forman, Angelina Godoy, Sara Goering, Michael Goodhart, Steven Greer, Lisa Hajjar, Stephen Hanson, John F. Hart, Steve

Herbert, Morris Jackson, Filiz Kahraman, Robert Keohane, Milli Lake, Hélène Landemore, Clark Lombardi, David Lucas, Stephen Macedo, Brad McHose, Anja Mihr, Gregg Miller, Adam Moore, Leslie Moran, Jan-Werner Müller, Lauren Hartzell Nichols, Arzoo Osanloo, Michael Paris, Alan Patten, Deborah Pearlstein, Wesley Pue, Anita Ramasastry, Mathias Risse, Emma Rodman, Jennifer Rubenstein, Kim Scheppele, Paige Sechrest, Stuart Streichler, Rebecca Thorpe, Wibren van der Burg, John Wallach, and David Watkins.

I was kindly invited to share my ideas at the Goethe University Frankfurt, Oberlin College, Princeton University, Purchase College, Rutgers University, the University of British Columbia, the University of California at Santa Barbara, and the University of Pittsburgh. I thank all those who attended these events, read the papers, and shared their opinions. My University of Washington colleagues gave me numerous opportunities to present my work, culminating in a manuscript workshop in January 2015. Thanks to all the participants, especially the workshop's organizers, Rachel Cichowski and Hilary Soderland, and the principal commentators—Rachel Cichowski, Anita Ramasastry, William Talbott, and Jack Turner.

At a crucial time, I was lucky to receive a Human Rights Teaching Fellowship from Columbia Law School. Equally indispensable were fellowships from Princeton University's Center for Human Values and the University of Washington's Simpson Center for the Humanities, along with research support from the University of Washington's Royalty Research Fund and Human Rights Education and Research Network. Jack Greenberg, the late Louis Henkin, Kwame Anthony Appiah, Kim Scheppele, and Kathleen Woodward created wonderful environments for learning and conversation at Columbia, Princeton, and the Simpson Center.

Brad Roth has tried valiantly to give me some understanding of international law. For informative discussions and expert advice on diverse topics, I thank Onur Bakiner, Clive Baldwin, James Caporaso, Anthony Tirado Chase, Emilie Combaz, Robert Crawford, Geoff Dancy, Elisabeth Ellis, Christopher Fariss, Brian Greenhill, Natalia Gubbioni, Martin Lederman, George Letsas, Jules Lobel, Glenn Mackin, Jeff McMahan, Jim Murdoch, Munkhsaikhan Odonkhuu, Darius Rejali, and Walter Walsh. I have been helped immeasurably by the *Law of Torture* listserv, founded by Martin Lederman and Kim Scheppele and co-managed by David Luban.

For skilled research assistance, I would like to thank Kate Barrett, Jacqueline Brehmer, Hayley Edmonston, Thayer Hastings, Kseniya Husak, Kristina

Johnson, Melissa Robe, Roya Yavari, and especially Laura Back, Adam Goch, and Tania Melo. Jennifer Driscoll's editing and proofreading assistance during the final weeks of revisions was superhuman and brilliant. Not only Jennifer, but also Julie Garbus, Morris Jackson, and William Talbott generously read the entire manuscript and made several crucial improvements. For excellent proofreading, I thank Ellen Ahlness, Jonathan Beck, Julie Garbus, David Lucas, and Vanessa Quince.

My editor at Penn Press, Peter Agree, guided me through the review and publication process with patience, enthusiasm, and skill. Alison Anderson, the managing editor, contributed excellent judgment and generous assistance. I thank the entire editorial team, as well as two anonymous readers for their helpful and discerning reviews.

I gratefully acknowledge permission to republish material from earlier articles and chapters: "The Mutual Dependence of External and Internal Justice: The Democratic Achievement of the International Criminal Court," *Finnish Yearbook of International Law* 12 (2001): 71–107; "Playing by Our Own Rules: How U.S. Marginalization of International Human Rights Law Led to Torture," *Harvard Human Rights Journal* 20 (2007): 89–140; "William Talbott's *Which Rights Should Be Universal?* An Overview and Appreciation," *Human Rights and Human Welfare* 7 (2007): 68–71; "The Democratic Legitimacy of International Human Rights Law," *Indiana International and Comparative Law Review* 19 (2009): 49–88; "The High Price of American Exceptionalism: Comparing Torture by the United States and Europe after 9/11," in *Human Rights in the 21st Century: Continuity and Change since 9/11,* ed. Michael Goodhart and Anja Mihr (London: Palgrave/Macmillan, 2011); "A Madisonian Argument for Strengthening International Human Rights Institutions: Lessons from Europe," *Global Governance, Global Government: Institutional Visions for an Evolving World System,* ed. Luis Cabrera (Albany: SUNY Press, 2011).

Thanks to my wonderful family—Peter Mack, Diane Mayerfeld, Michael Bell, Samuel Bell, Eleanor Mayerfeld, and Maggie Mack—for their love, inspiration, and brilliance. I remember my late parents, Ernest and Marilyn Mayerfeld, with love. I would be lost without the encouragement, support, and wisdom of my husband, Peter Mack. I dedicate this book to him with love.

www.ingramcontent.com/pod-product-compliance
Lightning Source LLC
Chambersburg PA
CBHW020337270326
41926CB00007B/217